INSTITUTIONS AND ORGANIZATIONS

FOURTH EDITION

*For Joy—who continues to construct and tend
institutions of value to many of us*

INSTITUTIONS AND ORGANIZATIONS

Ideas, Interests, and Identities

FOURTH EDITION

W. Richard Scott

Stanford University

Los Angeles | London | New Delhi
Singapore | Washington DC

Los Angeles | London | New Delhi
Singapore | Washington DC

FOR INFORMATION:

SAGE Publications, Inc.
2455 Teller Road
Thousand Oaks, California 91320
E-mail: order@sagepub.com

SAGE Publications Ltd.
1 Oliver's Yard
55 City Road
London EC1Y 1SP
United Kingdom

SAGE Publications India Pvt. Ltd.
B 1/I 1 Mohan Cooperative Industrial Area
Mathura Road, New Delhi 110 044
India

SAGE Publications Asia-Pacific Pte. Ltd.
3 Church Street
#10-04 Samsung Hub
Singapore 049483

Printed in the United States of America.

Library of Congress Cataloging-in-Publication Data

Scott, W. Richard.

Institutions and organizations: ideas, interests and identities / W. Richard Scott, Stanford University.—[Fourth edition].

pages cm
Includes bibliographical references and index.

ISBN 978-1-4522-4222-4 (pbk.)

1. Organizational sociology. 2. Social institutions. I. Title.

HM786.S3845 2013
302.3′5—dc23   2013006136

This book is printed on acid-free paper.

Acquisitions Editor: Patricia Quinlin
Editorial Assistant: Katie Guarino
Production Editor: David C. Felts
Copy Editor: Sarah J. Duffy
Typesetter: C&M Digitals (P) Ltd.
Proofreader: Jeff Bryant
Indexer: Virgil Diodato
Cover Designer: Candice Harman
Marketing Manager: Liz Thornton

13 14 15 16 17 10 9 8 7 6 5 4 3 2 1

Contents

Preface to the Fourth Edition

Institutional theory is among the most vibrant and rapidly growing areas in the social sciences today. Its intersection and intercourse with organizational studies beginning in the 1970s have transformed the areas of management theory, organization sociology, and institutional economics, and strongly impacted the neighboring areas of political studies of institutions, international business, accounting and society, social movement theory, and numerous other arenas.

I believe there to be a continuing need for a relatively brief, cogent, and coherent introduction to institutional theory as it relates to organizations—a need this volume endeavors to meet. If a naïve scholar strides into the maelstrom of institutional/organization scholarship and research without assistance, he or she will emerge with a migraine if not a concussion and will be hard pressed to ascertain what the central discussion is about, let alone how to productively join the conversation.

More fundamentally, there is a need in this area for theoretical/ conceptual clarification. How are we to understand institutions and institutional processes? The existing literature is a jungle of conflicting conceptions, divergent underlying assumptions, and discordant voices. Beginning with the first (1995) edition of this book presenting my Pillars framework, I have struggled to craft an inclusive definition of institutions and to develop an encompassing framework that incorporates the major clusters of institutional theories while indicating the ways in which they differ. I discuss the types of research associated with each and compare and contrast them. With each subsequent edition, I have worked to further clarify and elaborate these distinctive traditions while insisting on their underlying commonalities. Why is there a fourth edition? Because this field continues to pulse and throb, because new conceptions have been proposed and new types of empirical work conducted, because several have raised questions about the Pillars framework and deserve a response.

As with previous editions, I pursue three broad aims:

1. *To connect past and present work.* I attempt to capture the richness and diversity of institutional thought, viewed both historically and as a contemporary ongoing project, drawing on the insights of some of the greatest minds working from the late 19th to the beginning of the 21st centuries. I concentrate my efforts on detailing work carried out from the late 1970s to the present, but point out the ways in which this work is built on and informed by earlier contributions.

2. *To recognize the interdisciplinary nature of the field.* Since I am by temperament and training a sociologist, I give more attention to work in this vein, but attempt to describe and discuss contributions from other disciplines. An inclusive review of this work, both past and present, can be confusing and frustrating because scholars, within and between disciplines, use different definitions for the same term and also use different terms to convey the same meaning. Still, I think it is possible to discern the general directions of development in each of these arenas and to observe their strengths and limitations.

3. *To connect theory with empirical research.* I stress the connections between theoretical arguments and empirical research and devote much effort to describing examples of the kinds of studies carried out up to the present. It is impossible to do justice to the rich variety of work reported in the literature and, lamentably, many good studies have been excluded. I do, however, attempt to represent the diversity and creativity of the main strands of institutional research, and to signal trajectories of development that I believe to be promising.

As with previous editions of this work, it is not possible for me to acknowledge in detail and by name the many others—mentors, teachers, colleagues, and students—who have educated, entertained, and corrected me along the way. My teachers at the University of Kansas and the University of Chicago and my many students—undergraduate, graduate, and postgraduate—and colleagues at Stanford University have enriched both my mind and my life in numerous ways. The interdisciplinary community of organization scholars we created at Stanford during the period of 1970 to 2000 was, I believe, the strongest and most creative in the history of our field (see Schoonhoven and Dobbin 2010), and I and many others of us are still feeding on the ideas fostered at that time and in that place.

I continue to believe that institutional theory provides the most promising and productive lens for viewing organizations (as well as other aspects of contemporary life) in modern society. I attempt to communicate some of this intellectual promise and excitement in this book and hope it serves as an irresistible invitation to beginning and more senior scholars to join and advance our project.

W. Richard (Dick) Scott
Stanford, California

Introduction

Institutional theory has served as a conceptual framework and research tradition since the middle of the 19th century. Indeed, this approach dominated work in the social sciences during its foundational period from the 1850s into the 1920s. However, for reasons to be discussed in the text, it was eclipsed throughout many decades of the 20th century, only to be rediscovered and renewed in the 1970s. From that time until the present, institutional theory has not simply grown, but flourished to become the dominate frame guiding organization and management studies.

The approach addresses provocative questions about the world of organizations:

- Why do organizations of the same type, such as schools or hospitals, located in widely scattered locales so closely resemble one another?
- Institutions of various sorts have existed for thousands of years. What specific types of institutions are associated with the rise of organizations?
- How are we to regard behavior in organizational settings? Does it reflect the pursuit of rational interests and the exercise of conscious choice, or is it primarily shaped by conventions, routines, and habits?
- What is the relation between freedom and control in social life?
- Why do individuals and organizations conform to institutions? Is it because they are rewarded for doing so, because they believe they are morally obligated to obey, or because they can conceive of no other way of behaving?
- Why is the behavior of organizational participants often observed to depart from the formal rules and stated goals of the organization?

- Why is it, if formal rules are largely ignored, that resources and energy are expended to maintain these formal structures?
- Where do interests come from? Do they stem from human nature, or are they constructed/inflected by social context?
- Why and how do formal and informal control structures arise? Do individuals voluntarily construct rule systems that then operate to bind their own behavior?
- Do control systems function only when they are associated with incentives—rewards and punishments—or are other processes sometimes at work?
- How do differences in cultural beliefs shape the nature and operation of organizations?
- If institutions regulate and constitute individuals, how can individuals hope to alter the institutions in which they are embedded?

In addition to addressing these and other fundamental questions regarding organized social life, more than other theoretical perspectives, an institutional approach provides guidance and support for investigators, enabling efforts to

- link past and present processes and events,
- bridge differences between the social science disciplines and multiple subfields,
- span and connect micro- and macro-approaches to the understanding of social structure and process.

Chapters 1 and 2 review early theory and research on institutions and note the beginnings of the productive linkage between institutions and organizations. Chapters 3 and 4 introduce a conceptual framework that attempts to represent the central, distinctive elements and processes that comprise institutions, attending to their underlying assumptions, varying carriers, and multiple levels at which they work. Chapter 5 addresses questions of determinants: how and by whom are institutions constructed? Chapter 6 focuses on processes, in particular, on the ways in which institutions are maintained; how they spread, diffuse across time and space; and how they weaken, decay, and fall into disuse. Chapter 7 examines institutional consequences: how institutions shape organizational structures and processes. Chapter 8 expands the frame to consider institutional processes working at the level of organization fields—a productive new arena of study—and to illustrate the value of cross-level analyses. The final chapter reviews the distinctive emphases of the institutional perspective and summarizes major developments connecting institutions and organization research over the last half century. It concludes with a warning and a suggestion for institutional scholars as the work goes forward.

1

Early Institutionalists

Human beings do not pursue the course of their daily lives and perform the complicated actions of social life merely as automata conforming to the institutions and customs into which they have been born. There remains a vast field of study in the ideas, beliefs, emotions, and sentiments which act as the immediate motives of these actions.

—W. H. R. Rivers (1914, Vol. 2: 595)

N o attempt is made here to provide a comprehensive or thorough review of early institutional theory, but to completely neglect these ideas and arguments would be inexcusable. The beginning of wisdom for an institutional theorist is the recognition that current actors and events are greatly shaped by past efforts and their enduring products. What we refer to as the "present" context is the residue of the work of those who came before. Although some of the concerns of early institutionalists differ from today's agenda, a surprising number of contemporary ideas represent rediscoveries or recastings of the work of our intellectual forefathers and -mothers.

In reviewing this early work, it is good to recognize that contemporary students bring their own interests and concerns to the reading of these texts. As Alexander (1983, Vol. 1: 119) observes: "'Reading' is an important part of any theoretical strategy, and if the work in question is in any way open to varied interpretation then it certainly will be so interpreted." Conflicting interpretations are even more likely when the theorists in question change their views over time—so that, for example, there appears to be an "early" Durkheim and a "late" one—or when, like Weber, they simultaneously express contradictory or ambivalent views.

Somewhat arbitrarily, I sort the work into disciplinary categories—although, as will soon become apparent, greater divisions exist within than between disciplinary camps—and briefly review leading contributors to institutional thought from the late 19th to the mid-20th century in economics, political science, and sociology.

❖ EARLY INSTITUTIONAL THEORY IN ECONOMICS

European Quarrels

It is good at the outset to acknowledge the lack of logical coherence in the strands of work to be examined. In many respects, the "old" institutional economics bears a stronger intellectual kinship with the "new" institutional approaches advanced by sociologists and organizational scholars than to the "new" institutional economics. Conversely, the "new" institutional economics is more indebted to the critics of "old" institutional economics than to their early namesakes. The earliest institutional arguments arose in Germany and Austria in the late 19th century as one by-product of the famous *Methodenstreit:* a debate over scientific method in the social sciences. Drawing energy and inspiration from the earlier Romantic movement as well as from the ideas of Kant and Hegel, a collection of economists challenged the conventional cannon positing that economics could be reduced to a set of universal laws. Led by Gustav Schmoller (1900–1904), this Historical School insisted that economic processes operate within a social framework that is in turn shaped by a set of cultural and historical forces. Historical and comparative research was required to discern the distinctive properties of particular economic systems. Moreover, Schmoller and his associates called for economics to eschew its simplistic assumptions regarding "economic man" and embrace more realistic models of human behavior.

The principal defender of the classical approach in this debate was Carl Menger (1883/1963), the Viennese economist, who insisted on the utility of simplifying assumptions and the value of developing economic principles that were both abstract and timeless. Rather than denying the importance of broader societal institutional forces, Menger argued that institutions were themselves social phenomena in need of theoretical explanation. It is for this reason that Langlois (1986a: 5) concludes that Menger "has perhaps more claim to be the patron saint of the new institutional economics than has any of the original institutionalists."

As with many intellectual debates, the warring factions each sharpened and perfected their arguments, but neither succeeded in convincing the other. Attempts at reconciliation and synthesis occurred only among scholars of a later generation—principally in the work of Weber, to be discussed later.

American Institutional Economists

Many of the ideas of the Historical School were embraced and further developed by American institutional economists, a number of whom were trained in Germany. An earlier cohort working in the mid-19th century did not receive much attention, but by the turn of the century, three institutional economists had become quite influential: Thorstein Veblen, John Commons, and Westley Mitchell. While there were important differences in their views, all criticized conventional economic models for their unrealistic assumptions and inattention to historical change.

The focus of Veblen's work was on economic change, but he did not embrace the German Historical School, which he believed was inappropriately satisfied with developing a narrative account of industrial and capitalist development. Rather, he distanced himself both from this group and from neoclassical economists by insisting that economics must offer a theory of economic change that embraced a realistic model of individual actors and based their theories on dynamic rather than static models of the economy/society.

Veblen was highly critical of the underlying economic assumptions regarding individual behavior. He ridiculed "the hedonistic conception of man as that of a lightning calculator of pleasures and pain" (Veblen 1898: 398). Instead, he insisted that much behavior was governed by habit and convention. "Not only is the individual's conduct edged about and directed by his habitual relations to his fellows in the group, but these relations, being of an institutional character, vary as the institutional scene varies" (Veblen 1909: 245). Indeed,

Veblen (1919: 239) defined institutions as "settled habits of thought common to the generality of man." He embraced the pragmatic conception of individuals as knowing actors seeking "self-realization and expression in an unfolding activity" immersed in ongoing social environments (Veblen 1919: 74).

At the same time, Veblen (1898) insisted that economics should reorient itself as an evolutionary science, moving away from its taxonomic approach that viewed equilibrium as the normal state. He called for the creation of a science of *cumulative causation*. Also, like Marx, as discussed later, Veblen viewed much of the dynamism of the economy as driven by a set of internal contradictions—in Veblen's case, between the industrial system focusing on technology, production, and coordination on the one hand, and the business system with its emphasis on acquisition, competition, consumption, and marketing on the other. Veblen was critical of the tendencies of the business systems of economies, including speculation in financial markets, which he regarded as "inherently wasteful and detrimental to the community" (Hamilton and Petrovic 2009: 357).

Like Veblen, Commons (1924: 7) challenged the conventional emphasis in neoclassical economics on individual choice behavior, suggesting that a more appropriate unit of economic analysis was the *transaction*, a concept borrowed from legal analysis. "The transaction is two or more wills giving, taking, persuading, coercing, defrauding, commanding, obeying, competing, governing, in a world of scarcity, mechanisms and rules of conduct" (Commons 1924: 7). The "rules of conduct" to which Commons alludes are social institutions. Institutional rules were necessary to define the limits within which individuals and firms could pursue their objectives (Commons 1950/1970).

To Commons, the institutions existing at a specific time represent nothing more than imperfect and pragmatic solutions to reconcile past conflicts; they are solutions that consist of a set of rights and duties, an authority for enforcing them, and some degree of adherence to collective norms of prudent reasonable behavior (Van de Ven 1993: 142).

All three institutional economists emphasized the importance of change and were critical of their colleagues for not making its examination central to their work. Veblen embraced an evolutionary perspective and insisted that a valid economics would emphasize the role of technological change and trace the changing phases of the economy. Commons likewise stressed the centrality of change, viewing the economy as "a moving, changing process" (Commons 1924: 376) and the firm as a "going concern" (Ansell 2009: 474). Mitchell believed that conventional economics was a hindrance to understanding the nature of the business cycle, and he devoted much of his energies to studying economic change. Like most institutionalists (except for some varieties of rational choice scholars), he was reluctant to embrace an assumption of economic equilibrium. As one of the founders of the National Bureau of Economic Research and chair of the committee that published the voluminous report *Recent Social Trends* (President's Research Committee on Social Trends 1934), Mitchell pioneered the collection of empirical data on the operation of the economy and its ramifications in multiple sectors, insisting that economic principles should be grounded in facts, not solely in abstract, deductive theories.

The American institutionalists, particularly Veblen and Commons, were influenced not only by the German Historical School but also by the homegrown philosophy of pragmatism as espoused by John Dewey, William James, Charles Peirce, and others (Menand 1997). The central premise underlying pragmatist approaches is the utility of viewing human action as efforts by individuals to behave in sensible and purposeful ways within historical social contexts. We amplify these views in Chapter 3.

Jacoby (1990) argues that the approaches offered by the early institutionalists departed from those adopted by their mainstream, neoclassical colleagues in four important respects:

- *Indeterminancy vs. determinancy.* While the orthodox model assumed "perfect competition and unique equilibria, the institutionalists pointed to pervasive market power and to indeterminacy even under competition" (p. 318).
- *Endogenous vs. exogenous determination of preferences.* Neoclassical theorists posited individual preferences or wants, while institutionalists argued that such preferences were shaped by social institutions, whose operation should be the subject of economic analysis.
- *Behavioral realism vs. simplifying assumptions.* Institutional theorists argued that economists should use more pragmatic and psychologically realistic models of economic motivation rather than subscribe to naïve utilitarian assumptions.
- *Diachronic vs. synchronic analysis.* Rather than assuming the "timeless and placeless" assumptions of the neoclassical theorists, institutionalists insisted that economists should ascertain "how the economy acquired its features and the conditions that cause these features to vary over time and place" (p. 320).[1]

Regardless of whether they were correct in their accusations and assertions, the early institutional economists did not prevail within the discipline of economics: Neoclassical theory was victorious and continues its dominance up to the present time. Prior to the rise of the new institutional economics in the 1970s, only a few economists attempted to carry forward the institutionalists' agenda, the best known of whom are J. A. Schumpeter, Karl Polanyi, John Kenneth Galbraith, and Gunnar Myrdal (see Swedberg 1991). Arguably, the subfields of economics most affected by the legacy of the institutional theorists are those of labor economics, the field in which Commons specialized; industrial relations, which focuses on broader social and political factors affecting economic structures and processes; and the economics of industry, which examines the varying configurations of industrial structures and their effects on the strategies and performance of individual firms.

Why was the impact of the early institutionalists blunted? Modern-day commentators offer several explanations. The German Historical School no doubt overemphasized the uniqueness of economic systems and underemphasized the value of analytic theory. Even sympathetic critics acknowledge that Veblen exhibited "an explicit hostility to intellectual 'symmetry and system-building'" (Hodgson 1991: 211) and that Commons' arguments were hampered by his "idiosyncratic terminology and unsystematic style of reasoning" (Vanberg 1989: 343). But a more serious shortcoming was the tendency for the work to degenerate into naïve empiricism and historicism. Emphasizing the importance of the particular, of time and place and historical circumstance, institutional analysis came more and more to underline "the value of largely descriptive work on the nature and function of politico-economic institutions" (Hodgson 1991: 211).

Here then, we have the principal reason why the godfather of the "new" institutional economics, Ronald Coase (1983: 230), so cavalierly dismissed the "old" institutional economics: "Without a theory they had nothing to pass on except a mass of descriptive material waiting for a theory, or a fire."

The battle between the particular and the general, between the temporal and the timeless is one that contemporary institutional theorists continue to confront.

❖ EARLY INSTITUTIONAL THEORY IN POLITICAL SCIENCE

Institutional approaches dominated political science in both Europe and America during the latter half of the 19th century and the first two decades of the 20th century. I concentrate on the American scene, but first call attention to the work of a well-known but neglected student of institutions and organizations: Alexis de Tocqueville. Living in pre-revolutionary France in the mid-19th century, Tocqueville took advantage of an opportunity to visit the United States in the early 1830s ostensibly to study prison systems but primarily because he wanted to observe firsthand the emergence of a fledgling democracy (Brogan 2006). Tocqueville is best known for his study of the contribution of voluntary associations to American democracy, but considered more broadly his writings may be seen as an important early instance of the analysis of organizations operating under diverse institutional contexts (Swedberg 2009) as well as the relation between culture and institutions under equilibrium/disequilibrium conditions (Meyer 2003). Tocqueville distinguished between institutions, primarily laws but including associated routines and habits, and *moeurs* ("mores"), referring to norms, attitudes, and opinions. In his study of French aristocracy before the revolution, Tocqueville argues that the state's emphasis on institutions prevented them from noting the extent to which mores had departed from and no longer supported law. It was only the revolution of 1789 that brought these state/societal frameworks closer together. The concentration of power in the state, Tocqueville argues, made citizens so reliant on state action that they forgot how to form associations to pursue their own interests (Tocqueville 1856/1998, 2001). By contrast, as Tocqueville famously pointed out, the weakness of the state during the 19th century in America created the environment within which a robust collection of bottom-up movements and associations emerged, comprising an active civic sector (Tocqueville 1835/2004).

In contrast to this relatively sophisticated use of comparative institutional analysis, American political scientists, such as J. W. Burgess (1902), Woodrow Wilson (1889), and W. W. Willoughby (1896; 1904), pursued a more straightforward approach grounded in constitutional law and moral philosophy. In the heavy tomes produced by these scholars, careful attention was given to the legal framework and administrative arrangements characterizing particular governance (primarily nation-state) structures. Much of the work involved painstaking historical examination of the origins, controversies, and compromises producing specific regimes; some analyses were explicitly comparative, detailing how central problems or functions were variously managed by diverse governance mechanisms. But the underlying tone of the work was normative: "In the mainstream of political science, description was overshadowed by moral philosophy" (Simon 1991: 57).

As depicted by Bill and Hardgrave (1981; see also Peters 1999), the institutional school that developed at the turn of the 20th century exhibited several defining features. First, it was preoccupied with formal structures and legal systems. "Emphasis was placed upon the organized and evident institutions of government, and studies concentrated almost exclusively upon constitutions, cabinets, parliaments, courts, and bureaucracies" (Bill and Hardgrave 1981: 3). Second, the approach emphasized detailed accounts of particular political systems, resulting in "configurative description"—intricate descriptive accounts of interlinked rules, rights, and procedures (Bill and Hardgrave 1981: 3). Third, the approach was conservative in the sense that it emphasized origins but not ongoing change. "Political institutions were examined in terms of an evolutionary development which found fulfillment in the immediate present. But while these institutions had a past, they apparently had no future" (p. 6). They were regarded as completed products. Fourth, the work was largely nontheoretical, primary attention being given to historical reconstruction of specific institutional forms. Finally, the tone of these studies was more that associated with moral philosophy and less that of empirical science. These scholars devoted more attention to the explication of normative principles than to the formulation of testable propositions.

Although he acknowledges many of the same characteristics, Eckstein (1963) also insists that these early institutionalists did usher in the first crude form of positivism in political science. Unlike their own predecessors, primarily "historicists" who focused their interest on abstracted political systems derived from philosophical principles, they were looking at the real world, at hard facts:

> Primitive, unadulterated positivism insists upon hard facts, indubitable and incontrovertible facts, as well as facts that speak for themselves—and what facts of politics are harder, as well as more self-explanatory than the facts found in formal legal codes? (Eckstein 1963: 10)

In addition, these scholars attended to the real world in yet another sense: They placed great emphasis on formal political institutions, on charters, legal codes, and administrative rules, in part because "the nineteenth century was a great age of constitution-making" (Eckstein 1963: 10).

Beginning during the mid-1930s and continuing through the 1960s, the institutional perspective was challenged and largely supplanted by the behavioralist approach (not to be confused with behaviorism in psychology), which attempted to sever the tie to moral philosophy and rebuild political science as a theoretically guided, empirical science (see Easton 1965). More important for our concerns, the behavioralist persuasion diverted attention away from governmental structures to political behavior.

> Behaviorists argued that, in order to understand politics and explain political outcomes, analysts should focus not on the formal attributes of government institutions but instead on informal distributions of power, attitudes and political behavior. (Thelen and Steinmo 1992: 4)

Students of politics focused attention on voting behavior, party formation, and public opinion. Moreover, this reductionist shift in emphasis from rules and structures to behavior was accompanied by a more utilitarian orientation, viewing action as "the product of calculated self-interest" and taking an instrumentalist view of politics, regarding the "allocation of resources as the central concern of political life" (March and Olsen 1984: 735). To study politics was to study *Who Gets What, When, and How?* (Lasswell 1936).

These theoretical strands associated with behavioralism have been reinforced and deepened by the "rational revolution" arising in the 1970s and 1980s. As I discuss in later chapters, the rational choice approach—based on the application of economic assumptions to political behavior—has brought about fundamental changes in political science. Peters (1999) suggests that the attributes characterizing both movements, behavioral and rational, include (1) an emphasis on more rigorous and deductive theory and methodology; (2) a bias against normative, prescriptive approaches; (3) methodological individualism—the assumptions that individuals are the only actors and that they are motivated by individual utility maximization; and (4) "inputism": a focus on societal inputs to the political system (e.g., votes, interest group pressures, money) to the exclusion of attention to the internal workings of the system—the institutional political structures—as they may affect outcomes.

The new institutionalism in political science developed in reaction to the excesses of the behavioralist revolution, although one major variant employs rational choice approaches to account for the building and maintenance of institutions. Current institutionalists do not call for a return to "configurational history" but do seek to reestablish the importance of normative frameworks and rule systems in guiding, constraining, and empowering social and political behavior.

❖ EARLY INSTITUTITIONAL THEORY IN SOCIOLOGY

Attention to institutions by sociologists has been more constant than that exhibited by either economists or political scientists. While there are a number of different discernible strands with their distinctive vocabularies and emphases, we also observe continuity from the early work of Spencer and Sumner through Davis to the recent work of Friedland and Alford; from Cooley, Thomas, and Blumer to Hughes and his associates, including Abbott, Becker, and Freidson; from the early efforts of Marx, Durkheim, and Weber through Parsons to DiMaggio and Powell; and from the early work on the social sources of mind and self by Mead and Schutz to the emphasis on cognitive processes and knowledge systems by Berger and Luckmann as well as Meyer and Rowan.

Spencer and Sumner

Without question, the most influential conception of institutions pervading mainstream sociology throughout the 20th century has its origins in the work of Herbert Spencer. Spencer (1876, 1896, 1910) viewed society as an organic system evolving through time. Adaptation of the system to its context was achieved via the functions of specialized "organs" structured as institutional subsystems. Spencer devoted the main body of his work to a comparative study of these institutions, attempting to draw generalizations from comparing and contrasting their operation in different societies.

Spencer's general conceptions were embraced and amplified by William Graham Sumner (1906) in his major treatise, *Folkways*. Teeming with ethnographic and historical materials, the book generated numerous hypotheses concerning the origins, persistence, and change of folkways and mores (albeit many of these have a strong biopsychological basis). For Sumner, "an institution consists of a concept (idea, notion, doctrine, interest) and a structure" (p. 53). The concept defines the purposes or functions of the institution; the structure embodies the idea of the institution and furnishes the instrumentalities through which the idea is put into action. Societal evolution progresses from individual activities to folkways, to mores, to full-fledged institutions. Such institutions are "cressive"—evolving slowly through instinctive efforts over long periods of time (e.g., languages)—although institutions can also be "enacted"—the products of rational intention and invention (e.g., written constitutions).

Later generations of sociologists discarded the strong biological/evolutionary analogies and functional arguments devised by Spencer and Sumner, but nevertheless recognized the centrality of institutions as a sociological focus. Thus, in his influential mid-20th century text *Human Society*, Kingsley Davis (1949: 71) defined institutions as "a set of interwoven folkways, mores and laws built around one or more functions," adding that in his opinion, "the concept of institutions seems better than any other to convey the notion of segments or parts of the normative order." Every major sociological text and curriculum of the last hundred years has reflected not only the important distinction of levels (e.g., individuals, groups, communities, societies), but also the functional division of social life into spheres or arenas (e.g., kinship, stratification, politics, economics, religion) governed by varying normative systems. The conception of institutions as functionally specialized arenas persists in contemporary notions of organization *field* or *sector* (DiMaggio and Powell 1983; Scott and Meyer 1983; see Chapters 3 and 8) and is strongly represented in the work of Friedland and Alford (1991), who stress the importance for social change of the existence of multiple, differentiated, and partially conflicting institutional spheres, each governed by distinctive "logics."

Cooley, Thomas, and Blumer

Charles Horton Cooley and his followers emphasized the interdependence of individuals and institutions, of self and social structure. Although the great institutions—"language, government, the church, laws and customs of property and of the family"—appear to be independent and external to behavior, they are developed and preserved through interactions among individuals and exist "as a habit of mind and of action, largely unconscious because largely common to all the group. . . . The individual is always cause as well as effect of the institution" (Cooley 1902/1956: 313–314).

W. I. Thomas and Herbert Blumer were two other influential theorists who examined the complex and interdependent relations between social actors and action and social structure. Thomas (see Janowitz 1966) explored the relation between social organization and culture on the one hand and personality and individual behavior on the other. He emphasized, in particular, the role of interpretation: "If men define situations as real, they are real in their consequences" (Thomas and Thomas 1928: 572). Blumer, influenced by the American pragmatists, developed an early form of *structuration theory* (see Chapter 4), in which institutions provide a framework for human conduct, but must be interpreted through the development of shared meanings—through symbolic interaction.

Cooley, Thomas, and Blumer were early leading figures in the development of empirically based research on the micro-foundations of institutional processes. Their contributions merit more attention than they have received from contemporary institutional scholars.

Marx, Durkheim, Weber, and Parsons

The European tradition in institutional analysis was spearheaded by Karl Marx, whose influence permeated economics and political science as well as sociology. While Marx inspired a diverse array of theories and political movements, the work of primary importance to institutional theory involved his struggle with and reinterpretation of Hegel, the great German idealist philosopher. Hegel viewed history as the self-realization through time of abstract ideas or spirit (*Geist*). This self-creative spirit is reflected in the objective world, which most of us mistakenly take to be the true reality. It is the task of man to overcome this alienated state in which the world appears to be other than spirit (Hegel 1807/1967; Tucker 1972). Marx, famously, turned Hegel's arguments upside-down.

For Marx, the materialist world is the true one, and the alienation we experience occurs because humankind is estranged from itself in existing political and economic structures. Marx, working in the early decades of the industrial revolution, saw the key realm as economic: Productive activity had been transformed into involuntary labor. Under a capitalist system, work was no longer an expression of creative productivity, but alienated labor. The nature and meaning of work and work relations were seen to be transformed by structures of oppression and exploitation. These structures—including the accompanying beliefs, norms, and power relations—are the product of human ideas and activities, but appear to be external and objective to their participants. Ideas and ideologies reflect, and attempt to justify, material reality—not the other way around (Marx 1844/1972; 1845–1846/1972). Thus, in important (but historically specific) respects, Marx gave early expression to the social construction of reality.

Marx also borrowed from Hegel the idea of *dialectics*—the view that "conflict, antagonism, or contradiction is a necessary condition for achieving certain results" (Elster 1986: 34). The concept can be viewed as pertaining to the relation between ideas or viewed as a description of selected social conditions. Marx employed the concept in both senses, but emphasized the latter in his analysis of the conditions of social change. For example, Marx pointed to the paradox that capitalists want to pay their workers low wages to increase their profits but want other capitalists to pay high wages to their workers to create demands for products. Such paradoxes give rise to a *prisoner's dilemma* in which all capitalists lose by following their rational interest. In this and other analyses, Marx employed the idea of dialectics to analyze the unintended consequences of actors following their interests. A number of more contemporary scholars have appropriated Marxian views of dialectical processes operating in economic and political systems to help account for macro change in institutions, as we discuss in Chapter 8. More generally, Marx was the first major theorist to "highlight the broader social forces that act on and through organizations . . . [the] way the broader environment and the organization are structured by class relations and conflict" (Adler 2009: 78).

The other two major European figures engaged in establishing sociological variants of institutional analysis were Durkheim and Weber. The French sociologist Émile Durkheim was preoccupied with understanding the changing bases of social order that accompanied the industrial revolution, but, as previously noted, he appears to have modified his views over time. His early classic, *The Division of Labor in Society* (1893/1949), differentiated between the mechanical solidarity based on shared religious and cultural beliefs that integrated traditional societies and the newly emerging organic solidarity associated with an advanced division of labor. Initially, Durkheim viewed this new collective order as "based on the belief that action was rational and that order could be successfully negotiated in an individualistic way"—social order as "the unintended aggregate of individual self-interest" (Alexander 1983, Vol. 3: 131, 134). But his revised arguments led him away from an instrumentalist, individualist explanation to focus on collective, normative frameworks that supply "the noncontractual elements" of contract (Durkheim 1893/1949, Book 1, Chapter 7).

Durkheim's mature formulation emphasizes the pivotal role played by symbolic systems, systems of belief and "collective representations"—shared cognitive frames and schemas—that, if not explicitly religious, have a moral or spiritual character.

> There is something eternal in religion which is destined to survive all the particular symbols in which religious thought has successively enveloped itself. There can be no society which does not feel the need of upholding and reaffirming at regular intervals, the

collective sentiments and the collective ideas which make its unity
and its personality. (Durkheim 1912/1961: 474–475)

These systems, although a product of human interaction, are experienced by individuals as objective. Although subjectively formed, they
become crystallized. They are, in Durkheim's (1901/1950) terms, social
facts: phenomena perceived by the individual to be both external (to
that person) and coercive (backed by sanctions). And, as is the case
with religious systems, ritual and ceremonies play a vital role in
expressing and reinforcing belief. Rituals and ceremonies enact beliefs.
They "act entirely upon the mind and upon it alone" (Durkheim
1912/1961: 420) so that to the extent that these activities have impact
on situations, it is through their effects on beliefs about these situations.
    These symbolic systems—systems of knowledge, belief, and
"moral authority"—are for Durkheim social institutions.

Institutions, Durkheim writes, are a product of joint activity and
association, the effect of which is to "fix," to "institute" outside us
certain initially subjective and individual ways of acting and judg-
ing. Institutions, then, are the "crystallizations" of Durkheim's
earlier writing. (Alexander 1983, Vol. 2: 259)

The third major European figure contributing to institutional theory was Max Weber. As I will note in more detail in Chapter 2, more
contemporary analysts of institutions lay claim to Weber as their guiding genius than to any other early theorist. While Weber did not explicitly employ the concept of *institution*, his work is permeated with a
concern for understanding the ways in which cultural rules—ranging
in nature from customary mores to legally defined constitutions or rule
systems—define social structures and govern social behavior, including economic structures and behavior. For example, his justly famous
typology of administrative systems—traditional, charismatic, and
rational-legal—represents three types of authority systems differing
primarily in the kinds of belief or cultural systems that legitimate the
exercise of authority (see Weber 1924/1968: 215; Bendix 1960; Dornbusch
and Scott 1974: Ch. 2).
    There remains much controversy as to how to characterize Weber's
theoretical stance because he stood at the crossroads of three major
debates raging at the turn of the 20th century: first, that between those
who viewed the social sciences as a natural science and those who
argued that it was rather a cultural science (the *Methodenstreit* described
earlier); second, between idealist arguments associated with Durkheim

and the materialist emphasis of Marx; and third, between the institutionalist historical school of economics and the neoclassical interest in developing general theory. More so than any other figure of his time, Weber wrestled with and attempted to reconcile these apparently conflicting ideas.

Weber argued that the social sciences differ fundamentally from the natural sciences in that, in the former but not the latter, both the researcher and the object of study attach meaning to events. For Weber (1924/1968, Vol. 1: 4), action is social "when and in so far as the acting individual attaches a subjective meaning to his behavior." Individuals do not mechanically respond to stimuli; they first interpret them and then determine their response. Researchers cannot expect to understand social behavior without taking into account the meanings that mediate social action. Weber employed his interpretive approach to attempt a synthesis in which both the material conditions and interests stressed by materialists (such as Marx) and the idealist values (emphasized by Durkheim) combined to motivate and guide action (see Alexander 1983, Vol. 2; see also Chapters 3 and 9).

In developing his *Wirtschaftssoziologie* (economic sociology), Weber embraced the institutionalist arguments that economics needs to be historically informed and comparative in its approach, but at the same time he sided with Menger and the classicists in supporting the value of theoretical models that allowed one to abstract from specific, historically embedded systems to formulate and evaluate general arguments. Weber believed that economic sociology could bridge the chasm by attending to both historical circumstance and the development of analytic theory (Swedberg 1991; 1998). Weber suggested that by abstracting from the specificity and complexity of concrete events, researchers could create "ideal types" to guide and inform comparative studies. If researchers were careful not to mistake the ideal types for reality (e.g., that individuals under all conditions would behave as rational "economic men"), such models could provide useful maps to guide analysis and increase understanding of the real world (Weber, 1904–1918/1949). More precisely, "Weber views rational behavior as evolving historically, or, to phrase it differently, to Weber—unlike to today's economists—rational behavior is a variable, not an assumption" (Swedberg 1998: 36). Weber recognized that there was not one, but several variants of rationality—some (*Zweckrationalität*) primarily concerned with means-ends considerations, some (*Wertrationalität*) focusing more on the centrality of the end or ultimate value, and still others focusing on a belief in the importance of maintaining traditional structures (Clegg and Lounsbury 2009; Du Gay 2009; Kalberg 1980).

His insights paved the way for the construction of more recent formulations emphasizing the extent to which all sectors and their constituent organizations contain multiple, competing conceptions of rational behavior—varying institutional logics.

The American sociologist Talcott Parsons attempted to synthesize the arguments of major early theorists—in particular, Durkheim, Weber, and Freud—in constructing his voluntaristic theory of action (see Parsons 1937; 1951). Parsons was the most influential social theorist in sociology throughout the middle of the 20th century, although he is much less in vogue today.[2] Like Weber, he attempted to reconcile a subjective and an objective approach to social action by emphasizing that whereas normative frameworks existed independently of a given social actor, analysts needed to take into account the orientation of actors to them. A system of action was said to be *institutionalized* to the extent that actors in an ongoing relation oriented their actions to a common set of normative standards and value patterns. As such a normative system becomes internalized; "conformity with it becomes a need-disposition in the actor's own personality structure" (Parsons 1951: 37). In this sense, institutionalized action is motivated by moral rather than by instrumental concerns: "The primary motive for obedience to an institutional norm lies in the moral authority it exercises over the individual" (Parsons 1934/1990: 326). The actor conforms because of his or her belief in a value standard, not out of expediency or self-interest.

Viewed more objectively, from the standpoint of the social analyst, institutions are appropriately seen as a system of norms that "regulate the relations of individuals to each other," that define "what the relations of individuals ought to be" (Parsons 1934/1990: 327). Also, implicitly following the lead of Spencer and Sumner, Parsons developed his own abstract typology of norms oriented to the solution of the four generic problems of social systems: adaptation, goal attainment, integration, and latency (maintenance of cultural patterns) (see Parsons 1951; Parsons, Bales, and Shils 1953).

Contemporary theorists note several kinds of limitations with Parsons' formulation. Alexander (1983, Vol. 4: 242) concludes that although Parsons attempted to develop a multidimensional view of social action, his conception of institutionalization put too much weight on cultural patterns, overemphasizing the "control exerted by values over conditions." The importance of interests and of instrumental action and rational choice was underemphasized. DiMaggio and Powell (1991) praise Parsons for the contribution he made to the microfoundations of institutional theory in his attempt to understand the ways in which culture influences behavior. But they complain that his conception of culture failed to stress its existence as "an object of orientation exist-ing outside the individual" (p. 17). Instead, following Freud, Parsons viewed culture as acting primarily as "an internalized element of the personality system" (p. 17)—thus giving too much weight to a subjec-tive in contrast to objective view. Additionally, they argue that Parsons' analysis of culture neglected its cognitive dimensions in favor of its evaluative components: Culture was limited to "value-orientations" (DiMaggio and Powell 1991: 17). Each of these emphases drew Parsons away from examining the interplay of the instrumental and the norma-tive in social action.

Mead, Schutz, Bourdieu, Berger and Luckmann

George Herbert Mead, like Cooley, emphasized the interdepen-dence of self and society but gave particular attention to the role played by symbolic systems in creating both the human and the social. Mean-ing is created in interaction as gestures, particularly vocal gestures (language), call out the same response in self as in other; and self arises in interaction as an individual "takes on the attitudes of the other" in arriving at a self-conception (Mead 1934).

Working at about the same time as Mead, but in Vienna, Alfred Schutz also examined in detail the ways in which common meanings are constructed through interaction by individuals. However, Schutz (1932/1967: 139) also explored the wider "structure of the social world," noting the great variety of social relations in which we become involved. In addition to intimate, face-to-face, "Thou" relations, and "We" relations with persons thought to be similar to ourselves, we engage in multiple "They" relations with others known only indirectly and impersonally. Such relations are only possible to the extent that we develop an ideal type conception that enables us to deal with these others as needed, for example, to mail a letter or to stand beside them in an elevator. These relations are based upon typifications of the other and taken-for-granted assumptions as to the way the interaction will proceed. In this sense, the meanings are highly institutionalized (Schutz 1932/1967).

Moving closer to the present, the French scholar Pierre Bourdieu (1971; 1973) endeavored to combine the insights of Marx and Durkheim by examining the ways in which class interests express themselves in symbolic struggles: the power of some groups to impose their knowl-edge frameworks and conceptions of social reality on others. Bourdieu's work reached and began to influence organizational scholars about a decade later (see DiMaggio 1979). In particular, Bourdieu's concept of *field* (a social arena), was usefully appropriated by DiMaggio and Powell (1983) to better situate the locus of institutional processes shaping organizations (see Chapters 2 and 8).

Peter Berger and Thomas Luckmann, working in the United States, also provide a critical link between earlier work and that of later organizational scholars. Influenced by the work of Mead, but even more by that of Schutz,[3] Berger and Luckmann (1967: 15) redirected the sociology of knowledge away from its earlier concerns with epistemological issues or a focus on intellectual history to more mainstream sociological concerns, insisting that "the sociology of knowledge must concern itself with everything that passes for 'knowledge' in society." The concern is not with the validity of this knowledge, but with its production, with "the social creation of reality" (p. 15). Berger and Luckmann argue that social reality is a human construction, a product of social interaction. They underscore this position in their attention to language (systems of symbols) and cognition mediated by social processes as crucial to the ways in which actions are produced, repeated, and come to evoke stable, similar meanings in self and other. They define this process as one of *institutionalization.* In contrast to Durkheim and Parsons, Berger and Luckmann emphasize the creation of shared knowledge and belief systems rather than the production of rules and norms. Cognitive frameworks are stressed over normative systems. A focus on the centrality of cognitive systems forms the foundation for the sociological version of the new institutionalism in organizations (see Chapter 2).

❖ CONCLUDING COMMENT

This brief review attempts to identify some of the varying interests and emphases of the early institutional theorists—formulations developed between 1850 and the mid-20th century. As we will see, these theorists in numerous ways anticipated distinctions and insights rediscovered by later analysts. Contemporary economists—with the notable exception of economic historians—rejected the approaches promoted by the German Historical School, but some strands of the new institutionalism in economics reflect the interests of Menger and the Austrian School. Contemporary political scientists have left behind the moral philosophical roots of their institutional forebears, but a lively subset has rediscovered an interest in the historical and comparative study of political systems. An even larger collection of political scientists has adapted rational choice models devised by economists to better explain the emergence and functioning of political institutions.

Contemporary sociologists continue to pursue and refine the ideas of their numerous and varied predecessors. Some examine the diverse institutional spheres that make up society; others, the ways in which individuals are empowered and constrained by shared normative systems; and still others explore the ways in which symbolic systems—cultural rules and schemas—shape and support social life.

While there is continuity, there is also change, perhaps even progress. Most of the early work on institutions shared a common limitation: Little attention was accorded to organizations. Some theorists focused their analyses on wider institutional structures—on constitutions and political systems, on language and legal systems, on kinship and religious structures—while others emphasized the emergence of common meanings and normative frameworks out of localized social interaction. Few, however, treated organizations themselves as institutional forms or directed attention to the ways in which wider institutions shaped collections of organizations.

Theorists in the 1940s and 1950s began to recognize the existence and importance of particular collectivities—individual *organizations*—entities distinguishable from both broader social institutions on the one hand and the behavior of individuals on the other. Later developments, in the 1970s and 1980s called attention to the significance of organization *forms* and organization *fields*. The recognition of each of these levels has stimulated much fruitful development of institutional theory and research.

❖ NOTES

1. These generalizations—particularly the first and the fourth—are less applicable to the Austrian branch of economics led by Menger and Hayek. These theorists, while insisting on the importance of theory and of simplifying assumptions, were interested in understanding economic change and so were sympathetic to a more evolutionary approach and the study of economic processes (see Langlois 1986a). Their ideas fueled the development of evolutionary economics (see Chapter 2).

2. Camic (1992) argues that Parsons strategically selected these European predecessors—rather than American institutional scholars, such as Veblen and Mitchell, and his own teachers (Hamilton and Ayres), who shared their interests—because of the tarnished reputation of these institutional economists at the time when Parsons was constructing his theory of action. There is a politics to selecting intellectual forebears that helps to explain why some previous work is "drawn upon, while other work is overlooked" (p. 421).

Ironically, in a parallel fashion, Hall (1992) has accused sociological neoinstitutionalists of failing to acknowledge the influence of Parsons (whose reputation until recently was on the wane) as an important intellectual predecessor.

3. Berger (1992) reports that he and Luckmann were both junior members of the graduate faculty of the New School for Social Research (now New School University) in the early 1960s:

> We found ourselves in the lucky situation of being in the company of a small but lively group of young colleagues and graduate students who broadly shared a theoretical orientation, the one that all of us had learned from our teacher Alfred Schutz. One of Schutz's unrealized projects had been to formulate a new theoretical foundation for the sociology of knowledge in terms of his blend of phenomenology and Weberian theory. We intended to realize this project. (p. 1)

2

Institutional Theory Meets Organizations Studies

Neo-institutional approaches to organizations are part of a much wider intellectual endeavor that problematizes modernity, and questions the social origins of the whole constellation of institutions and at the same time seeks to grasp not the universal laws that generate social practices, but the social practices that generate universal laws and, in organizational theory, attendant management prescriptions.

—Frank R. Dobbin (1994a: 123)

As we have seen, institutions were identified and analyzed quite early by social scientists. Some of these scholars specifically attended to organizations as one type of social structure, including Weber, Tocqueville, and Parsons. However, the emerging field of organization studies in the 20th century drew primarily on the work of engineers, such as Taylor (1911; see Shenhav 1999); administrative theorists, such as Fayol (1919/1949) and the early work of Simon (1945/1997); former executives, such as Barnard (1938); and industrial psychologists like Mayo (1945). March (1965) dates the appearance of a distinctive academic focus on organizations to the period 1937 to 1947.

Most of these early formulations stressed the technocratic and instrumental characteristics of these forms, albeit some, such as Barnard and Mayo, pointed to the human and social dimensions of these systems. Little or no attention was given to the surrounding social/cultural environment of organizations.

The first section of this chapter reviews work connecting organizations and institutional arguments beginning in the 1940s and continuing up to the emergence of the "new" institutional approaches in the 1970s. Four strands of work are notable among early theorists of organizations. The first was stimulated by the translation into English of Weber's (1906–1924/1946; 1924/1947) work on bureaucracy, which aroused much interest among a collection of sociologists at Columbia University, especially Robert K. Merton and Philip Selznick.[1] Second, at the University of Chicago, Everett C. Hughes and colleagues were engaged in linking his interest in institutions to the ways in which work was organized in modern societies. Talcott Parsons, the reigning American sociological theorist of his time, at Harvard, became a third early conduit (beyond the role of translator of Weber and general social theorist) because he was encouraged by James D. Thompson to apply his own cultural-institutional theory of social systems to organizations. Thompson, the founding editor of *Administrative Science Quarterly*, a new interdisciplinary journal devoted to research on organizations, invited Parsons to prepare a two-part article for the inaugural issue in 1956. Lastly, Herbert Simon's pioneering work at the Carnegie Institute of Technology (now Carnegie Mellon University) on organizational decision making was expanded, in collaboration with James G. March, into an influential statement of the nature of rationality in organizations.

This early work, carried out during the 1940s to 1950s, which first explicitly connected institutions and organizations, is reviewed in the first section of this chapter. Then, in the second section, I consider the emergence during the 1960s to 1970s of a complex of new ideas that provided the basis for the more recent, somewhat novel, conception of institutions: neoinstitutional organization theory. As in Chapter 1, this review is roughly organized by disciplinary emphases.

❖ INSTITUTIONS AND ORGANIZATIONS: EARLY APPROACHES

The Columbia School: Merton's and Selznick's Institutional Models

Shortly after selections from Weber's seminal writings on bureaucracy were translated into English during the late 1940s, a collection of scholars at Columbia University under the leadership of Robert K. Merton revived interest in bureaucracy and bureaucratization, its sources and consequences for behavior in organizations (Merton, Gray, Hockey, and Selvin 1952).[2] It is generally acknowledged that a series of empirical studies of diverse organizations carried out by Merton's students—by Selznick (1949) of the Tennessee Valley Authority (TVA); Gouldner (1954) of a gypsum plant and mine; Blau (1955) of a federal and a state bureau; and Lipset, Trow, and Coleman (1956) of a typographical union—were instrumental in establishing organizations as a distinctive arena of study for sociologists (see Scott and Davis 2007: 9). Blau, Gouldner, and Lipset and colleagues conducted empirical studies of organizational and institutional construction and change (see Chapter 5), but it was Selznick who developed the most explicit theoretical treatment of institutions and their relation to organizations. We consider his work as it differed from but was influenced by Merton's own formulation.

Merton: Rules Trump Instrumentalism

As will be described below, Merton's (1936) early work on "the unanticipated consequences of purposive action" was helpful to Selznick, but his analysis of bureaucratic behavior was even more directly influential. Although Merton (1940/1957: 199) did not employ the term *institutionalization* in his well-known essay "Bureaucratic Structure and Personality," he provides a lucid discussion of processes within organizations leading officials to orient their actions around rules even "to the point where primary concern with conformity to the rules interferes with the achievement of the purposes of the organization." Merton depicts the multiple forces within bureaucracy producing discipline and orienting officials toward upholding a valued normative order. The strength of these pressures is such that officials are prone to follow the rules to the point of rigidity, formalism, even ritualism. Stimulated by the arguments of Durkheim, Merton (1940/1957) spells out his version of institutional processes within organizations:

> There may ensue, in particular vocations and in particular types of organization, the process of sanctification. . . . [T]hrough sentiment-formation, emotional dependence upon bureaucratic symbols and status, and affective involvement in spheres of competence and authority, there develop prerogatives involving attitudes of moral legitimacy which are established as values in their own right, and are no longer viewed as merely technical means for expediting administration. (p. 202)

Selznick: Means Become Infused With Value

The leading early figure in the institutional analysis of organizations was Philip Selznick, whose conception of institutional processes was strongly influenced by Merton's work.[3] His views evolved throughout the corpus of his writings. From his earliest writings, Selznick (1948: 25) was intent on distinguishing between organization as "the structural expression of rational action"—as a mechanistic instrument designed to achieve specified goals—and organization viewed as an adaptive, organic system, affected by the social characteristics of its participants as well as by the varied pressures imposed by its environment. "Organizations," created as instrumental mechanisms to achieve specific goals, to a variable extent and over time, are transformed into "institutions."

In his earliest formulation, Selznick borrows heavily on Merton's (1936) analysis of "the unanticipated consequences of purposive social action." Whereas some consequences of our actions occur as planned, others are unanticipated; social actions are not context-free but constrained, and their outcomes are shaped by the setting in which they occur. Especially significant are the constraints on action that arise from "commitments enforced by institutionalization. . . . Because organizations are social systems, goals or procedures tend to achieve an established, value-impregnated status. We say that they become institutionalized" (Selznick 1949: 256–257).

In his subsequent work on leadership, Selznick (1957) elaborates his views:

> Institutionalization is a process. It is something that happens to an organization over time, reflecting the organization's own distinctive history, the people who have been in it, the groups it embodies and the vested interests they have created, and the way it has adapted to its environment. . . . In what is perhaps its most significant meaning, "to institutionalize" is to *infuse with value* beyond the technical requirements of the task at hand. (pp. 16–17; emphasis in original)

As organizations become infused with value, they are no longer regarded as expendable tools; participants want to see that they are preserved. By embodying a particular set of values, the organization acquires a *character structure*, a distinctive identity. Maintaining the organization is no longer simply an instrumental matter of keeping the machinery working, but becomes a struggle to preserve a set of unique values. A vital role of leadership for Selznick, echoing Chester Barnard's

(1938) influential message in *The Functions of the Executive*, is to define and defend these values. Clearly, this set of ideas resonates with more recent work on organization culture (e.g., Martin 2002; Schein 1985) and on organization identity (Albert and Whetten 1985; Whetten and Godfrey 1999).

In addition to viewing institutionalization as a process, as something that happens to the organization over time, Selznick also treated institutionalization as a variable: Organizations with more precisely defined goals or with better developed technologies are less subject to institutionalization than those with diffuse goals and weak technologies (Selznick 1957). Organizations vary in susceptibility to and, hence, degree of institutionalization.

Contrasting Selznick's with Merton's conception, both emphasized quite similar processes of value commitments to procedures extending beyond instrumental utilities. However, while Selznick focused on commitments distinctive to the developing character of a specific organization, Merton stressed commitments associated with characteristics of bureaucratic (rational-legal) organizations generally. Selznick's approach calls for depicting a *natural history* of a specific organization, a description of the processes by which, over time, it develops its distinctive structures, capabilities, and liabilities. He himself studied the evolution of the TVA, noting how its original structures and goals were transformed over time by the commitments of its participants and the requirements imposed by powerful constituencies in its environment (Selznick 1949; see also Chapter 4). Selznick's students conducted similar case studies of the transformation of organizational goals, such as occurred in the Women's Christian Temperance Union (WCTU) (Gusfield 1955), a community college (Clark 1960), a voluntary hospital (Perrow 1961), and the YMCA (Zald and Denton 1963). In all of these studies, the official goals of the organization are shown to differ from—to mask—the "real" objectives, which had been transformed in interaction with interests both within and external to the organization. As Perrow (1986: 159) notes, Selznick's institutional school tends to produce an "expose" view of organizations: Organizations are not the rational creatures they pretend to be but vehicles for embodying (sometimes surreptitious) values.

Another of Selznick's students, Arthur Stinchcombe (1968), built on Selznick's formulation, making more explicit the role of agency and power. Stinchcombe defines an institution as "a structure in which powerful people are committed to some value or interest" (p. 107), emphasizing that values are preserved and interests are protected only if those holding them possess and retain power.

Institutionalization connotes stability over time, and Stinchcombe's analysis attempts to identify the ways in which power holders are able to preserve their power. He asserts: "By selection, socialization, controlling conditions of incumbency, and hero worship, succeeding generations of power-holders tend to regenerate the same institutions" (Stinchcombe 1968: 111).

Merton and Selznick laid the basis for a process model of institutions. Merton described processes operating in all or most bureaucratic organizations conducing officials toward overconformity, while Selznick focused on processes within particular organizations giving rise to a distinctive set of value commitments. Stinchcombe stressed the role of power and elaborated the mechanisms utilized by powerful actors to perpetuate their interests and commitments.

Hughes and the Chicago School

Following in the footsteps of Cooley as well as earlier Chicago sociologists, Thomas and Blumer, Everett Hughes developed an inter-dependent model of rule systems and concerted, situated interaction processes. Deftly defining institutions as an "establishment of relative permanence of a distinctly social sort" (Hughes 1936: 180), he identified their essential elements as "(1) a set of mores or formal rules, or both, which can be fulfilled only by (2) people acting collectively, in established complementary capacities or offices. The first element represents consistency; the second concert or organization" (Hughes 1939: 297).

Hughes insisted that institutions only exist and persist because they are carried forward by interacting individuals: "Institutions exist in the integrated and standardized behavior of individuals" (Hughes 1939: 319). More so than other students of organizations at this time, Hughes emphasized the openness and somewhat indeterminate nature of organizations. He resisted using the term "organization" because of its "implication that some known numbers of people are 'associated' or 'organized'" (Hughes 1962/1971: 54). Instead he preferred the name *going concerns*: "They occur in many forms, and may be in any stage of having, getting, or losing moral, social, legal, or simply customer approval" (Hughes 1962/1971: 54). In this manner, he anticipated later open-system modes of organizing, highlighting loose-coupling, organized anarchy, and network forms (see Scott and Davis 2007: Chap. 4) as well as the growing fusion of organization and social movement theories (Davis, McAdam, Scott, and Zald 2005).

In a similar vein, he believed that sociologists too often employed the term "institution" as "a great name, one deserved only by those things which embody the highest of human values"; but to do so, he argued, is misguided:

> If we close our lists there, we miss the main and more fascinating part of the sociologists' work, which is to understand how social values and collective arrangements are made and unmade: how things arise and how they change. To make progress with our job, we need to give full and comparative attention to the not-yets, the didn't quite-make-its, the not quite respectable, the unremarked and the openly "anti" goings-on in our society. (Hughes 1962/1971: 53)

Recent scholars, such as Barley (2008) and Ventresca and Kaghan (2008), see much of value in the work of Hughes and his students and associates. Hughes was among the first institutional scholars connecting institutions and organizations that viewed both as "explicitly dynamic" and "grounded in an ecological and evolutionary view of social/economic/organizational stability and change" (Ventresca and Kaghan 2008: 57–58).

Empirical work developing these insights by Hughes and his followers focused more on occupations—in particular, professions—than on organizations (see, e.g., Abbott 1988; Becker 1982; Freidson 1970; Hughes 1958). However, a number of studies examined "strong" organizational contexts, such as mental hospitals and medical schools (Becker, Geer, Hughes, and Strauss 1961). These studies explored "the microprocesses by which individuals attempt to limit the power of institutions," identifying "the cracks, the loopholes in social structures" that enable patients, students or other subordinate participants to construct meaningful selves and obtain some freedom even when confronting "total institutions" (Fine and Ducharme 1995: 125, 126; Goffman 1961), such as intense professional training programs or mental hospitals.

Parsons' Institutional Approach

Talcott Parsons applies his general "cultural-institutional" arguments to organizations primarily by examining the relation between an organization and its social and cultural environment—the ways in which the value system of an organization is legitimated by its connections to "the main institutional patterns" in "different functional contexts" (Parsons 1956/1960a: 20). While in most of his writing, as noted in Chapter 1, Parsons stressed the subjective dimension of institutions whereby individual actors internalize shared norms so that they become the basis for the individual's action, in his analysis of organizations, he shifts attention to what he terms the objective dimension: "a system of norms defining what the relations of individuals [or organizations] ought to be" (Parsons 1934/1990: 327).

Parsons (1956/1960a: 21) argues that these wider normative structures within societies serve to legitimate the existence of organizations but, "more specifically, they legitimize the main functional patterns of operation which are necessary to implement the values." Schools, for example, receive legitimacy in a society to the extent that their goals are connected to wider cultural values, such as training and education, and to the degree that they conform in their structures and procedures to established "patterns of operation" specified for educational organizations. Note that in some respects this argument replicates at the organizational level Parsons' discussion of institutionalization at the individual level since it focuses on the individual unit's—whether a person's or an organization's—orientation to a normative system. Organizations operating in different functional sectors are legitimated by differing values, exhibit different adaptive patterns, and are governed by different codes and normative frameworks. Moreover, value systems are stratified within a society such that organizations serving more highly esteemed values are thought to be more legitimate, and expected to receive a disproportionate share of societal resources (Parsons 1953).[4]

Parsons finds yet another use for the concept of institution. He argues that organizations tend to become differentiated vertically into three somewhat distinctive levels or layers: the *technical,* concerned with production activities; the *managerial,* concerned with control and coordination activities, procurement of resources, and disposal of products; and the *institutional,* concerned with relating the organization to the norms and conventions of the community and society. Every organization is a subsystem of "a wider social system which is the source of the 'meaning,' legitimation, or higher-level support which makes the implementation of the organization's goals possible" (Parsons 1956/1960b: 63–64). Parsons' typology of organizational levels was subsequently embraced by Thompson (1967/2003) and has been widely employed.[5]

Unlike Selznick's formulation, Parsons' theoretical work on organizations did not stimulate much empirical research. A few students, such as Georgopoulos (1972), employed Parsons' general conceptual scheme and described the importance of institutional underpinnings for specific types of organizations, but in general Parsons' insights were not so much built upon as rediscovered by later theorists.

Simon and the Carnegie School

Political scientist Herbert Simon developed his theory of administrative behavior to counteract and correct conventional economic theories that made heroic, unreasonable assumptions about individual rationality. Although Simon retained the assumption that value premises (preferences) are beyond the analyst's purview (are exogenous), he challenged the assumption that actors have complete knowledge of means and their consequences. He was among the first theorists to link the limits of individual cognitive capacity with the features of organizational structure. In his classic *Administrative Behavior*, Simon (1945/1997) described how organizational structures work to simplify and support decision making by individuals in organizations, allowing them to achieve higher levels of consistent, albeit "boundedly rational," behavior than would otherwise be possible. In accepting organizational membership, individuals are expected to adopt organizational value premises as a guide for their decisions; factual premises—beliefs about means-ends connections—are also commonly supplied, in the form of organizational rules, procedures, and routines (Simon 1945/1997, Ch. 5). Behavior is rational in organizations because choices are constrained and individuals are guided by rules.

Together with March, Simon developed his arguments concerning the ways in which organizations shape the behavior of participants, crafting *performance programs* to guide routine behavior and *search programs* to follow when confronting unusual tasks. March and Simon (1958: 141–142) argue that, in many circumstances, "search and choice processes are very much abridged. . . . Most behavior, and particularly most behavior in organizations, is governed by performance programs"—preset routines that provide guidance to individuals confronted by recurring demands. Such routines greatly reduce the discretion of most participants so that they make few choices and are circumscribed in the choices they do make. Imposed value assumptions, cognitive frames, rules and routines—these are the ingredients that conduce individuals to behave rationally. Indeed, "the rational individual is, and must be, an organized and institutionalized individual" (Simon 1945/1997: 111).

March and Simon's arguments, albeit among the earliest, remain among the most influential and clearest statements of the micro features and functions of neoinstitutional forms (see DiMaggio and Powell 1991: 15–26).

❖ FOUNDATIONS OF NEOINSTITUTIONAL THEORY

We have arrived at the point in our history when the ideas that have come to be recognized as neoinstitutional theory appeared. As we will see, they do not represent a sharp break with the past, although there are new emphases and insights. In this section, I review the proximate sources and founding conceptions linking neoinstitutional theory to organizational analysis in the mainstream disciplines of economics, political science, and sociology as well as in the related fields of cognitive psychology and cultural anthropology. Then, in Chapter 3, I attempt a more analytic synthesis of current conceptual approaches, noting areas of consensus and dispute.

Neoinstitutional Theory in Economics

Many diverse lines of work contribute to the mixture of ideas fueling neoinstitutional theory in economics. It is instructive, and rather ironic, that the newer economic work "reflects less the ideas of the early institutionalists than it does those of their opponents" (Langlois 1986a: 2). Most neoinstitutional economists do not seek to replace orthodox economic theory with the study of multiple and diverse institutional conditions, but rather to develop an economic theory of institutions.

In his useful review, Langlois (1986a) incorporates within neoinstitutional economics the contributions of Simon (discussed earlier); a focus on transaction cost and property rights inspired by Coase (1937), with a slight nod to Commons; the modern Austrian school as influenced by Hayek (1948); the work of Schumpeter (1926/1961) on innovation; and evolutionary theory as developed by Nelson and Winter (1982). Three more or less common themes underlie and link these contributions (see Knudsen 1993; Langlois 1986a):

1. A broader conception of the economic agent is embraced, replacing the assumption of maximizing within a set of known alternatives.

How broad a view is taken varies greatly among the identified schools. In his work on transaction costs, Williamson embraces Simon's conception of "bounded" rationality, while the Austrian and evolution-ary theorists utilize an even more expansive view that includes rule-based or "procedural" rationality (behavior is rational if specified procedures are followed, irrespective of outcome).

2. A focus on the study of economic processes rather than on the purely logical study of equilibrium states is preferred, fostering a recognition that economic systems evolve over time reflecting, in part, learning by the agents.

Conventional economics devotes the lion's share of its resources to the study of various types of economic systems that have attained an equilibrium (stable and well-coordinated behavior), but little to the question of how a state of equilibrium came into being or comes apart. Often, ad hoc stories are generated about how stability may have been achieved, but these are only tacked on to the formal model (see Knudsen 1993). Neoinstitutional economists, by contrast, are interested in developing and testing these process arguments. Rather than treating institutions mainly as exogenous variables affecting economic behavior, the newer scholarship considers how institutions affecting economic transactions arise, are maintained, and are transformed. Game theorists have also become interested in these questions, asking how norms or rules emerge as actors interact to devise treaties or regimes to deal with conflicts.

3. The coordination of economic activity is not simply a matter of market-mediated transactions, but involves many other types of institutional structures that are, in themselves, important topics of study.

In addition to the role of governmental systems, among the most important of these institutional structures are those embedded in organizations.

It is not possible here to consider in detail all of the specific approaches associated with these themes (for reviews, see Hodgson 1993; 1994; Mäki, Gustafsson, and Knudsen 1993; Silverman 2002; Zajac and Westphal 2002), but four of the more influential contributions will be briefly described.

Transaction Cost Economics

One branch of neoinstitutional economics is concerned with the rule and governance systems that develop to regulate or manage eco-nomic exchanges. These systems occur at many levels, from macro regimes at the international level to understandings governing micro exchanges between individuals. Accounting for the emergence and change of trading regimes among societies has been of primary interest to economic historians (e.g., North 1990), industry systems have been examined by industrial organization economists (e.g., Stigler 1968), and studies of the sources of organizational forms are being conducted by a growing set of organizational economists (see Milgrom and Roberts, 1992). While all of this work is properly regarded as institutional economics, it is the latter work, focusing on firm- and corporate-level structures, that is especially identified with the new institutionalism in economics.

By consensus, the pioneer theorist inaugurating this approach was Ronald Coase (1937), whose article "The Nature of the Firm" asks why some economic exchanges are carried out within firms under a governance structure involving rules and hierarchical enforcement mechanisms rather than being directly subject to the price mechanism in markets. Coase suggests that the reason must be that "there is a cost of using the price mechanism," namely "the costs of negotiating and concluding a separate contract for each exchange transaction which takes place in a market" (p. 389). It is because of these *transaction costs* that firms arise.

This insight lay fallow—in Coase's (1972: 69) own words, his article was "much cited and little used"—until it was resurrected in the 1970s by Oliver Williamson, who pursued its development by both conditionalizing and elaborating it. Williamson argued that transaction costs increase as a function of two paired conditions: when individual rationality, which is "bounded" (cognitively limited), is confronted by heightened complexity and uncertainty, and when opportunism— some actors' propensity to lie and cheat—is coupled with the absence of alternative exchange partners. Under such conditions, exchanges are likely to be removed from the market and brought within an organizational framework or, if already inside an organization, to stimulate the development of more elaborate controls (Williamson 1975; 1985). Williamson extends Coase's arguments by pushing them beyond the market versus firm comparison to consider a wide variety of alternative governance systems ranging from markets, to hybrid organizational forms (e.g., franchising or alliance arrangements), to various types of hierarchical structures (e.g., unified firms, multidivisional corporations) (Williamson 1985; 1991).[6] In this approach, Williamson builds on the previous work of Barnard (1938), who emphasized adaptation as a central problem facing organizations; Simon (1945/1997), with his conception of bounded rationality and organizational strategies for supporting decision making; and Chandler (1962), with his focus on matching a firm's structure to its strategy (Williamson 2005).

Thus, the Williamson variant of new institutional economics focuses primarily on the meso-analytic questions of "the comparative efficacy with which alternative generic forms of governance—markets, hybrids, hierarchies—economize on transactions costs" rather than on the more macro questions regarding the origins and effects of the "institutional rules of the game: customs, laws, politics" (Williamson 1991: 269)—the latter issues being left to economic historians and sociologists (see also Williamson 1994; 2005).

Although Williamson stretches conventional economics to take seriously the effects of varying institutional contexts, or governance structures, on economic behavior, unlike earlier economic institutionalists, he has remained firmly within the neoclassical tradition. Hodgson (1994) underlines the point:

> Like the work of other new institutionalists, Williamson's is constructed in atomistic and individualistic terms because its elemental conceptual building block is the given, "opportunistic" individual. He does not consider the possibility that the preference functions of the individual may be molded by circumstances, such as the structure and culture of the firm, or that this phenomenon may be significant in analyzing or understanding such institutions. (p. 70)

In addition, Williamson shows little interest in the processes by which varying governance structures arise or are transformed. His explanation for a structure is more often constructed as a functionalist one, "explaining" the choice of a given form by pointing to its consequences (Knudsen 1993; see also Chapter 5).

By contrast, other economists, such as Douglass North, have developed approaches that incorporate assumptions much more similar to those embraced by the turn-of-the-century economic institutionalists. As noted, North focuses on a higher level of analysis, examining the origins of cultural, political, and legal frameworks and their effects on economic forms and processes. As an economic historian, his focus is on development and change rather than on comparative statics (North 1989; 1990; see also Chapter 5). And while he attends to transaction costs in his analysis of economic systems, he is more prone to treat them as dependent variables—subject to the effects of varying wider institutional frameworks—than as independent variables to explain differences among actors' choice of governance mechanisms (see Hirsch and Lounsbury 1996).

Whereas Williamson (1994: 79) focuses attention on organizations as themselves institutional forms—governance systems devised to reduce transaction costs—that must take into account "background conditions" such as property rights, laws, norms and conventions, North (1990: 5) directs attention to these wider institutional frameworks—societal "rules of the game"—and views organizations as "players" who are attempting to devise strategies to win the game.

Game-Theoretic Approaches

Game theory is an important branch of the economic rational choice perspective that views institutions as an equilibrium phenomenon. Game theory examines situations in which individuals behave strategically in the sense that each person's outcomes depend on the choices made by other players. Games comprise sets of rules specifying the players (decision makers), their possible actions, and each player's preferences about outcomes. The objective is for each player to maximize her outcomes given the actions of other players. An equilibrium condition is reached when the behaviors of players are "self-reinforcing"—each player selecting a consistent option given her knowledge of how other players will behave. Games may support more than one equilibrium solution so that the testing of specific predictions may not be possible (Gibbons 1992). Economists and rational choice political scientists have modeled many types of game settings.

Elinor Ostrom has employed a game-theoric approach to examine a variety of institutional frameworks, focusing primarily on the "rules-in-use" in "action situations," including the regulation of the phone industry in the United States, the evolution of coffee cooperatives in Cameroon, the performance of housing condominiums in South Korea, and a comparison of nonprofit, for profit, and government day care centers in the United States (Ostrom 2005: 9, 138). She and her colleagues have devised an Institutional Analysis and Development (IAD) framework that focuses principally on (1) rules—"shared understanding by participants about enforced prescriptions concerning what actions (or outcomes) are required, prohibited, or permitted" (Ostrom 2005: 18)—but also attends to (2) the attributes of goods, such as whether they are easily divisible, transferable, or excludable, and (3) to the attributes of community, which include its culture, or the values shared within a community (Kiser and Ostrom 1982; Ostrom 2005). The framework is applied to action situations that include attention to the attributes of participants, positions, and actions of the actors involved. In short, the approach broadens and enriches mainstream game theory.[7]

Ostrom's attention to rule systems as the heart of institutional analysis recognizes that these systems operate at multiple levels. Her work stresses three as particularly important: *operational rules* that affect day-to-day decisions of participants in the setting, *collective-choice rules* that determine who is eligible to participate in decisions and which rules are to apply in changing situation, and *constitutional-choice rules* that lay out the deeper level frameworks specifying the capabilities and limits of the repertories of rules available (Ostrom 2005: 58–62). These frameworks have been employed to compare and contrast actions and outcomes not only in formal models and experimental simulations but also in examining rule-framed choice situations in a wide variety of qualitative field studies in diverse social and cultural settings.

Institutional scholars, such as Avner Greif (2006: 14), have embraced and adapted game-theoretic approaches because, rather than treating institutions as frameworks of rules or beliefs, they treat these as elements that help to "constitute the structure that influences behavior, while the behavioral responses of agents to this structure reproduce the institution." Greif points out that many rules are not obeyed; many beliefs do not affect the behavior of those who profess them. Thus, it is preferable to focus on

> *endogenous* institutions: those that are self-enforcing. In self-enforcing institutions all motivation is endogenously provided. Each individual, responding to the institutional elements implied by others' behavior and expected behavior, behaves in a manner that contributes to enabling, guiding, and motivating others to behave in the manner that led to the institutional elements that generated the individual's behavior to begin with. (pp. 15–16)

These types of institutions persist, unless there is exogenous change, because "the behavior of each actor is optimal, given the behavior and expected behavior of the other actors" (Greif 2003: 150). Such situations are of particular interest to economists because many equilibria are likely to exist: "What we observe does not have to be optimal and survival does not indicate efficiency" (Greif 2003: 150). In this manner, game theory offers a framework for examining the institutional foundations of markets from an equilibrium, rather than optimality perspective.

Greif is open to non-economic influences on choice behavior. The actor's motivations may stem from numerous influences, including many sociocultural attributes, including norms, beliefs, and cognitive ingredients. Because motivations vary greatly, "rational" decisions contribute to diverse choices among individuals of "optimal' outcomes.

Greif applies his approach to a variety of historical cases focusing on the institutional conditions contributing to or inhibiting economic development in the European and Muslim portions of the Mediterranean of the medieval period. In related work, Nee and Lian (1994) have utilized similar approaches to examine differences between the former Soviet Union and China in the emergence of the market economies. The former relied primarily on formal, top-down approaches, which have been far less successful than China's bottom-up incrementalist strategy, more closely tied to the interests of participating political and economic actors.

Evolutionary Economics

A third, important addition to neoinstitutional economic theory has been developed by Nelson and Winter (1982; Winter 1964). Their evolutionary approach distantly echoes the interests of Veblen, but is more solidly based on Schumpeter's (1926/1961) ideas on innovation and Alchian's (1950) arguments that economic agents such as firms are subject to adaptation and selection processes (Winter 2005). Nelson and Winter embrace an evolutionary theory of the firm analogous to biological models, in which a firm's routines are argued to be the equivalent of genes in a plant or animal. *Routines*—or capabilities—are made up of both the conscious and tacit knowledge and skills held by participants who carry out organizational tasks. To survive, a firm must be able to reproduce and modify its routines in the face of changing situations.

Nelson and Winter (1982: 36) locate their arguments at the industry or organizational population level of analysis in order to develop a theory of economic change processes. Their concern is to examine the ways in which competitive processes operate among firms so that those whose routines are best adapted to current conditions flourish while those with less adequate routines falter. A dynamic model of accumulating knowledge and capabilities is developed to displace the static model of orthodox economics. Firms are viewed as historical entities, their routines being "the result of an endogenous, experience-based learning process" (Knudsen 1995b: 203). Moreover,

> it is quite inappropriate to conceive of firm behavior in terms of deliberate choice from a broad menu of alternatives that some external observer considers to be "available" opportunities for the organization. The menu is not broad, but narrow and idiosyncratic;

it is built into the firm's routines, and most of the "choosing" is also accomplished automatically by those routines. (Nelson and Winter 1982: 134)

Nelson and Winter do not employ the term *institution* in their arguments, but it is quite clear that their conception of organizational routines can be treated as one mode of institutionalized behavior. Implicitly, as Langlois (1986a: 19) suggests, their view of institution is one of "regularities of behavior understandable in terms of rules, norms, and routines." Nelson and Winter embrace a much broader conception of factors shaping behavior and structure in organizations than do transaction cost economists. Also, their approach strongly favors a process orientation rather than one of comparative statics.

Resource-Based Theory

Whereas evolutionary approaches emphasize the power of exogenous forces such as variation, selection, and retention processes, resource-based theory stresses the possibility of organizational actors to strategically manage resources under their control. The level of analysis shifts from the organization population to the firm level.

This approach to the examination of organizations was pioneered by Edith Penrose (1959/1995), who recognized that the most important asset a firm possesses is its specialized use of resources (including worker skills) and its capacity to mobilize them, as required, in diverse combinations. More recently, this conception has been advanced and elaborated by scholars such as Jay Barney (1991) and David Teece (1982). Barney and colleagues argue that a firm's "resources and capabilities can be viewed as bundles of tangible and intangible assets, including a firm's management skills, its organizational processes and routines, and the information and knowledge it controls" (Barney, Wright, and Ketchen 2001: 643). A firm's competitive advantages "derive from the resources and capabilities a firm controls that are valuable, rare, imperfectly imitable, and not substitutable" (p. 643). This view contrasts with neoclassical economic arguments that assume that factors (resources) are elastic in supply, readily available if the price is right. Resource-based theorists insist that some resources are not elastic, developing over long periods of time, difficult to reproduce because based on tacit knowledge, their value dependent on linkages to complex constellations of other variables.

Both Barney and Teece argue that managerial skills are critical to building, maintaining, and modifying firm capabilities. Managers of firms operating in rapidly changing environments must master the skill of designing *dynamic capabilities*: sensing and shaping opportunities and threats, enhancing and reconfiguring the firm's intangible and tangible assets.

> Dynamic capabilities include difficult-to-replicate enterprise capabilities required to adapt to changing customer and technological opportunities. They also embrace the enterprise's capacity to shape the ecosystem it occupies, develop new products and processes, and design and implement viable business models. (Teece 2009: 4)

Resource-based scholars recognize the existence and importance of institutionalized elements within organizations, and point out the challenges these pose for organizational leaders: to nurture existing capabilities and to design and implement new institutional structures to meet changing challenges and opportunities.

In sum, there are important differences among contemporary institutional economists in the nature of their assumptions and the focus of their analytic attention. However, it is unquestionably the case that the new institutional economics is dominated currently by scholars who cling to the neoclassical core of the discipline while struggling to broaden its boundaries.

Neoinstitutional Theory in Political Science

As described in Chapter 1, neoinstitutionalism in political science may be viewed, at least in part, as a reaction to the behavioralist emphasis that dominated the field up through the mid-20th century. Resembling to some extent the situation in economics, the new institutionalists in political science and political sociology have grouped themselves into two quite distinct camps: the historical and the rational choice theorists.[8] The two perspectives differ along several dimensions.

Historical Institutionalism

The historical institutionalists, in many respects, hearken back to the turn-of-the-century institutional scholars who devoted themselves to the detailed analysis of regimes and governance mechanisms but also reflect the influence of Weber and his comparative approach as well as more recent sociocultural approaches (Lecours 2005; Thelen 1999). On the one hand, we find the more "materialist" approaches that focus attention on governance structures: electoral rules, party systems, relations between branches of government (e.g., Hall 1986; Steinmo, Thelen, and Longstreth 1992). Thelen and Steinmo (1992: 2), for example, view institutions as "both formal structures and informal rules and procedures that structure conduct." On the other side, some theorists adopt a more normative or ideational approach focusing on beliefs, values, and cognitive scripts (e.g., Finnemore 1993; March and Olsen 1984; 1989).

Although these differences exist, most historical institutionalists focus on the nature of political systems, examining the ways in which these structures shape the character and outcomes of conflicts—how they distribute power among actors and shape actors' conceptions of their interests (Hall and Taylor 1996). They emphasize that political institutions are not entirely derivative from other social structures such as class, but have independent effects on social phenomena (Evans, Rueschemeyer, and Skocpol 1985); that social arrangements are not only or even primarily the result of aggregating individual choices and actions; that many structures and outcomes are not those planned or intended, but the consequence of unanticipated effects and constrained choice; and that history is not usually "efficient"—a process "that moves rapidly to a unique solution" (March and Olsen 1984: 737)—but one that is much more indeterminate and context-dependent.

Some members of the historical group take a social-constructionist position that assumes "that capabilities and preferences, that is, the very nature of the actors, cannot be understood except as part of some larger institutional framework" (Krasner 1988: 72; see also Chapter 3). Individual preferences are not stable and often result from rather than precede or determine choices. Institutions construct actors and define their available modes of action; they constrain behavior, but they also empower it. Analysis from this perspective is aimed at providing a detailed account of the specifics of institutional forms since they are expected to exert strong effects on individual behavior: structuring agendas, attention, preferences, and modes of acting.

These analysts attempt to show that political systems are not neutral arenas within which external interests compete, but rather complex forms and forums that generate independent interests and advantages and whose rules and procedures exert important effects on whatever business is being transacted. In accounting for the origins of these structures, the approach is primarily that of historical reconstruction. Although individuals build these structures, there is no assurance that they will produce what they intend. Current choices and possibilities are constrained and conditioned by past choices (see, e.g., Ertman 1997;

Karl 1997; Skowronek 1982). Institutions, once established, have a "continuing effect on subsequent decision-making and institution-building episodes" (Campbell 2004: 25).

These insights have been derived from and applied to a wide variety of political systems, including private associations, nation-states, international organizations, and regimes such as monetary and trade agreements (e.g., Finnemore 1993; Keohane 1989; Schmitter and Lehmbruch 1979; Skowronek 1982). Critics point out that the work is too often historicist, focusing too much on the details of a single, complex case.

Rational Choice Theory

The second camp consists of the rational choice theorists (also termed "positive" theorists) and includes such scholars as Moe, Shepsle, and Weingast. These analysts view institutions as governance or rule systems, but argue that they represent deliberately constructed edifices established by individuals seeking to promote or protect their interests. The approach represents an extension of the neoinstitutional work in economics—including the transaction cost approach of Williamson and the work of agency theorists such as Alchian and Demsetz (1972)—and its application to the study of political systems. Tullock (1976: 5), an early advocate of importing economic models to explain political behavior, argues that "voters and customers are essentially the same people. Mr. Smith buys and votes; he is the same man in the supermarket and the voting booth" (see also Buchanan and Tullock 1962). Moe (1984) enumerates the major elements making up the paradigm adopted from the economists as including

> the contractual nature of organizations; markets vs. hierarchies, transactions costs, the rationality of structure, individualistic explanation, and economic methods of analysis. Standard neoclassical notions—optimization, marginality, equilibrium—are often central to work in this new tradition. (p. 750)

Political theorists recognize that economic models developed to account for economic organizations require modification if they are to be applied to political systems (Pierson 2004: 30–48). But they also insist that many of the basic questions are parallel: Why do public organizations exist? How are we to account for their varying forms and governance mechanisms? How can elected political officials, as "principals," control their bureaucratic "agents"? What are the effects of political institutions on political and social behavior? What are the mechanisms by which politicians secure their power positions? As Peters (1999: 45) observes, "Within this approach institutions are conceptualized largely as sets of positive (inducements) and negative (rules) motivations for individuals, with individual utility maximization providing the dynamic for behavior within the models."

Rational choice theorists recognize that "in the reality of politics social choices are not chaotic. They are quite stable" (Moe 1990a: 216). They are stable because "of the distinctive role that institutions play" (Moe, 1990a: 216). Many early scholars argued that much of the stability observed in the law-making process could be explained by the ways in which the rules of procedure and committee structures of legislatures structured the choices available to members (Ferejohn and Fiorina 1975; Riker 1980). Thus, the task becomes to understand the role of institutions and, "more fundamentally, to determine where these institutions come from in the first place" (Moe 1990a: 216). The general argument embraced by these theorists is that "economic organizations and institutions are explained in the same way: They are structures that emerge and take the specific form they do because they solve collective-action problems and thereby facilitate gains from trade" (Moe 1990a: 217–218).

Theorists disagree as to what is distinctive about political institutions. Weingast (1989) argues that politics differs from markets in that in the former, actors cannot simply engage in market exchange but must make decisions under some framework such as majority rule. Shepsle (1989) suggests that the most important task of political systems is to "get property rights right": to establish rule systems that will promote efficient economic organizations. Moe (1990a: 221) argues that political decisions are distinctive in that they are "fundamentally about the exercise of public authority," which entails access to unique coercive powers. Pierson (2004: 38) adds that politics is "a far, far murkier environment" than the economic realm, lacking "the measuring rod of price" and entailing the pursuit of often incommensurable goals with opaque processes. These and related researchers have attempted to account for the distinctive powers and influential procedures of congressional committees (Shepsle and Weingast 1987) and the performance (including the ineffectiveness) of some governmental bureaucracies (Moe 1990a; 1990b) as rational solutions to collective problems (see Chapter 5). Hall and Taylor (1996: 945) observe that one of the principal contributions of this approach has been to draw our attention to the crucial "role of strategic interaction in the determination of political outcomes" and to provide a set of tools for understanding how institutions structure such interaction.

An important arena of application for both historical and rational choice theorists has been that of international relations. Rational models view nation-states as self-interested actors attempting to maximize their own advantage in dealing with other nations. Rules are accepted when they lower the transaction costs of a participant and/or decrease the overall level of uncertainty (Hasenclever, Mayer, and Rittberger 1997; Rittberger 1993). By contrast, historical institutionalists, such as Krasner (1983) and Keohane (1989), emphasize the important independent effects of the emergence of cooperative norms among participating nations. In addition, as Keohane (1989: 382) points out, "institutions do not merely reflect the preferences and power of the units constituting them; the institutions themselves shape those preferences and that power."

In sum, while both historical institutionalists and rational choice theorists agree on the importance of institutions in political life, important differences in assumptions and perspectives remain. Rational choice theorists are more likely to stress the microfoundations of institutions, asking how institutions are devised to solve collective action problems experienced by individuals. Historical institutionalists are more likely to emphasize a macro perspective, tracing the evolution of an institutional form and asking how it affects individual preferences and behavior. Preferences are more likely to be treated by rational choice theorists as stable properties of actors, while for historical institutionalists, preferences are seen to be more problematic, emergent from the situation (endogenous), and context-specific. And the two camps are attracted to different sets of problems. Historical institutionalists "begin with empirical puzzles that emerge from observed events or comparisons"; rational choice theorists are more likely to be attracted to "situations in which observed behavior appears to deviate from what the general theory predicts" (Thelen 1999: 374). Finally, rational choice theorists give central place to the concept of equilibria and view institutions as central mechanisms in sustaining this condition, whereas historical institutionalists—like their 19th century counterparts—are more interested in historical change than in equilibrium—the factors producing political and economic change broadly viewed as "structured institutional change" (see Orren and Skowronek 1994).

Thelen (1999) cites evidence of convergence in the perspectives of the two camps in recent years, and Scharpf (1997) suggests that each approach is incomplete and proposes that in the long run they can be combined into a more complete explanation. At the present time, however, they remain relatively distinct approaches, more independent than overlapping in perspective and assumptions and more competitive than cooperative in demeanor.

Cognitive Psychology and Cultural Anthropology

Cognitive Theory

Simon's work on decision making in organizations paralleled developments in social psychology, as this field of study—both its psychological and sociological sides—experienced the "cognitive revolution." During the 1940s and 1950s, the stimulus-response (S-R) approach began to be revised to include attention to the participation of an active organism (S-O-R) that mediated between the provocation and the reaction (see Lewin 1951). Early research concentrated on how the state of the organism, as defined by various motivational and emotional variables, affected perception, selective attention, and memory. An early concern with "hot" cognition (for example, anger or fear) began to be superseded by attention to the effects of "cool" factors (such as attention and background assumptions) influencing everyday information processing and problem-solving behaviors.

> The idea of the human organism as an information processor became popular. The mind came to be viewed by many as a computerlike apparatus that registered the incoming information and then subjected it to a variety of transformations before ordering a response. (Markus and Zajonc 1985: 141)

The question became: What types of "software" provide the programs and transformation rules for these processes? Such factors ranged from the functioning of the brain and nervous system to the structure of individual cognitive processes. Early social theorists, like Durkheim, insisted that "the framework of the intelligence" was entirely provided by the forms of the society into which an individual was born: Social and cultural forms determine mental models (*collective representations*). This argument, with variations, has been echoed and elaborated by Mead, Parsons, and Bourdieu, among numerous others, up to the present time (Bergesen 2004). However, a large and growing body of psychological theory and research suggests that rather than providing a blank slate, humans (e.g., unsocialized infants) come equipped with a number of fundamental mental capabilities, such as conceptions of space, number, cause and effect relations, and recognition of categories (see Gopnik, Melzoff, and Kuhl 1999; Mehler and Dupoux 1994). In a related development, Chomsky (1986) has convinced most linguists that "the principles of language [syntax] are not learned but part of our bio-endowment" (Bergesen 2000: 73).[9]

Yet another debate concerns whether individual thought processes follow a logical axis involving abstract reasoning ("computational") model or a "pattern recognition" ("connectionist") model—the noting of similarities and differences in the situations encountered. The latter approach appears to be both more consistent with studies of human learning and better suited to explaining the ways in which social/ economic actors cope with the kinds of uncertainties they encounter (North 2005: 27). Related work points out that when similarities are encountered, they trigger preexisting "scripts"—a structure that describes appropriate sequences of actions in a well-known situation (Shank and Abelson 1977: 41).

Psychologists have long vacillated between positions that regard individuals as basically competent, rational beings and views emphasizing cognitive biases and limitations. The general impact of recent cognitive theory and research has been to emphasize the shortcomings of individuals as information processors and decision makers. Tversky and Kahneman (1974) pioneered in the identification of a number of specific types of biases likely to cause mistakes in assessing information and reaching conclusions. These and related problems were generalized by Nisbett and Ross (1980) into two common sources of inferential error: (1) a tendency to overuse simplistic strategies and fail to employ the logical and statistical rules that guide scientific analysis and (2) a "tendency to attribute behavior exclusively to the actor's dispositions and to ignore powerful situational determinants of the behavior" (p. 31).

Even though their views have stressed the intellectual limitations of individuals, cognitive psychologists have recognized that individuals do participate actively in perceiving, interpreting, and making sense of their world. By contrast, until fairly recently, sociologists have tended to give primacy to the effects of contextual factors, viewing individuals as more passive, prone to conform to the demands of their social systems and roles. *Identity theory* has emerged as a corrective to this oversocialized view by giving renewed attention to an active and reflexive self that creates, sustains, and changes social structures (see Burke and Reitzes 1981; Rosenberg 1979; Stryker 1994). Similar issues are addressed by *structuration theory*, discussed in Chapter 4.

Culture Theory

These advances by advocates of the nature persuasion have forced some retreats by, but have by no means defeated, the nurture advocates.

Irrespective of capacities and predispositions on the part of individual human actors, all scholars agree that learning occurs in a social context. The groundwork was laid by Franz Boas (1982), a cultural anthropologist working at the turn of the 20th century, who, "by stressing the plasticity of human culture . . . expanded human nature into an infinity of possibilities rather than a prison of constraints" (Ridley 2003: 202). One of the important developments in cultural theory involved a shift away from a more diffuse definition of culture as encompassing the entire way of life of a people to focus on its semiotic functions. Worthy successors to Boas, like Alfred Kroeber and Clyde Kluckhohn (1952: 357), carried forward this tradition, concluding that "culture consists of explicit and implicit patterns of historically derived and selected ideas and their embodiment in institutions, practices, and artifacts." Their more eloquent protégé, Clifford Geertz (1973: 5, 12), elaborated the message: "Believing, with Max Weber, that man is a social animal suspended in webs of significance he himself has spun, I take culture to be these webs. . . . Culture consists of socially established structures of meaning."

Donald (1991) has proposed a coevolutionary view in which the cognitive capacities of our species and the cultures we have developed have advanced in complementary ways. Advancing a "cognitive classification of culture," Donald suggests that human culture has progressed from

- an *episodic* one in which lives were experienced as a series of concrete episodes to
- a *mimetic* one resting on visuomotor skills that produced conscious, intentional, representational acts (e.g., tool-making, coordinated hunting) to
- the use of language that supports a *mythic* culture enabling an oral-narrative system allowing the creation of more comprehensive models of the nature of the world and our place in it to
- a *theoretic* culture involving written language and other forms of symbolic representation (maps, musical notation, architectural drawings) that allows for their externalization in media (books, films, digital media) that can be preserved, corrected, and transmitted over time and space.

Note that the emergence of theoretic culture supports new types of human enterprise, including the development of the sciences, numerous types of theoreticians, and a wide range of professions, which begin to specialize in the production, evaluation, and dissemination of various types of specialized knowledge (see Chapter 5). Each of these levels or phases represents not only advances in the complexity of culture but, simultaneously, improvement in cognitive capacity to the point where some scholars propose that

> genes are very far from being fixed in their actions. Instead, they are devices for extracting information from the environment. Every minute, every second, the pattern of genes being expressed in your brain changes, often in direct or indirect response to events outside the body. Genes are the mechanisms of experience. (Ridley 2003: 248)

All culture theorists underline the importance of symbolic systems in the ordering of social life, but a growing number also recognize that such systems embody not only content but also affect. The meanings embedded in systems are emotional as well as substantive. It is no doubt in recognition of this fact that Tocqueville (1835/2004), the justly famous student of American character and culture, referred to the cultural mores guiding its citizens as the "habits of the heart" (see also Bellah, Madsen, Sullivan, Swidler, and Tipton 1985). As D'Andrade (1984: 99) points out, "ideas, feelings, and intentions are all activated by symbols and are thus part of the meaning of symbols." Sociologist David Heise (1979) goes even further to assert that the meanings of settings, actors, and behaviors, indeed, of any social category, are primarily affective (see also Thoits 1989). Almost any type of stimulus evokes some sort of affective response, and many types of symbolic expressions—thanks, apologies, curses—specifically refer to feelings. Much of the motivation that propels action in any situation comes from the feelings evoked by the shifting patterns of meanings.

A limitation long present in the approach to culture taken by many sociologists is the assumption that culture is subordinate in interest and importance to social structure. The distinction between social structure, made up of the "relational system of interaction among individuals and collectivities," and culture, made up of "transmitted and created content and patterns of values, ideas, and other symbolic-meaningful systems" of symbolic and normative systems, is one of long standing (Kroeber and Parsons 1958: 583). Sociologists have tended to privilege social structure over symbolic systems in their accounts of behavior. The new cultural arguments stress the independent effects of cultural systems. Current institutionalists view the cultural and the social structural as interdependent.

Symbolic systems vary in the extent to which they exhibit uniformity and promote consistency of action. All too often, it is assumed that cultures are stable and constraining. However, more recent work stresses that culture can enable change. Swidler (1986: 277–278), for example, argues that whereas in "settled" times "culture accounts for continuities . . . organizing and anchoring patterns of action," in times of change, culture functions more like a "tool kit," providing repertoires "from which actors select different pieces for constructing lines of action."

Neoinstitutional Theory in Sociology

Sociological scholars have ranged rather widely in assembling the principal ingredients making up neoinstitutional approaches to organizational sociology. They have drawn upon developments in the neighboring disciplines of psychology and anthropology, as well as their homegrown subdiscipline, ethnomethodology.

Phenomenology and Ethnomethodology

Phenomenology, which began as a branch of philosophy, was incorporated into social science by scholars such as Schutz and Berger, who "stressed the in-depth exploration of the meanings associated with symbols" (Wuthnow 1987: 42). These scholars clearly embraced a view of culture as primarily a semiotic system. They also distanced themselves from the prevailing focus on shared norms and values, as exemplified in the work of Durkheim and Parsons, to emphasize shared knowledge and belief systems. Behavior is shaped not only by attention to rules and the operation of norms, but also by common definitions of the situation and shared strategies of action. As noted in Chapter 1, attention to cognitive frames and cultural frameworks rather than normative systems is one of the major distinguishing marks of neoinstitutional theory in sociology (see DiMaggio and Powell 1991: 15–18).

Corresponding to the changing conceptions of culture, in particular the "theoretic" mode, to use Donald's terminology, another important shift in emphasis involves the recognition that symbols exist not only as internalized beliefs but also as external frameworks. Much work in sociology (e.g., Parsons' value orientations and survey methodologies) treats beliefs as primarily internalized and subjective. By contrast, the types of data preferred by the new cultural scholars "are more readily observable kinds of behavior"—such as verbal utterances, rituals, codified bodies of knowledge, and cultural artifacts—"rather than [those] locked away in people's private ruminations" (Wuthnow 1987: 56). Such approaches direct attention away from the internalized, subjective nature of culture and treat symbols as external, objective phenomena.[10] This emphasis is particularly apparent in Berger and Luckmann's (1967) conceptualization of the construction of common meaning systems. They stress three moments or phases:

- *externalization*—the production, in social interaction, of symbolic structures whose meaning comes to be shared by the participants;
- *objectification*—the process by which this production "comes to confront him as a facticity outside of himself," as something "out there," as a reality experienced in common with others; and only then comes
- *internalization*—the process by which the objectified world is "retrojected into consciousness in the course of socialization." (pp. 60–61)

As noted in Chapter 1, Berger and Luckmann (1967) define this three-phase process as one of *institutionalization*. Institutions are symbolic systems that are "experienced as possessing a reality of their own, a reality that confronts the individual as an external and coercive fact" (p. 58).[11] A more recent manifestation of this recognition of the importance of culture as an external symbolic framework is a concern with the "production of culture"—an examination of the ways in which cultural items are produced, distributed, selected, and institutionalized (see Becker 1982; Caves 2000; Griswold 1992; Hirsch 1972; Lampel, Shamsie, and Lant 2006)

Closely related to phenomenology is the subfield of ethnomethodology. In an attempt to combat the prevalent models of social order advanced by Parsons and others, Harold Garfinkel (1974) coined the term *ethnomethodology*, corresponding to usage in cultural anthropology, to refer to the "common-sense knowledge" of how to operate within some social arena as developed and acquired by its participants. *Ethno-* stresses the local, indigenous production of meaning; *-methodology*, that the knowledge involves distinctions and rules necessary for carrying on the work at hand.

Researchers within this tradition have primarily studied behavior in work settings or that of other types of actors, such as jurors, engaged in some collective task. The questions posed by these researchers are: How do such individuals make sense of the situations they confront? How do they, collectively, construct the rules and procedures that allow them to cope with everyday demands? Detailed participant observation studies have been conducted—in police stations, welfare agencies, and psychiatric clinics, among other sites—to elicit these shared meanings (see Cicourel 1968; Garfinkel 1967; Zimmerman 1969).

As DiMaggio and Powell (1991: 20) emphasize, ethnomethodologists challenged and supplemented Parsons' model by stressing the cognitive rather than the evaluative-normative components of behavior; and they questioned the neoclassical economic model of rational decision making by emphasizing the tacit, routine nature of choice in organizational settings.

These then were the mix of ideas and themes that came together beginning in the 1960s to seed the development of neoinstitutional theory in sociology. Although, as noted, some of these ideas were being developed in and applied to organizations by ethnomethodologists, they did not penetrate the mainstream of organizational studies until the 1970s.

Neoinstitutional Theory and Organizations: Founding Conceptions

An important early attempt to introduce neoinstitutional arguments to the study of organizations was made by David Silverman (1971), who proposed an *action* theory of organization. Silverman attacked prevailing models of organization, including contingency arguments and Parsons' and Selznick's structural-functional views, as being overly concerned with stability, order, and system maintenance. Drawing on the work of Durkheim, Schutz, Berger and Luckmann, and Goffman, Silverman proposed a phenomenological view of organizations that focuses attention on meaning systems and the ways in which they are constructed and reconstructed in social action. Silverman contrasts his action approach with the prevailing systems view:

> The Systems approach tends to regard behaviour as a reflection of the characteristics of a social system containing a series of impersonal processes which are external to actors and constrain them. In emphasizing that action derives from the meanings that men attach to their own and each other's actions, the Action frame of references argues that man is constrained by the way in which he socially constructs his reality. (p. 141)

Adopting the insights of Durkheim, Silverman (1971) argued that meanings operate not only in the minds of individuals but are also objective *social facts* residing in social institutions. The environments of organizations need to be conceptualized not only as a supply house of resources and target of outputs but also as a "source of meanings for the members of organisations" (p. 19).

Silverman's critique and attempted redirection of organizational theory had more impact in European than U.S. circles (see Burrell and Morgan 1979; Salaman 1978).[12] Another European social theorist, Pierre Bourdieu, employed a general conception of *social field* to refer to social arenas governed by distinctive values and approaches. Bourdieu emphasized the contested nature of social fields and the role of power in resolving these contests (see Chapter 8). Fields can be examined as social phenomena external to any particular actor but also exist as subjective, internalized mental elements. In his analysis of social structures, Bourdieu (1977) places great importance on the internalization of cultural rules. His concept of *habitus* refers to the existence of a "system of lasting and transposable dispositions which, integrating past experiences, functions at every moment as a matrix of perceptions, appreciations and actions" (p. 95) allowing individuals to structure their behavior within situations (see also Bourdieu and Wacquant 1992: 94–149). Bourdieu's work was also much more influential in Europe than in the United States, until recently, when it served as one of the precursors to the development of the conception of organization field (see Chapters 4 and 8).

A subsequent effort to introduce the new institutional arguments into organizational sociology proved to be much more successful. Two seminal articles appearing in the same year introduced neoinstitutional theory into the sociological study of organizations. Articles by Meyer and Rowan (1977) and by Zucker (1977), like Silverman's work, built primarily on Durkheim's and, especially, Berger and Luckmann's conception of institutions.

John Meyer and Brian Rowan embrace the view of institutions as complexes of cultural rules. But in their formulation, not any and all cultural rules are supportive of organizations. Following Peter Berger's lead (see Berger, Berger, and Kellner 1973), Meyer and Rowan stress the importance of beliefs that are *rationalized*—formulated in ways that specify the design of rule-like procedures to attain specific objectives. The engines of rationalization include the professions, nation-states, and the mass media whose efforts support the development of larger numbers and more types of organizations. Organizations are not simply the product of increasing technical sophistication, as had long been argued, or even of increasingly complex relational patterns, but result from the increasing rationalization of cultural rules that provide an independent basis for their construction. Meyer and Rowan emphasize the impact on organizational forms of changes in the wider institutional environment.

While Meyer and Rowan developed the macro side of the argument, Lynne Zucker (a student of Meyer) emphasized the "microfoundations" of institutions (see Zucker 1991). She stressed the power of cognitive beliefs to anchor behavior: "Social knowledge, once institutionalized, exists as a fact, as part of objective reality, and can be transmitted directly on that basis" (Zucker 1977: 726; see Chapter 6).

Other influential contributions soon thereafter, by DiMaggio and Powell (1983) and by Meyer and Scott (1983b), elaborated the macro (environmental) perspective, which has become the dominant emphasis in sociological work. DiMaggio and Powell distinguished three important mechanisms—coercive, mimetic, and normative—by which institutional effects are diffused through a field of organizations, and emphasized structural isomorphism (similarity) as an important consequence of both competitive and institutional processes. Meyer and Scott proposed that all organizations are shaped by both technical and institutional forces, but that some types of organizations were more strongly influenced by one than the other. Both sets of authors identified the organization field or sector as a new level of analysis particularly suited to the study of institutional processes. Organization fields help to bound the environments within which institutional processes operate (see Chapters 4 and 8).

This early work in combination set in motion a wave of new effort linking institutions to organizations that has continued to fuel and guide an expanding set of studies with applications to new problems and fields of inquiry—from micro-mobilization to globalization processes. Like pioneering work in any arena, it has had an imprinting effect on much of the subsequent development of the field. But such influence has both its positive and its negative sides. As we will discuss in subsequent chapters, while the pioneering statements provided valuable insights to pursue, they also contained flawed or limiting assumptions that are still in the process of being corrected.

Powell and DiMaggio (1991) helped to underline the importance of these early papers by reprinting them as the foundational statements of the *new institutionalism in organizational analysis* in their influential edited volume. They also pointedly defined the differences between old and new institutionalism, the former represented by Selznick and his followers. The old model privileged conflicts of interest, power processes, informal structure, values, norms, and social commitments, and saw institutionalism as a process occurring within an organization. The new model emphasized cultural and constitutive processes, routines and schemas, legitimacy processes, and formal structure, and viewed institutionalism as a process occurring in the environment of organizations, often at the field level (DiMaggio and Powell 1991). These distinctions continue to be widely employed, although there have been numerous attempts to move beyond this oversimplified dichotomy (e.g., Greenwood and Hinings 1996; Hirsch and Lounsbury 1997).

Also active among sociologists are a set of investigators embracing a rational choice approach to social institutions. Their assumptions and approaches are quite similar to those already described as operating in economics and political science. While their numbers and influence are considerably smaller in sociology than in these other disciplines, they include a number of prominent sociologists, including Coleman (1990), Hechter (1987; Hechter, Opp, and Wippler 1990), and Nee (1998). As Coleman (1994) notes, these theorists embrace the "principle of actor maximization"—some in the stronger sense, others in the weaker, bounded rationality sense—as the "source of deductive power of rational choice theory." But unlike neoclassical economics, they replace the "assumption of a perfect market with social structures, sometimes regarded as endogenous, and other times as exogenous, which carries individual actions into systemic outcomes" (p. 167). And at least some of these analysts allow for the effects of "context-bound rationality within which individual interests and group norms develop" (Brinton and Nee 1998: xv).

❖ CONCLUDING COMMENT

Beginning in the 1950s with the emergence of organizations as a recognized field of study, scholars began to connect institutional arguments to the structure and behavior of organizations. These approaches both built on and departed from the work of earlier institutional theorists. Institutional arguments began to be connected to organizational studies through the work of Merton and his students, particularly Selznick; Hughes and colleagues; Parsons; and Simon and March.

The work that has come to be labeled neoinstitutional theory assumes quite varied guises across the social sciences. The main thrust of economic approaches embraces orthodox or slightly broadened, rationality assumptions and seeks to apply economic arguments to account for the existence of organizations and institutions. Williamson's development of transaction cost analysis exemplifies this approach to organizations. Political science remains split into two factions, the one applying rational choice economic models to political systems, and the other embracing a historical view of the nature of institutions, emphasizing their broad effects in constructing interests and actors.

Neoinstitutional approaches in sociology build on a loosely constructed framework of ideas stemming from cognitive psychology, cultural studies, phenomenology, and ethnomethodology. The newer conceptual models emphasize cognitive over normative frameworks and have focused primary attention on the effects of cultural belief systems operating in the environments of organizations rather than on intraorganizational processes.

In Chapter 3, I shift from a historical to an analytic approach. I begin with an attempt to develop an integrated model of institutions— drawing on and encompassing much of the contemporary work of the type just reviewed. I then identify several dimensions along which contemporary theories differ as they consider the relation of institutions to organizations.

❖ NOTES

1. Related work stimulated by Weber was also carried out at this time by Reinhard Bendix, an exile from Nazi Germany. As a young assistant professor at the University of California, Berkeley, Bendix applied Weber's historical-comparative approach to the study of work and authority systems in two matched pairs of societies, England and the United States, and Russia and East Germany. In many respects, his study of diverse managerial ideologies, *Work and Authority in Industry* (Bendix 1956/2001), was much more in accord with Weberian insights and research style than most other efforts at this time that invoked Weber's name (see Guillén 2001b).

2. Translations of some of Weber's important essays were made by Hans H. Gerth and C. Wright Mills (Weber 1906–1924/1946), who were both at Columbia University and connected to the circle of scholars gathered around Merton. Other important early translators were A. M. Henderson and Talcott Parsons (Weber 1924/1947).

3. In addition to his mentor, Merton, Selznick was also clearly influenced by the work of Robert Michels (1915/1949), a contemporary of Max Weber, who first examined the ways in which some members of organizations become more concerned with preserving the organization itself even at the cost of sacrificing its original goals. Michels observed this process in his study of the Social Democratic Party in Germany, which came to power but at the sacrifice of its original goals. He gloomily concludes: "Thus from a means, the organization becomes an end" (Michels 1915/1949: 390).

4. Values are expressions of goals or, more precisely, the criteria employed in selecting goals; norms are the generalized rules governing behavior that specify appropriate means for pursuing goals.

5. Parsons (1956/1960b: 65–66) notes that the "points of articulation" between the three system levels are characterized by "a qualitative break in the simple continuity of line authority" since "the functions at each level are qualitatively different." His discussion thus anticipates the recognition by later analysts that some structural elements are loosely coupled, or decoupled (see Meyer and Rowan 1977; Weick 1976).

6. A related line of theory and research, *agency theory*, also addresses the proper design of control structures to deal with the motivation and control of agents—those hired to assist the principal—the person expected to be the prime beneficiary of the collective work (see Alchian and Demsetz 1972; Jensen and Meckling 1976; Pratt and Zeckhauser 1985). Dealing with a problem common to all organizations, this approach focuses on the design of appropriate control and incentive systems to manage various kinds of work.

7. This IAD framework is rather similar to the Actor-Centered Institutionalism approach developed by Mayntz and Scharpf to analyze the operation of national policy settings (see Scharpf 1997).

8. Peters (1999) identifies six (!) institutional perspectives existing within political science: normative, rational choice, historical, empirical, international, and societal. This typology, in my view, gives too much weight to differences in methodology and/or topic. In a useful review, Hall and Taylor (1996) identity three new institutionalisms: historical, rational choice, and sociological.

9. Paradoxically, as Chomsky has shown, an innate, hard-wired language capacity provides the basis for a *generative grammar* capable of rich and flexible language usage (Bergesen 2000; 2005).

10. Informative reviews of cultural sociology are provided by Wuthnow, Hunter, Bergesen, and Kurzwell (1984), Wuthnow (1987), and DiMaggio (1990; 1997).

11. It is for this reason that phenomenologists such as Schutz and Bellah define themselves as *symbolic realists.*

12. In his subsequent work, Silverman (1972; Silverman and Jones 1976), shifted his focus toward a more micro, ethnomethodological emphasis, examining the multiple meanings and rationalities associated with participants' phenomenological accounts of their common situation (see Reed 1985).

3

Crafting an Analytic Framework I: Three Pillars of Institutions

Men make their own history, but they do not make it just as they please; they do not make it under circumstances chosen by themselves, but under circumstances directly encountered, given, and transmitted by the past.

—Karl Marx (1852/1963: 15)

To an institutionalist, knowledge of what has gone before is vital information. The ideas and insights of our predecessors provide the context for current efforts and the platform on which we necessarily craft our own contributions. However, as should be clear even from my brief review, the concepts and arguments advanced by our predecessors have been strikingly diverse, resting on varied assumptions and privileging differing causal processes. A number of theorists have proposed that we can clarify the arguments by boiling them down to a few dominant paradigms (see, e.g., Campbell, 2004; Hall and Taylor, 1996). However, as Campbell observes, these "schools" exhibit as many similarities as differences. Hence, my own approach to bringing some order into the discussion is to propose a broad definition of institutions that can encompass a variety of arguments, and then attempt to identify the key analytic elements that give rise to the most important differences observed and debates encountered. This chapter and the next identify and elucidate the three analytical elements that comprise institutions. Each element is important, and sometimes one or another will dominate, but more often—particularly in robust institutional frameworks—they work in combination. But because each operates through distinctive mechanisms and sets in motion disparate processes, I emphasize their differences in my initial discussion.

After introducing the principal distinctions around which the analysis will be conducted, I bravely but briefly consider their philosophical underpinnings. Varying conceptions of institutions call up somewhat different views of the nature of social reality and social order. Similarly, the institutional elements relate to disparate constructs of how actors make choices, the extent to which actors are rational, and what is meant by rationality. These issues, while too complex to fully explore, are too important to ignore.

The companion chapter, Chapter 4, completes the presentation of the analytical framework and associated issues. It begins by examining what types of institutional beliefs support the development of organizations. I then describe the concept of *structuration*, which can assist us in the effort to reconcile institutional constraints with individual agency. Finally, I identify the multiple levels at which institutional analysis takes place. It is important to recognize that even if an investigation focuses on a particular level, institutional forces operating at other levels—both "above" and "beneath" the level selected—will be at work.

Chapters 3 and 4 should be taken as a prolegomenon to the more problem-focused, empirically based discussions in the chapters to follow. They introduce concepts and definitions that will be employed to examine particular topics as well as preview controversies and issues that will be encountered as we review, in Chapters 5 through 8, developments in institutional theory and research from the 1970s to the present.

❖ DEFINING INSTITUTIONS

Let us begin with the following omnibus conception of institutions:

Institutions comprise regulative, normative, and cultural-cognitive elements that, together with associated activities and resources, provide stability and meaning to social life.

This is a dense definition containing a number of ideas that we will unpack, describe, and elaborate in this chapter and the next. In this conception, institutions are multifaceted, durable social structures, made up of symbolic elements, social activities, and material resources. Institutions exhibit distinctive properties: They are relatively resistant to change (Jepperson 1991). As Giddens (1984: 24) states, "Institutions by definition are the more enduring features of social life . . . giving 'solidity' [to social systems] across time and space." They can be transmitted across generations, maintained and reproduced (Zucker 1977). Institutions also undergo change over time.

Institutions exhibit stabilizing and meaning-making properties because of the processes set in motion by regulative, normative, and cultural-cognitive elements. These elements are the central building blocks of institutional structures, providing the elastic fibers that guide behavior and resist change. We examine the distinctive nature and contribution of each element in a subsequent section of this chapter.

Although symbolic systems—rules, norms, and cultural-cognitive beliefs—are central ingredients of institutions, the concept must also encompass associated behaviors and material resources. Although an institutional perspective gives heightened attention to the symbolic aspects of social life, we must also attend to the activities that produce, reproduce, and change them and to the resources that sustain them. Institutions are, in Hallett and Ventresca's (2006) useful metaphor, inhabited by people and their interactions. Rules, norms, and meanings arise in interaction, and they are preserved and modified by human behavior. To isolate meaning systems from their related behaviors is, as Geertz (1973) cautions, to commit the error of

> locking cultural analysis away from its proper object, the informal logic of actual life. . . . Behavior must be attended to, and with some exactness, because it is through the flow of behavior— or, more precisely, social action—that cultural forms find articulation. . . . Whatever, or wherever, symbol systems 'in their own terms' may be, we gain empirical access to them by inspecting events, not by arranging abstracted entities into unified patterns. (p. 17)

Similarly, for Berger and Luckmann (1967) institutions are "dead" if they are only represented in verbal designations and in physical objects. All such representations are bereft of subjective reality "unless they are ongoingly 'brought to life' in actual human conduct" (p. 75).

Sociological theorists Giddens (1979; 1984) and Sewell (1992) underline the importance of including resources—both material and human—in any conception of social structure so as to take into account asymmetries of power. Rules and norms, if they are to be effective, must be backed with sanctioning power, and cultural beliefs, or *schemas* in Sewell's terminology, to be viable, must relate to and are often embodied in resources. Conversely, those possessing power in the form of excess resources seek authorization and legitimation for its use. As Sewell observes, "Schemas not empowered or regenerated by resources would eventually be abandoned and forgotten, just as resources without cultural schemas to direct their use would eventually dissipate and decay" (p. 13)

The Giddens/Sewell formulation usefully stresses the duality of social structure, encompassing both idealist and material features of social life and highlighting their interdependence, an argument I elaborate in Chapter 4.

Most treatments of institutions emphasize their capacity to control and constrain behavior. Institutions impose restrictions by defining legal, moral, and cultural boundaries, distinguishing between acceptable and unacceptable behavior. But it is equally important to recognize that institutions also support and empower activities and actors. Institutions provide stimulus, guidelines, and resources for acting as well as prohibitions and constraints on action.

Although institutions function to provide stability and order, they themselves undergo change, both incremental and revolutionary. Thus, our subject must include not only institutions as a property or state of an existing social order, but also institutions as process, including the processes of institutionalization and deinstitutionalization (see Tolbert and Zucker, 1996). Scholars increasingly attend not only to how institutions arise and are maintained, but to how they undergo change. As we will see, much of the impetus for change occurs through endogenous processes, involving conflicts and contradictions between institutional elements, but institutions can also be destabilized by exogenous shocks, such as wars and financial crises.

Institutions ride on various conveyances and are instantiated in multiple media. These institutional *carriers* vary in the processes employed to transmit their messages. In addition, institutions operate at multiple *levels*—from the world system to interpersonal interaction. We examine these diverse carriers and levels in Chapter 4.

Important differences exist among the various schools of institutional scholars, as is apparent from our review of previous work in Chapters 1 and 2. In my view, the most consequential dispute centers on which institutional elements are accorded primacy.

❖ THE THREE PILLARS OF INSTITUTIONS

Regulative systems, normative systems, cultural-cognitive systems—each of these elements has been identified by one or another social theorist as *the* vital ingredient of institutions. The three elements form a continuum moving "from the conscious to the unconscious, from the legally enforced to the taken for granted" (Hoffman 1997: 36). One possible approach would be to view all of these facets as contributing, in interdependent and mutually reinforcing ways, to a powerful social framework—one that encapsulates and exhibits the celebrated strength and resilience of these structures. In such an integrated conception, institutions appear, as D'Andrade (1984: 98) observes, to be overdetermined systems: "overdetermined in the sense that social sanctions plus pressure for conformity, plus intrinsic direct reward, plus values, are all likely to act together to give a particular meaning system its directive force."

While such an inclusive model has its strengths, it also masks important differences between the elements. The definition knits together three somewhat divergent conceptions that need to be differentiated. Rather than pursuing the development of a more integrated conception,[1] I believe that more progress will be made at this juncture by distinguishing among the several component elements and identifying their different underlying assumptions, mechanisms and indicators.[2] By employing a more analytical approach to these arguments, we can separate out the important foundational processes that transect the domain.

Consider Table 3.1. The columns contain the three elements—three pillars—identified as making up or supporting institutions. The rows define some of the principal dimensions along which assumptions vary and arguments arise among theorists emphasizing one or another element. This table will serve as a guide as we consider each element.

The Regulative Pillar

In the broadest sense, all scholars underscore the regulative aspects of institutions: Institutions constrain and regularize behavior. Scholars more specifically associated with the regulatory pillar are distinguished by the prominence they give to explicit regulatory processes—rule-setting, monitoring, and sanctioning activities. In this conception, regulatory processes involve the capacity to establish rules, inspect others' conformity to them, and, as necessary, manipulate sanctions—rewards or punishments—in an attempt to influence future behavior.

Table 3.1   Three Pillars of Institutions

	Regulative	Normative	Cultural-Cognitive
Basis of compliance	Expedience	Social obligation	Taken-for-grantedness Shared understanding
Basis of order	Regulative rules	Binding expectations	Constitutive schema
Mechanisms	Coercive	Normative	Mimetic
Logic	Instrumentality	Appropriateness	Orthodoxy
Indicators	Rules Laws Sanctions	Certification Accreditation	Common beliefs Shared logics of action Isomorphism
Affect	Fear Guilt/ Innocence	Shame/Honor	Certainty/Confusion
Basis of legitimacy	Legally sanctioned	Morally governed	Comprehensible Recognizable Culturally supported

Sanctioning processes may operate through diffuse, informal mechanisms, involving folkways such as shaming or shunning activities, or they may be highly formalized and assigned to specialized actors such as the police and courts. Political scientists examining international institutions point out that legalization—the formalization of rule systems—is a continuum whose values vary along three dimensions:

- *obligation*—the extent to which actors are bound to obey because their behavior is subject to scrutiny by external parties
- *precision*—the extent to which the rules unambiguously specify the required conduct
- *delegation*—the extent to which third parties have been granted authority to apply the rules and resolve disputes (Abbott, Keohane, Moravcsik, Slaughter, and Snidal 2001)

I suggest that regulatory systems are those that exhibit high values on each of these dimensions while normative systems, considered below, exhibit lower values on them.

Economists, including institutional economists, are particularly likely to view institutions as resting primarily on the regulatory pillar. A prominent institutional economist, Douglass North (1990), for example, features rule systems and enforcement mechanisms in his conceptualization:[3]

[Institutions] are perfectly analogous to the rules of the game in a competitive team sport. That is, they consist of formal written rules as well as typically unwritten codes of conduct that underlie and supplement formal rules. . . . [T]he rules and informal codes are sometimes violated and punishment is enacted. Therefore, an essential part of the functioning of institutions is the costliness of ascertaining violations and the severity of punishment. (p. 4)

North's emphasis on the more formalized control systems may stem in part from the character of the customary objects studied by economists and rational choice political scientists. They are likely to focus attention on the behavior of individuals and firms in markets or on other competitive situations, such as politics, where contending interests are more common and, hence, explicit rules and referees more necessary to preserve order. These economists and political scientists view individuals and organizations that construct rule systems or conform to rules as pursuing their self-interests as behaving instrumentally and expediently. The primary mechanism of control involved, employing DiMaggio and Powell's (1983) typology, is that of *coercion*.

Although the concept of regulation conjures up visions of repression and constraint, many types of regulation enable and empower social actors and action, conferring licenses, special powers, and benefits to some types of actors. In general, regulatory processes within the private, market-based sector are more likely to rely on positive incentives (e.g., increased returns, profits); in their role vis-à-vis the private sector, public actors make greater use of negative sanctions (e.g., taxes, fines, incarceration). However, as we will see, public sector actors are capable of creating (constituting) social actors with broader, or more restricted, powers of acting.

Force, sanctions, and expedient responses are central ingredients of the regulatory pillar, but they are often tempered by the existence of rules that justify the use of force. When coercive power is both supported and constrained by rules, we move into the realm of *authority*. Power is institutionalized (Dornbusch and Scott 1975: Ch. 2; Weber 1924/1968).

Much work in economics emphasizes the costs of overseeing systems of regulation. Agency theory stresses the expense and difficulty entailed in accurately monitoring performances relevant to contracts, whether implicit or explicit, and in designing appropriate incentives (see Milgrom and Roberts 1992; Pratt and Zeckhauser 1985). Although in some situations agreements can be monitored and mutually enforced by the parties involved, in many circumstances it is necessary to vest the enforcement machinery in a third party expected to behave in a neutral fashion. Economic historians view this as an important function of the state. Thus, North (1990) argues:

> Because ultimately a third party must always involve the state as a source of coercion, a theory of institutions also inevitably involves an analysis of the political structure of a society and the degree to which that political structure provides a framework of effective enforcement. (p. 64)

However, North (1990: 54) also calls attention to problems that can arise because "enforcement is undertaken by agents whose own utility functions influence outcomes"—that is, third parties who are not neutral. This possibility is stressed by many historical institutionalists, such as Skocpol (1985), who argue that the state develops its own interests and operates somewhat autonomously from other societal actors. In this and other ways, attention to the regulative aspects of institutions creates renewed interest in the role of the state: as rule maker, referee, and enforcer.

In an attempt to broaden the conception of law as a regulatory mechanism, law and society theorists insist that analysts should not conflate the coercive functions of law with its normative and cognitive dimensions. Rather than operating in an authoritative and exogenous manner, many laws are sufficiently controversial or ambiguous that they do not provide clear prescriptions for conduct. In such cases, law is better conceived as an occasion for sense-making and collective interpretation (Weick 1995), relying more on cognitive and normative than coercive elements for its effects (see Suchman and Edelman 1997; see also Chapter 6). In short, institutions supported by one pillar may, as time passes and circumstances change, be sustained by different pillars.

The institutional logic underlying the regulative pillar is an instrumental one: Individuals craft laws and rules that they believe will advance their interests, and individuals conform to laws and rules because they seek the attendant rewards or wish to avoid sanctions. Because of this logic, the regulative pillar is one around which rational choice scholars gather.

Empirical indicators of the development, extent, and province of regulatory institutions are to be found in evidence of the expansion of constitutions, laws, codes, rules, directives, regulations, and formal structures of control. For example, Tolbert and Zucker (1983) determine whether municipalities are mandated by state law to adopt civil service reforms, and Singh, Tucker, and House (1986) and Baum and Oliver

(1992) ascertain whether voluntary service organizations are registered by oversight agencies. Dobbin and Sutton (1998) examine financial allocations to enforcement agencies as an indicator of regulatory enforcement.

As noted in Chapter 2, symbolic systems relate not only to substance but also to affect; they stimulate not only interpretive but emotional reactions. D'Andrade (1984) has pointed out that meaning systems work in representational, constructive, and directive ways—providing cognitive guidance and direction—but also in evocative ways, creating feeling and emotions. Emotions are among the most important motivational elements in social life. Much recent research on brain activity and cognitive behavior stresses the interdependence of cognition and emotion. Long regarded as separate spheres related to distinctive parts of the brain, this dichotomization now appears grossly oversimplified and misleading (Dolan 2003; LeDoux 1996). Attention to emotion in social life by social scientists has largely been associated with ongoing work on identity (see Chapter 2) and on "institutional work" (Lawrence, Suddaby, and Leca 2009)—emphasizing the importance of agency in maintaining and changing institutions (see Chapter 4). Contradictions between institutional demands at the macro level are experienced as conflicting role demands at the individual level—identity conflicts that need to be resolved (Creed, Dejordy, and Lok, 2010; Seo and Creed 2002). Emotions operate to motivate actors to change institutions in which they have become disinvested or to defend institutions to which they are attached (Voronov and Vince 2012). Note that attention to the emotional dimensions of institutions privileges work at the micro (individual and interpersonal) levels of analysis.

Are their distinctive types of emotions engendered by encounters with the regulative organs of society? I think so and believe that the feelings induced may constitute an important component of the power of this element. To confront a system of rules backed by the machinery of enforcement is to experience, at one extreme, fear, dread, and guilt, or, at the other, relief, innocence and vindication. Powerful emotions indeed!

In sum, there is much to examine in understanding how regulative institutions function and how they interact with other institutional elements. Through the work of agency and game theorists at one end of the spectrum and law and society theorists at the other, we are reminded that laws do not spring from the head of Zeus nor norms from the collective soul of a people; rules must be interpreted and disputes resolved; incentives and sanctions must be designed and will have unintended effects; surveillance mechanisms are required but are expensive and will prove to be fallible; and conformity is only one of many possible responses by those subject to regulative institutions.

A stable system of rules, whether formal or informal, backed by surveillance and sanctioning power affecting actors' interests that is accompanied by feelings of guilt or innocence constitutes one prevailing view of institutions.

The Normative Pillar

A second group of theorists views institutions as resting primarily on a normative pillar (again, see Table 3.1). Emphasis here is placed on normative rules that introduce a prescriptive, evaluative, and obligatory dimension into social life. Normative systems include both values and norms. *Values* are conceptions of the preferred or the desirable together with the construction of standards to which existing structures or behaviors can be compared and assessed. *Norms* specify how things should be done; they define legitimate means to pursue valued ends. Normative systems define goals or objectives (e.g., winning the game, making a profit) but also designate appropriate ways to pursue them (e.g., rules specifying how the game is to be played, conceptions of fair business practices) (Blake and Davis 1964).

Some values and norms are applicable to all members of the collectivity; others apply only to selected types of actors or positions. The latter give rise to *roles:* conceptions of appropriate goals and activities for particular individuals or specified social positions. These beliefs are not simply anticipations or predictions, but prescriptions—normative expectations—regarding how specified actors are supposed to behave. The expectations are held by other salient actors in the situation, and so are experienced by the focal actor as external pressures. Also, and to varying degrees, they become internalized by the actor. Roles can be formally constructed. For example, in an organizational context particular positions are defined to carry specified rights and responsibilities and to have varying access to material resources. Roles can also emerge informally as, over time through interaction, differentiated expectations develop to guide behavior (Blau and Scott 1962/2003: Chs. 1, 4). Normative systems are typically viewed as imposing constraints on social behavior, and so they do. But at the same time, they empower and enable social action. They confer rights as well as responsibilities, privileges as well as duties, licenses as well as mandates. In his essays on the professions, Hughes (1958) reminds us how much of the power and mystique associated with these types of roles comes from the license they are given to engage in forbidden or fateful activities—conducting intimate physical examinations or sentencing individuals to prison or to death.

The normative conception of institutions was embraced by most early sociologists—from Durkheim and Cooley through Parsons and Selznick—perhaps because sociologists are more likely to examine those types of institutions, such as kinship groups, social classes, religious systems, communities, and voluntary associations, where common beliefs and values are more likely to exist. Moreover, it continues to guide and inform much contemporary work by sociologists and political scientists on organizations. For example, March and Olsen (1989) embrace a primarily normative conception of institutions:

> The proposition that organizations follow rules, that much of the behavior in an organization is specified by standard operating procedures, is a common one in the bureaucratic and organizational literature. . . . It can be extended to the institutions of politics. Much of the behavior we observe in political institutions reflects the routine way in which people do what they are supposed to do. (p. 21)

Although March and Olsen's (1989) conception of rules is quite broad, including cultural-cognitive as well as normative elements—"routines, procedures, conventions, roles, strategies, organizational forms, and technologies . . . beliefs, paradigms, codes, cultures, and knowledge" (p. 22)—their focus stresses the centrality of social obligations:

> To describe behavior as driven by rules is to see action as a matching of a situation to the demands of a position. Rules define relationships among roles in terms of what an incumbent of one role owes to incumbents of other roles. (p. 23)

In short, scholars associated with the normative pillar stress the importance of a logic of "appropriateness" vs. a logic of "instrumentality." The central imperative confronting actors is not "What choice is in my own best interests?" but rather, "Given this situation, and my role within it, what is the appropriate behavior for me to carry out?"

Empirical indicators of the existence and pervasiveness of normative institutions include accreditations and certifications by standard setting bodies such as professional associations (Casile and Davis-Blake, 2002; Ruef and Scott 1998).

As with regulative systems, confronting normative systems can also evoke strong feelings, but these are somewhat different from those that accompany the violation of rules and laws. Feelings associated with the trespassing of norms include principally a sense of shame or disgrace, or for those who exhibit exemplary behavior, feelings of respect and honor. The conformity to or violation of norms typically involves a large measure of self-evaluation: heightened remorse or effects on self-respect. Such emotions provide powerful inducements to comply with prevailing norms.

Theorists embracing a normative conception of institutions emphasize the stabilizing influence of social beliefs and norms that are both internalized and imposed by others. For early normative theorists such as Parsons, shared norms and values were regarded as *the* basis of a stable social order. And as Stinchcombe (1997) has eloquently reaffirmed, institutions are widely viewed as having moral roots:

> The guts of institutions is that somebody somewhere really cares to hold an organization to the standards and is often paid to do that. Sometimes that somebody is inside the organization, maintaining its competence. Sometimes it is an accrediting body, sending out volunteers to see if there is really any algebra in the algebra course. And sometimes that somebody, or his or her commitment is lacking, in which case the center cannot hold, and mere anarchy is loosed upon the world. (p. 18)

Heclo (2008) also embraces a similar stance. Assuming what he terms an "inside-out" perspective on institutions—that is, viewing institutions from the standpoint of those participating in them—he affirms Selznick's (1957: 101) distinction "between strictly instrumental attachments needed to get a particular job done and the deeper commitments that express one's enduring loyalty to the purpose or purposes that lie behind doing the job in the first place." Heclo insists:

> Deeper than the agent/principal issues is the agent/principle perspective. It presupposes that as beings (which by existing we surely are) we humans are moral agents. That is to say, by virtue of being human, we experience our existence as partaking in questions of right and wrong. To say human life is to say morally-implicated life. (p. 79)

The Cultural-Cognitive Pillar

A third set of institutionalists, principally anthropologists like Geertz and Douglas and sociologists like Berger, DiMaggio, Goffman,

Meyer, Powell, and Scott stress the centrality of cultural-cognitive elements of institutions: the shared conceptions that constitute the nature of social reality and create the frames through which meaning is made (again, see Table 3.1). Attention to the cultural-cognitive dimension of institutions is the major distinguishing feature of neoinstitutionalism within sociology and organizational studies.

These institutionalists take seriously the cognitive dimensions of human existence: Mediating between the external world of stimuli and the response of the individual organism is a collection of internalized symbolic representations of the world. "In the cognitive paradigm, what a creature does is, in large part, a function of the creature's internal representation of its environment" (D'Andrade 1984: 88). Symbols—words, signs, gestures—have their effect by shaping the meanings we attribute to objects and activities. Meanings arise in interaction and are maintained and transformed as they are employed to make sense of the ongoing stream of happenings. Emphasizing the importance of symbols and meanings returns us to Max Weber's central premise. As noted in Chapter 1, Weber regarded action as social to the extent that the actor attaches meaning to the behavior. To understand or explain any action, the analyst must take into account not only the objective conditions but the actor's subjective interpretation of them. Extensive research by psychologists over the past three decades has shown that cognitive frames enter into the full range of information-processing activities, from determining what information will receive attention, how it will be in encoded, how it will be retained, retrieved, and organized into memory, to how it will be interpreted, thus affecting evaluations, judgments, predictions, and inferences. (For reviews, see Fiol 2002; Markus and Zajonc 1985; Mindl, Stubbart, and Porac 1996.)

As discussed in Chapter 2, the new cultural perspective focuses on the semiotic facets of culture, treating them not simply as subjective beliefs but also as symbolic systems viewed as objective and external to individual actors. Berger and Kellner (1981: 31) summarize: "Every human institution is, as it were, a sedimentation of meanings or, to vary the image, a crystallization of meanings in objective form." Our use of the hyphenated label *cognitive-cultural* emphasizes that internal interpretive processes are shaped by external cultural frameworks. As Douglas (1982: 12) proposes, we should "treat cultural categories as the cognitive containers in which social interests are defined and classified, argued, negotiated, and fought out." Or in Hofstede's (1991: 4) graphic metaphor, culture provides patterns of thinking, feeling, and acting: mental programs, or the "software of the mind."[4]

The stress in much of this work on cognition and interpretation points to important functions of the cultural-cognitive pillar but overlooks a dimension that is even more fundamental: its *constitutive* function. Symbolic processes, at their most basic level, work to construct social reality, to define the nature and properties of social actors and social actions. We postpone consideration of this function until the following section of this chapter, however, because it raises questions regarding the fundamental assumptions underlying social science research.

Cultural systems operate at multiple levels, from the shared definition of local situations, to the common frames and patterns of belief that comprise an organization's culture, to the organizing logics that structure organization fields, to the shared assumptions and ideologies that define preferred political and economic systems at national and transnational levels. These levels are not sealed but nested, so that broad cultural frameworks penetrate and shape individual beliefs on the one hand, and individual constructs can work to reconfigure far-flung belief systems on the other.

Of course, cultural elements vary in their degree of institutionalization—the extent of their linkage to other elements, the degree to which they are embodied in routines or organizing schema. When we talk about cognitive-cultural elements of institutions, we are calling attention to these more embedded cultural forms: "culture congealed in forms that require less by way of maintenance, ritual reinforcement, and symbolic elaboration than the softer (or more 'living') realms we usually think of as cultural" (Jepperson and Swidler 1994: 363).

Cultures are often conceived as unitary systems, internally consistent across groups and situations. But cultural conceptions frequently vary: Beliefs are held by some but not by others. Persons in the same situation can perceive the situation quite differently—in terms of both what is and what ought to be. Cultural beliefs vary and are frequently contested, particularly in times of social disorganization and change (see DiMaggio 1997; Martin 1992; 2002; Seo and Creed 2002; Swidler 1986).

For cultural-cognitive theorists, compliance occurs in many circumstances because other types of behavior are inconceivable; routines are followed because they are taken for granted as "the way we do these things." The prevailing logic employed to justify conformity is that of orthodoxy, the perceived correctness and soundness of the ideas underlying action.

Social roles are given a somewhat different interpretation by cultural than by normative theorists. Rather than stressing the force of mutually reinforcing obligations, cultural-cognitive theorists point to the power of templates for particular types of actors and scripts for action (Shank and Abelson 1977). For Berger and Luckmann (1967), roles arise as common understandings develop that particular actions are associated with particular actors:[5]

> We can properly begin to speak of roles when this kind of typification occurs in the context of an objectified stock of knowledge common to a collectivity of actors. . . . Institutions are embodied in individual experience by means of roles. . . . The institution, with its assemblage of "programmed" actions, is like the unwritten libretto of a drama. The realization of the drama depends upon the reiterated performance of its prescribed roles by living actors. . . . Neither drama nor institution exist empirically apart from this recurrent realization. (pp. 73–75)

Differentiated roles can and do develop in localized contexts as repetitive patterns of action gradually become habitualized and objectified, but it is also important to recognize the operation of wider institutional frameworks that provide prefabricated organizing models and scripts (see Goffman 1974; 1983). Meyer and Rowan (1977) and DiMaggio and Powell (1983) emphasize the extent to which wider belief systems and cultural frames are imposed on or adopted by individual actors and organizations.

Much progress has been made in recent years in developing indicators of cultural-cognitive elements. For many years, investigators such as social anthropologists and ethnomethodologists relied on close, long-term observation of ongoing behavior from which they inferred underlying beliefs and assumptions (e.g., Turner 1974). Later, quantitative researchers employed survey methodologies to uncover shared attitudes and common values (e.g., Hofstede 1984). More recently, however, a "new archival research" approach has emerged in which scholars employ formal analytical methodologies such as content, semiotic, sequence, and network analysis to probe materials such as discourse in professional journals, trade publications, organizational documents, directories, annual reports, and specialized or mainstream media accounts. This type of research has flourished due to the widespread availability of computer-analyzable documents. The best of this work illuminates "relevant features of shared understandings, professional ideologies, cognitive frames or sets of collective meanings that condition how organizational actors interpret and respond to the world around them" (Ventresca and Mohr 2002: 819).

The affective dimension of this pillar is expressed in feelings from the positive affect of certitude and confidence on the one hand versus the negative feelings of confusion or disorientation on the other. Actors who align themselves with prevailing cultural beliefs are likely to feel competent and connected; those who are at odds are regarded as, at best, "clueless" or, at worst, "crazy."

A cultural-cognitive conception of institutions stresses the central role played by the socially mediated construction of a common framework of meanings.

A Fourth Pillar? Habitual Dispositions

In a thoughtful essay, Gronow (2008) has proposed a fourth element, which he argues constitutes yet another basis for institutions. Building on the work of the American pragmatists, including Dewey, James, and others who influenced the work of early economic theorists Veblen and Commons (see Chapter 1), Gronow suggests that we add *habitual actions* to our framework. He suggests that "habitual dispositions are related to actions that have been repeated in stable contexts and therefore require only a minimal amount of conscious thought to initiate and implement" (p. 362). Although habits can be relatively automatic, Gronow points out that pragmatists insisted habits are not mere dead routines, but can include and overlap with reason and conscious choice.

While I welcome the strengthening of connections between pragmatism and institutional arguments and agree that more attention needs to be given to activities and practices, habits and routines, I am not persuaded of the need to add a fourth pillar to the conceptual framework. Shared dispositions are fundamentally cultural-cognitive elements closely tied to repetitive behavior. Like other such elements, they can be only semiconscious and taken for granted by the actors. Moreover, I take into account the important role of activities and routines by treating them as of one of the major carriers of institutional elements (see Chapter 4).

Combinations of Elements

Having introduced the three basic elements and emphasized their distinctive features and modes of working, it is important to restate the truth that in most empirically observed institutional forms, we observe not one, single element at work but varying combinations of elements. In stable social systems, we observe practices that persist and are reinforced because they are taken for granted, normatively endorsed, and backed by authorized powers. When the pillars are aligned, the strength of their combined forces can be formidable.

In some situations, however, one or another pillar will operate virtually alone in supporting the social order; and in many situations, a given pillar will assume primacy.

Equally important, the pillars may be misaligned: They may support and motivate differing choices and behaviors. As Strang and Sine (2002: 499) point out, "Where cognitive, normative, and regulative supports are not well aligned, they provide resources that different actors can employ for different ends." Such situations exhibit both confusion and conflict, and provide conditions that are highly likely to give rise to institutional change (Dacin, Goodstein, and Scott 2002; Kraatz and Block 2008). These arguments are pursued, illustrated, and empirically tested in subsequent chapters.

❖ THE THREE PILLARS AND LEGITIMACY

"Organizations require more than material resources and technical information if they are to survive and thrive in their social environments. They also need social acceptability and credibility" (Scott, Ruef, Mendel, and Caronna 2000: 237)—in short, they require legitimacy. Suchman (1995b: 574) provides a helpful definition of this central concept: "*Legitimacy* is a generalized perception or assumption that the actions of an entity are desirable, proper, or appropriate within some socially constructed system of norms, values, beliefs, and definitions." Legitimacy is a generalized rather than an event-specific evaluation and is "possessed objectively, yet created subjectively" (Suchman 1995b: 574). The "socially constructed systems" to which Suchman refers are, of course, institutional frameworks.

Max Weber was the first great social theorist to stress the importance of legitimacy. In his formulation of types of social action, he gave particular attention to those actions guided by a belief in the existence of a legitimate order: a set of "determinable maxims," a model regarded by the actor as "in some way obligatory or exemplary for him" (Weber 1924/1968, Vol. 1: 31). In his empirical/historical work, he applied his approach to the legitimation of power structures, both corporate and governmental, arguing that power becomes legitimated as authority to the extent that its exercise is supported by prevailing social norms, whether traditional, charismatic, or rational-legal (see Deephouse and Suchman 2008; Dornbusch and Scott 1975: Ch. 2; Ruef and Scott 1998). In his cultural-institutional perspective, Parsons (1956/1960b) broadened the focus of legitimation to include the goals of an organization, determining the extent to which they were congruent with the values extant in the society. And as we have seen, these arguments have been advanced and amplified by neoinstitutionalists, such as Berger and Luckmann (1967), Meyer and Rowan (1977), and Meyer and Scott (1983b) to include the legitimation of strategies, structures, and procedures.

In a resource-dependence or social exchange approach to organizations, legitimacy is typically treated as simply another kind of resource that organizations extract from their institutional environment (e.g., Dowling and Pfeffer 1975; Suchman 1995b). Scholars emphasizing the regulative pillar share, at least to some extent, this interpretation as they stress the benefits or costs of compliance. However, from a strong institutional perspective, legitimacy is not a commodity to be possessed or exchanged but a condition reflecting perceived consonance with relevant rules and laws or normative values, or alignment with cultural-cognitive frameworks. Like some other invisible properties such as oxygen, the importance of legitimacy become immediately and painfully apparent only if lost, suggesting that it is not a specific resource, but a fundamental condition of social existence.

Berger and Luckmann (1967) describe legitimacy as evoking a "second order" of meaning. In their early stages, institutionalized activities develop as repeated patterns of behavior that evoke shared meanings among the participants. The legitimation of this order involves connecting it to wider cultural frames, norms, or rules. "Legitimation 'explains' the institutional order by ascribing cognitive validity to its objectified meanings. Legitimation justifies the institutional order by giving a normative dignity to its practical imperatives" (pp. 92–93). In a similar fashion, Johnson, Dowd, and Ridgway (2006) compare and contrast the social psychological and the organizational views of legitimacy to arrive at a four-stage process: innovation, local validation, diffusion, and general validation. That is, for new actions to be legitimated, they must be locally accepted, and once they are "construed as a valid social fact, [they are] adopted more readily by actors in other local contexts" (p. 60). As a result of successful diffusion, "the new social object acquires widespread acceptance, becoming part of society's shared culture" (p. 61).[6] And emphasizing the cultural-cognitive dimension, Meyer and I propose that "organizational legitimacy refers to the degree of cultural support for an organization" (Meyer and Scott 1983a: 201).

This vertical dimension entails the support of significant others: various types of authorities—cultural as well as political—empowered to confer legitimacy. The reproduction of practices is supported by structures residing at multiple levels (Colyvas and Jonsson 2011). Who these authorities are varies from time to time and place to place but, in our time, agents of the state and professional and trade associations are often critical for organizations. Certification or accreditation by these bodies is frequently employed as a prime indicator of legitimacy (Dowling and Pfeffer 1975; Ruef and Scott 1998). In complex situations, individuals or organizations may be confronted by competing sovereigns. Actors confronting conflicting normative requirements and standards typically find it difficult to take action since conformity to one undermines the normative support of other bodies. "The legitimacy of a given organization is negatively affected by the number of different authorities sovereign over it and by the diversity or inconsistency of their accounts of how it is to function" (Meyer and Scott 1983a: 202).

There is always the question as to whose assessments count in determining the legitimacy of a set of arrangements. Many structures persist and spread because they are regarded as appropriate by entrenched authorities, even though their legitimacy is challenged by other, less powerful constituencies. Martin (1994), for example, notes that salary inequities between men and women are institutionalized in American society even though the disadvantaged groups perceive them to be unjust and press for reforms. "Legitimate" structures may, at the same time, be contested structures.

Stinchcombe (1968) asserts that, in the end, whose values define legitimacy is a matter of concerted social power:

> A power is legitimate to the degree that, by virtue of the doctrines and norms by which it is justified, the power-holder can call upon sufficient other centers of power, as reserves in case of need, to make his power effective. (p. 162)

It is important, however, to point out that power is not always a top-down process, but can involve bottom-up phenomena. Power, for example, can be *authorized* by superordinate parties (Stinchcombe 1968) or *endorsed* by those subject to the power-wielder (Dornbusch and Scott 1975; Zelditch and Walker 1984) who collectively enforce norms supporting compliance. Power can arise out of the mobilization of subordinate groups as they attempt to advance their own values and interests.

While power certainly matters, in supporting legitimacy processes as in other social activities, power is not the absolute arbiter. Entrenched power is, in the long run, hapless against the onslaught of opposing power allied with more persuasive ideas or stronger commitments.

Consistent with the preceding discussion, each of the three pillars provides a basis of legitimacy, albeit a different one (see Table 3.1).[7] The regulatory emphasis is on conformity to rules: Legitimate organizations are those established by and operating in accordance with relevant legal or quasi-legal requirements. A normative conception stresses a deeper, moral base for assessing legitimacy. Normative controls are much more likely to be internalized than are regulative controls, and the incentives for conformity are hence likely to include intrinsic as well as extrinsic rewards. A cultural-cognitive view points to the legitimacy that comes from conforming to a common definition of the situation, frame of reference, or a recognizable role (for individuals) or structural template (for organizations). To adopt an orthodox structure or identity in order to relate to a specific situation is to seek the legitimacy that comes from cognitive consistency. The cultural-cognitive mode is the deepest level since it rests on preconscious, taken-for-granted understandings.

The bases of legitimacy associated with the three elements, and hence the types of indicators employed, are decidedly different and may be in conflict. A regulative view would ascertain whether the organization is legally established and whether it is acting in accord with relevant laws and regulations. A normative orientation, stressing moral obligations, may countenance actions departing from mere legal requirements. Many professionals adhere to normative standards that motivate them to depart from the rule-based requirements of bureaucratic organizations. And whistle-blowers claim that they are acting on the basis of a "higher authority" when they contest organizational rules or the orders of superiors. An organization such as the Mafia may be widely recognized, signifying that it exhibits a culturally constituted mode of organizing to achieve specified ends, and it is regarded as a legitimate way of organizing by its members. Nevertheless, it is treated as an illegal form by police and other regulative bodies, and it lacks the normative endorsement of most citizens.

What is taken as evidence of legitimacy varies by which elements of institutions are privileged.

❖ BASIC ASSUMPTIONS ASSOCIATED WITH
    THE THREE PILLARS

Although the differences among analysts emphasizing one or another element are partly a matter of substantive focus, they are also associated with more profound differences in underlying philosophical assumptions. While it is not possible to do full justice to the complexity and subtlety of these issues, I attempt to depict the differences in broad outline. Two matters are particularly significant: (1) differences among analysts in their ontological assumptions—assumptions concerning the nature of social reality; and (2) differences involving the extent and type of rationality invoked in explaining behavior.

Regulative and Constitutive Rules

Truth and Reality

Varying ontological assumptions underlie conceptions of institutional elements. Thus, it is necessary to clarify one's epistemological assumptions: How do we understand the nature of scientific knowledge? My position on these debates has been greatly influenced by the formulation advanced by Jeffrey C. Alexander (1983, Vol. 1), who provides a broad, synthetic examination of the nature and development of theoretical logic in modern sociological thought. Following Kuhn (1970), Alexander adopts a *postpositivist* perspective viewing science as operating along a continuum stretching from the empirical environment on the one hand to the metaphysical environment on the other (see Figure 3.1).

At the metaphysical end reside the most abstract general presuppositions and models associated with more theoretical activity. At the empirical end, one finds observations, measures, and propositions. The continuum obviously incorporates numerous types of statements, ranging from the more abstract and general to the more specific and particular. But, more important, the framework emphasizes that, although the

Figure 3.1   The Scientific Continuum and Its Components

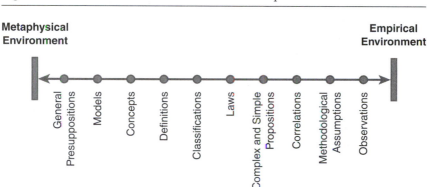

SOURCE: © Jeffrey Alexander. Used with permission.

mix of empirical and metaphysical elements varies, *every point on the continuum is an admixture of both elements.* "What appears, concretely, to be a difference in types of scientific statements—models, definitions, propositions—simply reflects the different emphasis within a given statement on generality or specificity" (Alexander 1983, Vol. 1: 4).

The postpositivist conception of science emphasizes the fundamental similarity of the social and physical sciences—both are human attempts to develop and test general statements about the behavior of the empirical world. It rejects both a radical materialist view that espouses that the only reality is a physical one, and also the idealist (and postmodernist) view that the only reality exists in the human mind. It also usefully differentiates reality from truth, as Rorty (1989) observes:

> We need to make a distinction between the claim that the world is out there and the claim that truth is out there. To say that the world is out there, that it is not our creation, is to say, with common sense, that most things in space and time are the effects of causes which do not include human mental states. To say that truth is not out there is simply to say that where there are no sentences there is no truth, that sentences are elements of human languages, and that human languages are human creations. (pp. 4–5)

Social Reality

Although the physical and social sciences share important basic features, it is essential to recognize that the subject matter of the social sciences is distinctive. In John Searle's (1995: 1, 11, 13) terminology, portions of the real world, while they are treated as "epistemically objective" facts in the world, "are facts only by human agreement." Their existence is "observer-relative": dependent on observers who share a common conception of a given social fact. Social reality is an important subclass of reality.[8]

Earlier in our discussion of cultural-cognitive elements, I introduced the concept of *constitutive* processes. Now we are in a position to develop this argument. Social institutions refer to types of social reality that involve the collective development and use of both regulative and constitutive rules. *Regulative rules* involve attempts to influence "antecedently existing activities"; *constitutive rules* "create the very possibility of certain activities" (Searle 1995: 27). Constitutive rules take the general form: X counts as Y in context C; for example, an American dollar bill counts as legal currency in the United States. "Institutional facts exist only within systems of constitutive rules" (p. 28). In general, as the label implies, scholars embracing the regulative view of institutions focus primary attention on regulative rules; for example, they assume the existence of actors with a given set of interests and then ask how various rule systems, manipulating sanctions and incentives, can affect the behavior of these actors as they pursue their interests. Cultural-cognitive scholars stress the importance of constitutive rules: They ask what types of actors are present, how their interests are shaped by these definitions, and what types of actions they are allowed to take. They thus differ in their ontological assumptions or, at least, in the ontological level at which they work.

The anthropologist David Schneider (1976) usefully describes the relation of constitutive culture to social norms:

> Culture contrasts with norms in that norms are oriented to patterns *for action,* whereas culture constitutes a body of definitions, premises, statements, postulates, presumptions, propositions, and perceptions about the nature of the universe and man's place in it. Where norms tell the actor how to play the scene, culture tells the actor how the scene is set and what it all means. Where norms tell the actor how to behave in the presence of ghosts, gods, and human beings, culture tells the actor what ghosts, gods, and human being are and what they are all about. (pp. 202–203)

Constitutive rules operate at a deeper level of reality creation, involving the devising of categories and the construction of typifications: processes by which "concrete and subjectively unique experiences . . . are ongoingly subsumed under general orders of meaning that are both objectively and subjectively real" (Berger and Luckmann 1967: 39). Such processes are variously applied to things, to ideas, to events, and to actors, and are organized into hierarchical linked arrangements and elaborate systems for organizing meaning. Games provide a ready illustration. Constitutive rules construct the game of football as consisting of things such as gridiron and goal posts and events such as first downs and offsides (see D'Andrade 1984). Similarly, other types of constitutive rules result in the social construction of actors and associated capacities and roles: in the football context, the creation of quarterbacks, coaches, and referees. Regulative rules define how the ball may legitimately be advanced or what penalties are associated with what rule infractions. Thus, cultural-cognitive theorists amend and augment the portrait of institutions crafted by regulative theorists. Cultural-cognitive theorists insist that games involve more than rules and enforcement mechanisms: They consist of socially constructed players endowed with differing capacities for action and parts to play. Constitutive rules construct the social objects and events to which regulative rules are applied.

Such processes, although most visible in games, are not limited to these relatively artificial situations. Constitutive rules are so basic to social structure, so fundamental to social life that they are often overlooked. In our liberal democracies, we take for granted that individual persons have interests and capacities for action. It seems natural that there are citizens with opinions and rights (as opposed to subjects with no or limited rights), students with a capacity to learn, fathers with rights and responsibilities, and employees with aptitudes and skills. But all of these types of actors—and a multitude of others—are social constructions; all depend for their existence on constitutive frameworks that, although they arose in particular interaction contexts, have become reified in cultural rules that can be imported as guidelines into new situations (see Berger and Luckmann 1967; Gergen and Davis 1985).

Moreover, recognition of the existence of such constitutive processes provides a view of social behavior that differs greatly from lay interpretations or even from those found in much of social science. As Meyer, Boli, and Thomas (1987) argue:

> Most social theory takes actors (from individuals to states) and their actions as real, a priori, elements. . . . [In contrast] we see the "existence" and characteristics of actors as socially constructed and highly problematic, and action as the enactment of broad institutional scripts rather than a matter of internally generated and autonomous choice, motivation and purpose. (p. 13)

In short, as constitutive rules are recognized, individual behavior is seen to often reflect external definitions rather than (or as a source of) internal intentions. The difference is nicely captured in the anecdote reported by Peter Hay (1993):

> Gertrude Lawrence and Noel Coward were starring in one of the latter's plays when the production was honored with a royal visit. As Queen Elizabeth entered the Royal Box, the entire audience rose to its feet. Miss Lawrence, watching from the wings, murmured: "What an entrance!" Noel Coward, peeking on tip-toe behind her, added "What a part!" (p. 70)

The social construction of actors also defines what they consider to be their interests. The stereotypic "economic man" that rests at the heart of much economic theorizing is not a reflection of human nature, but a social construct that arose under specific historical circumstances and is maintained by particular institutional logics associated with the rise of capitalism (see Heilbroner 1985).[9] From the cultural-cognitive perspective, interests are not assumed to be natural or outside the scope of investigation; they are not treated as exogenous to the theoretical framework. Rather, they are recognized to be endogenous, arising within social situations, as varying by institutional context and as themselves requiring explanation.

The social construction of actors and their associated activities is not limited to persons. Collective actors are similarly constituted, and come in a wide variety of forms. We, naturally, will be particularly interested in the nature of those institutional processes at work in the constitution of organizations and organization fields, processes considered in later chapters.

In their critique of the pillars framework, Phillips and Malhotra (2008) argue that because the different elements operate at varying ontological levels, they cannot be combined into an integrated framework. They propose that "authentic" institutional analysis involves exclusive attention to the cultural-cognitive elements:

> The fact that coercive and normative mechanisms are externally managed by other actors makes them very different from the taken-for-grantedness of cognitive mechanisms. Where coercive and normative mechanisms result in strategic action and often resistance, cognitive mechanisms function by conditioning thinking. (p. 717)

But is this true? In a world of words, many of the most important strategies involve choices as to how to frame the situation, how to construct a powerful narrative, how to brand the product. In contested situations, some of the most effective weapons available to contenders involve how to define the actions, the actors, and their intent. Are we seeking "Black power" or "civil rights"?

Cultural-cognitive elements are amenable to strategic manipulation. They are also subject to deliberative processes under the control of regulative and normative agents. Thus, members of the legislature or the judicial branch can change the rights and powers of individual and collective actors. Recently, the U.S. Supreme Court determined that corporations have political rights allowing them to exercise freedom of speech, including unrestricted expenditure of funds for political action committees. And professional authorities regularly create new institutions: new concepts, distinctions, and typologies that shape the types of measures we use; the kinds of data we collect; and the interpretations we make (Espeland and Sauder 2007; Scott 2008b).

In short, there are important differences among the pillars, as I have labored to explicate. I have attempted to construct what social theorist Charles Tilly (1984) defines as an *encompassing theoretical framework*, one that examines theories sharing broad objectives and attempts not simply to argue that they employ provide differing approaches, but to explicate the ways in which the approaches vary. I continue to believe that such a framework provides a fruitful guide for institutional analysis.

Rational and Reasonable Behavior

Theorists make different assumptions regarding how actors make choices: what logics determine social action. As discussed earlier and in Chapter 1, Weber defined social action so as to emphasize the importance of the meanings individuals attach to their own and others' behavior. For Weber and many other social theorists, "the central question that every social theory addresses in defining the nature of action is whether or not—or to what degree—action is rational" (Alexander 1983, Vol. 1: 72). A more basic question, however, is how is rationality to be defined? Social theorists propose a wide range of answers.

At one end of the spectrum, a neoclassical economic perspective embraces an *atomist* view that focuses on an individual actor engaged in maximizing his or her returns, guided by stable preferences and possessing complete knowledge of the possible alternatives and their consequences. This model has undergone substantial revision in recent decades, however, as over time economists have reluctantly acknowledged limitations on individual rationality identified by psychologists such as Tversky and Kahneman (1974), as described in Chapter 2. Validated by a Nobel Prize in economics (in 2002), this work has been incorporated into the mainstream as *behavioral economics*. Perhaps overstating the matter, a review of Kahneman's (2011) recent book concludes that his empirical investigations of human decision making "makes it plain that *Homo economicus*—the rational model of human behavior beloved of economists—is as fantastical as a unicorn" (*The Economist* 2011: 98). Nevertheless, this model, perhaps wearing a somewhat more modest cloak, continues to pervade much economic theorizing.

Embracing a somewhat broader set of assumptions, neoinstitutional analysts in economics and rational choice theorists in political science (e.g., Moe 1990a; Williamson, 1985) utilize Simon's (1945/1997: 88) model of bounded rationality, which presumes that actors are "intendedly rational, but only boundedly so." These versions relax the assumptions regarding complete information and utility maximization as the criterion of choice, while retaining the premise that actors seek "to do the best they can to satisfy whatever their wants might be" (Abell, 1995: 7). Institutional theorists employing these and related models of individual rational actors are more likely to view institutions primarily as regulative frameworks. Actors construct institutions to deal with collective action problems—to regulate their own and others' behaviors—and they respond to institutions because the regulations are backed by incentives and sanctions. A strength of these models is that rational choice theorists have "an explicit theory of individual behavior in mind" when they examine motives for developing and consequences attendant to the formation of institutional structures (Peters 1999: 45; see also Abell 1995). Economic theorists argue that, while their assumptions may not be completely accurate, "many institutions and business practices are designed as if people were entirely motivated by narrow, selfish concerns and were quite clever and largely unprincipled in their pursuit of their goals" (Milgrom and Roberts 1992: 42).

From a sociological perspective, a limitation of employing an overly narrow rational framework is that it "portrays action as simply an adaptation to material conditions"—a calculus of costs and benefits—rather than allowing for the "internal subjective reference of action" that opens up potential for the "multidimensional alternation of freedom and constraint" (Alexander 1983, Vol. 1: 74). Another limitation involves the rigid distinction in rational choice models made between ends, which are presumed to be fixed, and means. Sociological models propose, variously, that ends are modified by means, that ends emerge in ongoing activities, and even that means can become ends (March and Olsen 1989; Selznick 1949; Weick 1969/1979). In addition, rather than positing a lone individual decision maker, the sociological version embraces an "organicist rather than an atomist view" such that "the essential characteristics of any element are seen as outcomes of relations with other entities" (Hodgson 1994: 61). Actors in interaction constitute social structures, which, in turn, constitute actors. The products of prior interactions—norms, rules, beliefs, resources—provide the situational elements that enter into individual decision making (see the discussion of structuration in Chapter 4).

A number of terms have been proposed for this broadened view of rationality. As usual, Weber anticipated much of the current debate by distinguishing among several variants of rationality, including *Zweckrationalität*—action that is rational in the instrumental, calculative sense—and *Wertrationalität*—action that is inspired by and directed toward the realization of substantive values (Weber 1924/1968, Vol. 1: 24; see also Swedberg 1998: 36). The former focuses on means-ends connections; the latter on the types of ends pursued. Although Weber himself was inconsistent in his usage of these ideal types, Alexander suggests that they are best treated as analytic distinctions, with actual rational behavior being seen as involving an admixture of the two types. All social action involves some combination of calculation (in selection of means) and orientation toward socially defined values.[10]

A broader distinction has been proposed by March (1981), who differentiates between a logic of instrumentalism and a logic of "appropriateness" (see also March 1994; March and Olsen 1989), as noted earlier. An instrumental logic asks, "What are my interests in this situation?" An appropriateness logic stresses the normative pillar where choice is seen to be grounded in a social context and to be oriented by a moral framework that takes into account one's relations and obligations to others in the situation. This logic replaces, or sets limits on, individual-istic instrumental behavior.

Cultural-cognitive theorists emphasize the extent to which behavior is informed and constrained by the ways in which knowledge is constructed and codified. Underlying all decisions and choices are socially constructed models, assumptions, and schemas. All decisions are admixtures of rational calculations and nonrational premises. At the micro-level, DiMaggio and Powell (1991) propose that a recognition of these conditions provides the basis for what they term a theory of *practical* action. This conception departs from a "preoccupation with the rational, calculative aspect of cognition to focus on preconscious processes and schema as they enter into routine, taken-for-granted behavior" (p. 22). At the same time, it eschews the individualistic, asocial assumptions associated with the narrow rational perspective to emphasize the extent to which individual choices are governed by normative rules and embedded in networks of mutual social obligations.

The institutional economist Richard Langlois (1986b) proposes that the model of an intendedly rational actor be supplemented by a model of the actor's situation, which includes, importantly, relevant social institutions. Institutions provide an informational-support function, serving as "interpersonal stores of coordinative knowledge" (p. 237). Such common conceptions enable the routine accomplishment of highly complex and interdependent tasks, often with a minimum of conscious deliberation or decision making. Analysts are enjoined to "pay attention to the existence of social institutions of various kinds as bounds to and definitions of the agent's situation" (p. 252). Langlois encourages us to broaden the neoclassical conception of rational action to encompass what he terms "reasonable" action, a conception that allows actors to "prefer more to less [of] all things considered," but also that allows for "other kinds of reasonable action in certain situations" including rule-following behavior (p. 252). Social action is always grounded in social contexts that specify valued ends and appropriate means; action acquires its very reasonableness from taking into account these social rules and guidelines for behavior.

As briefly noted in our consideration of a fourth pillar, recent scholars have suggested that contemporary theorizing would be advanced by resurrecting and updating pragmatism, a theory promulgated during the late 19th and early 20th centuries by some of America's most ingenuous social philosophers and social scientists, including Oliver Wendell Holmes, William James, Charles Peirce, and John Dewey. Among their central tenants were that (1) "ideas are not 'out there,' waiting to be discovered, but are tools . . . that people devise to cope with the world in which they find themselves," and (2) that ideas are produced "not by individuals, but by groups of individuals—that ideas are social, . . . dependent . . . on their human carriers and the environment" (Menand 2001: xi). Indeed, as Strauss (1993) reminds us:

> In the writings of the Pragmatists we can see a constant battle against the separating, dichotomizing, or opposition of what Pragmatists argued should be joined together: knowledge and practice, environment and actor, biology and culture, means and ends, body and mind, matter and mind, object and subject, logic and inquiry, lay thought and scientific thought, necessity and chance, cognitive and noncognitive, art and science, values and action. (p. 72)

Ansell (2005) suggests that pragmatists favored a model of decision making that could be characterized as *practical reason*—recognizing that people make decisions in "situationally specific contexts," drawing on their past experiences, and influenced by their emotions as well as their reason.

❖ CONCLUDING COMMENT

While it is possible to combine the insights of economic, political, and sociological analysts into a single, complex, integrated model of an institution, I believe it is more useful at this point to recognize the differing assumptions and emphases that accompany the models currently guiding inquiry into these phenomena. Three contrasting models of institutions are identified—the regulative, the normative, and the cultural-cognitive—although it is not possible to associate any of the disciplines uniquely with any of these proposed models. We find researchers in each discipline emphasizing one or another of the pillars. The models are differentiated such that each identifies a distinctive basis of compliance, mechanism of diffusion, type of logic, cluster of indicators, affective response, and foundation for legitimacy claims.

While at a superficial level it appears that social analysts are merely emphasizing one or another of the multiple facets of institutional arrangements, a closer examination suggests that the models are aligned with quite profound differences in the assumptions made about the nature of social reality and the ways in which actors make choices in social situations. Two sources of continuing controversy are identified. First, analysts disagree as to whether to attend primarily to regulative rules as helping to structure action among a given set of actors with established interests or to instead give primacy to constitutive rules that create distinctive types of actors and related modes of action. Second, institutions have become an important combat zone in the broader, ongoing disputation within the social sciences centering on the utility of rational choice theory for explaining human behavior. Are we to employ a more restricted, instrumental logic in accounting for the determinants and consequences of institutions, or is it preferable to posit a broader, more socially embedded logic? There is no sign of a quick or easy resolution to either of these debates.

❖ NOTES

1. Such an integrated model of institutions is elaborated in Scott (1994b).

2. Not all analysts share this belief. In a rather abrasive critique of an earlier presentation of this argument (*Institutions and Organizations,* 1st ed., 1995), Hirsch (1997: 1704) pointed out that my approach runs the risk of enforcing a "forced-choice" selection of one element as against another, rather than recognizing the reality that all institutional forms are composed of multiple elements. Such is not my intent. I willingly accede to the multiplex nature of institutional reality while insisting on the value of identifying analytic concepts, which, I believe, will aid us as we attempt to sort out the contending theories and interrelated processes. Far from wishing to "rule out" or "discourage interpillar communication" or to make the "cross-fertilization of ideas unusual and unlikely," as Hirsch (1997: 1709) alleged, my intent in constructing this analytic scheme is to encourage and inform such efforts.

3. In his most recent work, however, North (2005: Ch. 3) greatly expands his interest in and attention to cultural-cognitive facets of institutions.

4. Note the similarity of these conceptions to Bourdieu's concept of *habitus,* discussed in Chapter 2.

5. Schutz analyzes this process at length in his discussion of "the world of contemporaries as a structure of ideal types" (see Schutz 1932/1967: 176–207).

6. However, as discussed in Chapter 6, it is essential that we not conflate diffusion and institutionalization.

7. Related typologies of the varying bases of legitimacy have been developed by Stryker (1994; 2000) and Suchman (1995b).

8. Searle's framework is, hence, a moderate version of social constructionism. This more conservative stance is signaled by the title of his book, *The Construction of Social Reality* (1995), which differs markedly from the broader interpretation implied by the title of Berger and Luckmann's *The Social Construction of Reality* (1967).

9. As succinctly phrased by the economic historian Shonfield (1965: 71): "Classical economics, which was largely a British invention, converted the British experience . . . into something very like the Platonic idea of capitalism."

10. Famously, Weber (1906–1924/1946: 280) captured this combination of ideas and interests in his "switchman" metaphor:

> Not ideas, but material and ideal interests directly govern men's conduct. Yet very frequently the "world images" that have been created by "ideas" have, like switchmen, determined the tracks along which action has been pushed by the dynamics of interests.

4

Crafting an Analytic Framework II: Logics, Agency, Carriers, and Levels

The fate of our times is characterized by rationalization and intel-lectualism and, above all, by the "disenchantment of the world."

—Max Weber (1906–1924/1946: 155)

I n Chapter 3, three institutional elements were defined and differ-ences described related to each in motivation for compliance, enforcement mechanisms, underlying logic, types of indicators, affect, and bases of legitimacy. Building on this framework, the pres-ent chapter examines the content of institutional models or logics conducive to the growth of organizations as well as other types of institutional models operating in the environment of organizations, considers the relation of agency to institutions, and describes varying types of carriers employed and levels of analysis utilized by institu-tional analysts.

❖ INSTITUTIONAL LOGICS AND ORGANIZATIONS

Rationalized Models

Institutions of one type or another can be traced back to the earliest stages of the history of humankind, whereas organizations as we know them are a relatively recent development. Clearly, then, not any and all institutional frameworks are conducive to organizational growth and sustenance. Numerous social theorists have attempted to specify what types of institutional logics are likely to give rise to formal organizations.[1]

Early views placed emphasis on regulatory and normative structures. Weber (1924/1968, Vol. 1: 24; Vol. 2: 953–954) stressed the emergence of a "legal order" consisting of a "system of consciously made rational rules" that support "instrumentally rational" action. Parsons (1951; Parsons, Bales, and Shils 1953) devoted much attention to detailing the value orientations and normative systems that support the development of more instrumental and impersonal social forms. His typology of "pattern variables"—basic value dimensions giving rise to different kinds of action orientations and supporting structures—identified universalism (vs. particularism), affective neutrality (vs. affectivity), achievement (vs. ascription), and specificity (vs. diffuseness) as normative orientations conducive to the rise of organizations.

Later theorists emphasized the cultural-cognitive systems supporting organizations. Ellul (1954/1964) noted the emergence of a "technicist" mentality, which encourages analytic approaches and the development of systematic, instrumental rules to pursue specific objectives. Berger and colleagues (Berger, Berger, and Kellner 1973) described the novel states of consciousness that accompany the emergence of technology and bureaucracy, including "mechanisticity," "reproducibility," "orderliness," and "predictability." Meyer (1983: 265–267) depicted the cultural elements ("rational myths") that underlie the creation of formal organizations as including "definable purposes," "culturally defined means-ends relationships or technologies," viewing things and people as "resources," and presuming the existence of a "unified sovereign" that gives coherence to collective actors.

What all of these arguments have in common is that they embody a rationalized conception of the world. Purposes are specified and then rule-like principles are devised to govern activities aimed at their pursuit. *Rationalization* involves "the creation of cultural schemes defining means-ends relationships and standardizing systems of control over activities and actors" (Scott and Meyer 1994: 3). Some of the principles, as in the "laws of mechanics," have an empirical base, whereas others, as in legal frameworks, are rooted in a consistent logical or philosophical structure. All such rationalized beliefs support the rise of organizations.

Institutional scholars argue that rationalization also entails the creation of entities—identifiable social units—endowed with interests and having the capacity to take action. These are products of the constitutive aspects of institutions that were discussed in Chapter 3. In the modern world, commencing with social processes associated with the Enlightenment, three primary categories of actors have been accorded primacy: individuals, organizations, and societies, the latter in the guise of the nation-state (see Meyer, Boli, and Thomas 1987). James S. Coleman (1974; 1990: Ch. 20) provided a valuable historical-analytical account of the emergence of organizations as significant collective actors accorded legal rights, capacities, and resources independent of those held by their individual participants.[2] Coleman views changes in the law not as causal factors, but as significant indicators of the growing independence of these new corporate forms as they became recognized as legal persons in the eyes of the law. Pedersen and Dobbin (1997) suggest that this process was fueled primarily by the growth of a scientific ethos that created abstract and general categories to classify and enumerate first the biological and physical universe and subsequently the social world. The rapid advance of commensuration—"the measurement of characteristics normally represented by different units according to a common metric" (Espeland and Stevens 1998: 315)—allowed the categorization and counting of all manner of material and social objects.

Professionals, initially from the engineering sciences (Shenhav 1995, 1999), attempted to tame the exotic, multiple, idiosyncratic instances of enterprise and fostered the emergence of, on the one hand, the generic category "organization" accompanied by its universal handmaiden "management" and, on the other hand, the differentiation of recognizable subtypes (e.g., schools, hospitals, public agencies, non-profit and for-profit corporations). The development of such templates or archetypes and the specification of their structural characteristics, utilities, capabilities, and identities has taken place over many years but, once established, they provide cultural models for the rapid molding of other similar forms. This professional project—treating all manner of collectivities as part of a more generic form "organization" and identifying meaningful subtypes—was later embraced and, necessarily, reinforced by the emergence in the mid-20th century of an academic discipline devoted to the pursuit of organizational studies. In short, you and I are part of this process!

Increasingly in modern societies, the belief grows that organizations are indispensable tools for concerted action. As Parsons (1956/1960a: 41) observed over a half century ago, "the development of organizations is the principal mechanism by which, in a highly differentiated society, it is possible to 'get things done,' to achieve goals beyond the reach of the individual." Meyer and colleagues concur:

> Whether in the public or private arena and in any social sector or industry, organization is possible and desirable. Empowered and rational people can be brought together in a managed and rationalized structure to take purposive collective action on many fronts in a scientized environment. (Meyer, Drori and Hwang 2006: 25)

Institutional Logics: Alternative Rationalized Models

Meyer and colleagues develop their arguments regarding the rationalizing power of cultural schemes at a very broad, world-system level considering the constitutive processes creating individuals, organizations, and nation-states. They depict the relentless trajectory of modernization forces during the past 300 years across all societies and sectors. However, a more complex and nuanced view of cultural schema has been developed by Alford and Friedland (1985; Friedland and Alford 1991). While they accept the importance of differentiating between individual, organization, and societal levels, they view the societal level as a complex pattern of "interinstitutional relations," encompassing a multiplicity of value spheres, each associated with a distinctive "institutional logic." They define *institutional logic* as "a set of material practices and symbolic constructions which constitutes its organizing principles and which is available to organizations and individuals to elaborate" (Friedland and Alford 1991: 248). They point to such varying societal logics as "capitalism," with its emphasis on commodification of human activity and accumulation; "democracy," with its stress on equality and participation; "family," with its stress on unconditional loyalty; and "religion," with its attention to epistemological, eschatological, and ethical matters. Each logic is associated with a distinctive mode of rationalization—defining the appropriate relation between subjects, practices, and objects.

Thornton and colleagues (Thornton, Ocasio, and Lounsbury 2012) have pursued and elaborated this perspective, employing the concept of institutional logics to identity a specific set of models for motivating and organizing social arenas or societal subsystems. These models differ in a number of respects, including their "root metaphor," their sources of

legitimacy and authority, and the types of norms and control mechanisms employed (Thornton and Ocasio 2008; Thornton et al. 2012:
54–56). The major types of rationalized institutional logics they identify
are the family, religion, state, market, profession, corporation, and community. Many of the most important tensions and change dynamics
observed in contemporary organizations and organization fields can be
fruitfully examined by considering the competition and struggle
among various categories of actors committed to contrasting institutional logics. Thus, many critics and would-be reformers of the state
seek to introduce market logics or corporate managerial forms in order
to improve its efficiency and accountability (Christensen and Laegreid
2001; Salamon 2002). And many organizations long operating under a
professional partnership mode have been invaded by corporate practices and subjected to greater market controls (Greenwood and
Suddaby 2006; Scott, Ruef, Mendel, and Caronna 2000; Thornton 2004;
Thornton, Jones, and Kury 2005). Even corporations find themselves
increasingly "managed by the markets," slavishly responding to financially based assessments of quarterly performance (Davis 2009). Others
address the conflicts between church and state (Wuthnow 2005), and
between family and corporate logics (England and Farkas 1986). In
short, an important source of the institutional tension and change experienced by both organizations and individuals in everyday life involves
jurisdictional disputes among the various institutional logics. These
and related change processes associated with competing institutional
logics are discussed in more detail in Chapters 6 and 8.

Differences in Time and Space

The socially constructed characteristics of both persons and collective actors, such as firms, vary over time and place as do the expected
relations among firms and between firms and the state (see Berger and
Huntington 2002; Hall and Soskice 2001a; 2001b; Hollingsworth and
Boyer 1997; Whitley 1999). Institutional rules in the West have
accorded greater individual autonomy and independence to social
actors—both persons and firms—than have related rules in East Asian
societies. Thus, although "the United States has institutionalized competitive individualism in its market structure," and most European
countries have developed a somewhat more "concerted" version of
industry structures, Asian economies "are organized through networks
of [interdependent and less autonomous] economic actors that are
believed to be natural and appropriate to economic development"
(Biggart and Hamilton 1992: 472). Relations among persons or firms

that Western eyes view as involving nepotism or collusion seem, by Eastern observers, normal, inevitable, and beneficial. Theoretical perspectives vary greatly in the extent to which they attend to differences among organizations and ways of organizing. Child (2000) contrasts what he terms "low context" perspectives, such as neoclassical economic theory and psychological universalism, with "high context" paradigms, such as cultural theory and institutional theory. The former minimize the impact of cultural and institutional differences and point to a convergence among forms over time (e.g., globalization erasing cultural differences), while the latter "share the strong presumption that management and organization will retain and develop its own distinct characteristics that derive from cultural preferences and embedded institutions" (p. 37).

In general, regulative and normative theorists give more attention to the examination of regulative rules, treating constitutive rules as background conditions. Thus, for example, neoinstitutionalist economists and rational choice political scientists inquire into the activities of a firm or agency and consider what kinds of structural arrangements or procedures are associated with specified behaviors, such as improved productivity or the passage of legislation. By contrast, economic historians and historical political scientists give much more attention to the origin of general types of social actors (e.g., "jobber, importer, factor, broker, and the commission agent"; Chandler 1977: 27), organizational archetypes (e.g., joint-stock companies, multidivisional and conglomerate firms), or changes in property or political rights (Campbell and Lindberg 1990). Similarly, neoinstitutional sociologists are more apt to focus on changes over time in the types of actors involved or the cultural rules establishing the logics of practice within a particular organizational context (e.g., Fligstein 1990; Schneiberg 2002; Scott et al. 2000). Scholars attending to constitutive rules insist that much of the coherence of social life is due to the creation of categories of social actors, both individual and collective, and associated ways of acting.[3]

❖ AGENCY AND INSTITUTIONS

Throughout the history of social science, there has existed a tension between those theorists who emphasize structural and cultural constraints on action and those who emphasize the ability of individual actors to "make a difference" in the flow of events. This is a version of the ancient antinomy between freedom and control. Obviously, the thrust of institutional theory is to privilege continuity and constraint in social structure, but that need not preclude attention to the ways in which individual actors take action to create, maintain, and transform institutions.

Early neoinstitutional scholars, such as Meyer and Rowan (1977), DiMaggio and Powell (1983), and Meyer and Scott (1983b), emphasized the ways in which institutional mechanisms constrained organizational structures and activities. However, more recent work, which I review in subsequent chapters—including that of DiMaggio (1988, 1991), Oliver (1991), and Christensen, Karnøe, Pedersen, and Dobbin (1997)—gives more attention to the ways in which both individuals and organizations innovate, act strategically, and contribute to institutional change.

Many theoretical frameworks treat freedom and constraint as opposing ideas, requiring us to "take sides"—to privilege one social value or the other. Fortunately, recent developments in sociological theory allow us to see the two thrusts as interrelated, compatible processes. In particular, the work of Anthony Giddens (1979, 1984) on "structuration" provides a productive framework for examining the interplay between these forces.

Although *structuration* is a rather infelicitous word, the term, coined by Giddens, reminds us that social structure involves the patterning of social activities and relations through time and across space. Social structures only exist as patterned social activities, incorporating rules, relations, and resources reproduced over time. Giddens (1984: 25) envisioned what he termed the "duality of social structure," recognizing it to be both product and platform of social action. Social structures exhibit a dual role in that they are "both the medium and the outcome of the practices they recursively organize" (p. 25). Individual actors carry out practices that are simultaneously constrained (in some directions) and empowered (in others) by the existing social structure. In Giddens' (1984: 21) model, social structures are made up of rules—"generalized procedures applied in the enactment/reproduction of social life"—and resources, both human and nonhuman, "that can be used to enhance or maintain power" (Sewell 1992: 9). Institutions are those types of social structures that involve more strongly held rules supported by stronger relations and more entrenched resources. Institutional practices are "those deeply embedded in time and space" (Giddens 1984: 13).

Structuration theory views actors as creating and following rules and utilizing resources as they engage in the ongoing production and reproduction of social structures. Actors are viewed as knowledgeable and reflexive, capable of understanding and taking account of everyday situations and routinely monitoring the results of their own and others' actions. *Agency* refers to an actor's ability to have some effect on the social world—altering the rules, relational ties, or distribution of resources. The presence of agency presumes a nondeterminant, "voluntaristic" theory of action: "to be able to 'act otherwise' means being able to intervene in the world, or to refrain from such intervention, with the effect of influencing a specific process or state of affairs" (Giddens 1984: 14). Agency provides for a consideration of the role of power in institutional processes.[4]

The basic theoretical premise underlying the concept of agency is strongly aligned with the phenomenological assumptions that undergird sociological versions of neoinstitutional thought. Between the context and response is the interpreting actor. Agency resides in "the interpretive processes whereby choices are imagined, evaluated, and contingently reconstructed by actors in ongoing dialogue with unfolding situations" (Emirbayer and Mische 1998: 966).

Structuration theory joins with numerous other theoretical arguments to support a more proactive role for individual and organizational actors, and a more interactive and reciprocal view of institutional processes. For example, to view behavior as oriented toward and governed by rules need not imply either that behavior is "unreasoned" or automatic. March and Olsen (1989) point out that rules must be both selected—often more than one rule may be applicable—and interpreted—adapted to the demands of the particular situation. Weick (1969/1979; 1995) emphasized that understandings and scripts emerge out of actions as well as precede them, and that collective symbols are as likely to be used to justify past behaviors as to guide current ones. As noted in Chapter 3, newer versions of culture theory view individuals as playing an active part, using existing rules and social resources as a repertory of possibilities for constructing strategies of action. Analysts have posited a "politics of identity," in which individuals or organized groups create goals, identities, and solidarities that provide meaning and generate ongoing social commitments (Aronowitz 1992; Calhoun 1991; Somers and Gibson 1994). They increasingly recognize the extent to which organizational participants do not always conform to conventional patterns, but respond variably, sometimes creating new ways of acting and organizing and being.

A collection of more recent scholars, while embracing the structuration framework, assert that too much attention has been accorded by institutionalists to the processes by which institutions guide and govern actors and not enough to the ways in which actors and their actions affect institutions. One approach to redirecting attention to this "second moment" of structuration suggests that renewed emphasis be given to "institutional work" that "highlights the awareness, skill and reflexivity of individual and collective actors" as they strive, variously, to create, maintain, or disrupt institutions (Lawrence and Suddaby 2006: 219; see also Lawrence, Suddaby, and Leca 2009). A focus on institutional creation has led some to revive DiMaggio's (1988) concept of "institutional entrepreneurship" as usefully stressing the ways in which some actors are able to mobilize resources to realize interests which they value (see Maguire, Hardy, and Lawrence 2004; see also Chapter 5). Attention to maintenance reminds us that the reproduction of institutions is never automatic—deinstitutionalization processes are often observed (Oliver 1992)—so that work is required for institutions to persist. A focus on institutional disruption has been fueled by the arrival of social movement theorists who have fruitfully comingled with institutionalists to examine the ways in which suppressed or marginalized interests and players mobilize resources to effect institutional change (Davis, McAdam, Scott, and Zald 2005). These and other examples of institutional work are discussed in subsequent chapters.

All actors, both individual and collective, possess some degree of agency, but the amount of agency varies greatly among actors as well as among types of social structures. Agency itself is socially and institutionally structured.

❖ VARYING CARRIERS

Institutions, whether regulative, normative, or cultural-cognitive elements are stressed, are conveyed by various types of vehicles or "carriers" (Jepperson 1991: 150). I identify four types: symbolic systems, relational systems, activities, and artifacts.[5] These distinctions are largely orthogonal to the three pillars, permitting us to cross-classify them (see Table 4.1). Theorists vary not only in which elements they favor, but in which carriers they emphasize, just as institutional frameworks differ in which elements are central and what type of carriers are utilized. It is readily apparent that carriers are important in considering the ways in which institutions change, whether in convergent or divergent ways. They point to a set of fundamental mechanisms that allow us to account for how ideas move through space and time, who or what is transporting them, and how they may be transformed by their journey.

A substantial literature exists that deals with the subject of carriers, but it is illusive because it is associated with a variety of labels, including diffusion of innovation, technology transfer, organizational

Table 4.1   Institutional Pillars and Carriers

	Pillars		
	Regulative	*Normative*	*Cultural-cognitive*
Symbolic systems	Rules Laws	Values Expectations Standards	Categories Typifications Schemas Frames

Relational systems	Governance
	    systems
	Power systems
		Regimes
		Authority systems
			Structural
			    isomorphism
			Identities

Activities	Monitoring Sanctioning Disrupting	Roles, jobs Routines Habits Repertoires of collective action	Predispositions Scripts

Artifacts	Objects complying
	    with mandated
	    specifications
		Objects meeting
		    conventions,
		    standards
			Objects possessing
			    symbolic value

learning, adoption of reforms, intermediaries, management fads and fashions, and processes of modernization. An emerging theme recognized by observers across all of these areas is that carriers are never neutral modes of transmission, but affect the nature of the message and the ways in which it is received. Thus, although analysts often employ what Reddy (1979) termed "conduit metaphors," such as delivering and circulating messages, how a message arrives affects its interpretation and reception. Thus, it makes a difference, as Abernethy (2000) details in his survey of European colonization efforts in Africa, whether Western ideas arrived in the guise of missionaries seeking to make converts, merchants looking for trading partners, or armies bent on the acquisition of booty and territorial conquest.

As ideas and artifacts move from time to time and place to place, they are altered, modified, combined with other ideas or objects, translated, and transformed (Czarniawska and Joerges 1996). In Sahlin-Andersson's (1996: 82) terms, they are *edited:* "The models are told and retold in various situations and told differently in each situation." Editing occurs because of differences in context, differences in logics or rationale, and differences in formulation or framing (Sahlin and Wedlin 2008). How and how much models are edited varies, however, by the type of carrier. The entries in Table 4.1 describe the content of the message—what is being transported. Carriers emphasize the features of the medium.

Note also that the entries in Table 4.1 do not refer to the simple transmission of an idea, a practice or an artifact. As Colyvas and Jonsson (2011: 28) point out, we should not conflate simple diffusion with institutionalization. Diffusion concerns itself with "spreading, or how things flow" whereas institutionalization is concerned with "stickiness, or how things become permanent." It is possible for materials to flow and for practices to be widespread that are not regarded as institutionally supported (e.g., fads, fashions, tastes), and for practices that are not prevalent to be legitimate (e.g., hiring in firms is supposed to be based on neutral and universalistic criteria but more often involves insider knowledge or favoritism). To address this issue, the typology proposed here emphasizes not only that materials and practices flow across boundaries of time and space, but so also do rules, norms, and beliefs. In short, the carriers we emphasize are those bearing institutional elements, not simply objects or activities.

Symbolic Carriers

As noted in Chapter 2, most recent students of culture treat it as a semiotic system: as collections of symbols. For institutionalists, the symbols of interest include the full range of rules, values and norms, classifications, representations, frames, schemas, prototypes, and scripts used to guide behavior. As the entries in Table 4.1 suggest, which aspects of symbolic systems are emphasized vary depending on which elements of institutions are accorded prominence. Cognitive theorists stress the importance of common categories, distinctions, and typifications as shaping perceptions and interpretations; normative theorists accent shared values and normative expectations that guide behavior; and regulative theorists point to the role played by conventions, rules, and laws.

The emergence of language as a human capacity greatly facilitated the transmission of symbols over time and place. As discussed in Chapter 2, spoken language provided the foundation for localized mythic cultures, but the power and mobility of words advanced immeasurably with the creation of a theoretic culture involving written language and its externalization in various media ranging from books to digital information. In his admirable survey of media and empire, economic historian Harold Innis (1972; 1995) described differences between reliance on an oral tradition versus all forms of writing:

Introduction of the alphabet meant a concern with sound rather than with sight or with the ear rather than the eye. Empires had been built up on communication based on sight in contrast with [the more geographically restricted] Greek political organization which emphasized oral discussion. (1995: p. 332)

With the invention of writing, the nature of medium employed to carry the words greatly affected transmission possibilities. Innis (1995: 325) observed how writing on stone or clay, for example, functioned to preserve knowledge over time, whereas writing on papyrus or paper was better suited to transport ideas across space. The appearance of the printing press opened up the possibility of mass dissemination of identical texts. Anderson (1983: 44–45) argues that the use of print languages created unified fields of exchange and communication employing languages "below Latin and above the spoken vernaculars" and the convergence of "capitalism and print technology" provided the basis for the systematic construction of nationalism.

Shifting to the present era, developments in information/communication technology have played a powerful role in broadcasting images and ideas worldwide, increasing the size of markets, lengthening supply chains by connecting and transforming organizations, and generally moving us more completely into a global economy and more interdependent political community. As Appadurai (1996) observed, the cinema and TV place a premium on the image, whereas the computer, cell phone, and texting privilege the word; however, the Internet can accommodate both in transcending distance. Myths, stories, songs, and images have long provided a repertory of models for living, but today's global media provides a richer mix of imagined possibilities: "More persons in more parts of the world consider a wider set of possible lives than they ever did before" (Appadurai 1996: 53). At the same time that new ideas arrive, however, they are translated, fused, and blended with local knowledge in a process termed *indigenization* or *glocalization*. Schemas are "transposable": "They can be applied to a wide and not fully predictable range of cases outside the context in which they are initially learned" (Sewell 1992: 17). Symbols are transportable, versatile, and malleable.

Relational Carriers

Institutions can also be carried by relational systems. Such systems are carriers that rely on patterned interactions connected to networks of social positions: role systems. Flows of immigrants bring new ideas, modes of behavior, and relational commitments across societal boundaries. Many robust relational systems transcend and intersect with the boundaries of organizations, as is the case with occupational and professional connections and communities of practice (Brown and Duguid 2000).

Rules and belief systems are coded into positional distinctions and roles; relational systems incorporate—instantiate—institutional elements. As with symbolic systems, some relational arrangements are widely shared across many organizations, creating structural isomorphism (similar forms) or structural equivalence (similar relations among forms). Other forms may be distinctive to a particular organization, embodying localized belief systems and creating a unique organizational "character structure" (Selznick 1957) or "identity" (Albert and Whetten 1985).

Which aspects of relational structures are emphasized depends on which elements of institutions are featured. Cognitive theorists stress structural models. Classifications and typifications are often coded into organizational structures as differentiated departments and roles. For example, codified knowledge systems support the development of differentiated academic departments in universities. Normative and regulatory theorists are apt to view relational systems as "governance systems," emphasizing either the normative (authority) or the coercive (power) aspects of these structures. Such governance systems are viewed as creating and enforcing codes, norms, and rules, and as monitoring and sanctioning the activities of participants. Social psychologists such as Strauss (1978) examined the construction of "negotiated orders" in specific settings. The new institutional economists, such as Williamson, emphasize relational systems erected to exercise governance as the principal carriers of institutional forces.

A more complex and consequential role of relational systems for institutional structures and processes is suggested by Powell and colleagues (Owen-Smith and Powell 2008; Powell, Koput, and Smith-Doerr 1996; Powell, White, Koput, and Owen-Smith 2005). These investigators have examined the emergence of the biotechnology field in several locations in the United States with its evolving structure of relations among small biotech companies, large corporations, U.S. institutes of health, venture capital firms, and universities. The connections among and the relative centrality of these players have changed over time as the field has gradually gained coherence and relations solidified. They argue that in such cases networks and institutions are "co-constituted," that actors possessing different kinds of capital and driven by different logics find ways to gradually make sense of their world, resolve ambiguities, and develop mutually reinforcing modes of interacting (Owen-Smith and Powell 2008; see also Chapter 8). Institutional categories and norms shape, and are shaped by, shifting relational systems.

Activities as Carriers

As discussed in Chapter 1, early economic institutionalists such as Veblen and Commons, borrowing from the American pragmatist tradition early in the 20th century, emphasized the importance of habit, routine, and convention in social behavior. These scholars stressed the centrality of behavior, of social action. Cohen (2007; 2009) suggests that a momentous shift in organization studies occurred with the decision by Herbert Simon (1945/1997: 1) to shift primary attention from action, "getting things done," to decision making, "the choice that prefaces all action." With this choice, Simon turned his back on the pragmatist tradition of John Dewey and others, who had emphasized the centrality of action, including habit and routine, instead privileging cognition. (In spite of this turn, as we discussed, in his later work with March, Simon recognized the importance of "performance programs" for codifying rational recipes for acting.) As for neoinstitutional theorists, as we have emphasized, much contemporary institutional theory privileges symbols and beliefs over social behavior. Indeed, scholars such as John Meyer assume that institutionalization frequently involves changes in rules and formal structures (symbolic and relational systems) that have little effect on—are decoupled from—participant actions (Drori, Meyer, and Hwang 2006; Meyer and Rowan 1977).

Although dominant intellectual currents in organization studies from the 1950s on were at work to privilege symbols over behavior and structure over action, counter trends developed that have grown stronger and more insistent over time. These include, in rough time ordering, the work of social psychologists like Strauss (Strauss, Schatzman, Bucher, Erlich, and Sabshin 1964), with his focus on "negotiated order"; Weick (1969/1979), with his attention to "organizing" (as opposed to "organization"); Silverman (1971), with his preference for "action" over "systems" accounts of organization; Giddens (1979), with his work on "structuration" as an alternative to "structure"; evolutionary economists Nelson and Winter (1982), with their emphasis on "routines"; Bourdieu's (1977) work on "practices"; Barney's (1991) resource-based theory, with its attention to "capabilities"; and Lawrence and Suddaby's (2006) focus on "institutional work."

While earlier work on activities connected to organizations and institutions placed most emphasis on repetitive actions—habits and routines—that provided a basis for order and continuity, more recent work, partly under the influence of social movement theorists, has insisted that institutional scholars should also take into account actions that construct new institutions or disrupt existing ones. Movement theorists have been less interested in how institutions persist than in the processes by which they are disrupted and overturned, giving way to new institutional forms—the processes of insurgency, contentious action, and mobilization (e.g., McAdam, McCarthy, and Zald 1996; McCarthy and Zald 1977; Tilly 1978). On reflection, in effect, it appears that for many years organization/institutional theorists and movement scholars have been attending to different moments of the same process (McAdam and Scott 2005: 8–14).

Considering activities in relation to the three pillars, it is obvious that, for the regulative pillar, attention must be focused on the monitoring and sanctioning behavior of "principals," on the one hand, and on compliance/deviance responses of "agents" on the other. As discussed in Chapter 3, high costs are associated with oversight, and the choices made in what activities to monitor can have a significant influence on the effectiveness of control systems as well as which aspects of performance agents attend to. But it also happens that the agents can have their own agenda and can seek to evade or even disrupt the rule systems and authorities in place. (I discuss in Chapter 7 a wider array of possible responses to institutional pressures.)

Activities associated with the normative pillar include all the ways in which social action is structured in institutional settings, including, most important, roles, generally, and jobs, more specifically. Also, as emphasized by early economic institutionalists, institutions may be embodied in—carried by—structured activities in the form of habitualized behavior and routines. Routines are carriers that rely on patterned actions that reflect the tacit knowledge of actors—deeply ingrained habits and procedures based on unarticulated knowledge and beliefs. Rather than privileging symbolic systems, many early institutionalists, such as Veblen, viewed habitualized action, routines, standard operating procedures, and similar patterned activities as the central features of institutions.

Later, March and Simon (1958) identified repetitive "performance programs" as the central ingredient accounting for the reliability of organizations. More recently, evolutionary theorists, such as Nelson and Winter (1982), have emphasized the stabilizing role played by participants' skills and organizational routines: activities involving little or no conscious choice and behavior governed by tacit knowledge and skills of which the actor may be unaware. Viewing routines as the "genes" of organizations, Winter (1990: 274–275) points out that they range from "hard"—activities encoded into technologies—to "soft"—organizational routines such as airplane inspection or fast-food procedures—but all involve "repetitive patterns of activity." These patterns include a broad range of behaviors, extending from standard operating procedures and skill sets of individual employees to "organizational activity bundles such as jobs, assembly lines, airline reservations systems, accounting principles or rules of war" (Miner 1991: 773). Such routines involve more than acquiring a "system of rules or representations"; they entail the "learning of modes of acting and problem-solving" (Hanks 1991: 20). These types of skills underlie much of the stability of organizational behavior—accounting for both their reliable performance as well as their rigidities.

Routines are typically learned within, and sustained and renewed by, relational systems. Experiential learning and on-the-job training often take place in situations allowing novices to engage in what Lave and Wenger (1991) term "legitimate peripheral participation":

> By this we mean to draw attention to the point that learners inevitably participate in communities of practitioners and that the mastery of knowledge and skill requires newcomers to move toward full participation in the sociocultural practices of a community. (p. 29)

The fact that they are learned in and sustained by a community means that routines are not readily transportable to new and different settings involving new actors and relationships. Routines tend to be more "sticky" and less easily carried across settings, but they are transportable.

In related work, Clemens (1997: 39) borrows from social movement scholars the concept of "repertoire" to refer to the "set of distinctive forms of action employed by or known to members of a particular group or society." She argues that specific forms of organizations are associated with distinctive repertoires of activity providing "templates, scripts, recipes, or models for social interaction" (p. 49). These repertoires act to facilitate collective action as collections of actors know what they are to do while their counterparts know what to expect from them.

Artifacts as Carriers

Anthropologists have long recognized the importance of "material culture" or artifacts created by human ingenuity to assist in the performance of various tasks. We adopt Suchman's (2003: 98) definition: "An artifact is a discrete material object, consciously produced or transformed by human activity, under the influence of the physical and/or cultural environment." Early forms were often as primitive as shaped rocks and sticks, but more recent artifacts include complex technologies embodied in both hardware and software. Organizational students of technology earlier treated these features as a unidirectional and deterministic influence impacting organizational structure and behavior (see, e.g., Blau, Falbe, McKinley, and Tracy 1976; Woodward 1958). Later theorists reacted by emphasizing the socially constructed nature of technology and the extent to which its effects are mediated by situational factors and interpretive processes (Bijker, Hughes, and Pinch 1987). In any case, the most important characteristic of artifacts is that they "all embody both technical and symbolic elements" (Suchman 2003: 99; see also Gagliardi 1990).

Orlikowski (1992) usefully proposed that artifacts and technology can be examined within the same theoretical framework devised by Giddens (1984) to accommodate social structure and human agency. Viewing artifacts as an instance of structuration allows analysts to recognize that such inventions are products of human action, but also that, "once developed and deployed," they become reified and appear "to be part of the objective, structural properties" of the situation (Orlikowski 1992: 406). This perspective is often obscured from participants and analysts because the actors and actions that create the new instruments may be removed in time and space from those that employ them to accomplish work. Analysts focusing on artifact creation are better able to see the multiple possibilities: the path selected versus the "roads not taken"; analysts focusing on artifact use see primarily the constraints imposed by the design selected on those who employ it. Although such differences do exist, they should not obscure the extent to which users interact with and modify the meaning and use of artifacts. Orlikowski (1992) observes:

> While we can expect a greater engagement of human agents during the initial development of a technology, this does not discount the ongoing potential for users to change it (physically and socially) throughout their interaction with it. In using a technology, users interpret, appropriate, and manipulate it in various ways. (p. 408)

Barley (1986) provides an instructive empirical study of the adoption of "identical" technologies (CT scanners) by radiological departments in two community hospitals, examining the ways and extent to which the technologies were associated with somewhat divergent changes in the decision making and power structure of the departments (see Chapter 8).

Artifacts, like other carriers, can be viewed as associated with, and affected by, each of the three pillars. The design and construction of some artifacts and technologies is mandated by regulative authorities often in the interests of safety. Modern societies contain a wide range of agencies— ranging from those that attempt to ensure the reliability of atomic plants to those that set performance and safety standards for commercial aircraft and passenger cars—which oversee product quality. Social contracts, existing in the shadow if not the substance of law, can be examined as social artifacts, as Suchman (2003) demonstrated. Technologies are also shaped by and embody normative processes. Trade and industrial groups often convene to set standards for a wide range of machines and technical equipment, as discussed previously. Such agreements serve to ensure compatibility and can create added value for participants to the extent that many players adopt the standard (Katz and Shapiro 1985). Artifacts can embody and represent particular constellations of ideas. Indeed, the symbolic freight of some objects can outweigh their material essence (e.g., the significance of the bread and wine in the communion service or the goal posts in the football match).

These arguments and distinctions suggest some of the many ways in which organizations are deeply embedded in institutional contexts. A given organization is supported and constrained by institutional forces. Also, a given organization incorporates a multitude of institutionalized features in the form of symbolic systems, relational systems, activities, and artifacts within their own boundaries. Hence, it is appropriate to speak of the extent to which organizational components or features are institutionalized. These views are shared by all or the great majority of institutional theorists. That subset endorsing a cultural-cognitive perspective adds an additional, even more fateful, assertion: The very concept of an organization as a special-purpose, instrumental entity is a product of institutional processes—constitutive processes that define the capacities of collective actors, both generally and as specialized subtypes. This version of institutional theory, in particular, tends to subvert or undermine the conventional distinction between organization and environment. Organizations are penetrated by environments in ways not envisioned by many theoretical models.

❖ VARYING LEVELS OF ANALYSIS

Differentiating Levels

One of the principal ways in which the several varieties of institutional theory differ is in the level at which they are applied. The recognition of varying levels is particularly important for institutional scholars who argue that the wider contexts within which social events occur, not simply their immediate circumstances, are of utmost import in explaining these events. Differentiation among types of contexts helps to specify these cross-level arguments.

While the notion of levels is both familiar and useful, the metaphor has a materialist flavor. It can encourage investigators to take social boundaries too seriously and may obscure one of the central insights associated with institutional analysis: Order is often created by shared meanings rather than by physical or material causes. Thus, it is over-simplifying, if not misleading, to describe nation-states or organizations or their participants as if they were operating independently of institutional systems at other levels. The levels that we define and circumscribe are *open systems*. The systems are porous in the sense that activities and meanings occurring on one level are often linked to and activate activities and meanings at other levels. Analysts employing the levels distinction should be mindful of the ways in which it can enable, but also distort, our attempt to understand the nature of the processes at work.

In defining levels, the key underlying dimension is the scope of the phenomena encompassed, whether measured in terms of space, time, or numbers of persons affected. For institutions, level may be usefully operationalized as the range of jurisdiction of the institutional form. Given the complexity and variety of social phenomena, any particular set of distinctions among levels is somewhat arbitrary. Nevertheless, for our purposes, it is useful to identify six categories: the levels of world system, society, organization field, organizational population, organization, and organizational subsystem (see Figure 4.1).

Most of these levels are widely employed and recognizable to social analysts; all are of interest to students of organizations. In institutional scholarship during the modern period (since the 1970s), the more macrolevels have received the lion's share of attention, but during the past decade, this imbalance is being addressed: More analysts are examining microlevel processes (Elsbach 2002; Fiol 2002; Powell and Colyvas 2008; Zilber 2002). Let's briefly review each level:

- The *world system* level is also meant to encompass work at the "global," "international," and "transnational" levels: scholarship that examines structures and processes occurring cross-societally and over longer periods of time. The early work of Wallerstein (1974) on world systems has been supplemented by

Figure 4.1   Institutional Pillars and Varying Levels: Illustrative Schools

the work of Meyer and colleagues on world society (Drori et al. 2006) and has recently been joined by that of a growing number of international business scholars (e.g., Peng 2003).

- The *society* level focuses on structures and processes pertaining to societies or nation-states. Social theorists such as Sorokin (1937–1941) and Parsons (1951) pioneered these approaches, which have long been the province of political sociologists (Skocpol 1985) and political scientists (Dahl and Lindblom 1953; March and Olsen 1984).

- Perhaps the least familiar, yet a level of great significance to institutional theory, is that of the *organization field*, a level that identifies a collection of diverse, interdependent organizations that participate in a common meaning system (DiMaggio and Powell 1983; Scott and Meyer 1983; see also Chapter 8).

- Another level of analysis somewhat distinctive to organizational research and often employed in institutional studies is that of the population. *Organizational populations* are defined as a collection or aggregate of organizations that are "alike in some respect," in particular to "classes of organizations that are relatively homogeneous in terms of environmental vulnerability" (Hannan and Freeman 1977: 934; see also Hannan and Freeman 1989). Newspaper companies and trade unions are examples of organizational populations.
- Not surprisingly, *organization*-level studies were among the first to appear in early work on institutions and organizations, as pioneered by Selznick (1949; 1957) and his students. In this work, institutional processes operating at the level of a specific organization are the focus of attention. Early work has been supplemented by later work on "organization culture" (Kunda 1992; Martin 2002).
- Work focusing on *organizational subsystems,* or component units of organizations such as departments or teams, was pioneered by industrial relations scholars such as Roethlisberger and Dickson (1939) and Seashore (1954) and has been continued and extended by students of work and organization such as Barley (1986), Heimer (1999), and Kellogg (2011). It has become an increasingly common focus of institutional scholarship.

To reiterate, all six levels are of interest to those who study organizations. As with the notion of carriers, the levels distinction is orthogonal to and can be cross-classified with the set of institutional elements.

Levels and Pillars: Illustrative Studies

Beginning with scholars examining the operation of *regulative processes* at differing levels, working at the trans-societal level, North and Thomas (1973) examined how the institution of property rights and associated state regulatory apparati developed in the Western world during the 15th through the 17th centuries. At the societal level, Skocpol (1979) examined differences in the organization and operation of the state as it affected the course of revolutions occurring in France, Russia, and China. Working at the organization field level, Guthrie and Roth (1999) examined the dynamic interaction of state institutions and employers regarding the development of maternity leave policies for employees. At the organization population level, Barnett and Carroll (1993) studied the effects on the development of early telephone companies of various regulatory policies pursued by state and federal authorities. Focusing on the organization level, Williamson (1975; 1985; 1991) developed his markets and hierarchies framework to explain the emergence of varying types of organizational forms to govern and reduce the costs of economic transactions at the level of the firm. And examining organization subsystems, Shepsle and Weingast (1987) studied the institutional foundations of committee power in Congress.

Turning to theorists emphasizing *normative elements*, Brunsson and Jacobsson (2000) examined the construction of "standards" (normative frameworks) at the transnational level by professional associations and international nongovernmental organization, while Tate (2001) detailed the continuing persistence of varying standards at the national level. Parsons (1956/1960b) described differences in value systems and normative frameworks at the societal level and their consequences for organizations. At the organization field level, Mezias (1990) studied changes in normative beliefs regarding financial reporting requirements for corporations occasioned by the actions of state agents and professional accounting societies, and Stern (1979) and Starr (1982) examined the effects of the rules and conventions promulgated by trade and professional associations on organization fields, specifically college athletics and medicine. Singh, Tucker, and House (1986) examined the effects on survival rates in a population of voluntary social service organizations of being certified by public agencies. At the organization level, Selznick (1949) studied the ways in which procedural requirements became "infused with value" in the Tennessee Valley Authority. And at the organization subsystem level, Roy (1952) and Burawoy (1979) examined the institutionalization of normative frameworks regarding production and restriction of output among workers in a machine shop of a manufacturing plant (see also Burawoy and Verdery 1999).

Among those scholars examining *cultural-cognitive* aspects of institutional processes, Meyer and colleagues (Drori et al. 2006) examined cultural processes operating at the transnational level giving rise to organizations and shaping organization structures and processes in a wide variety of contexts. Dobbin (1994b) studied the varying cultural belief systems that undergirded societal policies affecting the construction of railway systems in the United States, England, and France. Working at the level of the organization field, researchers such as Deephouse (1996) and Hoffman (1997) employed discourse analysis and other types of content analytic techniques to assess meaning systems in banking and corporate environmentalism. Examining organization populations, Carroll and Hannan (1989) employed data on the density or prevalence of newspapers—viewed as an indicator of the taken-for-grantedness of this form—to examine its effects on the growth rates of newspapers in selected U.S. cities. At the organization level, Clark (1970) examined the distinctive cultural values cultivated by a set of elite colleges and their effects on organizational viability, whereas Kunda (1992) studied the "engineering culture" of a high-tech company. Zimmerman (1969), working at the subsystem level, described the development of typifications and shared interpretations among intake work in a social welfare agency.

Cross-Level Analyses

Some of the most important types of institutional research involves multiple levels, as investigators work to show the effects of conditions or events at one level on actors and actions at a lower level. For many theorists the core thesis of an institutional perspective is that the behavior of actors—whether individual or collective—is not to be attributed to their characteristics or motives but to the context within which they act (Schneiberg and Clemens 2006). For example, in their research on rationalizing processes at the world system level, Meyer and colleagues (Drori et al. 2006; Meyer, Boli, Thomas, and Ramirez 1997) employ historical and comparative research to show that the basic structures, policies, and program adopted by societies is primarily predicted not by their domestic demographic or economic characteristics but rather by events occurring at the world system level and the nature and strength of a society's connections to this system. Similarly, many studies by institutional scholars of organizations are designed to show how that organization's structure and behavior are shaped, variously, by its relation to the nation-state or society, the organizational population to which it belongs, or its location in and connections to the organization field in which it operates. Much of the research reviewed in subsequent chapters reports the findings of such cross-level approaches.

Levels and Pillars: Illustrative Schools

More generally, as illustrated in Figure 4.1, it is possible to associate various schools or types of work with different locations in the property space created by the cross-classification of pillars and levels. Most of the institutional work conducted by sociologists in the recent period is guided by the combination of a cultural-cognitive emphasis and attention to the macro- and cross-levels: processes operating at transorganizational, societal, and field levels. Moreover, this work stresses cultural elements—widespread beliefs, conventions, and professional knowledge systems—but also attends to the impact of macrostructural carriers such as international organizations, the state, and trade and professional associations.

Organizational ecologists have directed attention to the organizational population level of analysis, and in their recent work have appropriated institutional arguments to account for important features of the density dynamics of organizational populations. The familiar slow take-off and then more rapid growth rate of a specified organization population has been interpreted by Carroll and Hannan (1989) as reflecting the increasing cognitive legitimacy of a particular template or archetype for organizing this type of work (see Chapter 6). (Population ecologists also attend to noninstitutional processes, such as competition for scarce resources.)

Attention to cognitive elements at the organization or organizational subsystem level was pioneered by ethnomethodologists and has been continued by students of corporate culture (see Martin 1992; Trice and Beyer 1993). Ethnomethodologists, along with some evolutionary economists, focus on habits and skills and so attend more closely to activities as carriers of scripts and schema at the organizational and suborganizational levels (see Barley 1986). Those who examine corporate culture, of course, give primacy to carriers of symbolic systems.

The traditional institutional approach in sociology—work associated with Becker, Hughes, Parsons, and Selznick—is defined by a focus on normative elements and attention to levels ranging from the individual organization to the society. This mode of analysis is very much alive and well and continues to be emphasized by such scholars as Brint and Karabel (1991) and Padgett and Ansell (1993). Both symbolic and relational carriers are emphasized in this approach.

Economists and rational choice political scientists are most likely to emphasize the regulative view of institutions. Economic historians focus on the macrolevels, examining the origins and functions of transnational regimes, national rules, and enforcement mechanisms that are developed to regulate economic behavior of firms and individuals. Historical institutionalists in both sociology and political science emphasize the study of regulatory regimes and governance mechanisms that operate at the societal and industry levels. The new institutionalists in economics, along with the rational choice theorists in political science, focus primarily on regulatory processes operating at the organizational or suborganizational level. The economic historians and historical institutionalists emphasize symbolic and relational carriers, whereas the new institutional economists emphasize primarily relational carriers.

We discover, then, substantial differences among current schools aligned with the new institutionalism. Organizational sociologists pursuing this line of work emphasize a cultural-cognitive conception, symbolic carriers, and macro- and cross-level forces. By contrast, neo-institutional economists and most political scientists stress a regulative conception, relational carriers, and a microfocus. Rather different perspectives to be sharing the same label!

❖ CONCLUDING COMMENT

Organizations have arisen and gained prominence in part because of the development of distinctive cultural logics that endeavor to rationalize the nature of the physical and social worlds. Valued ends are to be pursued systematically by codified, formalized means, and organizations are viewed as providing appropriate social entities to promote and oversee such projects. As such beliefs become more widespread and invade ever more arenas of social life, organizations become ubiquitous vehicles of collective action.

Although institutional conceptions underline the sources of social stability and order, the structuration framework advanced by Giddens and embraced by most institutionalists enables us to theorize and examine the sources of both social order and social change. Contemporary work attends to the agency of actors as well as to the constraints of structure. To complement the concept of elements or pillars, two other sets of distinctions are introduced in an attempt to recognize the variety of forms and processes exhibited by institutions as well as the great variety of scholarly approaches currently in use. First, institutions are viewed as varying in their mode of *carrier*. Institutions may be borne by symbols, relational structures, activities, and artifacts. Second, institutions are described as capable of operating—having jurisdiction over—differing *levels*. Some are restricted to operating within an organizational subunit, whereas others function at levels as broad as that of world systems. The variety of institutional elements, the diversity of their carriers, and the multiple levels at which they operate help to account for why institutions receive so much attention and why they generate so much confusion and inconsistency among their observers.

❖ NOTES

1. Other theorists have called attention to the role played by technological innovations and associated developments, such as labor specialization in the role of organizational forms (see Kerr, Dunlop, Harbison, and Myers 1964; Rosenberg and Birdzell 1986; for a review, see Scott 2003b: 154–163).

2. Krasner (1988) and Meyer and colleagues (Meyer et al. 1997; Meyer, Drori, and Hwang 2006) provide an institutional perspective on the emergence of nation-states.

3. Note that one methodological consequence of this different focus is that scholars focusing on regulative processes are more apt to examine similar types of organizations cross-sectionally or over shorter time periods (often assuming equilibrium conditions), whereas scholars focusing on more constitutive processes embrace longer time periods or utilize comparative designs.

4. In addition to Giddens, the other major social theorist at this time emphasizing the role of power processes in the construction and reconstruction of stable social systems was Pierre Bourdieu (1977; Bourdieu and Wacquant 1992).

5. Jepperson (1991) identified a somewhat different set of carriers: cultures, regimes, and organizations.

5

Institutional Construction

Much of the social science literature on institutions has the character of a play that begins with the second act, taking both plot and narrative as an accomplished fact. Very little research asks how a play comes to be performed, or why this particular story is being staged instead of some other.

—Walter W. Powell, Kelley Packalen,
and Kjersten Whittington (2012: 434)

The lion's share of theory and research in recent decades has been devoted to questions of how existing institutions affect the structure and functioning of organizations, organizational populations, or organization fields—work that we review in subsequent chapters. The current chapter considers the question of institutional determinants—how institutions arise and achieve stability, legitimacy, and adherents. Where do institutions come from? How are they constructed? Who are the actors who create them, and what are the forces by which new types of institutions emerge?

❖ CREATING INSTITUTIONS

It is somewhat arbitrary to distinguish the processes involved in creating institutions from those employed to change them. Institutions do not emerge in a vacuum; they always challenge, borrow from, and, to varying degrees, displace prior institutions. The difference lies largely in the investigator's focus. If attention is directed primarily to the processes and conditions giving rise to new rules, understandings, and associated practices, then we have a study of institutional creation. As Greif (2006: 17) points out: "Beliefs, norms, and organizations inherited from the past will constitute part of the initial conditions in the processes leading to new institutions." However, if the analyst examines how an existing set of beliefs, norms, and practices comes under attack, undergoes delegitimation, or falls into disuse, to be replaced by new rules, forms, and scripts, we have a study of institutional change. Processes of creation are discussed here; other types of change processes are reviewed in later chapters.

Naturalistic Versus Agent-Based Accounts

As noted in Chapter 1, writing at the beginning of the 20th century, William Graham Sumner (1906) observed that although many institutions are "cressive," evolving as a result of unintended, interdependent actions over long periods of time, others are "enacted," intendedly designed by purposive actors. This distinction has recently been revived and renewed by Strang and Sine (2002), who distinguish between "naturalistic" and "agent-based" accounts of institutional construction. *Naturalistic* accounts treat institutionalization as a "natural and undirected process" (Strang and Sine 2002: 502). Such views are embodied in the work of Schutz (1932/1967) and Berger and Luckmann (1967), who stress the unconscious ways in which activities evolve as multiple actors first engage with and attempt to make sense of their common situation and then develop responses that over time become habitualized, reciprocally reinforced and passed on to others as "the way we handle this type of issue." Another type of naturalistic process is described by ecologists, such as Carroll and Hannan (1989), who interpret the increasing pervasiveness of an organization form—its higher "organizational density"—as evidence of its "taken-for-grantedness": its institutionalization (see Chapter 6). In these accounts, institutions are not created by the purposeful actions of interest-based agents, but rather emerge from the collective sense-making and problem-solving behavior of actors confronting similar situations.

By contrast, analysts embracing an *agent-based* view stress the importance of identifying particular actors as causal agents, emphasizing the extent to which intentionality and self-interest are at work. Following Stinchcombe's early formulation giving heightened attention to power (see Chapter 2), DiMaggio (1988) also emphasized the importance of "bringing agency back in" to accounts of institutional processes. He noted that studies of highly institutionalized organizations or organization fields can easily overlook the role of self-interest and power processes because opposing interests have been suppressed and dissenters silenced. The play of power is more visible during times of institutional change and, especially, institutional construction (DiMaggio 1991).

> Put simply . . . institutionalization is a product of the political efforts of actors to accomplish their ends. . . . [T]he success of an institutionalization project and the form that the resulting institution takes depends on the relative power of the actors who support, oppose, or otherwise strive to influence it. . . . Central to this line of argument is an apparent paradox rooted in the two senses in which the term institutionalization is used. Institutionalization as an outcome places organizational structures and practices beyond the reach of interest and politics. By contrast, institutionalization as a process is profoundly political and reflects the relative power of organized interests and the actors who mobilize around them. (DiMaggio 1988: 13)

Limits of Institutional Design

It is certainly the case that actors frequently work to create institutions that will reflect, protect, and advance their interests, that "parties often need institutions to help capture gains from cooperation" (Weingast 2002: 670). However, numerous considerations undermine the ability of actors to achieve their intended ends. Paul Pierson (2004) provides a useful synthesis and summary of the kinds of limitations that beset attempts to design institutions:

- "Specific institutional arrangements invariably have multiple effects" (p. 109), many of which are unexpected, unintended, and may be unwelcome.
- "Institutional designers may not act instrumentally" (p. 110), but be guided by norms of "appropriateness," by fads, or by misguided attempts to apply ready-made solutions that do not fit current circumstances.

- "Institutional designers may have short time horizons" (p. 112), whereas the institutions they develop have long-term effects that frequently differ from those originally sought.
- The plans of institutional designers may lead to unexpected effects because the situations to which they apply have undergone change.
- Institutional designs presume that actors and their interests will remain unchanged, whereas over time actors come and go and interests change.

Another general argument long made by organization theorists points to the erosion of the founders' mission over time by an "organizational imperative" to protect and grow the organization, even at the sacrifice of its original objective. Beginning with the influential work of Michels (1915/1949) and extending through the work of Merton and Selznick up to the studies by Brint and Karabel (1991) and Kraatz, Ventreca, and Deng (2010), analysts point to ways in which environment pressures can result in the transformation of organizational goals. (These and related studies are described below and in subsequent chapters dealing with organization and institutional change.)

Such concerns should make us mindful of the assumptions we make when assessing the role of agency, interest, and rationality in the design of institutions.

Institutional Entrepreneurs[1]

An important facet of the discourse surrounding institutional construction was initiated by Eisenstadt (1980) and Paul DiMaggio (1988) with their introduction of the concept of "institutional entrepreneur." Because it links such construction to the seminal early work of Schumpeter and also reenergizes the "structure-agency" debate, this concept has received extensive attention and elicited much debate and inquiry (Battilana and D'Aunno 2009; Ruef and Lounsbury 2007a).

Schumpeter (1926/1961) defined the "entrepreneurial function" as the creation of "new combinations" of existing resources, whether material, social, or symbolic. Usefully, Schumpeter emphasized functions and activities rather than personal characteristics, allowing for the possibility that the functions may be distributed across actors and recognizing that the entrepreneurial process does not "create" new resources, but combines existing resources in novel ways (Aldrich 2005; Becker and Knudsen 2009). Such a stance resonates with institutional views that stress that actors are embedded in existing contexts and operate with available materials.

A neglected aspect of the entrepreneurial function in building institutions has been identified and elaborated by Fligstein (2001b), who examines the kinds of "social skills" required to induce cooperation among others with varying agendas and interests. Such individuals are able to focus attention on "evolving collective ends," constructing shared meanings as common agendas are configured, and broker agreements among diverse individuals and interests (p. 113). These types of social skills may be as or more important than the technical skills commonly emphasized.

In order to clarify the conceptual terrain, I have proposed the following distinctions (Scott 2010: 32–33):

- *Organizational entrepreneurs* are actors who pursue their objectives by founding a new enterprise—a new organization, but within an existing institutional mold. Such efforts entail the mobilization of resources and the assumption of risk for the value of the resources invested. The efforts produce what Aldrich and Ruef (2006: 67) term a "reproducer organization."
- Following Maguire, Hardy, and Lawrence (2004: 657), *institutional entrepreneurship* refers to "the activities of actors who have an interest in particular institutional arrangements and leverage resources to create new institutions or to transform existing ones."

I find it useful to differentiate between two subtypes of institutional entrepreneurs:

- *Technical and organizational population–level institutional entrepreneurs* combine human and technical resources in novel ways to create new types of products, processes, or forms of organizing, giving rise to "innovative organizations" (Aldrich and Ruef 2006). To be successful, such entrepreneurs must devote much attention to gaining acceptance from wider audiences for their creations.
- *Field-level institutional entrepreneurs* create or significantly transform institutional frameworks of rules, norms, and/or belief systems either working within an existing organization field or creating frameworks for the construction of a new field.

The population and field levels are not the only ones at which institutional construction occurs, as noted below, but they are among the more important for scholars examining institutional processes and organizations.

Accounts and Pillars

Whether a naturalistic or an agent-based approach is employed appears to vary, on first examination, by what types of elements—whether regulative, normative, or cultural-cognitive pillars—are invoked. Those examining regulative elements are more likely to be methodological individualists and assume that individuals function as agents, constructing rules and requirements by some kind of deliberative, strategic, or calculative process. Pros and cons are weighed, causes and effects evaluated and argued, and considered choices are made. Majorities or authorities rule. Such analysts would appear to lean toward an agent-based view. Analysts examining institutions made up of normative elements are more likely to posit a more naturalistic process, as moral imperatives evolve and obligatory expectations develop in the course of repeated interactions. Cultural-cognitive institutions seem to emerge from the operation of even more ephemeral, naturalistic processes. Particularly in early accounts, shared understandings, common meanings, and taken-for-granted truths seem to have no parents, no obvious sources, no obvious winners or losers.

Although there are differences in the processes associated with each pillar, these characterizations, on reflection, appear to be oversimplified and can be misleading. Consider regulative rules. If they appear rational and transparent, this reflects the extent to which certain types of social settings and procedures have been constructed to be—are institutionalized to serve as—seats of collective authority or as forums variously constituted for decision making. A more comprehensive analysis of regulatory rule-making would examine the constitutive roots of the specific governance apparatus—how the forums developed, the rules evolved for decision making and for selecting participants—as well as all the backstage activities (the fodder of historical institutionalists) that enter into the creation of laws and legal rulings. Conversely, although norms often evolve through nonpurposeful interaction, they can also be rationally crafted. Professional bodies and trade associations act to create and amend their normative frameworks and standards via more conscious and deliberative processes, as documented below. As with regulatory authorities, some social groups are endowed with special prerogatives allowing them to exercise moral leadership in selected arenas, whether they are environmental scientists dealing with global warming or medical scientists dealing with the control of contagious diseases. Cognitive elements also result from both more and less rational choice processes; they may evolve from inchoate collective interactions but they can also be consciously

designed and disseminated by highly institutionalized cultural authorities (Scott 2008b). Folkways are produced by the former; scientific
truths and laws, by the latter.

In sum, it appears that the two accounts of institutional construction should best be regarded as the endpoints of a continuum along
which institutional work takes place. Most "rational agents" do not
fully understand their situation or the consequences that follow from
the alternatives they select, and most "naturalistic" actors are motivated to advance their own interests whether or not they can articulate
the reasons for their choices (Emirbayer and Mische 1998). Institutions
have many fathers and mothers, only some of which recognize and
acknowledge their parental role.

Types of Agents

DiMaggio and Powell (1983: 147) astutely observe that the nation-
state and the professions "have become the great rationalizers of the
second half of the twentieth century," but other types of actors also
play important roles. As defined above, institutional entrepreneurs are
individuals or organizations who participate in the creation of new
types of organizations or new industries, tasks that require marshalling
new technologies, designing new organizational forms and routines,
creating new supply chains and markets, and gaining cognitive, normative, and regulative legitimacy. Clearly, we are not talking about a single actor, but a variety of roles and functions distributed across diverse
players.

I briefly describe some of the major categories of institutional
agents currently at work.

The Nation-State

From some perspectives, the state is simply another organizational
actor: a bureaucratically organized administrative structure empowered to govern a geographically delimited territory. However, such a
view is limited and misleading. In our own time, and since the dawn
of the modern era, the nation-state has been allocated—is constituted
in such a way as to exercise—special powers and prerogatives (Krasner
1993). As Streeck and Schmitter (1985: 20) pointed out, the state is not
simply another actor in the environment of an organization: Its "ability to rely on legitimate coercion" make it a quite distinctive type of
actor. All organizations are correctly viewed as "governance structures,"
but the state is set apart. Lindblom (1977: 21) succinctly concludes:

"The special character of government as an organization is simply . . . that governments exercise authority over other organizations."

In terms of institutional construction, states (in collaboration with legal professionals) possess extraordinary *constitutive* powers to define the nature, capacity, and rights enjoyed by political and economic actors, including collective actors. For example, during the past three centuries, states have worked to shape the powers and rights of the joint stock, limited liability corporate actor that has long since become the preferred form for organizing economic activity (see Coleman 1974; 1990; Micklethwait and Wooldridge 2003; Seavoy 1982). Such activity is ongoing. Only recently, the U.S. Supreme Court extended the free speech rights of corporations and unions by prohibiting any restrictions on their independent expenditures in support of issues or candidates.

More generally, Campbell and Lindberg (1990) detail the ways in which, by defining and enforcing property rights, the state influences the economic behavior of organizations. Property rights are "the rules that determine the conditions of ownership and control of the means of production" (p. 635), including labor laws defining the power of workers to organize, antitrust laws that limit ties between competitors, and patent laws that limit access to new technologies.

> The state provides the legal framework within which contracts are written and enforced. . . . The state's influence, quite apart from sporadic interventions, is always present in the economy insofar as it provides an institutional and legal framework that influences the selection of different governance regimes and thereby permanently shapes the economy. (Campbell and Lindberg 1990: 637)

Even the *regulatory* powers of the state can lead to the creation of new institutional forms. Fligstein (1990) underlined the role of antitrust legislation, including the Sherman Act of 1890, which prevented the development of the cartel-like forms that emerged in Europe at this time—unlike the United States, the German (as well as other European) states emphasized "the benefits of industrial cooperation" (Chandler 1990: 395)—and the Celler-Kefauver Act of 1950, which encouraged diversification (supported by the multidivisional corporate form) as a growth strategy for U.S. corporations after World War II (see Chapters 7 and 8).

States also exert highly significant effects not only on individual firm structures and behaviors, but also on the structuration of organization fields. Baron, Dobbin, and Jennings (1986) provide a historical account of the powers of the state to shape industry (field) and firm structure in their study of the evolution of modern personnel systems in the United States. The high water mark of state influence occurred in connection with the mobilization for World War II, when the federal government intervened to stabilize employment. Agencies such as the War Production Board, the War Labor Board, and the War Manpower Commission "engaged in unprecedented government manipulation of labor markets, union activities, and personnel practices. These interventions . . . fueled the development of bureaucratic controls by creating models of employment and incentives to formalize and expand personnel functions" (Baron et al. 1986: 369). In short, the pressures created were cultural-cognitive and normative, inducing conformity among professional managers as well as regulative controls involving coercion.

Later chapters detail other ways in which states influence the structure and behavior of firms and fields.

Corporations and Other Business Organizations

In capitalist economies, in particular, business firms exert enormous power over the organization and mobilization of economic resources. They create hierarchical frameworks to exert direct coercive and regulatory authority over their paid personnel, but also form alliances, enter into networks, negotiate contracts, and design and redesign a variety of governance frameworks to oversee their enterprise (Child 2005; Scott and Davis 2007). At the firm level, they exercise control over the allocation of assets at their disposal; collectively, at the industry level, they work both competitively and cooperatively to influence policies and programs that affect their welfare.

Fligstein (1990, 1991) stressed the role of corporate elites who are in a position to negotiate—with their competitors and within constraints imposed by the state—an institutional framework working to curb cut-throat competition and allow multiple firms to operate in a given field or arena, albeit with differing advantages. The ability of elites to manage these negotiations depends "on the resources that organizations command and the types of network and dependency relations the organization has to other organizations" (Fligstein 1991: 314).

Elite organizations can also mobilize politically to advance their collective interests (Cawson 1985). Vogus and Davis (2005) described the efforts of corporate elites to defend themselves against state legislation favorable to takeover attempts. The better organized the local corporate elite—assessed in terms of number of board interlocks—the more likely was the state to adopt management-friendly legislation regulating hostile takeovers.

During the second half of the 20th century, many firms reorganized to operate as multinational corporations to produce goods and services for a global market through facilities located around the world. This development, as Gereffi (2005:163) points out, has moved the global economy from a "shallow integration" manifested largely through international exchanges of money and materials to a "deep integration" involving "the production of goods and services in cross-border value-adding activities that redefine the kinds of production processes contained within national boundaries." Supply and value chains are devised linking raw materials and final products in ever-changing combinations of firms as supply sources fail or demand changes. These flexible networks represent important new types of institutional arrangements.

The Professions

In modern societies, professional occupations have come to play a unique and distinctive role. They have displaced the seers and wise men and women of earlier times to serve in a variety of capacities as institutional agents. We emphasize here their role as creators of new institutional frameworks. Employing the pillars framework, we observe that different types of professionals make use of differing combinations of elements (see Scott 2008b). Some professionals operate primarily within the *cultural-cognitive* sphere by creating new conceptual systems: "Their primary weapons are ideas. They exercise control by defining reality—by devising ontological frameworks, proposing distinctions, creating typifications, and fabricating principles or guidelines for action" (Scott and Backman 1990: 29).

The knowledge systems constructed vary greatly in their content and in the extent of their empirical grounding, with physical and biological scientists working at the more empirically constrained end and philosophers and literary critics operating in less confined arenas. Strang and Meyer (1993: 492) stress the importance of the role of *theorization*: "the development and specification of abstract categories, and the formulation of patterned relationships such as chains of cause and effect" in the construction and diffusion of new institutions.

The types of professionals who emphasize the construction of *normative frameworks* include theologians and ethicists, many legal scholars, and accountants. However, in addition to these specialists, a great many other professional groups work within their associations to create and promulgate "standards" in their areas of expertise, which range from the threading of screws to the education of children and the control of AIDS (Brunsson and Jacobsson 2000).

Other professionals, including many legal experts, military officers, and managers, exercise substantial influence on the construction of *regulatory frameworks.* Lawyers in many countries (especially the United States) have a near monopoly on positions within policy-setting and state regulatory bodies: authorities empowered to create and enforce new kinds of institutional regimes. Managerial professionals increasingly are in a position to craft new governance structures for overseeing their enterprises. Institutional economists are ready to supply design criteria to executives seeking to craft more effective and efficient governance systems to reduce production and transaction costs.

Students of occupations have long claimed that, although their compositional boundaries are somewhat unclear and shifting over time, the professions, as a category, have been guided by normative codes that emphasize disinterested service, embracing a "social trusteeship" model (Brint 1994; Freidson 2001). Similarly, Meyer (1996) argues that the professions often act as disinterested "others" rather than self-interested actors, attempting to speak, for example, for the protection of the environment or for social justice. However, there are disturbing signs that these codes and logics are weakening in part because of a shift in generalized beliefs about the relative value and morality of public service and private gain, and as more professionals place emphasis on their "technical expertise" as validated by the market (Brint 1994; Scott 2008b).

Associations

Joining nation-states and professions as important classes of institutional actors exercising authority in cultural-cognitive, normative, and regulative domains are an increasingly diverse array of associations operating at national and international levels. In general, associations are organizations established to more effectively pursue the interests of their members. Many associations take the form of "meta-organizations": organizations whose members are themselves organizations (Ahrne and Brunsson 2008). Many associations operate by promulgating standards—sometimes regarding the behavior of their own members (e.g., business associations) but often attempting to affect the behavior of wider publics (e.g., professional associations). Associations vary significantly across countries and over time in their ability to establish and enforce standards of practice (Tate 2001). Their efforts are historically situated and follow distinctive trajectories influenced in particular by the closeness of their connection to the state. Those in liberal regimes are more likely to pursue voluntary and cooperative

approaches, whereas those working within more coordinated economies are more likely to seek and receive the backing of the coercive
power of the state (Hall and Soskice, 2001b).

As globalization proceeds apace, associations of all sorts now operate at the transnational level, organized as international nongovernmental organizations (INGOs). Such organizations existed throughout
the 20th century, but have grown rapidly in numbers and influence
since World War II (Boli and Thomas 1997; Smith 2005). How do INGOs
obtain and exercise their influence? Boli and Thomas (1997; 1999) point
out that, at the present time, they do not presume to displace or replace
nation-states, and, unlike states, they cannot make or enforce law.
Unlike global corporations, they are not able to exercise coercive power
and lack economic resources to employ as sanctions. Rather, "INGOs
are more or less authoritative transnational bodies employing limited
resources to make rules, set standards, propagate principles, and
broadly represent 'humanity' vis-à-vis states and other actors" (Boli and
Thomas 1997: 172; see also Brunsson and Jacobsson 2000).

While they lack coercive power or regulative authority, in an era
where neo-liberal ideologies limit the sphere within which nation-
states may exercise control, systems of "private regulation," relying on
mutual surveillance and voluntary compliance provide valuable alternative regulatory regimes. Bartley (2003) details efforts between 1990
and 2000 involving two contrasting industry associations, forest
products and apparel manufacturing, which have worked with the
assistance of INGOs to develop and enforce environmental and labor
standards within their respective industries. Numerous nation-states,
acting both directly and indirectly, have supported such arrangements,
recognizing their own inability to take action under current political-
economic conditions.

Social Movements

Whereas earlier theory and research emphasized the actions of
established and authoritative actors, such as professionals or state officials, engaged in institutional design or redesign projects, a wave of
scholars drawing from social movement ideas and arguments have
recently significantly reshaped the narrative to include new kinds of
players employing different techniques and tools (Davis, McAdam,
Scott, and Zald 2005). Whereas established authorities rely on coercive,
normative, and memetic processes to diffuse their models and frameworks creating isomorphic structures, movement actors employ issue-
framing, mobilization, and contestation to champion new ways of
organizing. Social movement theory came into its own during the

1960s, a time of extraordinary social upheaval in the Western democracies, bringing together ideas and arguments from political science and sociology to examine the sources and mechanisms of bottom-up social and institutional change. Also, as Schneiberg and Lounsbury (2008) point out, although movement scholars adopt some of the premises of those who study institutional entrepreneurs—for example, their emphasis on agency and deliberate, strategic action—a social movement approach is likely to be more structural, stressing constraints and openings ("opportunity structures") in existing political structures and the importance of collective mobilization around a common concern.

Two types of approaches have evolved: (1) studies that treat movements as "forces against institutions, that is, forces operating outside established channels to assert new visions and disrupt or directly contest existing arrangements," and (2) studies that examine movements operating within established institutional systems, working to exploit existing differences and contradictions and introduce reforms (Schneiberg and Lounsbury 2008: 652). A good example of a study of the first type is provided by Clemens (1993; 1997). Clemens points out that suppressed interests are often denied conventional modes of exercising voice or influence and, as a consequence, are forced to employ unconventional approaches. She examines the emergence of the women's movement in the United States at the beginning of the 20th century. Prohibited from the ballot box and from mainstream electoral politics, activist women borrowed from the tactics employed by disreputable lobbyists, only to perfect them into a repertoire of actions now used by all interest groups. They embraced conventional organizing forms (e.g., women's clubs), but used them to advance the political education of their members, mobilize public opinion, gain procedural mastery of the legislative process, and devise ways to intervene in shaping policy and hold political officers accountable for their votes and decisions.

The second type, movements developing within institutionalized systems, is well illustrated by the research of Scully and Creed (2005), who examined the ways in which a subset of existing employees were able to secure the adoption of gay-friendly policies by organizations. In their work, they emphasize the central role played by the construction of social identities—the processes by which workers began to recognize/construct a set of shared identities allowing them to work within and across organizations to, first, legitimate their identity and, then, create and diffuse repertories of action to instigate and gain support for new policies. Researchers noted that "agents talked of innovation but were startlingly alike in their approaches and outcomes" (p. 311), having informally shared ideas and tactics. "The social construction of a collective identity involves defining the field of action that the actors inhabit, as well as their interests, ends, and means" (p. 312).

Marginal Players

Network theorists stress the importance of marginality to fostering innovation and learning processes. Those who locate gaps or missing connections in social networks—"structural holes" (Burt 1992)—or who are associated with persons or organizations unlike themselves—forming "weak ties" (Granovetter 1973)—are likely to garner influence and be exposed to ideas different from their own. Just as the locations where sea water meets fresh water are particularly supportive of varied forms of marine life, so the areas of overlap and confluence between institutional spheres generate rich possibilities for new forms. Morrill (forthcoming) depicted the emergence of a new organization field staffed by new types of actors at the boundary where conventional legal structures overlap with social welfare forms. The field of alternative dispute resolution emerged between 1965 and 1995 in response to a growing number of minor disputes that were clogging the law courts. A community mediation model, championed by the social work community, and a multidoor-courthouse model, supported by lawyers, competed for the jurisdiction of this interstitial arena. Morrill detailed the processes by which new roles and practices were created (innovation), legitimation and resources were acquired from players in the existing fields (mobilization), and a stable uncontested institutional settlement achieved (structuration). Morrill concluded:

> In the interstices created by overlapping resource networks across organizational fields, rules, identities, and conventional practices are loosened from their taken-for-granted moorings and alternative practices can emerge, particularly in the face of perceived institutional failure.

Demand- and Supply-Side Explanations

Mark Suchman (1995a) provides an illuminating general discussion of conditions giving rise to new institutional arrangements. He suggests that the impetus for institutional creation is the development, recognition, and naming of a recurrent problem to which no preexisting institution provides a satisfactory repertoire of responses (see Figure 5.1). These cognitive processes can be viewed as giving rise to collective *sense-making* activities, as elucidated by Weick (1995), as actors attempt to interpret and diagnosis the problem and, subsequently, propose what are, at the outset, various ad hoc solutions. Once these responses have been "generalized into solutions," it may be possible for the participants to engage in "a more thoroughgoing 'theorization' of the situation—in other words, to formulate general accounts of how the system works and, in particular, of which solutions are appropriate in which contexts" (Suchman 1995a: 43). Solutions generated in one context may then diffuse to other situations regarded as similar. Note the extent to which Suchman's discussion maps onto and builds from Berger and Luckmann's (1967) general formulation of institutionalization, as discussed in Chapters 2 and 3.

Figure 5.1   A Multistage Model of Institutionalization

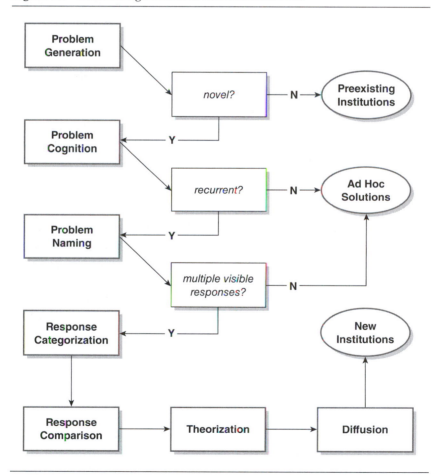

SOURCE: Suchman, Mark. 1995. Localism and globalism in institutional analysis. In *The Institutional Construction of Organization*, ed. W. R. Scott and S. Christensen (p. 44). Thousand Oaks, CA: Sage. Copyright © 1995 by Sage Publications, Inc.

The foregoing description is meant to be sufficiently abstract to be applicable to any level of analysis—from the organizational subsystem to the world system. Suchman (1995a: 41) proposed that the question of *where* institutions arise—at what level—is determined by "where in the social structure particular shared understandings arise." That is, this question is to be settled empirically by observing the locus of the social processes at work. At a broader level, Suchman's general model embodies a "demand-side" argument: Institutions are crafted by actors in response to recurrent problems for which no existing "off-the-shelf" solutions are available.

A contrasting view of institutional construction offered by John Meyer (1994) is that institutional creation can also be driven by "supply-side" processes. His arguments are developed primarily at the world system level, but are applicable to other levels. He suggests, as noted earlier, that certain types of actors—particularly those in the sciences and professions—occupy institutionalized roles that enable and encourage them to devise and promote new schemas, rules, models, routines, and artifacts. They see themselves as engaged in the great project of rationalization, whereby more and more arenas of social life are brought under the "rubric of ideologies that claim universal applicability" (p. 42). The adoption of these generalized principles and procedures is promoted as evidence of "modernization," irrespective of whether local circumstances warrant or local actors "need" or want these developments. At the international and societal levels, general rules and principles are promulgated by professional associations and a wide range of NGOs. At the level of the organization field, organizational population, and individual organization, the carriers and promoters include foundations, management schools, accounting and auditing firms, and consulting companies (see DiMaggio and Powell 1983; Sahlin and Wedlin 2008). These purveyors of solutions must often begin their work by convincing potential adopters that they have a problem.

❖ SELECTED STUDIES OF INSTITUTIONAL CONSTRUCTION

Transnational-Level Studies

Early studies of institutional building at the transnational level were pursued by political scientists employing a "realist" approach. These scholars focused attention on nation-states as the primary actors and assumed that, to the extent that they constructed or participated in international institutions and regimes, such as the World Trade Organization, they were rationally pursuing their interests/preferences (e.g., Morgenthau 1948). Subsequent scholars, such as Keohane and Nye (1977), broadened the canvas to include non-state players such as INGOs and the independent role played by economic actors and processes. And more recently, realist approaches have been joined and challenged by "constructivist" scholars who are more open to a diverse range of actors in shifting and overlapping networks with an increased attention to normative and cultural-cognitive forces at work (Katzenstein, Keohane, and Krasner 1998; Widmaier, Blyth, and Seabrooke 2007).

Meyer and colleagues have pursued a broad agenda of research that emphasizes the role of cultural forces at work at the transnational level. In a series of studies, they have developed and tested a theory of the processes by which rational models of organization and organizing have emerged during the past several centuries—since the Enlightenment—giving rise to a collection of nation-states and a limited range of organizational forms that are, despite enormous disparities in technical and economic development among societies, remarkably similar in their formal structures and modes of operation (Drori, Meyer, and Hwang 2006; Meyer, Boli, Thomas, and Ramirez 1997; Thomas, Meyer, Ramirez, and Boli 1987). Institutions are viewed as "cultural rules giving collective meaning and value to particular entities and activities, integrating them into the larger schemes" (Meyer, Boli, and Thomas 1987: 13). In contrast to the realist account of organizations as distinctive entities designed to efficiently pursue specific objectives, the approach views nation-states and organizations as being constituted by the wider environment. Organization is not just about productivity and exchange, but serves to signal rationality and legitimacy. A wide-ranging series of empirical studies document the worldwide diffusion of models for organizing—ranging from the structuring of nation-states, to educational systems, to procedures for protecting the natural environment, advancing women's rights, husbanding human resources, and ensuring transparency of governing units (Berkovitz 1999; Drori et al. 2006; Frank, Hironaka, and Schofer 2000; Meyer et al. 1997).

A contrasting approach is associated with the work of Djelic and colleagues, who focus attention on the recent emergence of a wide range of governance mechanisms to manage economic and political activities at the international level. In their view, recent developments in globalization are not "only about adaptation and change of national institutions. [They are] also about institution building in the transnational arena—a space traditionally and typically pictured and described as anomic and adversarial" (Djelic and Quack 2003c: 3). These scholars have examined institution-building in such varied realms as the regulation of competition, central banking, control of carbon emissions, and business education (Djelic and Quack 2003b; Djelic and Sahlin-Andersson 2006). The scenario developed is not one of increasing global uniformity—the dominance of a single model—but a more variegated "multilevel and multilayered historical process" marked by "competing and conflicting actors and logics" (Djelic and Quack 2003a: 303) involving both negotiation and the emergence of novel forms. They emphasize that, at the transnational level at the current time, we are witnessing a period of vibrant institution-building.

Societal-Level Studies

An early influential study of institution-building at the societal level is the historical account provided by North and Thomas (1973) of "the rise of the Western world." These economic historians argued that economic growth does not occur unless there are mechanisms that closely align social and private rates of return. Individuals are motivated to undertake socially desirable activities only if they provide private benefits that exceed private costs. This situation, in turn, requires that appropriate property rights be established and enforced. The need for such regulatory institutions, however, does not guarantee their development. Creating such structures is costly and challenging politically. Since the rise of the nation-state, governments have assumed responsibility for enforcing property rights. However, the interests and fiscal needs of rulers may encourage them to establish and enforce agreements that do not promote economic growth. Hence, "we have no guarantee that productive institutional arrangements will emerge" (North and Thomas 1973: 8).

North and Thomas (1973) review historical evidence from the high Middle Ages to the beginning of the 18th century, noting developments in the political economy of Europe that advanced or depressed economic growth. They examined a number of cases and drew on a variety of historical materials, but their most detailed discussion contrasted political and economic developments during the period 1500 to 1700 in England, the Netherlands, Spain, and France. They concluded that, by the beginning of the 18th century, "a structure of property rights had developed in the Netherlands and England which provided the incentives necessary for sustained growth" (p. 157). In England, for example, Tudor kings became dependent on political support from the House of Commons, increasingly dominated by the rising merchant class, and political compromises pressed on the rulers resulted in expanded markets, both internal and colonial. By contrast, French kings developed methods of taxation that did not require them to extend markets, eliminate hereditary land tenure, or challenge the power of guilds and nobility in order to secure adequate revenue to support army and court. The interests of the fledgling bourgeoisie were not recognized or protected. Such recognition had to await a long-delayed and tempestuous revolution.

Although their particular interpretation of history has not gone unchallenged (see, e.g., Wallerstein 1979), North and Thomas provide a careful examination of ruling societal elites located in contrasting historical conditions who made choices that gave rise to markedly different institutional arrangements regulating economic activity with important consequences for each society.

Field-Level Studies

Dezalay and Garth (1996) provide a detailed historical account of the creation of an institutional framework at the international level for resolving disputes between businesses in different countries: transnational commercial arbitration rules and practice. Although their scope is international, they focused on the creation of a specific organizational field. Their history depicts the construction of an "international legal field"—the gradual and conflictual development of an arena with defined boundaries, central players, and accepted ground rules for dispute resolution.

The focus of their history is the transformation that began to occur in the 1970s as an elite "club" of "grand old men" centered in Paris confronted increased demand for arbitration services fostered by burgeoning international trade and globalization. This demand brought into the arena a new generation of "technocrats" housed in U.S. corporate law firms. The delicate transition was negotiated by the International Chamber of Commerce, which succeeded in transferring the legitimacy of the former elite to an expanding set of arbitrators in a classic instance of increased bureaucratization and rationalization of the field. Personal charisma was gradually replaced by routinized, impersonal, specialized expertise. Maintaining legitimacy was essential for the continued success of arbitration if it was "to provide a basis to govern matters that involve powerful economic and political entities" (Dezalay and Garth 1996: 33). Dezalay and Garth provide a finely nuanced account of "the contests through which the field and the markets of arbitration are constituted" (p. 41). Although all participants are depicted as attempting to pursue their respective interests, the tale told is not one of rational design, but of improvisation, contestation, and compromise resulting in an eventual institutional settlement.

DiMaggio's (1991) study of the efforts by professionals to create the cultural conditions that would support the development and maintenance of art museums during the late 19th century in America is also cast at the organization field level, but limited to a single society. In his historical account, DiMaggio gave primary attention to cultural-cognitive aspects of the professional project: the creation of distinctions between high and low forms of art, and the creation and selection among cultural models for constituting art museums as distinctive types of organizations. Struggles are depicted among contending professional factions debating the merits of a "curator" versus an "educational" model of museum, and between the interests of new types of professionals—curators, art historians, and acquisition experts—and those of trustees and museum managers. Significantly, these struggles took place primarily at the field level, involving the collective efforts of professionals pursuing a common project, rather than within individual museum organizations. Philanthropic foundations, specifically the Carnegie Corporation, are shown to play a pivotal role as they sided with the interests of the new museum professionals. This study underlines DiMaggio's contention that agency and interests are more apparent—more amenable to study—during the creation of a new institutional field in contrast to the routine operation of an existing field.[2]

Another informative study of contending models for organizing at the field level is provided by Rao's (1998) account of the emergence of consumer protection organizations in the United States during the early part of the 20th century. The Consumers' Union (CU) embodied the model of watchdog as radical critic, overseeing both consumer interests and worker rights. By contrast, Consumer Research (CR) advanced the model of watchdog as impartial evaluator, limiting their purview to consumer goods. Pressure from conservative media and political bodies forced CU to abandon its more radical agenda and, like CR, operate as a "rational" scientific agency employing impartial testing methods to evaluate consumer products. Rao emphasizes that the institutionalization of such consumer interest agencies could not take place until a settlement had been reached between these competing institution-building projects.

Additional field-level studies of institutional construction and change are discussed in Chapter 8 (see also Thornton, Ocasio, and Lounsbury 2012; Wooten and Hoffman 2008).

Population-Level Studies

At the population level, institutional construction concerns primarily the creation of new organizational forms. In his now classic discussion of organizations and social structure, Stinchcombe (1965) identified organizational forms as an important topic of study and pointed out that organizational foundlings of the same type tend to be concentrated in particular historical periods. Moreover, because new organizations must rely on existing ideas, technologies, and social routines, organizations take on a similar character—are imprinted by their institutional environment—reflecting the historical conditions of their origin. And, most important, although these differences exhibit the somewhat arbitrary conditions of their birth, they tend to persist over time. Organization forms exhibit substantial inertia. Stinchcombe assembled data on differences in the labor force composition of varying industries to illustrate this effect, demonstrating that industries founded in different periods tended to exhibit differing labor force characteristics and that these differences were maintained over long time periods.

These insights provided an important touchstone for both population ecologists and institutional theorists. Ecologists are necessarily concerned with identifying meaningful organizational forms. After all, it is difficult to enumerate organizational populations if their identification is problematic. Theorists like McKelvey (1982) proposed the creation of a broad general taxonomy, but most ecological scholars utilize a more pragmatic approach that focuses on identifying similarities in key properties, such as stated goals, structural features, and core technologies in a collection of organizations (see Hannan and Freeman 1989).

Institutionalists Greenwood and Hinings (1993: 1055) stress the cognitive dimension in their attempt to identify distinctive organizational forms or *archetypes*, which they define as "a set of structures and systems that consistently embodies a single interpretive scheme." Although they emphasize the importance of environmental niches associated with distinctive patterns of resource usage, ecologists also increasingly recognize that organization forms and the boundaries between them are institutionally defined and constructed. While the differences involved may have their origins in technologies, the characteristics of clients served, or the resources consumed, particular arrangements come to be seen as the "natural" way to carry out certain types of activities. Institutionalizing processes ensue,

transforming arbitrary differences into differences with real social consequences. In this sense, nominal classifications become real classifications. They become real in their consequences when they serve as bases for successful collective action, when powerful actors use them in defining rights and access to resources, and when members of the general population use them in organizing their social worlds. Thus, the clarity of a set of boundaries is not a permanent property of a set of classifications. Rather, the realism of distinction among forms depends on the degree of institutionalization that has occurred. (Hannan and Freeman 1989: 57)

And in their most recent formulation, Hannan and colleagues propose that organization form is a taken-for-granted category, shared by internal and external audiences, specifying the characteristics of appropriate actors and activities. Organizations violating these rules are penalized by their audiences, experiencing an "illegitimacy discount" (Hannan, Pólos, and Carroll 2007; see also Rao and Kenney 2008; Zuckerman 1999).

In the following chapter, we consider the way in which ecologists measure degree of institutionalization.

Mohr and Duquenne (1997) illustrate the application of such arguments in their study of the emergence of differentiated populations of welfare organizations in New York City during 1888 to 1917 (see also Mohr 1994). They suggest that differentiation in these populations occurred along three axes: the sorts of statuses recognized and the merit they were accorded, the kinds of social needs or problems identified, and the kinds of solution repertoires recognized. Client differentiation was driven by power struggles surrounding these three socially constructed dimensions. The subtypes of welfare organizations provided the "containers" within which these dimensions were poured and provided the frameworks around which providers and clients negotiated and struggled.

As another example of a study of institutional construction at the population level, Suchman (1995a; Suchman, Steward, and Westfall 2001) combined both historical and analytic approaches in his study of the creation of organizational forms for semiconductor firms in California's Silicon Valley. Creating a new organization requires not only resources, but also ideas or models on how to organize. Conventional histories celebrate the role of Stanford University engineers in providing the designs and early material resources for start-up companies (see, e.g., Saxenian 1994). While acknowledging this contribution, Suchman and colleagues laid the groundwork for a "genetics of organization" that examines the flows of both operational resources and "constitutive information":

Just as mating patterns shape organic populations by structuring the flow of constitutive genetic blueprints, institutional patterns—definitions, typologies, accounts of relevance, theories of causation, and so on—shape organizational populations by structuring the flow of constitutive cognitive models. Cognitive models carry the scripts for organizational competences, and in structuring the transmission of such models, cognitive institutions function as organizational reproduction mechanisms. (Suchman et al. 2001: 358–359)

They proceed to outline an organizational genetics, concerned with the development and preservation of distinctive species or forms, to supplement organizational ecology, which focuses on competition among existing species or types of organizations. In established organization fields, most new organizations are "reproducer rather than innovative" forms because they largely copy routines and competences from existing organizations (Aldrich and Ruef 2006: 67). They follow what Suchman and colleagues (2001: 359) term a "filiation" mode of reproduction: Here "new organizations draw competences directly from specific existing organizations that embody those competences themselves." But when fields are in their early stages of development, organizations cannot simply copy successful recipes. Under such circumstances, Suchman suggests, a process of "compilation" may be employed, whereby "information intermediaries" such as consultants or lawyers observe existing, relatively heterogeneous practices and attempt to distil a core set of organizing principles. In their historical account, Suchman and Cahill (1996) described how lawyers and venture capitalists in Silicon Valley functioned as "dealmakers," linking clients with various transactional partners and as "counselors," formulating and disseminating standardized solutions to recurrent problems.

Shifting to a quantitative approach, Suchman (1995a; Suchman et al. 2001) analyzed data on 108 venture-capital financing contracts from two Silicon Valley venture-capital funds. Such contracts bring together the venture capitalists, lawyers, and entrepreneurs in the crucial founding event, constituting the structure of relations among these parties as they jointly form the start-up company. The contracts were coded along numerous dimensions, and these scores were then used to calculate measures of contractual standardization as an indicator of increasing institutionalization. Suchman's analysis reveals that standardization was strongly correlated to both date of filing and location of the law firm that drafted the contract. In general, standardization of contracts was greater the later in the time period they were filed and the closer the location of the law firm drafting the contract was to the core of Silicon Valley.

Organization-Level Studies

Following the lead of Coase (1937), Oliver Williamson addressed a question often overlooked by social scientists: Why do firms exist at all? Why are not all economic transactions mediated by markets? As discussed in Chapter 2, Williamson (1975; 1994), embracing (boundedly) rational choice assumptions, proposed that economic agents select or devise frameworks in order to minimize transaction costs. When exchanges are simple and easy to monitor, markets will be preferred. However, if exchanges are uncertain or partners cannot be trusted, then more complex "governance systems"—namely, organizational frameworks of rules and authoritative controls—although costly to construct, will be preferred.

Walker and Weber (1984) tested Williamson's arguments that transactions involving higher uncertainty and greater asset specificity (specialized skills or machinery)—more likely to increase vulnerability vis-à-vis partners—would be more likely to be brought within the firm rather than purchased from outside. That is, organizational designers will elect to have such tasks governed by the firm's hierarchy rather than by the market. Their study of 60 "make or buy" decisions within a division of a large automobile company found results generally consistent with these predictions, although, unexpectedly, the researchers found that comparative production costs had a larger impact on these decisions than did transaction costs.[3]

Williamson's framework extends beyond the simple choice of markets versus hierarchies to consider various types of organizational structure. Following Chandler's (1962) early insights and historical research, Williamson (1975) argued that firms adopting a multidivisional (M-form) structure would be more capable of separating strategic from operational decision making, allowing them to better allocate capital among divisions and monitor divisional performance. To test these arguments, Armour and Teece (1978) studied a sample of diversified firms in the petroleum industry and found that those firms adopting the M-form structure performed better financially. Teece (1981) extended the test to evaluate the performance of pairs of firms matched by size and product line in 20 industries. The performance of the firm first adopting the M-form (the lead firm) was compared with that of the matched firm for two time periods. Again, the results confirmed the hypotheses.[4]

Like Williamson, Moe (1990a) focuses on the level of the individual organization. He has been particularly inventive in applying rational choice perspectives to the design of public agencies. Adopting the perspective of institutional economists, Moe views organizations primarily as governance systems, emphasizing regulatory elements. Moe pointed out that governmental structures differ from those in the private sector in that, unlike the world of voluntary exchange, "people can be forced to [give up resources involuntarily] by whoever controls public authority" (p. 221). The legitimate use of coercive power distinguishes public from private authorities. The problem confronted by political actors in democratic systems is that, although they can use their power to design institutional arrangements that serve their interests, the possibility exists that opposing parties will come to power and employ the same instruments to serve their own ends. To deal with this problem of the uncertainty of political control, Moe argued, public authorities often restrict the discretion of agencies and envelop them in detailed rules and procedures.

> Obviously, this is not a formula for creating effective organizations. In the interests of political protection, agencies are knowingly burdened with cumbersome, complicated, technically inappropriate structures that undermine their capacity to perform their jobs well. Nor, obviously, is this a formula for effective hierarchical control by democratic superiors. Insulationist devices are called for precisely because those who create public bureaucracy *do not want* a truly effective structure of democratic control. (Moe 1990a: 228; italics in original)

These pathologies are particularly likely to develop in political systems based on the separation of power, such as the United States, compared to parliamentary systems, such as the United Kingdom.

The "politics of structural design" become even more perverse in situations where the Congress and the White House are controlled by opposing parties. Moe (1989) provided a detailed historical account of the creation of the Consumer Product Safety Commission (CPSC), an agency created when Richard Nixon, a Republican, was president, but was compelled to work with a Democratic Congress. Consumer interests, allied with Congress, were successful in their struggle to create an independent agency, separate from cabinet departments that were viewed as overly conservative. Strict procedural rules were imposed to ensure that the agency would attend to consumer interests. However, business interests, with the support of the administration, made sure that ample provision was made for their input and review of all pending decisions, and that enforcement powers were not vested in the Commission, but in an independent agency, the Justice Department. The initial design of the agency reflected the contending interests of the parties, and subsequent modifications were governed by the shifting political power of consumer versus business interests.

Philip Selznick, like Moe, also examined the design of a public agency. However, in his well-known account of the evolution of the Tennessee Valley Authority (TVA), Selznick (1949) eschewed a rational choice framework, as he depicted processes that undermine rational design. He provided a historical account of the development over time of a distinctive ideology and set of normative commitments on the part of TVA officials. As I noted in reviewing Selznick's views in Chapter 2, his approach describes how the original structure and goals of this innovative government corporation were transformed over time by the commitments of its participants to the means of action. In Selznick's (1957: 17) work, to institutionalize is "to infuse with value beyond the technical requirements of the task at hand" in that intrinsic worth is accorded to a structure or process that originally possessed only instrumental value. Although Selznick emphasized normative beliefs and values in his analysis, he also attended to the importance of cognitive features of organizations. His discussion of the role played by the grassroots ideology in framing decisions and garnering support from important constituencies is central to his argument (see Selznick 1996).

Selznick's approach focuses on internal relations, especially informal structures rather than on formal structures, and on the immediate environment of the organization—the "organization set"—rather than on more general cultural rules or characteristics of the wider organizational field (see DiMaggio and Powell 1991). The carriers of institutionalized values are relational structures, in particular, informal structures and cooptative relations linking the organization with salient external actors, both individual and collective.[5] Selznick's argument stresses the importance of power processes—the vesting of interests in informal structures and the cooptation of external groups that acquire internal power in return for their support. His analysis of the TVA examines the ways in which particular constituencies, such as the agricultural interests, on whom the organization was dependent, were able to modify agency programs in ways that compromised its conservation agenda. Selznick views this as a failure of "institutional leadership." Founders are seen to abandon their mission for the sake of protecting the survival of their organization.

Selznick's interest in organizations that become defined by their commitments to distinctive values has been pursued by a new generation of researchers interested in "organizational identity." Defined as a commitment to values that are "central, enduring, and distinctive," organizational identity provides participants with a core set of normative elements around which to craft their narratives and sense-making activities (see Albert and Whetten 1985; Whetten and Godfrey 1999).

Diane Vaughn (1996) wove together normative commitment and power arguments to account for the continued use of a flawed design by Morton Thiokol engineers and the fateful decision by NASA officials to launch the Challenger missile, which exploded shortly after takeoff, killing all crew members aboard. Her richly detailed historical account of the organizational routines—both technical and decision making—leading up to the disaster depicted the development of a culture within which "signals of potential danger" were "repeatedly normalized by managers and engineers alike" (p. xiii). Although production pressures played an important role, these pressures "became institutionalized and thus a taken-for-granted aspect of the worldview that *all* participants brought to NASA decision-making venues" (p. xiv; italics in original).

Interpersonal- and Intraorganization-Level Studies

Employing a game-theoretic approach, Axelrod (1984) used the prisoner's dilemma situation to examine the conditions under which individuals who pursue their own self-interest in the absence of a central authority will evolve norms of cooperation. The prisoner's dilemma involves a situation in which two players make one of two choices: cooperation (c) or noncooperation (n). The payoff matrix is such that if both players opt for c, then both receive an intermediate reward; if both select n, they receive a low reward; but if one player selects c when the other selects n, the former (sucker) receives no reward and the latter (exploiter) receives a high reward. Players are not allowed to exchange any type of information other than their choices, and the game is played over a number of trials. The challenge for each player is to provide incentives and encourage the formation of norms to induce his or her partner to cooperate. However, the knowledge of each player is limited, and any normative structure that develops must be fashioned incrementally, based on inferences from previous interactions.

In a novel design, Axelrod (1984) invited other game theorists from many disciplines to compete in a computer tournament to select the best game strategy by submitting a program that embodies rules to select the cooperative or noncooperative choice on each move. Such a program provides a complete process description of the sequence of decisions during the course of the encounter. Of the 14 strategies submitted, the most successful was the "TIT FOR TAT" decision rule: a strategy that starts with a cooperative choice and thereafter selects whatever the other player did on the previous move. This simple strategy provided the best payoff to the player adopting it under a wide range of simulated conditions. Axelrod summarized its virtues:

What accounts for TIT FOR TAT's robust success is its combination of being nice, retaliatory, forgiving, and clear. Its niceness [never initiating noncooperation] prevents it from getting into unnecessary trouble. Its retaliation discourages the other side from persisting whenever defection is tried. Its forgiveness helps restore mutual cooperation. And its clarity makes it intelligible to the other player, thereby eliciting long-term cooperation. (p. 54)

Although it may be argued that the prisoner's dilemma is "just a game," it encapsulates an important dilemma built into many real-world situations, from the school yard to international diplomacy. It is to cope with such situations that security regimes and similar types of institutions develop (see Krasner 1983; Scharpf 1997). A particularly important element of the conditions supporting the rise of stable cooperative norms is that "the future must have a sufficiently large shadow" (Axelrod 1984: 174). The anticipation of future interaction provides an important stimulus to evoke norms of reciprocity. Indeed, such norms are argued to undergird the stability of much ongoing economic and social behavior, making it less necessary for parties to resort to such expensive alternative regulatory structures as the legal system and police force (see Macaulay 1963).

Elsbach (2002: 37) defines intraorganizational institutions as "taken-for-granted beliefs that arise within and across organizational groups and delimit acceptable and normative behavior for members of those groups." This definition encompasses a wide range of organizational research beginning during the 1930s and variously labeled studies of work group behavior and subgroup identities, human relations, organizational culture, organizational identity, and sense-making processes (see, e.g., Dutton and Dukerich 1991; Frost, Moore, Louis, Lundberg, and Martin 1985; Martin 1992; Roethlisberger and Dickson 1939; Roy 1952; Schein 1985; Weick 1995). Earlier studies tended to emphasize the normative facets of institution-building, whereas later approaches have given more attention to shared schemas and identities—cultural-cognitive elements.

Comparative Comments

The studies briefly summarized here differ in a number of important respects. They are arranged by level of analysis, but it is important to emphasize that level is defined by the nature of the dependent variable: the level of the unit whose structure or behavior is to be explained. In many of the studies reviewed, multilevel processes are shown to be involved with, for example, societal structures affected by transnational phenomena or, alternatively, field-level processes being influenced by the actions of organizations embedded within the field. We believe that a hallmark of the more sophisticated institutional approaches is their openness to such multilevel causal processes.

The studies reviewed also vary in terms of the assumptions made about rationality of actors and salience of institutional elements. Among the various studies reviewed, Moe and Williamson assume a higher level of rational choice exercised by actors in designing institutional arrangements. In these studies, actors are assumed to be pursuing their individual interests armed with substantial knowledge of alternatives and their relation to consequences. Hence, the critical question is: When and why is it in an actor's self-interest to construct and maintain institutional structures that will govern not only others', but one's own, behavior? Other theorists embrace a less restrictive conception of rationality, assuming that while individuals attempt to pursue their interests, they do so with imperfect knowledge and intelligence. Errors in judgment occur and unintended consequences result. Rather than conceiving of institutions as "sets of predesigned rules," these theorists are more apt to see them as "unplanned and unintended regularities (social conventions) that emerge 'organically'" (Schotter 1986: 118). Among the studies reviewed, North and Thomas and Axelrod best exemplify these assumptions.

Although analysts in all of the studies presume that participants have interests and examine the processes by which contending interests are resolved, researchers such as Dezalay and Garth, DiMaggio, Mohr, Selznick, and Suchman view such interests not simply as preexisting, but as being constructed in the course of the interaction and negotiation processes.

With respect to institutional elements, North and Thomas, Moe, and Williamson place primary emphasis on regulatory structures. Axelrod, Dezalay and Garth, Selznick, and Vaughn attend largely to normative elements, although the latter three also consider cultural-cognitive elements. DiMaggio, Mohr and Duquenne, and Suchman highlight the role of cultural-cognitive processes of institutional creation.

❖ CONCLUDING COMMENT

From an early focus on how existing institutions affect organizations, institutional theorists have recently expanded their purview to include attention to the ways in which institutions are constructed. Accounts of construction processes vary according to how much intent and conscious design is emphasized, as opposed to less intentional, more evolutionary processes.

Institutional agents include both individual and collective actors, and they differ in whether they employ primarily regulative, normative, or cultural-cognitive tools in their construction efforts. The nation-state and the professions play high-profile roles in institutional constructions, whereas a variety of other types of actors, including other elites as well as social movement organizations and marginal players, have a hand in the building of institutions.

Investigators have examined these processes at work across multiple levels. Institution-building at the transnational level represents a relatively new focus of interest and is one of the most active construction arenas as we enter the 21st century.

❖ NOTES

1. This discussion draws extensively on Scott (2010).

2. A possible limitation of this study is that it does not attend to potential sources of influence in field construction stemming from outside the United States. It is generally recognized that Americans at this time looked to Europe for their models of high culture.

3. More recent research suggests that this specific prediction may no longer hold in certain industries, including automobile manufacturing. To protect and develop specific assets, partnering relations with suppliers are now more likely to be used than vertically integrated structures (Helper, MacDuffie, and Sabel 2000).

4. Critics of Williamson's arguments, including David (1992) and Granovetter (1985) point out that Williamson makes heroic assumptions regarding the ability of those who construct firms to predict the consequences of their institutional designs, and note the problems associated with "functionalist" explanations that "explain" the existence of structure by the *consequences* observed (see also Elster 1983).

5. In his monograph on the TVA, Selznick emphasized the cressive, unplanned, and unintended nature of institutional processes. Value commitments were generated over time, unplanned structure having unintended consequences. However, in his later, more prescriptive writing on leadership, Selznick (1957) argued for a more intentional model: Effective leaders are those who can define and defend social values and obtain the support of others in preserving them.

6

Institutionalization

Institutions do not merely influence behavior and outcomes—including policies—at a given moment in time. They are also the engine of history as they shape change. Institutions affect the timing and nature of institutional change and influence the details of new institutions. Institutions impose constraints and provide opportunities for intentional institutional change, as well as unleash processes of unintentional changes.

—Avner Greif (2006: 380)

Zucker (1977: 728) observed that "institutionalization is both a process and a property variable." It refers both to a process occurring over time as well as to a set of social arrangements "that has attained a certain state or property . . . ; social patterns that, when chronically reproduced, owe their survival to relatively self-activating social processes" (Jepperson 1991: 145). We concentrate in this chapter on institutionalization as process.

We begin by reviewing three versions of institutionalization as process—each relying on assumptions and arguments associated with one of the three pillars. These perspectives embrace not simply differing conceptions of the elements or ingredients involved, but of the processes underlying their construction, maintenance, and change.

❖ THREE CONCEPTIONS OF INSTITUTIONALIZATION: UNDERLYING MECHANISMS

How and why does institutionalization occur? An important part of the answer to these questions is to examine the mechanisms involved in creating and sustaining institutions. *Mechanisms* focus attention on how effects are produced. Elster (1989: 3) regards mechanisms as the "nuts and bolts" of social processes, which Hernes (1998: 74) appropriately amends to "the cogs and wheels . . . the wheelwork or agency by which an effect is produced." A less colorful, but more useful, definition is provided by McAdam, Tarrow, and Tilly (2001: 24): "Mechanisms are a delimited class of events that alter relations among specified sets of elements in identical or closely similar ways over a variety of situations." Increasing attention to mechanisms is particularly salutary for institutional theorists who too often have neglected to address questions of the "who" and "how" with regard to institutional effects. We consider three general alternative mechanisms underlying the process of institutionalization within social systems.

Institutionalization Based on Increasing Returns

A compelling version of institutionalization has been put forward by institutional economists to account for the development and persistence of institutional systems based on the process of positive feedback. The specific argument was first proposed by David (1985; 2000) and Arthur (1994) to explain unusual features detected in some types of technological trajectories.[1] They observed that, under specified conditions, technologies develop in such a manner that it is difficult, if not impossible, to reverse course or to consider the use of alternative approaches even if these would provide "superior" solutions. Such a path-dependent process is argued to occur because of "positive feedback": Further developments in the same direction are rewarded, whereas the costs of switching to an alternative increase over time. The necessary conditions supporting positive feedback as described by Arthur (1994) are (a) the presence of high setup costs—once an approach is available, the development of alternatives involves additional, often substantial, costs; (b) learning effects—individuals who invest time and effort in learning a particular approach are reluctant to consider alternatives; (c) coordination effects—the multiple advantages that accrue to a user because others have adopted the same option; and (d) adaptive expectations—as latecomers perceive that a particular approach is widely accepted, they are more inclined to adopt it themselves. Important consequences that follow from this process include indeterminacy (a number of solutions [multiple equilibria] are possible), inefficiencies (inferior technologies may be adopted), lock-in (the difficulty in withdrawing from the selected solution), and the primacy of early events (small differences and chance events can create unlikely trajectories that are difficult to alter).

North (1990) suggests that, with modification, this framework is applicable to the analysis of institutional change. He argues that all of the factors identified by Arthur apply to institutions—perhaps even more so than to technologies. The learning and coordination effects, coupled with the associated growth of formal and informal rules, all reinforce the buy-in of multiple players. As a result of this combination of processes, North asserts that "the interdependent web of an institutional matrix produces massive increasing returns" (p. 95).

In addition to the effect of increasing returns, institutional processes (more than technologies) are shaped by the existence of imperfect markets. If markets are competitive, North asserts, then imperfect institutions are detected and eliminated. However, if markets are flawed—if feedback is fragmentary, if subjective evaluations dominate objective information, and if transaction costs are high—then imperfect institutions are likely to persist. The combination of path dependence and suboptimal markets is employed by North (1990: 92) to account for (a) the substantial differences we observe in the "evolution of societies, polities, or economies over time"; and (b) the persistence of systems that, at least by standards stressing the value of economic growth, exhibit persistently poor performance.

The central thrust of the increasing returns argument for institutionalization is to highlight the role of *interests* and *incentives* as a motivating force in social life. This argument is at the core of the approach of scholars, such as Greif (2006: 14), who view institutions as "equilibrium phenomena" in the sense that they "constitute the structure that influences behavior, while the behavioral responses of agents to this structure reproduce the institution."

Institutionalization Based on Increasing Commitments

Rather than emphasizing the role of incentives (costs and benefits), scholars embracing the normative pillar focus on the mechanism of commitments. Possible loci of commitment include norms and values, structures and procedures, and individuals and collective actors. The theorist who has most explicitly pursued this view of institutionalization is Philip Selznick (1948; 1949; 1957; 1992).

As described in Chapters 2 and 5, Selznick (1957: 16–17; italics in original) argues that, "in its most significant meaning, 'to institutionalize' is to *infuse with value* beyond the technical requirements of the task at hand." In a more general statement, Selznick (1992) asserts:

> Institutionalization is the emergence of orderly, stable, social integrating patterns out of unstable, loosely organized, or narrowly technical activities. The underlying reality—the basic source of stability and integration—is the creation of social entanglements or commitments. Most of what we do in everyday life is mercifully free and reversible. But when actions touch important interests and salient values or when they are embedded in networks of interdependence, options are more limited. Institutionalization constrains conduct in two main ways: by bringing it within a normative order, and by making it hostage to its own history. (p. 232)

Selznick argues that organizations are transformed into institutions through a two-step process. First, the creation of a formal structure provides an "institutional" solution to problems of economy and coordination. Explicit goals and rules, coordination mechanisms, and communication channels—these provide the modes of governance referenced by institutional economists such as Williamson. But for Selznick (1992), this first step is only a beginning.

> Beyond lies what we may call "thick" institutionalization. . . . Thick institutionalization takes place in many different ways. Familiar examples are: by sanctifying or otherwise hardening rules and procedures; by establishing strongly differentiated organizational units, which then develop vested interests and become centers of power; by creating administrative rituals, symbols, and ideologies; by intensifying "purposiveness," that is, commitment to unifying objectives; and by embedding the organization in a social environment. (p. 235)

Thick institutionalization is a cumulative process taking place over time. Knudsen notes the strong resemblance of Selznick's version of institutionalization to Nelson and Winter's evolutionary views and Teece and Barney's resource-based perspective, described in Chapter 2. In all of these conceptions, the firm is modeled as a "hereditary mechanism" that accumulates more and more complex behavioral patterns over a period of time. The organization structure of a firm can therefore no longer be regarded as determined by its transaction costs, but rather by its accumulated competences or capabilities. (Knudsen 1995a: 144–145)

The mechanism of commitment also plays a large role in discussions of relational contracts and network forms of organizing. Relational contracts are agreements between two parties in which as much or more attention is paid to preserving the relationship as to honoring the contract. Womack, Jones, and Roos (1991) provide a useful description of the types of relational contracts that developed between Toyota and its multiple suppliers in the 1970s and 1980s. In contrast to U.S. automobile companies, at least at that time, Toyota worked with a much smaller set of suppliers with whom it entered into long-term, flexible agreements, sharing proprietary information, providing equipment and training, and exchanging employees. The assembly plant–supplier relations were marked by reciprocity, trust, and mutual concern for the other's welfare—in short, by long-term commitments.

Similarly, in contrast to conventional markets or hierarchies, network forms of organization rely more heavily on mutuality. In Powell's (1990) description:

In network forms of resource allocation, individual units exist not by themselves, but in relation to other units. These relationships take considerable effort to establish and sustain, thus they constrain both partners' ability to adapt to changing circumstances. As networks evolve, it becomes more economically sensible to exercise voice rather than exit. Benefits and burdens come to be shared. . . . As Macneil (1985) has suggested, the "entangling strings" of reputation, friendship, interdependence, and altruism become integral parts of the relationship. (pp. 303–304)

If the increasing returns argument privileges the role of incentives, then the commitment argument highlights the role of *identity:* Who am I (or who are we), and what is the appropriate way for me (us) to behave in this situation?

Institutionalization as Increasing Objectification

Anchored in the work of Berger and Luckmann (1967), scholars embracing the cultural-cognitive pillar emphasize the role of increasing objectification of shared beliefs in institutionalization. As described in Chapter 2, Berger and Luckmann identify *objectification*—the processes by which the meanings produced in social interaction "come to confront [the actor] as a facticity outside of himself"—as one of the three phases of institutionalization. Berger and Luckmann stress the importance of transmission of shared beliefs to third parties—individuals who played no role in constructing them—as they are informed not "This is the way we do this," but rather "This is how these things are done." In the process of transmission to others—to a new generation—the objectivity of the institutional world "thickens and hardens" (p. 59). In the following section, we discuss how, as recipes or templates diffuse, in the form of best practice or advanced modes for organizing, their degree of institutionalization increases.

In an expanded view of the processes associated with objectification, Tolbert and Zucker (1996) propose a multistage model of institutional processes that occur within as well as between organizations (see Figure 6.1).[2] In response to changes in political, technological, or market conditions, actors in organizations innovate, advancing new ideas, solutions, and practices. They also scan the environment to determine what similar organizations are doing. Many of the proposed solutions invented or adopted prove to be unsatisfactory and are dropped. However, some innovations will prove more viable and come to the attention of others. They become more broadly accepted or habituated and, in interactions within and between organizations, become the object of formal "theorization"—a formulation of why and how the innovation is effective and an identification of the class of problems or organizations for whom it is suitable (Strang and Meyer 1993). These preinstitutionalization processes, if they proceed successfully, set the stage for objectification.

> Objectification involves the development of some degree of social consensus among organizational decision-makers concerning the value of a structure, and the increasing adoption by organizations on the basis of that consensus. . . . The impetus for diffusion shifts from simple imitation to a more normative base. . . . [The innovation is viewed as possessing] both general cognitive and normative legitimacy. (Tolbert and Zucker 1996: 182–183)

In this sense, we are no longer considering simple diffusion—widespread adoption—of the innovation as sufficient for institutional legitimation, but taking into account agents' underlying motives and rationales. "In a final stage of institutionalization, termed 'sedimentation,'

Figure 6.1 Component Processes of Institutionalization

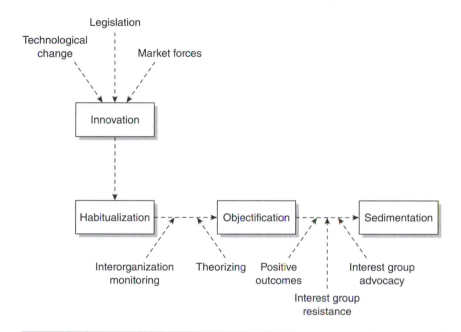

SOURCE: Tolbert, Pamela S., and Lynn Zucker. 2006. Component processes of institutionalization. In *Handbook of Organization Studies,* ed. Stewart Clegg, Cynthia Hardy, and Walter R. Nord (p. 182). Thousand Oaks, CA: Sage.

the innovation is perpetuated across several generations and spreads to virtually all of the relevant population of potential adopters" (Tolbert and Zucker 1996:184).[3]

Objectified beliefs often become embedded in routines, forms and documents (e.g., the types of classifications employed), and artifacts— tools, hardware, and machinery. We organize our material world in accordance with our mental categories, and the two become self-reinforcing.

While the increasing returns argument focuses on the role of interests and incentives and the increasing commitment approach emphasizes identity, the increasing objectification view favors *ideas*. Cultural-cognitive theorists stress that ideas—beliefs, schema, and assumptions—play a powerful role in institutional processes. Campbell (2004) points out that ideas play this role in multiple ways. Among the most powerful are the taken-for-granted assumptions that reside in the background of debates. Such ideas "remain largely accepted and unquestioned, almost as principles of faith" (p. 93). As Abraham Lincoln observed: "Public sentiment is everything. With public sentiment, nothing can fail, without it nothing can succeed." Such deep-seated beliefs go largely unnoticed unless and until others, holding contrasting assumptions, enter the scene pursuing unusual goals or employing unfamiliar or unacceptable means. Personnel or companies working in foreign cultures are likely to encounter surprising and inexplicable behavior stemming from differences in background beliefs (Hofstede 1991; Orr and Scott 2008). A collection of political scientists interested in foreign policy have departed from the conventional arguments of their colleagues who embrace a *realpolitik* perspective that believes that all foreign policies are guided by a nation's material and political interests. They suggest, rather, that these interests are grounded in and framed by ideas, including "world views" (e.g., individualistic and secular premises), "principled beliefs" or normative ideas (e.g., religious and humanitarian concerns), and "causal beliefs" (ideas about how things happen) (Goldstein and Keohane 1993). The importance of ideas as an element of institutions is, of course, highlighted by the current attention to institutional logics, as discussed in Chapter 4 (see Freidland and Alford 1991; Thornton, Ocasio, and Lounsbury 2012).

The role of ideas in shaping behavior has a long intellectual pedigree, and during the 19th century was largely coded under the concept "ideology," associated with the work of Karl Marx (see Chapter 1). Although most contemporary institutional theorists have steered clear of this highly loaded term, as more scholars attend to the role of power in the shaping of institutions, the connection between ideas, institutional logics, and ideology is again being addressed (Meyer, Sahlin, Ventresca, and Walgenbach 2009b). While some theorists have suggested that any and all broad belief systems and shared conceptual systems are ideologies (e.g., Simons and Ingram 1997), most scholars insist that many commonly shared conceptual frameworks cross group and class boundaries providing a kind of "common cultural ground" (van Dijk 2001). I prefer to follow the early lead of Berger and Luckmann (1967: 123), who argued that "when a particular definition of reality comes to be attached to a concrete power interest, it may be called an ideology." Or, relatedly, the views of Thompson (1996: 7), who defines ideology as "meaning in the service of power" (see also Meyer, Sahlin, Ventresca, and Walgenbach 2009a). Not all institutional ideas (or logics) are ideological, but many are constructed to serve the interests of one or another contesting power.[4] Analysts take note!

In sum, arrayed in line with the three pillars, we encounter three rather different accounts of the mechanisms leading to institutionalization. Although different aspects of institutions are privileged and different mechanisms are evoked, these arguments are not necessarily in conflict. Robust institutionalization is often the product of multiple mechanisms that interact with and reinforce each other. In addition to the broad classes of mechanisms identified as associated with institutionalization, other more specific mechanisms have been and will be identified. We discuss below some of the mechanisms and carriers associated with institutionalization, and Chapters 7 and 8 will describe other mechanisms, including those involving cross-level processes.

❖ MAINTAINING AND DIFFUSING INSTITUTIONS

Maintenance

The concept of institution connotes stability and persistence. Are these conditions problematic? Once an institutional structure is in place, is there anything else to be said? A good many students of organizations assume that institutionalization is an absorbing state and, once completed, requires no further effort at maintenance. Simon (1945/1997), for example, describes a number of reasons for the persistence of behavioral patterns once established. He emphasizes, in particular, cognitive patterns: "The activity itself creates stimuli that direct attention toward its continuance and completion" (p. 106). Such individual-level, attention-directing processes also act to decrease the individual's sensitivity to external stimuli. Organizational ecologists also assume that stability or, in their terms, *inertia* is a normal state for organizations. Inertia is the product of such organization-level processes as sunk costs, vested interests, and habitualized behavior shored up by the external constraints imposed by contractual obligations to exchange partners and regulatory regimes (Hannan and Freeman 1984; 1989). Change is assumed to be both difficult and dangerous for organizations.

Other theorists, however, argue that persistence cannot be taken for granted. Zucker (1988b: 26), for example, suggests that entropy—"a tendency toward disorganization in the social system"—is the more normal condition. Things—structures, rules, and routines—tend to break down. She argues, as a corollary, that deinstitutionalization is prevalent and has many roots. (These ideas are considered in a later section of this chapter.) Persistence is seen to be tenuous and problematic. Theorists such as Giddens (1984) take an intermediate position. He emphasizes the extent to which the persistence of rules, norms, and beliefs requires actors to actively monitor ongoing social activities and continuously attend to maintaining the linkages with the wider socio-cultural environment. Structure persists only to the extent that actors are able to continuously produce and reproduce it.

In his work on the institutionalization of economic systems, Avner Greif (2006: 14) embraces and elaborates this intermediate position, combining agency and structural views, by proposing an equilibrium perspective. Greif argues, as I have proposed, that institutions are supported by varying elements, including rules, beliefs, and norms. "These institutional elements are exogenous to each individual whose behavior they influence." But they are also "endogenous institutions," which are self-reinforcing.

> Each individual, responding to the institutional elements implied by others' behavior and expected behavior, behaves in a manner that contributes to enabling, guiding, and motivating others to behave in the manner that led to the institutional elements that generated the individual's behavior to begin with. Behavior is self-enforcing in that each individual, taking the structure as given, finds it best to follow the institutionalized behavior that, in turn, reproduces the institution in the sense that the implied behavior confirms the associated beliefs and regenerates the associated norms. (Greif 2006: 15–16)

In my reading of the institutional literature, most institutional scholars accord little attention to the issue of institutional persistence. Lawrence (2008: 190) suggests that one reason for this neglect is that much of the work of maintenance is performed by non-elite actors: "the institutional janitors and mechanics who deal with the mess and breakdowns of institutional mechanisms that occur as an everyday occurrence." Also, as expected, those who do consider maintenance disagree over what mechanisms underlie stability. In particular, the underlying conception of institution—whether cultural-cognitive, normative, or regulative—affects views of maintenance mechanisms. Cultural-cognitive theorists tend to emphasize the important role played by unconscious, taken-for-granted assumptions defining social reality. Jepperson (1991: 145), for example, insists that the hallmark of an institution is its capacity for automatic maintenance and self-restoration. Institutional mechanisms are those requiring no conscious mobilization of will or effort. Similarly, Zucker (1977: 726) argues: "Internalization, self-reward, or other intervening processes need not be present to ensure cultural persistence because social knowledge once institutionalized exists as a fact, as part of objective reality, and can be transmitted directly on that basis."

To evaluate this claim, Zucker conducted an experimental study to assess the extent to which the degree of institutionalization was observed to affect the extent of uniformity, maintenance, and resistance to change exhibited by subjects. Her study utilized the classic Sherif (1935) stimuli, asking subjects to evaluate the amount of apparent movement by a stationary light in a darkened room. Extent of institutionalization was manipulated by instructions given to the subjects. To create lower levels of institutionalization, the subject was told only that the other participant (a confederate) was "another person"; to create intermediate levels, the subject was told that she and her coworker (the confederate) were both "members of an organization," but their positions were unspecified. And to create higher levels of institutionalization, the subject was told that she and her coworker were both participants in an organization, and the coworker (confederate) was given the title of "Light Operator." Zucker (1977) reasoned:

> Settings can vary in the degree to which acts in them are institutionalized. By being embedded in broader contexts where acts are viewed as institutionalized, acts in specific situations come to be viewed as institutionalized. Indicating that a situation is structured like situations in an organization makes the actors assume that the actions required of them by others actors in that situation will be . . . more regularized and that the interaction will be more definitely patterned than if the situation were not embedded in an organizational context. Any act performed by the occupant of an office is seen as highly objectified and exterior. When an actor occupies an office, acts are seen as nonpersonal and as continuing over time, across different actors. (pp. 728–729)

Note the extent to which Zucker's experiment is built on a cultural-cognitive conception of institutionalization. The only factor manipulated to account for the behavior of subjects was their cognitive framing of the situation, including their own identity within it. No sanctions or other types of regulative controls or normative pressures were involved in producing the observed effects.

Zucker found that extent of institutionalization exhibited the expected effects: Subjects working in more institutionalized (organization-like) conditions were more likely to transmit the standards they had learned in an initial series of trials (with the confederate supplying the standard) to a new naïve subject, maintain their standards over time (subjects were asked to return one week later to perform the same type of activity), and resist attempts to change their judgments (having adopted the confederate's standard in the initial period, subjects were exposed to a second confederate who attempted to alter the standard).

Zucker shows that in ongoing social systems, transmission of beliefs and practices to new actors is a vital process underlying persistence. Further, more highly institutionalized practices, being more "objectified," are more easily transmitted than less institutionalized behavior (Tolbert and Zucker 1996).

Others stressing cultural-cognitive mechanisms in the institutional maintenance point to processes like "mythologizing" work, such as recounting the legends of early leaders, and "embedding and routinizing" processes, such as training and refresher courses (Lawrence and Suddaby 2006). Zilber (2002) describes a process of "reinterpretation" and "reframing" in which a rape crisis center was able to maintain and legitimate its activities by shifting from a feminist perspective that motivated its creation to a therapeutic perspective as new personnel were recruited. The professional ideology provided a stronger basis for framing and motivating the center's activities for new workers than the social movement ideology.

Theorists taking a normative view emphasize the stabilizing influence of shared norms that are both internalized and imposed by others. For example, in his examination of "the reproduction of inertia" in a multinational corporation, Kilduff (1993) stresses the role of social networks, whose members draw "on shared normative frameworks, [and] continually monitor interpersonal behavior," and of accounts that provide "an interpretive and normative base" to support ongoing behavior. The ease of maintenance and transmission of institutional practices is affected by the extent to which new recruits share similar beliefs and interpretive frameworks of current personnel. The more different the new members are, the more effort must be expended to transmit existing beliefs and practices. In her study of law firms, Tolbert (1988) found that firms employing recruits from more heterogeneous training backgrounds were more likely to utilize special training programs, mentoring systems, more frequent evaluations, and other socialization mechanisms than were firms employing recruits primarily from the same law school.

Other theorists focus on cross-level effects, stressing the central role of the environment not only in fostering the acceptance of innovations (see below), but in supporting and sustaining changes once they have occurred. In a study of public school districts in California, Rowan (1982: 261) demonstrates that districts were more likely to adopt and retain innovations—new programs and personnel—when they were supported by "key members of the institutional environments of local systems," specifically by state and federal legislatures, state educational agencies, state-level professional associations, and teacher training institutions. If support was lacking from one or more of these external constituencies, districts were less likely to adopt and more likely to drop the innovation when viewed over a 40-year period. Legitimating organizations, such as professional associations who set and enforce standards, confront at least two important challenges (Trank and Washington 2009). They must "offer constituents meaning-ful consequences, either through sanctioning participation in the field or by facilitating constituent organizations' capacity to acquire resources"; and because they are likely to confront other claimants to their authority, they must "engage in deliberate, conscious action to maintain their field-level power and their gatekeeping role if confronted with a contender legitimation organization" (Trank and Washington 2009: 239–240).

Regulatory theorists are more likely to stress conscious control efforts, involving interests, agency and power, and the deployment of sanctions. Actors employ power not just to create institutions, but also to preserve and maintain them over time (see DiMaggio 1988; Stinch-combe 1968). Regulatory actors engage in "enabling" work, creating rules that facilitate, supplement, and support institutions, "policing work" that attempts to ensure compliance through enforcement, and "deterring, valourizing and demonizing" work in order to expose devi-ants and celebrate high achievers (Lawrence and Suddaby 2006: 230). Neoinstitutional economists, including both transaction cost and agency theorists, emphasize how important it is to devise appropriate governance structures and develop incentives and controls suited to the situation (see Pratt and Zeckhauser 1985). However, if regulation is institutionalized, the rewarding and sanctioning take place within a framework of rules. Power is stabilized and legitimized by the devel-opment of rules.

Some studies attend to the full range of forces supporting persis-tence: cultural-cognitive, normative, and regulative. In Miller's (1994) examination of a Pietist mission that has survived for almost two cen-turies, all of the institutional elements appear to be at work. The Basel Mission was founded in the early 19th century to educate missionaries and establish evangelical outposts in various parts of the world. Miller examined the records of this organization, focusing on the period from 1815 to 1915, to ascertain the basis for its longevity. He argues that participants were recruited from a relatively homogenous social base; given intensive socialization so that participants came to share similar beliefs and values; placed in a strong authority structure combining aspects of charismatic, traditional, and bureaucratic control elements together with formalized procedures of "mutual surveillance"; and encouraged to develop a sense of "specialness and separation" that insulated them from being corrupted by the secular world.

In their study of the evolution over a 35-year-period of a new industry devoted to the cochlear implant—a device to restore hearing to the deaf—Van de Ven and Garud (1994) analyze a series of events coded as creating variation (novel technical events), selection (rule-making events), and retention (rule-following events). The latter events, retention, are indicators of institutional persistence because they refer to an event that "was programmed or governed by existing institutional rules and routines" (p. 429).[5] Viewed over the period of study, their data show how novel technical events dominated during the developmental period from 1956 to 1983, rule-making and rule-following events grew in an oscillatory fashion during the middle period from 1983 to 1986, and then, by 1989, "no more institutional rule-making events occurred while rule-following events continued to occur" (p. 430). They also describe how institutional rules operated to suppress innovation and to "constrain the flexibility of private firms to adapt to changing circumstances" as existing technologies were "locked in" to specific technological paths (p. 439).

Institutional Diffusion

In a thoughtful analysis of diffusion studies, Strang (2010: 6) points out that the widespread interest in diffusion processes "resonates" with contemporary institutional understandings of social action, assuming a modern "world of sovereign actors who decide whether or not to do something new." While these actors take one another into account, they are relatively independent agents who operate in "a culturally integrated world of voluntaristic action." In his examination of a large bank, Strang observed the behavior of officers serving on numerous managerial teams charged with developing proposals for corporate innovation in more than a dozen distinct domains. Far from being "cultural dopes" or mindless sponges, Strang's teams were observed to be expert comparison shoppers, carefully locating best practices in other successful organizations and then customizing these models to fit into their own organization. While such behavior may not be typical or even widespread, evidence that it occurs means that traditional diffusion models need to be modified to recognize the agency of individual adopters, changes over time in conceptions of the innovation, and the importance of distinguishing between formal adoption and implementation.

Much attention has been accorded to diffusion processes—to the ways in which institutional patterns spread over time and space. Much less effort has been given to understanding the processes by which a given institutional pattern or model is created, to who and what processes are involved, and to how the model itself undergoes transformation over time. Pizarro (2012) provides an instructive example of these processes in his analysis of the crafting of an "environmental conservation regime": a template for countries to employ in devising policies to enable the creation of geographic zones for the protection of biological diversity. Prior to World War II, two competing models had emerged—a British model based on game preservation in the colonies, and an American model emphasizing the protection of scenic wonders. Following the war, a growing collection of nation-states came together in an international series of conferences, forming the International Union of Conservation of Nature in 1956. A series of resolutions over the next half-century, reflected not only the convergence around a common template to support diversity protection efforts by its members, but also a continuing evolution of this template as newer and differing countries entered into the process. For example, in later years, much more emphasis was placed on the rights of indigenous peoples within the protected areas. A "fortress model" gradually gave way to a more inclusive ecosystem view with attention to these parks as a source of economic development and cultural value. The "model" widely diffused among nation-states around the world, but which version of the model was adopted differed over time as the regime was continually reconstructed.

The diffusion of an institutional form across space or time has a triple significance in institutional analysis. First, extent of diffusion of a set of rules or structural forms is often taken as an indicator of the growing strength of an institutional structure. In this sense, studies of institutional diffusion are often regarded as studies of increasing institutionalization. Recall, however, as emphasized by Colyvas and Jonsson (2011) and noted in Chapter 4, that diffusion in and of itself does not equal legitimation. Practices must be accompanied and supported by changing rules, norms, and/or beliefs operating at multiple levels. Second, because the diffusing elements are being adopted by and incorporated into organizations, studies of diffusion are also treated as studies of institutional effects. In such studies, early or later adoption is often argued to follow different principles because of the changing strength of the institutions and also because of the varying characteristics of the adopting organizations. Studies of factors affecting the adoption behavior of individual organizations are discussed in Chapter 7. Third, the spread of a new form or practice is also an instance of institutional change—but change of a particular kind. It is *convergent change:* change that reinforces and diffuses existing patterns (see Greenwood and Hinings 1996). Most institutional theory and research has emphasized convergent processes. Only recently has attention turned to disruptive and divergent change, a topic I consider below and in later chapters.

Several distinctions are helpful in understanding the various ways in which institutions are diffused. DiMaggio and Powell's (1983) useful typology focuses attention on three contrasting mechanisms—coercive, normative, and mimetic—that identify varying forces or motives for adopting new structures and behaviors. As discussed in Chapter 3, these mechanisms map well onto the three types of institutional pillars I identify. Other analysts, such as Brown (1981) and Meyer (1994), distinguish between demand- and supply-side explanations of diffusion (see Chapter 5). Demand-side approaches focus attention on the characteristics or conditions of new adopters, whereas supply-side approaches focus on the nature and efforts of agents attempting to spread the innovation. For many types of diffusion processes, it is more useful to examine the attributes or behavior of the diffusion agent or the "propagator" than those of the target or recipient units.

Early researchers tended to view diffusion as a rather mechanical process: the movement of technologies, models, and ideas from one place to another. Attention to the intermediary role of carriers, with the recognition that the mode of transmission affects the message transmitted, has helped to correct this misconception (see Chapter 4 and the following section). As noted in our earlier discussion, information is modified, edited, and translated in transmission by the carrier (Czarniawska and Joerges 1996; Sahlin-Andersson 1996). Even more important, there is increasing recognition that the end user also alters the innovation, sometimes in small and other times in major ways. Institutional effects are not one-sided and determinant, but multifaceted and related to a nonergodic world (precise predictions assume constant states, whereas social contexts are constantly changing; North 2005). As Latour (1986) concludes:

> The spread in time and space of anything—claims, orders, artifacts, goods—is in the hands of people; each of these people may act in many different ways, letting the token drop, or modifying it, or deflecting it, or betraying it, or adding to it, or appropriating it. (p. 167)

These ideas are employed to frame a brief review of selected diffusion studies.

Regulative Processes

To be effective, the use of coercion requires relatively clear demands, effective surveillance, and significant sanctions. Beyond this, it also matters whether the mechanisms employed are primarily those of power, involving imposition of authority—where the coercive agent is viewed as a legitimate agent of control—or rely on the use of threats or inducements (Scott 1987). We would expect institutional effects—the depth or shallowness of institutionalization—to vary by these mechanisms, higher penetration being associated with authority. Numerous institutional forms are diffused by some combination of these mechanisms in the world of public and private organizations. Djelic (1998) describes variation among Germany, France, and Italy in their response after World War II to the U.S. efforts to export the American model of corporate enterprise. Mechanisms involved included coercion, inducement (the Marshall Plan), and mimicry.

Nation-states with statist or corporatist traditions are more likely to successfully employ coercive, regulative power in introducing innovations and reforms than pluralist or individualist systems (Hall and Soskice 2001a; 2001b; Jepperson and Meyer 1991). Private organizations such as firms and corporations routinely utilize their legitimate authority as well as carrots and sticks to introduce new forms and practices within their establishments. Coercive mechanisms emphasize supply-side processes, directing attention to the characteristics of the diffusion agent and to relational carriers, noting the alignment of interests between principal and agent, and the adequacy of information, inspection, and control systems.

Three empirical studies are employed to illustrate the study of diffusion supported by regulatory authority. In their well-known study of civil service reforms, Tolbert and Zucker (1983) examine the diffusion of municipal civil service reform in the United States at the turn of the century, from 1885 to 1935. They contrast two types of diffusion processes: the situation in which particular states adopted the reform and mandated that cities under their jurisdiction embrace it, and the situation in which a state allowed individual cities to choose whether to adopt the reform. States mandating the reform employed legal procedures and official sanctions to enforce compliance; the institutional arrangement was that of a hierarchically structured authority system. By contrast, cities in states lacking mandates were responding to change processes resembling a social movement—a decentralized model of reform relying on normative and cultural-cognitive influences (beliefs that it is the right or modern thing to do and an awareness that other cities were adopting the reform). As expected, cities in states mandating the reform were much more likely to adopt civil service provisions than those in states lacking such mandates. They did so much earlier and more completely: Mandated reforms were adopted by 60% of the municipalities within a 10-year period (all did so within 37 years), whereas it took 50 years for nonmandated reforms to approach the 60% level (Tolbert and Zucker 1983: 28–29).

In her study of profound social change in Japan in the late 19th century, during the Meiji period, Westney (1987) provides a historical account of the conscious selection by Japanese officials of various Western models regarded as successful for organizing particular organization fields, such as police systems and postal services. These models, or organizational archetypes, were then imposed on the relevant sectors, employed as a basis for restructuring existing organizational arrangements. The diffusion of these models exhibited differing patterns, affected by the variable authority of the propagating officials, the presence of compatible preexisting cognitive models supplied by indigenous organizations (e.g., the army for the police), and the availability of a supportive organizational infrastructure in the immediate environment. Westney emphasizes that, although the original intent of the reformers had been to simply imitate and import successful practices from other societies, much inventiveness was required to fit these models into their new circumstances: both imitation and innovation were observed.

Cole (1989) examined differences among firms in Japan, Sweden, and the United States in the adoption and retention of innovative small-group activities, such as quality circles. His analysis emphasizes the role played by varying national infrastructures—governmental agencies, trade associations, and union organizations—in legitimating, informing, and supporting the innovations. Japan more than Sweden and Sweden more than the United States possessed such supportive structures, with the result that the innovations spread more widely and were more stable in the former than the latter societies. Although these three countries varied in the relative strength of regulatory statist authority, Cole's analysis also points to important differences in the extent to which trade associations and unions were mobilized to provide normative support for these innovations. This also illustrates the importance of the wider organization field structure in explaining the behavior of individual organizations (see Chapter 8).

Normative Processes

Analysts focusing on normative processes stress the importance of network ties and commitments—relational structures as carriers. Many of the studies emphasizing normative processes focus on professional or collegial networks, interlocking directorates (individuals who serve on multiple director boards), or the support provided by informal ties.

Institutional scholars argue that regulatory activities thought to embody coercive pressures often depend more on normative and cognitive elements. Examining the effects of governmental influence on employers in the United States, Dobbin and Sutton (1998: 443) call attention to the "strength of a weak state" because the state's inability to craft clear unambiguous legislation on employment gave rise to processes by which managers "recast policy-induced structures in the mold of efficiency." The state's role in eliciting change is overshadowed and augmented by managers' interests in collectively crafting a normative justification that creates a market rationale for their conformity. In a related discussion, Edelman, Uggen, and Erlanger (1999: 407) suggest that it is not accurate to view legal actions by the state, such as the U.S. regulation of employment practices, as operating independently and from "on high." Rather, when law is contested, "organizations actively participate in the meaning of compliance" in ways that "renders law endogenous: the content and meaning of law is determined within the social field that it was designed to regulate" (p. 407). The meaning of laws "mandating" equal opportunity or affirmative action were negotiated and socially constructed by the actions and reactions of personnel managers who created national networks, first involving firms tied together by military contractors and later involving their professional and business associations.

In effect, the personnel professionals acted as a kind of social movement, developing and testing, and then diffusing best practices from firm to firm (Dobbin 2009). While the legislature and the courts played a role, it was a supporting one. "Judges rarely did more than give the nod to programs already popular among leading firms. Courts followed—they did not lead" (Dobbin 2009: 4). The diffusion of new forms and procedures was more responsive to the spread of norms carried by professional networks (e.g., a firm's membership in personnel associations) than to changes in regulatory policies (e.g., the weakening of regulatory enforcement during the Reagan years had little effect on diffusion). In his recent study covering more than 30 years of personnel reforms, Dobbin (2009) shows that similar reform processes have operated from the 1960s, from efforts to define and enforce equal opportunity systems through more recent efforts to curtail sexual harassment. Although created by normative mechanisms, most of the reforms have been codified into law-like rules enforced by corporations "governing hiring, promotion, discharge, discipline, maternity leave, sexual harassment," and others—a set of private governance mechanisms responsive to broadly shared compliance norms (p. 11).

Westphal and Zajac (1994) examine the emergence in business circles, during the period from 1970 to 1990, of an informal norm that the compensation of chief executive officers should be linked to the financial performance of their companies. Although based on theoretical arguments by agent-principal economists and supported by some empirical data showing effects of such incentive plans on short-term stock prices, the argument took on moral weight as more and more boards of Fortune 500 companies adopted them. Corporate boards not taking such actions were regarded as negligent in their protection of stockholders' interests. The practice spread rapidly among companies, and those adopting the new model were rewarded by the stock market. Often there is competition among those who promulgate normative models. For example, as discussed in Chapter 5, DiMaggio (1991) described the contests occurring among professional camps holding competing visions for developing art museums during the early 20th century in the United States. Following Bourdieu, DiMaggio and Powell (1983: 152) view professionalization as "the collective struggle of members of an occupation to define the conditions and methods of their work." Research by Lounsbury, Ventresca, and Hirsch (2003), described in Chapter 8, provides another apt example.

Normative standards may arise slowly and incrementally over time but they may also be explicitly established by self-appointed arbiters employing more or less representative bodies and deliberative procedures. Professional and trade associations present clear modern instances of such groups and processes. For example, after considerable struggle and compromise extending over many years, various medical associations joined forces with a managerial association, the American Hospital Association, to form the Joint Commission on Accreditation of Healthcare Organizations (JCAHO). Whereas licensure is a governmental, regulatory process, accreditation is a "nongovernmental, professional-sponsored process"—a normative process aimed at promulgating high standards for the industry (Somers 1969: 101). Although accreditation is not legally mandated, in professionally dominated arenas such as health care, organizations lacking accreditation are suspect and ineligible for reimbursement from governmental funding sources. Empirical studies show that organizations such as hospitals, for example, accredited by appropriate professional bodies were considerably more likely to survive than those lacking such normative support (see Ruef and Scott 1998).[6] Research by Westphal, Gulati, and Shortell (1997), discussed in more detail in Chapter 7, details the strong role played by the JCAHO in the adoption of total quality management programs by U.S. hospitals during the period 1985 to 1993. Of the roughly 2,700 hospitals in their sample, those adopting some version of total quality management increased from virtually none in 1985 to nearly 2000 in 1993. Greenwood, Suddaby, and Hinings (2002) describe negotiations and debates within the professional association of Canadian accountants as they worked to theorize and institute new models of governance for accounting firms. These changes resulted from a contested, deliberative process that was enacted into a set of codified rules regarding the structure of professional service corporation. Once this settlement was in place, the new models began to diffuse widely.

As discussed in Chapter 5, we are witnessing a period of active institution-building at the transnational level. An important attribute of the new systems being constructed is that they rely much more on "governance" systems than on "governmental" forms. The newer structures utilize "soft" rather than "hard" laws—depending on the actions of private rather than (or in combination with) public organizations, and on network rather than hierarchical structures (Mörth 2004). In short, they substitute normative for regulatory systems. These softer laws are circulated by and embodied in a variety of types of carriers and mechanisms, including "reporting and coordinating procedures," "monitoring," and "agenda setting" in which arenas are created in which "good and desirable" practices are proposed and disseminated (Jacobsson and Sahlin-Andersson 2006). Sometimes combinations of NGOs and firms form cooperative associations to develop and promulgate standards that are enforced by self-policing as well as by inspections conducted by external oversight units. Compliance is rewarded by certifications in industries as varied as forestry products, the apparel industry, coffee companies, and organic farming. Bartley (2003: 434), who studied the development of environmental and labor standards in the apparel and forest products fields, argues that such systems of private regulation have developed rapidly since the 1990s because the spread of neoliberal and fair trade belief systems has "led both state and nonstate actors to support private, rather than public forms of regulation."

Most empirical work focuses on factors affecting the diffusion of a successful normative model, with much less attention given to proposed models that fail to catch on. Representative empirical studies of institutional diffusion of organizational forms and practices, perhaps the most widely studied aspect of institutional processes, are discussed in Chapter 7.

Cultural-Cognitive Processes

Following Berger and Luckmann, Strang and Meyer (1993) stress the centrality of cultural-cognitive elements in institutional diffusion processes. They argue that diffusion is greatly affected by theorization processes. For diffusion to occur, the actors involved need to regard themselves as similar in some important respect (the creation of categories such as the generic "organization" or particular subtypes such as "hospitals" facilitates this process). Theorization also provides causal accounts, explanations for why some kinds of actors need to add specific components or practices. As discussed earlier in this chapter, theorization contributes to "objectification" (Tolbert and Zucker 1996).

Organizational ecologists have embraced the cultural-cognitive conception of institutions by recognizing that "organizational density"—the numbers of organizations exhibiting a given organizational form—can be interpreted as a measure of the legitimacy of that form: the extent to which it is institutionalized. Many studies by organization ecologists have documented the importance of "density dependence," demonstrating that the number of organizations of a given type was positively correlated with the founding of additional organizations of the same type. Research on numerous, diverse populations of organizations revealed that as a new form emerged, numbers increased slowly at first, then more rapidly, finally tailing off or declining (for a review of these studies, see Baum and Shipilov 2006; Hannan and Freeman 1989). Carroll and Hannan (1989) were the first to provide a theoretical interpretation of this empirical finding, arguing that organizational density serves as an indicator of the cognitive status of the form: its cognitive legitimacy. They propose that

an organizational form is legitimate to the extent that relevant actors regard it as the "natural" way to organize for some purpose. From this perspective, rarity of a form poses serious problems of legitimacy. When few instances of a form exist, it can hardly be the "natural" way to achieve some collective end. On the other hand, once a form becomes prevalent, further proliferation is unlikely to have much effect on its taken-for-grantedness. Legitimacy thus grows monotonically with density but at a decreasing rate. (pp. 525–526)

However, as the numbers continue to increase in a given environment, legitimation processes give way to competitive processes—the dampening of new foundings and the consolidation of existing forms—so that the density curve levels out or declines over time.

This interpretation of density as connoting legitimacy has proved to be controversial. Zucker (1989) argues that Carroll and Hannan provide no direct measure of legitimacy, simply assuming the connection between prevalence and legitimacy (see also Baum and Powell 1995). Baum and Oliver (1992) suggest that prevalence may be only a proxy for other, related effects such as embeddedness. Their study of day care centers in Toronto found that when measures of the latter, such as the number of relations between centers and governmental institutions, are included, then density effects disappeared. Carrol and Hannan (1989; Hannan, Carroll, Dundon, and Torres 1995b) responded by noting the widespread use of indirect indicators in the sciences, the support for the association between prevalence and legitimacy provided by historical accounts related to the early experience of the populations studied, and the advantage offered by its generality—its applicability to any type of population.

Many other institutional scholars have studied the diffusion of ideologies or belief systems, forms or archetypes (conceptions as to how to organize), and processes or procedures. Nothing is as portable as ideas. They travel primarily by symbolic carriers, although they also are conveyed by relations and artifacts. They may circulate via specific social networks, but they also ride on more generalized media (see Boxenbaum and Jonsson 2008; Czarniawska and Joerges 1996; Sahlin and Wedlin 2008; Sahlin-Andersson and Engwall 2002).

Mauro Guillén (1994) carried out detailed historical analyses comparing the diffusion of managerial ideologies in the first half of the 20th century in the United States, Germany, Great Britain, and Spain. He differentiated between management theory, transmitted among intellectuals and indexed by the flow of books, articles, and professional discourse, and management practice, the use of techniques by practitioners as indicated by surveys and case studies. Scientific management, one of the early major managerial ideologies, was discovered to be more highly diffused among practitioners than intellectuals and to have penetrated the United States and Germany much earlier than Great Britain and Spain. Guillén argued that differences among the four societies in international pressure, labor unrest, state involvement, and professional groups, among other factors, help to account for the differences in diffusion patterns observed.

Shocked out of their complacency by the fierce competition provided by Japanese automobile and electronics manufacturers in the mid-1970s, American firms began to explore and experiment with a range of practices that came to be labeled total quality management (TQM; see Cole and Scott 2000). As described by Cole (1999), American business was not quick to respond, unsure of the nature of the challenge it faced or what to do about it. A period of sense-making ensued as communities of actors crafted and sifted interpretations. Although expert gurus offered insights, consulting companies proffered advice, professional associations (e.g., the American Society for Quality) offered normative justification, and award programs (e.g., the Baldrige National Quality Award) offered prestige and financial incentives, little consensus developed regarding the core ingredients of TQM. The movement was not sufficiently theorized or supported by adequate normative and regulative structures to diffuse widely or to have deep effects in this country (see Cole's [1989] comparative research, described earlier in this chapter). Some practices, such as quality circles, were widely discussed, but tended to receive more lip service than use. Companies felt the need to change, but the directions and recipes offered did not provide clear guidelines. Perhaps the most important change associated with TQM was in the cognitive framing of quality, shifting attention from the concerns and criteria of internal engineers to external customers and from a "detect-and-repair" to a "prevent-and-improve" mentality. Although the quality fad seems to have run its course, it provided the basis for some useful organizational learning (see Cole 1999). Not all attempts at institutional diffusion succeed.

❖ DEINSTITUTIONALIZATION PROCESSES

As noted, persistence of institutional beliefs and practices cannot be presumed. *Deinstitutionalization* refers to the processes by which institutions weaken and disappear. As we would expect, some analysts emphasize primarily the depletion and increasing disuse of regulative systems, noting enfeebled laws, diluted sanctions, and increasing noncompliance. Others stress eroding norms and evidence of the diminished force of obligatory expectations. Still others point to the erosion of cultural beliefs and the increasing questioning of matters once taken for granted. Regardless of which elements are emphasized—of course, these elements interact, and various combinations may be involved—analysts should attend to both beliefs and behaviors: to schemas and resources. Beliefs and behaviors are loosely coupled, as generations of sociologists have emphasized, but changes in our ideas and expectations put pressure on related activities and vice versa.

The possible causes of deinstitutionalization are multiple. As noted, Zucker (1988b) emphasizes the general phenomenon of entropy associated with "imperfect transmission" and modification of rules under the pressure of varying circumstances and the erosion of roles by the personal characteristics of occupants. Oliver (1992) describes three general types of pressures toward deinstitutionalization: functional, political, and social. *Functional* pressures are those that arise from perceived problems in performance levels associated with institutionalized practices. For example, U.S. public schools have clearly suffered loss of legitimacy in recent years due to lower scores on standardized educational tests compared to children in comparable societies (see National Commission on Excellence in Education 1983). Reduced legitimacy allows increased consideration of alternative policies (e.g., No Child Left Behind) and approaches such as vouchers. There is an ecology of institutions, organizations, and actions. When institutional structures are determined by some important constituency to be inadequate in the guidelines they provide, these structures are candidates for reform or replacement as problems accumulate.

Functional pressures can also arise from changing consumer preferences. Kraatz and Zajac (1996) studied the effect on private liberal arts colleges of changes in student educational goals beginning in the 1970s as students became less motivated by humanistic purposes and self-fulfillment goals and more concerned with making a living and succeeding financially. Data from over 600 U.S. colleges during the period 1971 to 1986 revealed that, despite strong normative and cultural-cognitive commitments to the value of liberal arts programs, virtually all the schools responded to student enrollment pressures by introducing vocationally oriented professional programs. As expected, those more dependent on student tuition were more likely to add such programs, whereas the more prestigious colleges were most resistant to these changes. Kraatz and Zajac interpret their findings as demonstrating the limits of institutional arguments: In the face of changes in consumer preferences, strongly institutionalized values and their associated structures gave way to market pressures. An alternative interpretation, which I prefer, is that their study depicts the undermining (delegitimation) of one institutional logic—the virtues of the liberal arts—and its gradual replacement by a second—embracing market-oriented institutional logics. Deinstituionalization can be reframed as institutional change.

Functional demands often pit pressures emanating from the environment, which threaten the survival of the organization, against those internal constituents committed to protect the mission: the values and goals for which the organization was established. These values are, to a variable extent, "precarious," as Michels (1915/1949) and Selznick (1949) have emphasized, and require "institutional leadership" if they are to prevail. Kraatz and colleagues (Kraatz, Ventresca, and Deng 2010) examine changes in liberal arts colleges that allowed financial criteria to invade admissions department decisions, which had been insulated from such pressures. A "mundane" administrative change created "enrollment management" departments bringing formerly autonomous departments into a conjoint decision context with the result that many colleges abandoned their previous mission of admitting students based primarily on their academic performance to favor those better able to meet tuition costs. Colleges resisting these changes were led by more powerful and professionalized faculty and admissions personnel and by longer-tenured presidents. Because of the response of such leaders, in a sample of 515 private liberal arts colleges over the period 1987 through 2006, the diffusion of enrollment management programs abated over time.

Political pressures result from shifts in interests or underlying power distributions that provide support for existing institutional arrangements. Changing voter preferences can lead to new political alignments and changing majorities in legislative groups can result in changes in regulatory legislation or enforcement practices. Thus, as discussed in Chapter 7, when the U.S. Surgeon General finally summoned the courage and political resources to "blow the whistle" on tobacco companies, although the Big Six companies responded collectively to defend themselves, all companies attempted to adapt to the new environment in a variety of individual ways (Miles 1982). The Big Six companies survived, many by diversifying into other markets. Population ecologists remind us, however, that it is important not to focus exclusive attention on the largest companies in an industry. Research by Hannan and Freeman (1989: 23–33) reports that, during the period of interest, "of the 78 companies in the U.S. tobacco business in 1956, 49 had left the industry by 1986." About a quarter of these shifted into other business lines, but the rest failed to survive.

Business interests can lobby legislative bodies to change corporate governance frameworks, as discussed in Chapter 5. As noted in our review of social movement contributions in Chapter 5, changes in the alignment of political groups can weaken support for existing institutional settlements and provide welcome opportunities for new players and divergent interests to enter the arena. The rise of environmental interests during the 1960s and the responsiveness of the political establishment to the increasing demands for clear air and water led to a major shift in the institutional environment within which the petrochemical industries operated, resulting in changes in the organizational structure and strategies of these companies and the institutional logics employed by their managers, as Hoffman (1997; 1999) details (see also Chapter 7).

Social pressures are associated with differentiation of groups and increasing fragmentation of normative consensus, causing divergent or discordant beliefs and practices. In our health care study, we show how the long-term reduction in physician membership in the American Medical Association, associated with the rise of specialty associations, resulted in the weakening and fragmentation of normative consensus among physicians and, as a consequence, a disintegration of the unified voice of "American medicine" regarding health care matters (Scott, Ruef, Mendel, and Caronna 2000). The presence of multiple competing and overlapping institutional frameworks undermines the stability of each (Kraatz and Block 2008).

We are beginning to see more empirical studies of deinstitutionalization. As might be expected, the indicators employed to assess the extent of deinstitutionalization range from weakening beliefs to abandonment of a set of practices. Geertz (1971) describes a subtle and barely discernible pattern of deinstitutionalization underway in two Islamic societies as fundamentalist belief systems gradually loosen their hold on believers:

What is believed to be true has not changed for these people, or not changed very much. What has changed is the way in which it is believed. Where there once was faith, there now are reasons, and not very convincing ones; what once were deliverances are now hypotheses, and rather strained ones. There is not much outright skepticism around, or even much conscious hypocrisy, but there is a good deal of solemn self-deception. (p. 17)

Analyzing changes over time in the normative and cultural-cognitive conventions governing grand opera, Robinson (1985: 10) describes how the use of "two clocks"—the real-life tempo of the recitative as "things move along more or less as they do in real life," in contrast to the "slow time" devoted to an aria or ensemble number—which characterized 17th- and 18th-century productions gave way to the "continuous" musical style of the 19th century. Transitional composers paved the way by employing, but ridiculing, earlier styles. Thus, in his opera *The Barber of Seville* (1816), Rossini self-consciously adhered to 18th-century conventions, but employed them to comic effect so that "one sees in Rossini an operatic convention at the very end of its artistic life: he makes fun of it; the next generation simply abandons it."

Sine and Tolbert (2006: 7) describe an intermediate stage of deinstitutionalization based on changing practices. They examine a decline in the use of tenure systems in American institutions of higher education from 1965 to 1995. Although only a few colleges and universities abandoned the tenure system, "many higher education institutions have, in the last three decades, steadily increased the number and proportion of non-tenure-track faculty positions." The tenure institution, strongly supported by the normative structures of the teaching profession, persists, but its scope is narrowing so that the protections apply to ever smaller numbers of faculty members. Using data from 1989 to 1995, Sine and Tolbert show that, although there are costs, primarily labor costs, associated with compliance to the tenure system, other costs, primarily legitimacy costs, attend to reduced compliance.

Outright abandonment of an institutionalized practice represents the extreme case of deinstitutionalization. Ahmadjian and Robinson (2001) examine the gradual abandonment, by Japanese companies, of their celebrated practice of permanent employment, viewed as a cornerstone of their distinctive employment system (Abegglen 1958; Cole 1979; Dore 1973; Ouchi 1981). For many years during the post–World War II period, Japanese firms had an implicit contract with their mainline employees, who were given extensive in-company training, to provide them with employment until retirement. This commitment was viewed by many observers, including Cole and Ouchi, as a critical contributor to the remarkable productivity associated with the Japanese industry during this period. However, under the pressure of a severe economic downturn during the 1990s, Japanese firms began to abandon their normative commitment to employees. In their examination of over 1,500 companies arrayed across diverse industries, Ahmadjian and Robinson found that, while downsizing strategies were first utilized by poorly performing companies and more slowly adopted by larger and more prestigious firms, as time passed, more and more companies abandoned the commitment to permanent employment. Over time, "social and institutional concerns gave way to economic pressures as downsizing became increasingly widespread across the population, and firms found safety in numbers"

(Ahmadjian and Robinson 2001: 644). However, as was the case with the study of the dilution of the liberal arts curriculum within colleges, although economic pressures played a role in destabilizing existing practices—whether regarding curriculum or personnel practices—the changes observed do not reflect the naked play of market forces or the adaptive efforts of independent, individual organizations, as Kraatz and Zajac (1996) would have us believe, but the emergence and diffusion of a new institutional logic concerning the right way to conduct the activities in question. As Burdros (1997: 230) makes clear in his study of U.S. corporate adoption of downsizing programs, these practices are supported by beliefs espoused by neoliberal arguments and advanced by investment managers which have proved persuasive to many businesses, although "available research indicates that these events generally have adverse human and organizational effects" (see also Campbell and Pedersen 2001). Deinstitutionalization is associated not only with the growing recognition that current institutional patterns are ineffective, but also with the development of a challenging alternative institutional logic.

Dacin and Dacin (2008: 327) point out that "institutional processes are rarely if even completely extinguished. The practice continues albeit weaker in scope (extent of diffusion) or potency." They note that there often exists a set of "custodians" who view it as their personal mission to perpetuate and, as necessary, reinvent the core elements of the traditions so as to ensure its continuation. Institutions, by definition, are "sticky."[7]

❖ CARRIERS AND INSTITUTIONAL MECHANISMS[8]

Four types of carriers were identified in Chapter 4: symbolic systems, relational systems, activities, and artifacts. As I have emphasized, type of carrier affects the message being carried in multiple ways and, hence, the trajectory of institutionalization processes.

Symbolic Systems

Attention to symbolic systems as carriers of institutional rules and beliefs emphasizes the important role played by such mechanisms as interpretation, theorization, framing, and bricolage—"mechanisms that operate through alterations of individual and collective perception" (McAdam, Tarrow, and Tilly 2001: 26). For ideas to move from place to place and time to time through the use of symbols, they must be encoded into some type of script that is then decoded by recipients who are necessarily embedded in different situations and possessed of differing agendas. As discussed in Chapter 5, Strang and Meyer (1993) employ the concept *theorization* to refer to this coding process. The process of theorization applies both to actors, because diffusion occurs more readily when "the actors involved are perceived as similar (by themselves, and others), and within social institutions more generally" (p. 491), and to the diffusing practices themselves, as practices are abstracted, codified, and converted into models.

> Under these conditions, we suppose that what flows is rarely an exact copy of some practice existing elsewhere. When theorists are the carriers of the practice or theorization itself is the diffusion mechanism, it is the theoretical model that is likely to flow. Such models are neither complete nor unbiased depictions of existing practices. Instead, theoretical models systematically capture some of the features of existing practices and not others, or even fundamentally revise the practices altogether. (Strang and Meyer 1993: 495)

A general problem encountered in focusing exclusively on isolated symbolic materials is that to do so disembeds them from their social context. As Brown and Duguid (2000: 31) note, "This makes [the information] blind to other forces at work in society." Thus, for example, although the appearance of a newspaper makes it appear to be a simple record of what happened on a given day,

> news is not some naturally occurring object that journalists pick up and stick on a paper. It is made and shaped by journalists in the context of the medium and the audience. . . . The newspaper, then is rather like the library—not simply a collection of news, but a selection and a reflection. And the selection process doesn't just "gather news," but weaves and shapes, developing stories in accordance with available space and priorities. (Brown and Duguid 2000: 185–186)

Brown and Duguid point out that the older usage of the word *media* was employed to refer not only to the information, but also the associated technology and social institutions. Yet in today's digital world, any reference to media does not typically conjure up the background role of actors and social institutions. Such inattention to social context is not just a problem on the input side, where symbolic information is created, but also on output side, where it is translated and applied. In her study of the implementation of Western models in Meiji Japan, discussed earlier, Westney (1987: 25) points out that departures from models occurred in part because the models needed to be adapted to "a different societal scale" and also because social organizations and institutional frameworks that provided essential support for the models were missing in Japan.

Students of social movements and institutions have recently stressed the important role played by the *framing* of information or issues. Adapting Goffman's (1974) original concept, Snow and colleagues (Snow and Benford 1992; Snow, Rochford, Worden, and Benford 1986) emphasize the ways in which meaning is mediated by the use of varying cognitive frames. Campbell (2005: 48–49) usefully defines *frames* as "metaphors, symbols, and cognitive cues that cast issues in a particular light and suggest possible ways to respond to these issues." Frames are employed by disseminators to distil and sharpen messages and by recipients to capture and interpret them, so that a critical component of successful transmission involves processes of "frame alignment" (Snow et al. 1986). While symbolic frames may emerge from a more informal *sense-making* process (Weick 1995) as actors collectively work to interpret some event, they can also be created by more strategic *sense-giving* processes in which contesting groups struggle to define and disseminate ideological positions to internal and external constituents (Gioia and Chittipeddi 1991). As Fiss and Zajac (2006: 1173) emphasize, strategic change within organizations entails not only a "shift in structures and processes, but also a cognitive organizational reorientation." Their study examines how the alignment of interests within German firms affected the extent to which they adopted and enacted the shareholder model or, alternatively, blended it with the prevailing broader stakeholder model. Government-owned companies, companies owned by domestic banks that themselves endorsed the stakeholder model, and family-owned companies were more likely to adopt a blended strategy, while companies having greater visibility, as measured by media coverage, were more likely to embrace the globally favored shareholder model (Fiss and Zajac 2006).

Bricolage involves the creative combination of symbolic and structural elements garnered from varying sources and traditions (Douglas 1986; Levi-Strauss 1966). Actors may arrive with ideas and templates derived from their previous experience, but when applying them to new situations often join them with local structures and ideas to form new hybrid combinations. Stark (1996) provides a graphic description of this process as Eastern European capitalists struggled to craft new types of enterprise after the collapse of the socialist framework. He found that rather than completely discarding all aspects of the former enterprises, Hungarian businesspeople mixed and matched selected elements from the socialist and capitalist repertories of structures and routines, constructing hybrid public-private organizations. Unclear as to which models to follow, they employed "organizational hedging that crosses and combines disparate evaluative principles" (Stark 1996: 1014). Crafting new combinations of symbolic and structural elements, Hungarian agents were engaged in "rebuilding organizations and institutions not *on the ruins* but *with the ruins* of communism as they redeploy available resources in response to their immediate practical dilemmas" (Stark 1996: 995; italics in original).[9]

Relational Systems

Connections or linkages characterize all manner of things, from words and sentences in paragraphs, to websites, and the food chain. Here we emphasize social connections among individuals, groups, and organizations and the ways in which these channels carry institutional materials. McAdam et al. (2001: 22) stress the value of a relational perspective that allows us to view "social interaction, social ties, communication, and conversation not merely as expressions of structure, rationality, consciousness, or culture but as active sites of creation and change." Strang and Meyer (1993) distinguish between relational and symbolic carriers of institutions. They point out that designs emphasizing relational carriers are based on social realist models, which assume that social actors are relatively independent entities who must be connected by specific networks or communication links if diffusion is to occur. By contrast, if symbolic carriers are privileged, "diffusion processes often look more like complex exercises in the social construction of identity than like the mechanistic spread of information" (Strang and Meyer 1993: 489).

In recent years, researchers interested in the diffusion of institutional ideas and forms have made extensive use of network measures and methods in examining these flows. Measures, including distance, centrality, clustering, density, structural equivalence, and centralization, have been employed to examine their effects on the rate of flow or type of information disseminated.[10] For example, researchers have pointed out that similar or closely related ideas are likely to flow between friends and close associates. "Particularly when organized by homophily, strong ties lead actors to take the perspective of the other and to exert powerful pressures for conformity" (Strang and Soule 1998: 272). By contrast, following research by Granovetter (1973) and others, contacts with individuals or organizations differing from oneself—"weak" ties—are associated with the transmission of new or different ideas so that, as noted in Chapter 5, institutional agents introducing innovations are likely to be situated in networks that cross conventional boundaries.

A multitude of studies on interlocking directorates in corporations—organizations that share board members—suggests that such connections are more likely to function as "weak" ties, providing organizations with information regarding the ways in which other organizations are dealing with one or another problem. Differing kinds of information travel through different networks. For example, a study by Davis and Greve (1997) compared the diffusion patterns of two recent governance innovations, "golden parachutes" and "poison pills," adopted by many U.S. corporations in response to the takeover waves of the 1980s.[11] Parachutes, perceived to principally advantage incumbent executives of takeover targets, were found to diffuse among Fortune 500 firms slowly during the period 1980 to 1989. Their adoption was primarily related to geographic proximity: "Firms adopted to the extent that other firms in the same metropolitan area had done so" (p. 29). By contrast, pills, perceived as protecting the integrity of the firm against hostile takeover attempts, diffused rapidly after their introduction in 1985, their spread being strongly related to the pattern of board interlocks among firms. Thus, the spread of parachutes was associated with firm ties to local (regional) companies, whereas the spread of pills was associated with links to national elite networks. More important, Davis and Greve propose that the two innovations were associated with different carriers and exhibited different diffusion patterns because they involved different institutional elements. Pills acquired "substantial normative legitimation in the eyes of the directors adopting them" (p. 33) and diffused via formally constituted national networks, whereas the spread of parachutes was based more on their cognitive legitimacy—the information available locally to managers that others occupying the same role had secured such protections.

Gaps or "structural holes" often exist in networks. Such conditions provide important opportunities for actors who can seize the chance to link together two or more previously unconnected social sites (Burt 1992). As McAdam et al. (2001: 26) point out, *brokerage* is an important relational mechanism for relating groups and individuals in stable sites; alternatively, *mobilization* can be employed during periods of unrest to bring together previously disconnected parties.

A largely neglected topic playing a central role in relational carriers is the existence and increasing importance to a wide variety of *intermediary roles*—roles defined almost entirely by the activities they perform in carrying information between central players in organizational fields. Ranging from consultants to librarians to lobbyists to advertising and rating agencies, the existence of these and other information intermediaries is vital to the functioning of any complex field (see Sahlin-Andersson and Engwall 2002). For example, McDonough, Ventresca, and Outcalt (2000) examined the role played by high school counselors, private counselors, and college admissions officers in mediating the selection and flow of students in the field of higher education. By focusing on contrasting interests and roles and on conflicts over values and meanings, they attempt to speed "the shift away from more disembodied social processes to situated social practices, [which] directs our attention to *how* activities take shape, the mechanisms by which forms emerge, acquire stability, and experience challenges to that stability" (p. 378).

Activities

Building on the work of ethnomethodologists (see Chapter 2), a new cadre of scholars led by Bruno Latour (1987) and Michel Callon (1998) have reformulated the cognition-action duality to give priority to action: suggesting that the "doing" often precedes and constructs the "knowing." This work emphasizes that categories and classifications often follow from, rather than guide, action by actors attempting to cope with their ongoing situations. They propose that action can be *performative,* contributing to the construction of the reality that it describes (Powell and Colyvas 2008). In these and other ways, scholars from the action-network and institutional work schools, have worked to reestablish the equal status, if not the priority of, action over structure. And, as noted, scholars stressing "institutional work" (e.g., Lawrence, Suddaby, and Leca 2009), have effectively enlarged the repertory of activities having significant institutional repercussions. In addition to activities that *reproduce* ongoing institutions, thereby acting to maintain and reinforce them, they add others such as *creation* or *innovation* and *disruption*. The act of consciously and publically disrupting existing societal beliefs, rules, and norms can destabilize a long-lasting regime, as demonstrated by the self-immolation of a Libyan street vendor setting off the social upheavals of the "Arab spring." Other activity-based mechanisms identified by social movement scholars such as McAdam and colleagues (2001) include *repression* and *radicalization.*

Structuration theorists attempt to reconnect culture and behavior, ideas, and actions by theorizing their mutuality and interdependence. Feldman and Pentland (2003: 101–102) applied these arguments to routines, suggesting that routines incorporate an ideal or schematic ("ostensive") aspect and a "performance" aspect—"the specific actions taken by specific people at specific times when they are engaged in an organizational routine." Thus, routines involve both a generalized idea and a particular enactment. In this manner, they propose to reintroduce ideas, but also agency, back into the concept of routines. To carry out a routine is not simply to "reenact" the past, but to engage with and adapt to the context in ways that require "either idiosyncratic or ongoing changes and reflecting on the meaning of actions for future realities" (p. 95).

As discussed in Chapter 4, routines are indispensable in carrying information residing in the tacit knowledge of actors. Such information travels by direct contact among actors occupying similar roles and engaged in closely related activities. We have already described the importance of on-the-job training for many types of work. The concept of "communities of practice" (Brown and Duguid 1991) helps to extend such learning opportunities beyond the confines of a single organization. A good part of the power and attraction of network forms of organization are the opportunities they afford organizations and their participants to acquire the "sticky" knowledge embedded in the routines of other organizations—offset with the concern that there may be a "leakage" of their own proprietary knowledge to alliance partners or subsidiaries (see Oxley 1999).

Artifacts

As noted in Chapter 4, although artifacts—tools, equipment, and technology—appear as hard and unyielding, like activities they lend themselves to a structuration perspective. As Orlikowski (1992) detailed, artifacts in use are adapted and modified by their users. Barley (1986) notes that technologies are not determinant, but rather their introduction provides an occasion for structuration. The introduction of the same technology produced different effects on the practices of uses, as well as on the organization structures incorporating them. Previously discussed mechanisms such as interpretation, bricolage, and translation can be applied to artifacts as well as other types of carriers.

Artifacts, like resources, contain important material aspects, but their meaning and use can vary over time and space. As Sewell (1992: 19) argues, they "embody cultural schemas whose meaning . . . is never entirely unambiguous."

❖ CONCLUDING COMMENT

Because institutions are comprised of multiple elements, they spread through differing mechanisms. Regulatory institutions advance largely because they provide increasing returns to those who manage them. Normative institutions flourish on the basis of increasing shared commitments among the parties and the shaping of identities for the actors involved. Cultural-cognitive institutions depend, for their power and influence, on widening the circle of those who accept their claims as valid and self-evident.

How institutions persist, once created, is an understudied phenomenon. Our current understanding of social structures is that their persistence is not to be taken for granted. It requires continuing effort—both to "talk the talk" and to "walk the walk"—if structures are not to erode and dissolve. The ecological explanation for persistence—inertia—seems on reflection to be too passive and unproblematic to be an accurate aid to guide studies of this topic.

By contrast, the diffusion of institutional forms over time and space has attracted considerable research attention across diverse scientific communities. Diffusion is of interest to the more theoretically oriented as a palpable indicator of increasing institutional strength, although more attention needs to be given to the strength of normative and cultural supports for these changes. To those of a more practical bent and in a culture emphasizing modernity, such changes are viewed as a sign of progress and receptivity to innovation. Each of the elements—regulatory, normative, and cultural cognitive—has been shown to enable and support the diffusion of institutional ideas and forms. Most studies of diffusion embrace a demand-side perspective, focusing attention on the characteristics of adopting systems. However, a supply-side approach, focusing on the nature of the dissemination agents, appears as useful, if not more useful, in examining instances of contemporary institutional diffusion.

Diffusion, of necessity, highlights the role of institutional carriers who, depending on the type of message and the type of messenger, utilize various mechanisms, including theorization, framing, bricolage, brokerage, and mobilization, that affect the meaning of the messages transmitted. Institutions are modified in transmission.

❖ NOTES

1. "Unusual" features refer, in particular, to the persistence of technical systems that, by objective tests, were demonstrably inferior to available alternatives. The canonical example is the continuing dominance of the QWERTY keyboard of the typewriter (and the word processor) (David 1985).

2. Note that their model resembles that developed by Suchman (1995a), as discussed in Chapter 5 (see Figure 5.1).

3. A related, empirical study of the adoption by Canadian law firms of a new organizational template employs the concept of "sedimentation" somewhat differently to refer to situations in which an existing template is not replaced by the new, but rather layered on the old, providing a different, hybrid structure (Cooper, Hinings, Greenwood, and Brown 1996).

4. Some have suggested that the new version of the "golden rule" is he or she who holds the gold makes the rules (Pfeffer 1992: 83). Still rules can operate to constrain the arbitrary exercise of power (see Dornbusch and Scott 1975).

5. This is not meant to imply that institutional processes are only relevant to the retention phase. They also play a significant role in the variation phase (e.g., affecting the cognitive frames determining which models are devised) as well as the selection phase (where concerns for legitimacy often determine which models survive).

6. This study also shows that the endorsement of management associations came over time to be more strongly associated with hospital survival than those of medical associations, indicating, we believe, a change during the study period (1950–2000) in the salience of prevailing institutional logics in the health care field.

7. In addition to those noted above, see also Davis, Diekmann, and Tinsley's (1994) examination of the processes involved in the delegitimation of the conglomerate form in business enterprise; Greve's (1995) analysis of the abandonment by radio stations of one format for another; Zilber's (2002) study of changes over time in the meanings associated with organizational action; and Simons and Ingram's (1997) study of the gradual abandonment of ideological commitments regarding the use of labor by Israeli kibbutzim.

8. This section draws on materials first published in Scott (2003a).

9. For a helpful discussion of these and related mechanisms, see Campbell (2004: Ch. 3).

10. For a summary of definitions and measures employed in network studies, see Scott and Davis (2007: Ch. 11) and Smith-Doerr and Powell (2005).

11. "Golden parachutes" provide severance benefits to top executives unemployed after a successful takeover. "Poison pills" give shareholders the right to buy shares at a two-for-one rate in the event of a hostile takeover attempt (Davis and Greve 1997: 10).

7

Institutional Processes and Organizations

The device by which an organism [or organization] maintains itself stationary at a fairly high level of orderliness . . . really consists in continually sucking orderliness from its environment.

—Erwin Schrödinger (1945: 75)

To date, the lion's share of research on institutional processes by organizational scholars has focused on their effects on individual organizations. It is not surprising that at the onset, organizational scholars should attend to institutions only insofar as they affect the structure and functioning of organizations, although this narrow focus broadened over time. In this chapter, I review representative arguments and associated evidence. Earliest studies emphasized the effects of institutional context on all organizations within the relevant environment. The institutional environment was viewed as unitary and as imposing structures or practices on individual organizations to which it was obliged to conform either because it was taken for granted that this was the proper way to organize, because to do so would result in normative approbation, or because it was required by legal or other rule-like frameworks. Later scholars came to recognize that many if not most organizations operate in complex institutional environments and confront fragmented and contending institutional pressures. Also, later studies began to examine differences among organizations, recognizing that whether, when, and how organizations responded depended on their individual characteristics or connections. Recent theorists and researchers have stressed the varied nature of organizational responses to institutional demands. In some situations, individual organizations respond strategically, either by decoupling their structures from their operations or by seeking to defend themselves in some manner from the pressures experienced. In others, the demands are negotiated as organizations collectively attempt to shape institutional requirements and redefine environments. I review examples of studies that address these issues.

❖ ORGANIZATIONS AND INSTITUTIONS: THREE VIEWS

Three views are encountered in current writings about the relation between organizations and institutions. The first, most clearly developed by Douglas North (1990: 4–5) and embraced by many institutional economists, is based on a game analogy: Institutions provide the rules of the game, whereas organizations act as the players. Organizations may well assist in constructing the rules, attempting to devise rules favorable to themselves, and they often attempt to change the rules by political and other means. However, a consideration of rules and rule-setting and enforcement processes is to be clearly distinguished from concern with the players' response to an existing set of rules. In his own work, North has attended primarily to the processes involved in constructing institutional rule systems.

Occupying a somewhat intermediate position, theorists such as Oliver Williamson (1975; 1985) view organizations, and their structures and procedures, as institutions: systems designed to exercise governance over production systems and minimize transaction costs. As noted, Williamson (1994) emphasizes the regulative aspects of institutions. However, rather than focusing attention on the "background conditions" involving property rights, contract law, and the like—the wider institutional environment—he attends to the impact of these rules on the organization of economic activities at the level of individual economic enterprises. Designers of organizations construct institutional forms—governance structures—to more effectively manage economic transactions. In a parallel manner, but emphasizing normative forces as described in Chapter 6, Selznick (1957) examines the ways in which individual organizations devise distinctive character structures over time, developing commitments that channel and constrain future behavior in the service of their basic values. For scholars such as Williamson and Selznick, organizations are relatively distinct institutions that are either designed by or evolve out of the choices made by organizational agents.

Sociologists including Meyer, Zucker, and Dobbin act to elide the distinction between organizations and their institutional environments by stressing the strong connection between processes occurring at societal (and even transnational) levels and the structure and operation of individual organizations. Focusing on the cultural-cognitive aspects of institutions, organizational sociologists emphasize the extent to which the modern organization is itself an institutionalized form—in Zucker's (1983: 1) phrase, "the preeminent institutional form in modern society." Unlike economists, who view organizational systems as reflecting "natural" economic laws, these sociologists insist that "rationalized organizational practices are essentially cultural, and are very much at the core of modern culture precisely because modern culture is organized around instrumental rationality" (Dobbin, 1994a: 118). Not only is our overall conception of an instrumental organization based on a cultural model, but many of the components comprising any given organization are not locally designed to produce efficiency in a specific context, but taken "off the shelf" of available patterns. As Meyer and Rowan (1977) point out:

> The growth of rationalized institutional structures in society makes formal organizations more common and more elaborate. Such institutions are myths which make formal organizations both easier to create and more necessary. After all, the building blocks for organizations come to be littered around the societal landscape; it takes only a little entrepreneurial energy to assemble them into a structure. (p. 345)

Again we see the wide range of assumptions and arguments guiding contemporary institutional studies.

❖ LEGITIMACY, ISOMORPHISM, AND COUPLING

Suchman (1995b: 571) correctly points out that legitimacy has become "an anchor-point of a vastly expanded theoretical apparatus addressing the normative and cognitive forces that constrain, construct, and empower organizational actors." The general concept of legitimacy is defined and discussed in Chapter 3. Weber was among the first social theorists to call attention to the central importance of legitimacy in social life. In his theoretical and historical work, he gave particular attention to those forms of action that were guided by a belief in the existence of a legitimate order, a set of "determinable maxims" providing models viewed by the actor as "in some way obligatory or exemplary for him" (Weber 1924/1968, Vol. 1: 31). In his analysis of administrative systems, both public and private, Weber examined the changing sources of legitimation as traditional values or a belief in the charismatic nature of the leader increasingly gave way to a reliance on rational/legal underpinnings. Organizations were regarded as legitimate to the extent that they were in conformity to rational (e.g., scientific) prescriptions and legal or law-like frameworks.

Parsons (1956/1960a) applied the concept of legitimacy to the assessment of organizational goals. As specialized subsystems of larger societal structures, organizations are under normative pressure to ensure that their goals are congruent with wider societal values, as described in Chapter 2. The focus of the organization's value system "must be the legitimation of this goal in terms of the functional significance of its attainment for the superordinate system" (Parsons 1956/1960a: 21). This conception of legitimacy, emphasizing the consistency of organizational goals with societal functions, was later embraced by Pfeffer and colleagues (Dowling and Pfeffer 1975; Pfeffer and Salancik 1978).

Meyer and Rowan (1977) shifted the focus from organizational goals to the structural and procedural aspects of organizations. The structural vocabulary of modern organizations—their emphasis on formality, offices, specialized functions, rules, records, and routines—was seen to be guided by and reflect prescriptions conveyed by wider rationalized institutional environments. These rule-like prescriptions are based on "norms of rationality"—on cultural beliefs, not only on the technical requirements associated with adapting to complex networks and social exchanges. These structures signal rationality irrespective of their effects on outcomes. The master proposition they advanced was that, "independent of their productive efficiency, organizations which exist in highly elaborated institutional environments and succeed in becoming isomorphic with these environments gain the legitimacy and resources needed to survive" (p. 352).

The principle of isomorphism was first applied to organizations by human ecologist Amos Hawley (1968), who argued that "units subjected to the same environmental conditions . . . acquire a similar form of organization" (see also Hawley 1950). Ecologists proposed that isomorphism resulted from competitive processes because organizations were pressured to assume the form best adapted to survival in a particular environment (see Hannan and Freeman 1989), whereas neoinstitutionalists Meyer and Rowan (1977) emphasized the importance of "social fitness": the acquisition of a form regarded as legitimate in a given institutional environment. DiMaggio and Powell (1983: 147) reinforced this emphasis on institutional isomorphism, focusing attention on coercive, normative, and mimetic mechanisms that "make organizations more similar without necessarily making them more efficient." More so than Meyer and Rowan, DiMaggio and Powell recognized that the models developed and the mechanisms inducing isomorphism among structural features operate most strongly within delimited organization fields, rather than at more diffuse, societal levels. (Chapter 8 is devoted to the discussion of organization fields.)

Meyer and Rowan (1977) also argued that while organizations conform to institutional pressures by adopting appropriate structures and rules, the activities of participants are often "decoupled" from these formal structures. That is, the actual behavior of organizational members frequently does not conform to official prescriptions or accounts. They propose two explanations for this departure: (1) local demands for efficiency of performance may conflict with externally generated pressures for ceremonial structural conformity; and (2) because the ceremonial rules "may arise from different parts of the environment, the rules may conflict with one another" (p. 355).

Meyer and Rowan's isomorphism and decoupling arguments help to account for two notable features of all contemporary organizations. First, there exists a remarkable similarity in the structural features of organizational forms operating within the same organizational field. One college tends to resemble another college, and one hospital is much like other hospitals. The recognition that organizations must not only be viable in terms of whatever competitive processes are at work, but must also exhibit structural features that make them both recognizable and in conformity with normative and regulative requirements, goes a long way to explaining observed similarities among organizations in the same arena. Second, students of organizations at least since Barnard (1938) have long observed the presence of formal and informal structures, the former reflecting officially sanctioned offices and ways of conducting business, the latter actual patterns of behavior and work routines. An uneasy tension exists between these structures. What was not clear until the work of the neoinstitutionalists is why such tensions exist. Even more fundamentally, if they are disconnected from the work being performed, why do the formal structures exist at all? By positing an environment consisting not only of production pressures and technical demands (the "task" environment), but also of regulative, normative, and cultural-cognitive elements (the "institutional" environment), the relatively independent sources of informal versus formal structures are revealed.

Arguments regarding decoupling have been controversial and attracted considerable attention from the outset of neoinstitutional theory. It is useful to put them in a larger perspective. Since the rise of the "open system" perspective in the late 1950s, scholars have recognized that "loose coupling"—a realization that these systems "contain elements that are only weakly connected to others and capable of fairly autonomous actions" (Scott and Davis 2007: 93; see also Buckley 1968; Weick 1976)—is a conspicuous feature of all social systems. Organizations, in particular, incorporate human actors of varying types and interests who are capable of independent action, and these actors are located in multiple units, many of which operate with only minimal central control. They are known to deal with external demands by developing specialized administrative units that deal with divergent demands by "mapping" these concerns into their own structures; for example, firms develop an internal legal unit to deal with legal demands (Buckley 1967; Thompson 1967/2003).

Organizations under pressure to adopt particular structures or procedures may opt to respond in a ceremonial manner, making changes in their formal structures to signal conformity, but then buffering internal units, allowing them to operate independent of these pressures. Although this is certainly a possible response, Meyer and Rowan imply that this response is widespread. Indeed, some theorists treat decoupling as the hallmark of an institutional argument. I believe this interpretation to be incorrect.

To begin, these decoupled responses are often seen to be merely symbolic, the organizational equivalent of smoke and mirrors (see Perrow 1985). However, to an institutionalist, the adjective *merely* does not fit comfortably with the noun *symbolic*. The use of symbols involving processes by which an organization connects to the wider world of meaning exerts great social power (see Brunsson 1989; Pfeffer 1981). Second, numerous studies suggest that, although organizations may create boundary and buffering units for symbolic reasons, these structures have a life of their own. Personnel employed in these units often play a dual role: They both transmit and translate environment demands to organizations, but also represent organizational concerns to institutional agents (see Hoffman 1997; Taylor 1984). In addition, the very existence of such units signals compliance. Edelman (1992) elaborates this argument in her discussion of organizational responses to equal employment opportunity/affirmative action (EEO/AA) requirements:

> Structural elaboration is merely the first step in the process of compliance. Once EEO/AA structures are in place, the personnel who work with or in those structures become prominent actors in the compliance process: they give meaning to law as they construct definitions of compliance within their organizations. . . . But while actors within organizations struggle to construct a definition of compliance, structural elaboration signals attention to law, thus helping to preserve legitimacy. (p. 1544)

Rather than assuming that decoupling automatically occurs, we should treat this as an empirical question: When and under what conditions do organizations adopt requisite structures but then fail to carry out the associated activities? Consistent with our pillars framework, which elements are involved can be expected to affect the response. Organizations are more likely to practice decoupling when confronted with external regulatory requirements than with normative or cognitive-cultural demands. Thus, research by Coburn (2004: 233), who studied the effect of curricular changes in elementary school reading programs, found that teachers were more likely to respond to "normative messages than to regulative messages by incorporating them into their classroom and doing so in ways that altered their preexisting practice." Organizations are also more likely to decouple structure from practice when there are high symbolic gains from adoption but equally high costs associated with implementation. Westphal and Zajac (1994) studied the behavior of 570 of the largest U.S. corporations over two decades when such firms were adopting long-term CEO compensation plans in an attempt to better align CEO incentives with stockholder interests. Although many companies adopted these plans, a substantial number failed to use them to restructure executive compensation within a subsequent 2-year period. Adoption of a plan was found to enhance organizational legitimacy with stockholders and stock purchasers. Westphal and Zajac (1994; 1998) found that plan adoptions, regardless of whether they were used, resulted in improved market prices, and they found adoption to be associated with greater

CEO influence over the board. At the same time, use of these plans could negatively impact CEO compensation. Accordingly, the researchers found that nonimplementation was also associated with greater CEO influence. In addition, Westphal and Zajac (1994) observed the familiar pattern involving late versus early adoption: Late adopters were less likely to implement the plan than early adopters, suggesting that decoupling is more likely to occur among reluctant adopters responding to strong normative pressures. (For reviews of other studies concerning the conditions under which decoupling occurs, see Boxenbaum and Jonsson 2008.)

Finally, a helpful approach to examining coupling processes in organizations is proposed by Hallett and Ventresca (2006), who revisit Gouldner's (1954) classic study of industrial bureaucracy (see Chapter 2). They suggest that too much neoinstitutional research concentrates attention on wider environmental institutional frames—macro institutional orders—and so defocalizes the ways in which new meaning systems—micro institutional orders—arise through social interaction. As an alternative, they propose "a doubly constructed view": on the one hand, institutions provide templates and guidelines for organizations; on the other hand, "the meaning of institutions are constructed and propelled forward by social interactions" among organizational participants (Hallett and Ventresca 2006: 213). Gouldner studied a gypsum company being subjected to wider rationalizing pressures and describes how these institutional forces were mediated and interpreted by participants within varying organizational subsystems (in particular, the office versus the mine), giving rise to diverse meanings and responses.

In sum, there are good theoretical reasons for attending to isomorphism among organizational models and formal structures, and in the following sections I review additional research examining isomorphic pressures. However, to treat the existence of structural isomorphism as the litmus test for detecting institutional processes oversimplifies the complexity and subtlety of social systems. Varying, competing institutions and multiple institutional elements are often at work. Although they constitute new forms, they also interact with a variety of previously existing forms with varying characteristics and in differing locations. Similarly, to treat decoupling as an automatic response to external institutional pressures has been shown to be oversimplified and misleading. Participants in organizations interpret these pressures in varying ways and construct a variety of responses, some of which may be strategically motivated, as discussed in a later section.

Varying Elements and Organizational Legitimacy

The meaning of legitimacy and the mechanisms associated with its transmission vary somewhat with the three institutional elements, as previewed in Chapters 3 and 6. General effects of institutional processes on organizational structures are readily apparent, but often overlooked. They become most visible when a longer time period is considered. A clear instance of the effects of regulatory forces—combined with cultural-cognitive constitutive processes—on for-profit organizations is represented by the structuring influence of incorporation statutes. These social arrangements, allowing for the pooling of capital from many sources along with limitations on liability for those who managed these assets, were created early in the 18th century in England, but the misadventures of the South Sea Company set back the acceptance of these forms until the mid-1800s (Micklethwait and Wooldridge 2003: Ch. 2). In its early development, the corporate form was restricted to enterprises pursuing broadly public purposes, such as turnpikes and canals, but gradually it was appropriated for use by private firms, as detailed by social historians Seavoy (1982) and Roy (1997). Individually crafted charters granted by state legislatures were replaced by generic statutes providing a legal template for incorporation available to a wide range of organizations. These legal (and cultural) changes were associated with the rapid expansion of business enterprise in England and the United States during the second half of the 19th century, fueled in good part in America by competition among the several states to pass legislation favorable to businesses wishing to incorporate.

The effect on organizational structure of normative influences is illustrated by the distinctive features of the American community hospital. During the late 19th and early 20th centuries, American physicians consolidated their social and cultural authority, upgraded their training systems, and exercised increasingly strong jurisdictional controls over the medical domain (Starr 1982). Although they became increasingly dependent on hospitals, which provided the technical equipment, laboratory facilities, and nursing services required for effective acute care, physicians were able to remain independent of administrative controls, organizing themselves into an autonomous medical staff to oversee clinical activities. This dual control structure—one administrative, the other professional-collegial—provided the organizing principle for community hospitals in the United States throughout the 20th century (White 1982). Only during the most recent decades have managerial interests begun to exert more direct controls over rank-and-file physicians in hospitals (see Scott, Ruef, Mendel, and Caronna 2000).

The power of shared cultural models as a basis for organizing is highlighted in Knorr-Certina's (1999) study of high-energy physics and molecular biology laboratories. She argues that, more so than most types of organizations, the structural blueprint for these knowledge societies is object- rather than person-centered. The work takes place in the context of shared scientific knowledge—"distributed cognition, which then also functions as a management mechanism: through this discourse, work becomes coordinated and self-organization is made possible" (p. 242–243). Moreover, legitimation of these organizations is based on the congruence between the theories and practices of these laboratories and the wider scientific community of which they are a part. Many of the distinctive features of professional organizations are possible because of the unobtrusive controls exercised by shared symbolic systems linking actors to the objects of their work based in understandings grounded in their invisible colleges.

We can supplement these more historical and process-oriented accounts with studies employing quantitative approaches. These studies provide evidence of the increasing variety and sophistication of indicators employed. With regard to studies emphasizing the cultural-cognitive pillar, as noted, some scholars infer legitimacy from the prevalence of an organizational form (Carroll and Hannan 1989), and others interpret the increasing diffusion of a form as an indication of increasing legitimacy (Tolbert and Zucker 1983). These indirect and somewhat controversial measures tap into the cultural-cognitive and, to some extent, the normative dimensions of legitimacy. However, more direct measures of cultural cognitive support are based on a variety of archival materials utilized to measure changes in meaning systems and legitimating ideologies. For example, in studies described in Chapter 8, investigators have measured changes in legitimating "institutional logics" as assessed by changes in professional discourse or media coverage (e.g., Rao, Monin, and Durand 2003; Scott et al. 2000). In an imaginative approach, Zuckerman (1999) assessed the "illegitimacy discount" imposed by stock analysts on those firms whose markets did not match conventional industry-based classifications.

Employing a more individual-level approach to legitimacy processes, Elsbach (1994: 58) conducted studies combining impression management and institutional theories to examine how organizational agents "use verbal accounts or explanations to avoid blame or gain credit for controversial events that affect organizational legitimacy."

Managers of companies in the cattle industry in California were asked to respond to a number of controversial events occurring within the industry, and their responses were evaluated by informants representing influential groups (e.g., media, public officials). These qualitative studies provided the inputs for an experiment in which varying combinations of situations (vignettes) and company responses were reported to experimental subjects who then rated the legitimacy accorded to the organization. Acknowledgments of problems in contrast to denials, and references to widely institutionalized procedures in contrast to technical measures, led to higher legitimacy scores.

Analysts emphasizing the normative pillar have stressed measures that assess certification and accreditation procedures utilized by professional associations (e.g., Casile and Davis-Blake 2002; Mezias 1995; Ruef and Scott 1998), opinions expressed by the public media (e.g., Hybels and Ryan 1996), and the endorsement of established community organizations such as schools and religious organizations (e.g., Baum and Oliver 1992). Ventresca and Mohr (2002: 811) point out that the latter shift analysts' attention away from measures that "emphasize organizations as independent objects toward the measurement of relations among objects and the inherent connectivity of social organization."

Scholars favoring the regulative view of institution utilize measures that stress the extent to which organizations are under the jurisdiction of a given authority (e.g., Hannan and Carrol 1987; Tolbert and Zucker 1983), whether enforcement is vigorous or lax (Dobbin and Sutton 1998), and whether a specific organization has been approved by a licensing body or, conversely, has been subject to sanctions by an enforcement authority (e.g., Deephouse 1996; Singh, Tucker, and House 1986).

These and related studies demonstrate that it is possible to develop measures of legitimating processes in modern society, such that these institutional forces need not simply be asserted or assumed, but are subject to being assessed with empirical evidence. (For additional summaries and discussions of such studies, see Boxenbaum and Jonsson 2008; Deephouse and Suchman 2008; Greenwood, Raynard, Kodeih, Micelotta, and Lounsbury 2011; Kraatz and Block 2008.)

Varying Sources and Salience

The sources of legitimation are many and diverse in today's complex and differentiated societies. Virtually all are themselves organizations, including the state and professional associations, although some organizations, such as the media and rating agencies, serve as conduits for collecting the assessments of members of more general or specialized publics (Deephouse and Suchman 2008). Who—which agencies or publics—has the right to confer legitimacy on organizations of a given type may not be a simple question in environments characterized by complexity or conflict. It is a truism of modern organization studies that organizations are highly differentiated, loosely coupled systems, in part because they must relate to many different environments. Universities, for example, relate not only to educational accreditation agencies and professional disciplinary associations, but also to federal agencies overseeing research grants and contracts and student loans, to the National Collegiate Athletic Association for sports activities, to local planning and regulatory bodies for building and roads, among many other oversight bodies (see Richardson and Martinez 2009; Stern 1979; Wiley and Zald 1968).

In his study of commercial banks operating in the Minneapolis– St. Paul metropolitan area, Deephouse (1996) examined the effects of two different sources of legitimation: state regulatory agencies that made onsite assessments of the safety and soundness of a bank's assets and metropolitan newspapers who reported information to the public about banking activities. Both sources were found to be positively associated with isomorphism in the asset strategies pursued by banks. Banks that experienced fewer enforcement actions from regulatory agencies and banks that received a higher proportion of positive reports in the public media were more likely to exhibit conformity to the industry average in their strategies for distributing assets across various categories of borrowers, such as commercial, real estate, and individual loans. This finding held up after the differences in their age, size, and performance (return on assets) was taken into account. Both of the legitimation sources were significantly associated with strategic isomorphism, although there was only a modest association of .34 between measures of regulatory assessment and public endorsement. This result suggests that legitimation sources vary in the attributes to which they attend in conferring legitimacy.

The salience of such legitimation agents can vary among organizational subunits or programs, and also over time. In our study of hospitals in the San Francisco Bay area, for example, Martin Ruef and I (Ruef and Scott 1998) found that accreditation by an assortment of medical bodies, such as the American College of Surgeons, was independent of (and, in some cases, negatively associated with) accreditation by various managerial bodies, such as the American Hospital Association. Although the endorsement of both types of accreditation agencies was positively associated with hospital survival throughout the period 1945 to 1995, the strength of this relation was found to vary over time. During the period before 1980, when professional medical associations exercised greater influence in the field, medical association accreditations were more strongly associated with hospital survival than were managerial endorsements, whereas after 1980, managerial accreditations were a stronger predictor of survival than medical endorsements. We argue that market and managerial logics have become more prevalent in the health care field since 1980, challenging and, to some degree, supplanting the logics of the medical establishment. It appears that the influence of various regulatory and normative bodies varies depending on the institutional logics dominant within the wider institutional environments.

In summary, individual organizations exhibiting culturally approved forms and activities (including strategies), receiving support from normative authorities, and having approval from legal bodies are more likely to survive than organizations lacking these evaluations. Legitimacy exerts an influence on organizational viability independent of its performance or other attributes or connections.

In the following section, I review arguments and related research concerning the effects of the institutional context on organizational structures. In much of this work, the underlying rationale implied is that the effects are due to legitimacy processes. However, other causal processes may also be at work.

❖ INSTITUTIONAL CONTEXT AND ORGANIZATIONAL STRUCTURE

Imprinting

Stinchcombe (1965) was the first theorist to call attention to the strong influences of social (including institutional) conditions present at the time of its founding on the structural form of an organization. He argued that "the organizational inventions that can be made at a particular time in history depend on the social technology available at the time" (p. 153). It is for this reason that organizations of the same type are founded in "spurts" followed by relatively slower growth. These organizations tend to exhibit similar structural characteristics, to be of roughly the same size, and to exhibit similar occupational and labor force characteristics. For example, new universities were founded in the United States mainly from 1870 to 1900, and those arriving either earlier or later were likely to exhibit different forms (p. 154). Of even more interest, the structural features adopted by organizations during the founding period are highly stable, tending to persist over long periods of time. In this sense, organizations are "imprinted" with the characteristics present at the time of their founding. The primary explanation for organizational imprinting is that of path dependence, the increasing returns associated with continuing in the same direction and the costs associated with developing alternative approaches (see Chapter 6). Moreover, as more organizations of the same time are created, their cognitive legitimacy increases (Carroll and Hannan 1989), so that their structural templates are reinforced.

These arguments have recently been extended to examine continuities in organizational forms created within a given societal context. Entire political economies have been observed to reflect particular configurations of beliefs, norms, and rules that persist over time and tend to shape both the types of organizations established and the ways in which they relate to one another. Thus, Whitley (1992b; 1999) has examined differences among societies in their prevailing "business recipes," their typical ways of structuring internal firm organization, relations among firms, and relations between firms and political authorities, and documents the persistence of these diverse arrangements over time. And Hall and Soskice (2001b) examine the persistence of differences in the ways in which societies structure and govern their market economies, with some countries favoring a "liberal" mode relying on arm's-length exchange of goods and services, whereas others opt for a more "coordinated" approach in which political authorities play a larger role. These divergent "varieties of capitalism" tend to persist over long periods of time, resisting the homogenizing pressures of globalization.

Schneiberg (2007) challenges those who would attempt to characterize entire societal systems in terms of their central institutional tendencies, pointing out that alternative forms of organizing often coexist within societies and their sectors and may persist over time. Noting that most accounts of U.S. industrial development stress the dominance of large firm, mass production, and for-profit corporations, he points out that across several industries and in several states, alternative cooperative or state-owned enterprises developed, were successful, and have been reproduced over time. Ranging from state-owned electric utilities to cooperative organizations in dairy, grain, and other agricultural sectors, to mutual insurance companies, these types of organizations flourished in many midwestern states from the 1830 to the 1920s. The existence and persistence of these alternative forms is explained by the success of the actions of a variety of religious and social movements, including the Populist Party and the Grange, that challenged dominant economic and political groups to carve out a space for more communal forms.

While earlier discussions viewed organizational imprinting as a relatively determinant, top-down process, these more recent treatments emphasize the role of active agents who shape the paths along which development occurs. Like Schneiberg, Johnson (2007) stresses the role of social and cultural entrepreneurs who piece together particular combinations of the social resources provided by macro-level conditions. Her analysis of the imprinting process that gave rise to the Paris opera stresses the creative bricolege required to create the hybrid form combining a royal charter's academic form with a commercial theatre model. She points out that

> an actor-based approach to organizational imprinting . . . calls for attention to the sequence and character of key moments in the founding processes and offers a corrective to the telescoping of founding processes into "founding conditions" typical of many ecological and some entrepreneurship studies. (p. 118)

Other studies emphasize the importance of founding entrepreneurs who actively shape the structure and strategy of the firms they found. For example, Boeker (1989) studied factors affecting the institutionalization of power differences present at the time of founding in a sample of 53 semiconductor companies. Boeker contrasts the impact of entrepreneurial and environmental effects present at the time of the firm's founding on current firm strategy. He found that the previous functional background of the entrepreneur influenced the selection of the firm's strategy, but also that this decision was independently influenced by the industry's stage of development at the time the firm was founded. Firm strategies were significantly impacted by industry stage in three of the four stages examined. For example, firms founded during the earliest era were more likely to embrace and continue to pursue first-mover strategies, whereas firms founded during the most recent period studied were more likely to develop and to pursue a niche strategy.

Cultural models of organizing precede the creation of organizations. Most organizational fields present not a single, but a (limited) number of organizational models or archetypes. Research by Baron, Hannan, and Burton (1999) assessed the types of models or blueprints governing employment practices present in the mind of the founding

CEOs in a sample of start-up firms engaged in computer hardware, software, and semiconductors in Silicon Valley. Examining the characteristics of these firms after their first few years of operation revealed that companies whose CEOs held a more bureaucratic conception of employment practices were more likely to exhibit higher managerial intensity (proportion of managers to full-time employees) than companies whose CEOs valued more egalitarian "commitment" models.

Environmental Complexity

Gradually, both theorists and researchers have come to realize that, although organizations confront and are shaped by institutions, these institutional systems are not necessarily unified or coherent. More generally, with the arrival of open system perspectives in the 1950s, organization theorists gradually shifted attention to not only the organization within an environment but the *organization of the environment.* Scholars such as Dill (1958), Emery and Trist (1967), Pfeffer and Salancik (1978), and Thompson (1967/2003) attempted to identify abstract dimensions along which organizational environments might vary, including amount of homogeneity-heterogeneity, stability-variability, extent of connectedness, and degree of munificence-scarcity of resources. However, these dimensions proved difficult to assess empirically and did not take into account the varying location or position of organizations operating within the "same" environment.

Many of these problems became more tractable as researchers recognized that environments vary greatly depending on type of organization: We began to focus attention on more discrete contexts such as the particular sector or field within which the organization was operating. I devote Chapter 8 to discussing more fully the concept of organization field and to research conducted at this level. Here I call attention to two different but potentially compatible foci of research on environmental complexity: relational structure and institutional logics.

Relational Complexity

In developing our approach to the analysis of "societal sectors," Meyer and I wished to call attention to the effects on organizations of the wider relational systems within which they were embedded. Prior research had concentrated on local exchanges among organizations in the same community (e.g., Warren 1967), whereas we emphasized the importance of nonlocal and vertical ties, for example, the connections of local schools to district and state systems, or the ties of local banks to corporate headquarters and regulatory agencies (Scott and Meyer 1983). We identified a number of variables, such as centralization of decision making and fragmentation of the decision-making structure—among authorities at the same or differing levels and among types of decisions (e.g., programmatic vs. funding)—arguing that organizations operating in more complex and fragmented systems were more likely to develop more complex and elaborated internal administrative structures, holding constant the complexity of their work processes. Powell (1988) found evidence consistent with this prediction in his study comparing a scholarly book publishing house and a public TV station. He concluded that "organizations, such as [the public television station] WNET, that are located in environments in which conflicting demands are made upon them will be especially likely to generate complex organizational structures with disproportionately large administrative components and boundary-spanning units" (p. 126). And Meyer, Scott, and Strang (1987) employed data on the administrative structure of districts and elementary and secondary schools to demonstrate that schools and districts depending more on federal funding, which involves many independent programs and budgetary categories, had disproportionately large administrative structures compared to schools relying primarily on state funding, which tended to be more integrated.

This research stream was pursued by Scott and Meyer (1987) and has been revived by Pache and Santos (2010), who consider the combined effects of fragmentation and centralization to suggest that the highest level of complexity for organizations is created by high fragmentation combined with moderate centralization. Such conditions are exemplified by scientific and professionally dominated organizations dependent on federal, state, and private funding, for example, arts organizations such as museums (Alexander 1996) and symphony orchestras (Glynn 2000), drug abuse treatment centers (D'Aunno, Sutton, and Price 1991), health care organizations (Scott et al. 2000), and biotechnology firms (Powell 1999). How organizations respond to such conditions is considered below.

Cultural Conflict

With the appearance of Friedland and Alford's influential essay in 1991, institutional scholars have attended increasingly to another, related facet of environmental complexity: conflicts in the cultural prescriptions available to guide and motivate organizational actions. As discussed in Chapter 4, such conflicts were seen as residing in "potentially contradictory interinstitutional systems," such as political, economic, or religious prescriptions. Interest in this topic has rapidly grown, as evidenced by the empirical and theoretical work of Thornton and colleagues (Thornton 2004; Thornton, Ocasio, and Lounsbury 2012) and by the review article by Greenwood and associates (2011), who discuss some 40 empirical studies conducted since 1991. Greenwood and colleagues point out that these studies vary in (1) the multiplicity of logics considered (are there more than two?), as well as (2) the degree to which such logics are incompatible (p. 332). Related to the latter difference is a variety of potential areas of disagreement, for example, over goals, means, appropriate material resources, appropriate human resources, the control of work, or the definition of organizational boundaries (Meyer and Scott 1983a: 204). Among the major types of conflicting logics examined have been various modes of artistic or aesthetic logics versus commercial logics (e.g., Jones and Thornton 2005; Lampel, Shamsie, and Lant 2006), various modes of professional logics (editorial, legal, medical) versus market logics (e.g., Brock, Powell, and Hinings 1999; Greenwood and Suddaby 2006), varying styles of business logics (collectivist vs. corporate; Haveman and Rao 1997), and conflicting cultural logics confronting multinational corporations operating in diverse countries (Seo and Creed 2002; see also Chapter 8).

Of course, a major issue posed for organizations operating in conflicting environments is how to secure and maintain their legitimacy. In an early formulation, Meyer and I suggested that "organizational legitimacy refers to the degree of cultural support for an organization—the extent to which the array of established cultural accounts provide explanations for its existence, functioning, and jurisdiction, and lack or deny alternatives" (Meyer and Scott 1983a: 201). A pluralistic, conflicted environment thus poses a major challenge for organizations in such contexts.

Organizational Responses to Complexity

The next section presents more general types of responses made by organizations to institutional demands, but here I concentrate particularly on responses to conflicting environmental prescriptions. Kraatz and Block (2008) provide a helpful classification of possible responses, including attempts (1) to eliminate or neutralize some of the demands made on them; (2) to compartmentalize, with different, loosely coupled subunits managing one or another set of demands, or by responding sequentially to them; (3) to "balance" disparate demands, playing constituencies off against each other; and (4) to embrace a hybrid or composite model, "forging a durable identity of their own, and to emerge as institutions in their own right" (p. 251). This latter alternative builds on Selznick's views that some organizations, under appropriate leadership, can craft their own identity around a distinctive set of value commitments (see Chapter 2). It also addresses the problem confronting every organization in its search for legitimacy: how to meet the changing demands of external constituencies while at the same time maintaining its commitments to its core values, being a "hostage to [its] own history" (Selznick 1992: 232).

Environmental forces induce changes not only by stimulating actions to redesign the structural features of organizations but by shaping the identities of organizations and their participants. As described in Chapter 5, some types of organizations successfully craft a recognizable identity that provides guidance to both participants and constituents. Organization identity emphasizes those features of an organization that differentiate it from other members of the same population and can shape both internal priorities as well as repertories of possible responses (Albert and Whetten 1985; Dutton and Dukerich 1991; Greenwood et al. 2011; King, Clemens, and Fry 2011). Environmental forces also impinge on organizations by introducing new identities into the mix of participants or by altering the identities of current members (see Glynn 2008). In his research on the effect of the environmental protection movement on chemical and petroleum industries, for example, Hoffman (1997) describes the changes that occurred as these energy companies began to hire environmental engineers and, gradually, to include them in their decision-making processes. More generally, Greenwood and Hinings (1996) point out that an important component of institutional change is the way in which environmental forces shape internal organizational power processes, as new types of actors are added, or as current actors are undercut or empowered by changing circumstances.

Another lens for examining effects on organizations of conflicted environments is found in the research of Heimer and Staffen (Heimer 1999; Heimer and Staffen 1998). They provide a detailed qualitative study of decision making in neonatal intensive care units at two Illinois teaching hospitals, artfully combining institutional and decision-making ideas and arguments. They focus on the conflicts occurring among three institutional spheres: families concerned with the welfare of their infant children, medical providers, and legal authorities, including both state regulators and private attorneys. They observed that these institutional systems influenced organizational decisions at three levels: (1) by shaping general rules and procedures, (2) by shaping the elements affecting decisions, and (3) by affecting the interests and relative power of the participants in the decision processes.

With respect to rules and procedures, many of the most fateful effects of legal and medical institutions occur in their impact on medical structures, including staffing patterns, mandated procedures, and documentation routines. While some of these features are ceremonial and may be decoupled from actual activities, many are hardwired and routinely enforced and enacted. In these respects many of the ways in which legal and medical institutions influence behavior in this setting are unobtrusive but pervasive. Civil law, for example, penetrates deeply into medical settings because medical insurers and risk managers insist that quality assurance specialists be employed to monitor outcome statistics and to investigate unexpected incidents. To consider the "elements affecting decisions," Heimer and Staffen employ Cohen, March, and Olsen's (1972) well-known "garbage can" model, which stresses the importance of who has the right to participate and whether or not they are present, who is able to authoritatively determine that a problem exists, who determines that a choice needs to be made, and who defines what an acceptable solution is. Considering these types of elements, medical personnel have a decided advantage since most of the decision situations occur in arenas controlled by them, and they are more likely to be present when a decision situation occurs. Medical personnel and state agents are "repeat players," while families are "almost consummate novices, using unfamiliar decision tools on unfamiliar medical problems" (Heimer 1999: 44). Finally, the interests and relative power of participants reflect in general the advantages of advanced training and control of turf, although family members, especially mothers, can claim extraordinary rights to protect the interest of their child.

❖ INTERACTIVE PROCESSES

Although all organizations in a given institutional field or sector are subject to the effects of institutional processes within the context, not all experience them in the same way or respond in the same manner. Just as social psychologists call attention to "individual differences"— differences among individuals in their definition of and response to the same situation—students of organization have increasingly attended to differences among organizations in their response to the same environment. I review here studies examining how adoption responses vary because of differences among organizations in the amount of pressure they experience, in their characteristics, or in their location within the field. In a later section of this chapter, I consider a broader array of responses by organizations to their institutional environments.

The general question addressed is: Why are some structures or practices adopted by some organizations, but not others in similar situations? Granted, simple adoption of a practice is not a strong indicator of "deep institutionalization" (Owen-Smith and Powell 2008: 596); diffusion is a necessary if not sufficient indicator of institutional change. This question is of interest not only to institutionalists, but also to students of the diffusion of innovation (see Abrahamson 1991; Rogers 1995; Strang and Soule 1998) and organizational learning (see Haunschild and Chandler 2008; Haunschild and Miner 1997; Ingram 2002; Levitt and March 1988). The latter ask in this connection: How do organizations learn both from their own experience and from the experience of others? Institutional arguments, emphasizing the effects of rules, norms, or constitutive beliefs, shade off into stratification and instrumental arguments, for example, that organizations imitate others whom they perceive to be successful or prestigious (see, e.g., Burns and Wholey 1993; Deephouse and Suchman 2008; Haunschild and Miner 1997; Haveman 1993). Many motives conduce toward conformity: fads, fashion, status enhancement, and vicarious learning. Not all mimetic behavior involves institutional processes.

A study by Kellogg (2011) details the ways in which new regulations adopted by the American Council for Graduate Medical Education to restrict the work hours of hospital residents to an 80-hour week were variously implemented in three hospitals in urban centers of the same region. Kellogg shows how the same macro-level normative pressures for reform were dependent for their success on the mobilization of reformers within the organization willing to fight for change against internal defenders. Macro-level reforms require the vigorous support of micro-level leaders if change is to be realized.

Variable Institutional Pressures

All organizations in the same field are not equally subject to the institutional processes at work there. Organizations vary in the extent to which they are under the jurisdictional authority or on the radar screen of oversight agencies. Regulative requirements regarding employee protections such as health and safety rules often apply only to organizations of a given size. Equal opportunity laws apply more clearly to public sector organizations and to organizations receiving federal grants and contracts than to other employers (see Dobbin 2009;

Dobbin, Edelman, Meyer, Scott, and Swidler 1988; Edelman 1992). As another example, Mezias (1990) examined the adopting of new procedures for reporting income tax credits by the 200 largest nonfinancial firms in the United States from 1962 to 1984. He discovered a number of organization-level factors that influenced adoption, including whether the firm was under the jurisdiction of the Interstate Commerce Commission. Casile and Davis-Blake (2002) found that business schools located in public universities were more responsive to changes in accreditation standards than those affiliated with private colleges.

Variation in institutional pressures also comes from differences over space and time in the strength of cognitive beliefs or normative controls. As described earlier in this chapter and in Chapter 5, both ecologists and institutional scholars view the increasing prevalence of a form or practice as an indicator of increasing legitimation. This process occurring over time has given rise to an interesting line of research that contrasts the characteristics of early versus late adopters. Two studies were particularly influential in shaping the arguments.

The first was the study of the diffusion of civil service reforms among municipalities at the turn of the 20th century conducted by Tolbert and Zucker (1983), portions of which were discussed in Chapter 6. Turning their attention to those states in which civil service was not mandated, Tolbert and Zucker show that its adoption by cities during the initial period varied according to their characteristics: Larger cities, those with higher proportions of immigrants and a higher proportion of white-collar to blue-collar inhabitants, were more likely to adopt the reform. The authors argue that these cities were rationally pursuing their interests, some local governments confronting more severe governance problems that encouraged them to adopt changes that would buffer them from "undesirable elements." Although such city characteristics were strongly predictive of adoption during the earliest period (1885–1904), in each subsequent period, the associations became weaker, so that by 1935, these variables no longer had any predictive power. The authors interpret these weakening correlations as evidence of the development of widespread and powerful cultural beliefs and norms supporting civil service reform, such that all cities were under increasing pressure to adopt the reform regardless of their local needs or circumstances.

The second study, by Fligstein (1985), was briefly discussed earlier, but merits more detailed examination. Fligstein tested a number of alternative arguments for why large firms adopted the multidivisional (M-form) structure. His data were collected to reflect five periods, each a decade between 1929 and 1979, and included information on the 100 largest U.S. industrial corporations for each period.[1] During the earlier periods, firms that were older, pursuing product-related strategies in their growth patterns, and headed by managers from sales or finance departments were more likely to adopt the M-form than firms lacking these characteristics. During the 1939 to 1949 time period, these same factors continued to operate, but another variable also became relevant. If firms were in industries in which other, similar firms had adopted the M-form, they were more likely to adopt this structure. All of the factors, with the exception of age, continue to be significantly correlated with M-form adoption during the last two decades included in the study.

Fligstein's study provides empirical support for two different versions of institutional arguments. The findings linking structural forms to strategies support Williamson's (1975) arguments that organizational managers attempt to devise governance structures that will economize on transactions costs—the alignment of structure with strategy. The findings relating M-form adoption to the number of other similar firms employing the structure are consistent with DiMaggio and Powell's (1983) views of mimetic—and normative—processes operating in uncertain environments.

These findings have been replicated in a number of later studies, some of which are described below. They suggest the following general pattern. In the early stages of an institutionalization process, adoption of the practice by organizations represents a choice on their part that can reflect their varying specific needs or interests. As the institutionalization process proceeds, normative and cultural pressures mount to the point where adoption becomes less of a choice and more of a requirement. Differences among individual organizations are of less consequence when confronted by stronger institutional imperatives. Although in one sense the logic of action has shifted from one of instrumentality to appropriateness, in another sense, the situation confronting each organization has changed so that it is increasingly in the interest of all to adopt the practice. Not to do so would be regarded as deviant, inattentive, or behind the times, resulting in a loss of legitimacy and, perhaps, attendant material resources. More generally, as Colyvas and Jonsson (2011: 33) conclude, "The analytic insight is that factors associated with adoption are likely to shift over time."

The question of what types of benefits are associated with early and late adoption is further explored in a study of over 2,700 U.S. hospitals encouraged to adopt total quality management (TQM) procedures in response to increased normative pressures from the Joint Commission on Accreditation of Healthcare Organizations. Westphal,

Gulati, and Shortell (1997) found that late adopters—hospitals slower to adopt these practices—conformed more highly to the pattern of practices implemented by other hospitals to which they were connected or to a particular, standardized approach, compared to early adopters. That is, hospitals adopting early were more likely to customize their TQM practices to their specific situation; those adopting later exhibited a more ritualistic pattern, mechanically following standard TQM models or imitating the practices of other hospitals with whom they were connected in alliances or systems. The adoption of TQM improved hospital legitimacy (overall ratings by the Joint Commission) for both early and late adopters, but only early adopters of TQM also improved their productivity and efficiency, as measured by a number of objective and subjective indicators. We see again that, although early and late adoption showed different effects, all hospitals adopting TQM improved their legitimacy and some improved their performance.

Organizational Factors Associated With Adoption

A generation of studies has attempted to identify what organizational features are associated with early adoption. Of course, these features vary greatly depending on the nature of the innovation. Most of the studies reviewed examine the adoption of some type of administrative innovation (e.g., new managerial structures or employment systems). A number of general characteristics appear to be associated with adoptive behavior. Without attempting to be comprehensive, I identify three classes of variables that have received attention from recent scholars.

Attributes

Organizations vary in many ways, but only a few of these differences have been found to be regularly associated with early adoption. Numerous studies have found that organization size is important, larger organizations being more prone to early adoption. Size effects have varying interpretations, each of which is conducive to receptivity. Larger organizations tend to be more resource-rich; larger organizations are more differentiated and, hence, more sensitive to environmental changes; and larger organizations are more visible to external publics, including governance bodies (see Dobbin et al. 1988; Edelman 1992; Greening and Gray 1994). Organizations that operate within or are more closely aligned with the public sector are more likely to be responsive to institutional pressures, particularly legal and regulatory requirements, but also normative pressures (see Dobbin et al. 1988; Edelman 1992; Casile and Davis-Blake 2002). Organizations possessing differentiated personnel offices are more likely to be receptive to innovations, particularly those pertaining to employment matters (Baron, Dobbin, and Jennings 1986; Baron, Jennings, and Dobbin 1988; Dobbin et al. 1988; Edelman 1992; Kalleberg, Knoke, Marsden, and Spaeth 1996). Unionization has been shown to affect selected types of adoption, in particular, grievance procedures and internal labor market practices (Pfeffer and Cohen 1984; Sutton, Dobbin, Meyer, and Scott 1994; Kalleberg et al. 1996). In private sector organizations, the characteristics of CEOs have been found to affect adoptive behavior. CEO background—for example, whether business experience comes from production, marketing, or finance (Fligstein 1985; 1990) and CEO power vis-à-vis the corporate board (Westphal and Zajac 1994)—is associated with the adoption of new structural forms and with CEO compensation protections and incentive systems. Firms experiencing turnover in their top management teams are more likely to adopt new accounting procedures (Mezias 1990). Finally, organizational performance has been found to influence the adoption of CEO income protection and incentive plans (Westphal and Zajac 1994).

For diffusion to occur, individuals and organizations need to be able to recognize and absorb innovations from their environment. Research by Cohen and Levinthal (1990) suggests that organizations vary in their "absorptive capacity"—the ability to assimilate and exploit new knowledge. Their study of a sample of firms in the U.S. manufacturing sector found that those with higher R&D expenditures were better able to take advantage of new technical advances than those with a lower investment in basic research. They suggest that such investments are made not so much in the expectation of producing new innovations themselves, but in order to broaden "the firm's knowledge base to create critical overlap with new knowledge and providing it with the deeper understanding that is useful for exploiting new technical developments that build on rapidly advancing science and technology" (p. 148).

Linkages

Relations among organizations exhibit structure. Linkages among organizations vary by frequency and nature of exchanges, multiplicity and absence of connections, and central and peripheral location. Organizational participants are linked together with their counterparts in other organizations both at high levels (e.g., interlocking boards of directors, friendship, and school ties among executives) and low levels (e.g., occupational affiliations and communities of practice that cross organizational boundaries). These ties affect organizational decisions.

For example, Haunschild (1993) demonstrates that corporations sharing directors were more likely to make acquisitions during the 1980s, and Palmer, Jennings, and Zhou (1993) reported that interlocking directors predicted the adoption by corporations of an M-form structure during the 1960s. Rao and Sivakumar (1999) report that firms with similar ties were more likely to create an investor relations office when they learned about it from other board members.

The distinction between being connected and being similar to another social unit is an important one to network theorists. The former, referred to as *cohesion,* pertains to the presence of exchange relations or communication links between two or more parties. The latter, termed *structural equivalence,* refers to social units that "occupy the same position in the social structure"; they "are proximate to the extent that they have the same pattern of relations with occupants of other positions" (Burt 1987: 1291). In situations where information is widely available (e.g., via the mass media), social contagion—the diffusion of some practice or structure—may be more influenced by the behavior of those we regard as similar to ourselves than by those with whom we are in contact (recall the similar arguments made by Strang and Meyer, 1993, discussed in Chapter 6).

The relative importance of cohesion versus structural equivalence is evaluated in a study by Galaskiewicz and Burt (1991), who examined factors affecting diffusion of norms and standards among contributions officers in corporate firms pertaining to the evaluation of nonprofit organizations seeking donations. The study examines how common norms develop within an organization field, affecting how individual officials come to view their social environment, adopt standards, and arrive at similar evaluations. Results were based on evaluations made by 61 contributions officers of 326 local nonprofit organizations eligible to receive donations from corporations. Judgments by officers (as to whether they recognized the nonprofits and, if so, regarded them as worthy prospects) were correlated with the evaluations of other officers who were either (a) in contact or (b) in equivalent structural positions. "The results show weak evidence of contagion by cohesion and strong evidence of contagion by structural equivalence" (Galaskiewicz and Burt 1991: 94). Differences in judgment were also influenced by differences in the personal characteristics of officers, such as gender and prominence, but these did not eliminate the structural effects.

Reference Groups

These and related studies raise this general question: If organizations imitate the behavior of other organizations, how do they determine which organizations to emulate? Clearly, organizations must choose among their many network connections, and they must decide what criteria to employ to assess similarity. A number of recent scholars explore these questions by utilizing network approaches. Notably, much of this research focuses on the adoption by market-based organizations of various competitive strategies, including acquisition behavior, entry into new markets, choice of an investment banker, or construction of a comparison set (e.g., for justifying CEO compensation). Illustrative findings are that organizations are prone to imitate the behavior of organizations that are geographically proximate (Davis and Greve 1997; Greve 1998); perceived to be similar to themselves (e.g., operating in the same industry) (Haunschild and Beckman 1998; Palmer et al. 1993; Porac, Wade, and Pollock 1999); closely connected by ties, including resource, information, and board interlocks (Galaskiewicz and Bielefeld 1998; Haunschild 1993; Kraatz 1998; Uzzi 1996); have high status or prestige (Burns and Wholey 1993); and are more (visibly) successful (Haunschild and Miner 1997; Haveman 1993; Kraatz 1998). In contrast, firms may select less successful others as a comparison set to justify or place their own actions in a favorable light (Porac et al. 1999).

The arguments associated with reference group variables include institutional pressures, status processes, vicarious learning, and political maneuvering. More important, however, these studies begin to show the ways in which institutional processes interact with interest-based motivations to guide organizational choices and behaviors (see also Baum and Dutton 1996; Dacin, Ventresca, and Beal 1999).

Institutional and Organizational Processes Shaping Responses to Environmental Demands

The public policy literature contains numerous studies providing examples of the ways in which organizations both engage in regulatory activities and respond to attempts to control their behavior. Some of these accounts take a top-down perspective, focusing on the structure and tactics of the enforcement agency (e.g., Wilson 1980), whereas others take a bottom-up view, examining how the policies are interpreted and carried out at local sites (e.g., Lipsky 1980). Organizations operate at every level in these accounts: as policymakers, units of the implementation machinery, and targets of policy reform. Although these studies have received scant attention from mainstream organizational scholars, they contain important insights concerning how organizations participate in and respond to regulatory efforts (see, e.g., Hoffman and Ventresca 2002; Landy, Roberts, and Thomas 1990; McLaughlin 1975; Peterson, Rabe, and Wong 1986). Pierson (2004: Ch. 1) provides a perceptive discussion of political organizations, public policy setting, and institutional processes.

A more general process-oriented perspective is provided by organizational scholars who focus attention on organizations as information systems: as symbol-processing, sense-making, and interpretation systems. Pfeffer and Salancik (1978) stress the importance of the information system developed by the organization: the specialized units and processes that determine the variety and types of information routinely collected by the organization. Information is more likely to be salient and used simply because it is available. The availability of information thus influences the "attention structure" of decision makers. Because "time and capabilities for attention are limited," as March (1994: 10) notes, "theories of decision making are often better described as theories of attention or search than as theories of choice." Rather than assuming a straightforward, unified, demand-response model, a more ambiguous, complex, and nuanced portrait is painted of organizations staffed by multiple actors with conflicting agendas and interests confronting diverse and imperfect information. Demands or requirements trigger not automatic conformity, but multiple questions: Does this apply to us? Who says so? Is this something to which we should respond? What might we do about it? Who else may be in the same situation? What are they doing? They become occasions for interpretation and initiate sense-making processes (Barley 1986; Daft and Weick 1984; Whetten and Godfrey 1999). Weick (1995) provides a penetrating and provocative analysis of these processes—reminiscent of Suchman's (1995a) discussion of theorization—that occur within and across organizations.

Related efforts to foster the development of more interactive and subtle models of the ways in which organizations relate to institutional environments have been carried out by law and society scholars, who complain that institutionalists too often embrace a "legal formalism" stressing the external, objective, rational nature of law. Rather, as Suchman and Edelman (1997; see also Edelman and Suchman 1997) propose, laws and regulations are socially interpreted and find their force and meaning in interactions between regulators and regulatees. This approach is well illustrated in a series of studies examining the response of a diverse sample of U.S. organizations to equal employment opportunity/affirmative action laws passed in the early 1960s (see Dobbin 2009; Dobbin et al. 1988; Dobbin, Sutton, Meyer, and Scott 1993; Edelman 1992; Edelman, Uggen, and Erlanger 1999; Sutton et al. 1994). All laws are subject to variable interpretation, but these statutes—in part reflecting underlying, unresolved political conflicts—were particularly ambiguous to the point where even cooperative organizational managers could not determine what it meant to be in compliance. The passage of the legislation set in motion an elaborate sense-making process in which personnel managers engaged in discourse with their counterparts—within their organizations, in their professional journals, at conventions—attempting to discern what measures would be found acceptable. Proposals were floated, prototype programs were developed, and, over time, these responses were evaluated by the federal courts (yet another collection of state-based, professional actors), which served as the final arbiters of adequate compliance. Personnel managers were much more willing to initiate procedural rather than substantive solutions (that focused on the consequences of employer actions; Edelman 1992), although their proposals were often couched in language emphasizing their contributions to organizational efficiency (Dobbin and Sutton 1998).

When eventually selected kinds of programs were declared to meet the requirements of the law—governance processes having shifted to the judiciary—these models diffused rapidly through the field. The overall process that occurred was one in which legal changes could best be understood as an endogenous process engaging various actors and working through sense-making and problem-solving activities within the organization field. This process was guided more by normative constructions among professional actors than by coercive mechanisms emanating from the state, and it was better understood as a structuration process changing rules and behaviors across the entire field, rather than as a simple process by which individual organizations were confronted by and conformed to centralized directives. Colyvas and Jonsson (2011) point out:

> A notable feature in the institutionalization of EEO [equal employment opportunity] is how much governance occurred at multiple levels: in the field, through the assimilation of the principles and practices into law; at the organizational level as a rationalized response to legal mandates; and among individuals by its integration into everyday procedures and employee expectations.

> Such complexity is often obscured in traditional models that map
> these macro- and micro-dynamics onto levels of analysis. (p. 41)

Much of the value in an institutional approach resides in its recognition of the interplay of structures and processes across levels.

❖ STRATEGIC RESPONSES

Studies emphasizing institutional processes rather than effects, such as those described earlier, begin to suggest that organizations may not be quite so powerless or passive as depicted in earlier institutional accounts. Noting the oversocialized conception of organizations and the limited response repertoire proffered by early formulations—in effect, "Conform, either now or later!"—a number of scholars have joined voices in calling for more attention to power and agency, particularly on the part of individuals and organizations subject to institutional pressures (see DiMaggio 1988; Perrow 1986). Pfeffer (1981; Pfeffer and Salancik 1978) was among the first to emphasize that managers often manipulated symbols to "manage" their legitimacy in the larger environment.

In an important codification of these arguments, Christine Oliver (1991) called for an expansion of the choice set available to organizations. Drawing on resource-dependence arguments, she outlined a broad range of potential responses, emphasizing throughout the possible use of more self-interested, strategic alternatives.[2] I begin by reviewing her arguments and typology. However, because they focus on responses by individual organizations, I conclude by pointing to the possibility of more collective strategic actions.

Individual Organizational Responses

Although it is useful to recognize that organizations can react to institutional pressures in a number of ways, it is also important to observe the extent to which institutional environments operate to influence and delimit what strategies organizations can employ. Just as institutions constitute organizations, they also define and set limits on their appropriate ways of acting, including actions taken in response to institutional pressures. Strategies that may be appropriate in one kind of industry or field may be prohibited in another. For example, public agencies are frequently encouraged to coordinate services, whereas private organizations are expected to refrain from becoming overly cozy (or collusive). Tactics that can be successfully pursued in one setting may be inconceivable in another. In short, like other organizational processes, organizational strategies are institutionally shaped.

Oliver (1991: 152), however, concentrates primarily on types of strategies that organizations can pursue irrespective of such field-level constraints. She delineates five general strategies available to individual organizations confronting institutional pressures:

- *Acquiescence* or conformity is the response that has received the lion's share of attention from institutional theorists.

As we have seen, it may entail either imitation of other organizations selected as models or compliance to the perceived demands of cultural, normative, or regulative authorities. It may be motivated by anticipation of enhanced legitimacy, fear of negative sanctions, hope of additional resources, or some mixture of these motives.

- *Compromise* incorporates a family of responses that include balancing, placating, and negotiating institutional demands.

Compromise is particularly likely to occur in environments containing conflicting authorities. Research by D'Aunno, Sutton, and Price (1991) describes hybrid programs devised by mental health agencies incorporating drug abuse programs. Although this may seem a special case, as I noted in Chapter 6, in liberal, pluralist societies like the United States, inconsistent and contested institutional frameworks are commonplace (Berman 1983). This implies that organizations will frequently find themselves in situations in which they have considerable room to maneuver, interpret, bargain, and compromise. For example, Abzug and Mezias (1993) detail the range of strategies pursued by organizations responding to court decisions regarding comparable worth claims under Title VII of the Civil Rights Act of 1972. The federalized structure of the court systems, permitting quasi-independent rulings by federal, state, and local courts, allowed a greater variety of appeals and also provided avenues for reform efforts to continue at one level if blocked at another.

Alexander (1996: 803) describes a combination of compromise strategies as being pursued by curators of fine arts museums in the United States, whose organizations increasingly rely on diverse funding streams—wealthy individuals, corporations, governments, and foundations—each of which holds different goals in providing support. Alexander finds that curators, whose prestige "rests on the scholarliness and quality of their work, including the exhibitions they mount," tend to alter the format of exhibitions to please their funders—for example, creating "blockbuster" and traveling exhibitions to please corporate and government sponsors—but to compromise less on the content of exhibitions. Other specific strategies employed included "resource shifting," "multivocality" (sponsoring exhibitions with many facets that appeal to a variety of stakeholders), and "creative enactment" (inventing linkages between particular types of art and the specific interests of a potential sponsor).

- The strategy of *avoidance,* as defined by Oliver (1991), includes concealment efforts and attempts to buffer some parts of the organization from the necessity of conforming to the requirement.

I described a range of these strategies earlier in the discussion of decoupling and loose coupling.

- The strategy of *defiance* is one in which organizations not only resist institutional pressures to conform, but do so in a highly public manner.

Defiance is likely to occur when the norms and interests of the focal organizations diverge substantially from those attempting to impose requirements on them. Covaleski and Dirsmith (1988) describe one organization's attempt to defy the state's efforts to impose a new budgetary system on them. The University of Wisconsin system attempted to devise and obtain public support for an alternative budgetary system that would more clearly reflect their own interests in research and educational programs and retaining top-flight faculty. In the end, state power prevailed, and the university was forced to accept the state's enrollment-based approach.

- Organizations may respond to institutional pressures by attempting to *manipulate*—"the purposeful and opportunistic attempt to co-opt, influence, or control" the environment (Oliver 1991: 157).

Numerous scholars, from Selznick (1949) to Pfeffer and Salancik (1978) to Alexander (1995), have examined the ways in which organizations attempt to defend themselves and improve their bargaining power by developing linkages to important sources of power. Of special interest to institutional theorists are the techniques used by organizations to directly manage views of their legitimacy. Elsbach and Sutton (1992: 702) report a process study of impression-management techniques employed by Earth First! and ACT UP, two militant reform organizations that employed "illegitimate actions to gain recognition and achieve goals." Their analysis suggests that such techniques were employed to gain media attention to the organization and its objectives. Once such attention was forthcoming, spokespersons for each organization stressed the more conventional aspects of the organization and attempted to distance their organization's program from the illegal activities of some of its members. They sometimes claimed innocence or justified their actions in the light of the greater injustices against which they were contending. Endorsements and support received from other constituencies were emphasized. In these and related ways, organizations attempt to manage their impressions and improve their credibility. However, as Ashforth and Gibbs (1990) point out, organizations that "protest too much" run the risk of undermining their legitimacy. Suchman (1995b) has described a range of strategies employed by organizations to gain, maintain, and regain their legitimacy.

One final caution: In recognizing the possibility of strategic action by organizations confronting institutional pressures, it is also important that institutional theorists not lose sight of the distinctive properties of institutions, in particular those associated with the cultural-cognitive forms. As Goodrick and Salancik (1996) point out:

> A problem with the direct incorporation of a strategic choice perspective into institutional theory is that it discounts the social-fact quality of institutions. Rather than being social facts that make up the fabric of social life, they assume the special and arbitrary positions of dominant social agents. . . . The notion that organizations act at times without choice or forethought is lost. . . . The institutional context [then becomes] . . . of no special importance for understanding organizational action. It is simply a constraint to be managed like any other constraint, a choice among many choices. (p. 3)

Goodrick and Salancik (1996) examined the behavior of various types of California hospitals in adopting Cesarean operations from 1965 to 1995, a time when the rates for this procedure increased greatly. Professional practice norms encourage the use of Cesarean sections for high- but not low-risk births. Comparing Cesarean rates among for-profit and nonprofit hospitals, the researchers observed differences among them only for births of intermediate risk. For-profit hospitals were more likely to carry out these relatively profitable procedures under these conditions than nonprofit forms. But this self-interested, strategic behavior only occurred for intermediate-risk patient conditions for which professional norms did not provide clear guidelines. Institutional rules set the limits within which strategic behavior occurs.

More generally, there is clear tension between a strategic approach and the view of many institutional theorists. As previewed in Chapter 3, a strategic perspective views legitimacy as another type of resource—a cultural resource—to be extracted from the environment. As Suchman (1995b: 576) points out, given the "almost limitless malleability and symbols and rituals," in contrast to the hardness of material resources and outcomes, the former provides ready targets for manipulation by managers. Institutionalists, however, emphasize the limits of this view.

In a strong and constraining symbolic environment, managers' decisions are often constructed by the same belief systems that determine audience reactions. Consequently, rather than examining the strategic legitimation efforts of specific focal organizations, many institutionalists tend to emphasize the collective structuration (DiMaggio and Powell 1983) of entire fields or sectors of organizational life (Suchman 1995b: 576).

Collective Responses

More so than the actions of single organizations, concerted responses by multiple organizations have the potential to shape the nature of the demands and even to redefine the rules and logics operating within the field. I review several studies dealing with these collective responses to institutional environments, but reserve for Chapter 8 a discussion of more general field-level changes.

Earlier in this chapter, I discussed a number of empirical studies depicting the ways in which organizations subject to some type of normative or regulative pressure respond in ways that reshape or redefine these institutional demands. Recall the behavior of personnel officers confronted by equal opportunity legislation. I suspect that such processes—in which rules or normative controls are proposed or legislated, interpretations and collective sense-making activities take place among participants in the field to which they are directed, and then the requirements are redefined and clarified—are more often the rule than the exception.

A study by Kaplan and Harrison (1993) examines the reactions by organizations to changes in the legal environment that exposed board members to a greater risk of liability suits. Corporations pursued both proactive strategies, adapting so as to conform to environmental requirements, and reactive strategies, attempting to alter environmental demands. Both involved collective as well as individual efforts. The Business Roundtable, a voluntary governance association, "took the lead in coordinating the conformity strategy by making recommendations on board composition and committee structure" consistent with the concerns raised by such regulatory bodies as the Security and Exchanges Commission (p. 423). Proactive collective strategies included lobbying efforts directed at states to broaden the indemnification protection for outside directors as well as the creation of insurance consortia to underwrite the costs of providing director and officer liability insurance to companies. The strategies pursued were judged to be highly successful: "New legislation and the insurance consortia enabled most corporations to substantially improve director liability protection. As a result, most board members are less at risk of personal liability now than they were a decade ago" (pp. 426–427).

A somewhat more contentious process of negotiation and compromise is detailed by Hoffman (1997) in his historical account of reactions by the U.S. chemical and petroleum firms and industries, during the period 1960 to 1995, to increasing regulatory pressures intended to reduce treats to the natural environment. Trade journals were examined to assess industry response to these challenges. During the 1960s, industry media devoted relatively little attention to environmental concerns; most accusations and concerns were dismissed as groundless. However, with the formation of the Environmental Protection Agency in 1970—in response to a number of highly visible environmental accidents—governmental scrutiny of both industries increased dramatically, as did the mobilization of environmental activists. The Chemical Manufacturers Association and the American Petroleum Institute initially pursued primarily confrontational strategies in an attempt to influence regulatory behavior—in particular, standard-setting—but by the late 1980s, a more cooperative framework had evolved as the industries and related corporations began to embrace a policy of corporate environmentalism. Public agencies and corporate actors accommodated to one another's interests, erecting new types of understandings, norms, and hybrid public/private governance arrangements.

More conflict-laden collective reactions have occurred whose resolution has proved more difficult. Miles (1982) examined the interesting case of the response by the Big Six tobacco companies in the United States to the Surgeon General's report linking smoking and cancer. Each of these companies reacted individually, some developing their foreign markets and others diversifying their products. But they also engaged in collective action, creating the Tobacco Industry Research Committee to conduct their own scientific studies and cooperating to hire lobbyists and create political action committees to guide legislation and resist the passage of punitive laws. Collective efforts to shape the regulative and other governance structures to which they are subject continue up to the present day in response to heightened activities on the part of federal and state officials.

A different kind of negotiation process and redefinition of the organization field is described by Halliday, Powell, and Granfors (1993) in their study of U.S. state bar associations These associations were formed at the turn of the 20th century as market-based organizations competing for the support of lawyer members. However, during the early decades, failure rates were high. A different model of organizing was developed in the early 1920s, which relied on state support: Membership in the association was mandated as a condition for practicing in the state, and annual fees were imposed on all members. This new form, which required either legislative action or a ruling by the state supreme court, rapidly diffused through a number of states, although it did not supplant the market-based form in all states. Event-history analysis revealed that the state-based mode was more likely to be adopted in states in which the market-based form had attracted only a small proportion of lawyers (i.e., states favorably disposed to licensing professions) and in rural states. The state-based form was also promoted by a centralized, propagator association, the American Judicature Society, created to advance legal reform and diffuse the new structure. Collective action in this case resulted in the transformation of an organizational form, moving it out of the competitive marketplace and under the protective wing of the state.

❖ SOURCES OF DIVERGENCE

Collecting arguments from this and previous chapters, we see that, although institutional pressures under many conditions conduce toward isomorphic organization structure and practices, there are many ways in which "identical" institutional forces can result not in convergent, but divergent outcomes. Among the mechanisms and processes discussed, consider the following:

- Varying carriers whose characteristics or mode of transmission alters the message
- Varying translations of institutional rules

- Misunderstandings or errors in the application of rules
- Varying exposure or susceptibility to institutional rules
- Varying attributes or relational connections that affect knowledge of or response to institutional pressures
- Adaptations or innovations by users adopting institutional forms
- Competing models being combined into varying hybrid forms
- Strategic responses by individual organizations to institutional pressures
- Strategic responses by networks or associations of organizations

Given the variety and prevalence of these factors, it would appear that if more nuanced institutional arguments are used, investigators may discover that it is easier to account for divergence than convergence of response by organizations to "common" institutional pressures.

❖ CONCLUDING COMMENT

Although organization analysts early embraced an open systems conception of organizations, it has taken a long time for us to comprehend the extent to which organizations are creatures of their distinctive times and places, reflecting not only the technical knowledge, but also the cultural rules and social beliefs in their environments.

Much of the important work by institutional theorists over the past two decades has been in documenting the influence of social and symbolic forces on organizational structure and behavior. Empirical research has examined how institutional systems shape organizations, variably, as a function of their location in the environment, their size and visibility, and their nearness to the public sphere, structural position, and relational contacts.

Organizations are affected, and even penetrated, by their environments, but they are also capable of responding to these influence attempts creatively and strategically. By acting in concert with other organizations facing similar pressures, organizations can sometimes counter, curb, circumvent, or redefine these demands. Collective action does not preclude individual attempts to reinterpret, manipulate, challenge, or defy the authoritative claims made on them. Organizations are creatures of their institutional environments, but most modern organizations are constituted as active players, not passive pawns.

In this chapter, I have tried to reflect the gradual but significant shift in scholarly treatments of institution-organization relations. From a concern with one-way, determinant institutional effects, most contemporary researchers are instead crafting research designs to examine the complex recursive processes by which institutional forces both shape and are shaped by organizational actions.

❖ NOTES

1. Note that this sample design is unusual in that each of the decades represents a different set of firms. In subsequent analyses, Fligstein (1990, 1991) examined the strategic behavior of firms that had entered and left so that the characteristics of "stayers" and "leavers" could be compared.

2. This conception was instrumental in attracting the attention of management scholars to institutional ideas. After all, an approach that views organizations as shaped largely by environmental forces—whether ecological or institutional—may appeal to academic social scientists, but is unlikely to attract scholars who consult with present and prepare future business managers for leadership responsibilities.

8

Institutional Processes and Organization Fields

The theory of fields is a generic theory of social organization in modernity

—Neil Fligstein (2001a: 29)

I believe that no concept is more vitally connected to the agenda of understanding institutional processes and organizations than that of organization field. Previously defined in Chapter 4 and referred to from time to time in subsequent chapters, the concept of field—both as a conception and a level of analysis—figures sufficiently large in institutional approaches to organizations to merit extended attention. Like so many aspects of institutional theory, the conception of organization field is a work in progress. While its introduction into organization theory can be dated with precision, it builds on previous work and has been subject to criticism, amendment, and improvement up to the present moment. It is, at one and the same time, widely accepted and hotly contested.

❖ CONCEPTUALIZING ORGANIZATION FIELDS

Our discussion begins with the general concept of field and then moves to its application to organizations, considering both its contributions to conceptualizing the environment within which a particular organization operates as well as its value as a new object of study.

Fields and Organization Fields

Field Conceptions

The concept of a "field approach" to explaining the behavior of an object has a long history in both the physical and social sciences. As detailed by Martin (2011), its origins lay in work during 19th century on electromagnetism and fluid mechanics in the physical sciences and, somewhat later, by German gestalt theory in psychology. What was common to these and related approaches is that the behavior of the objects under study is explained not by their internal attributes but by their location in some physically or socially defined space. The objects, or actors, are subject to varying vectors of force (influences) depending on their location in the field and their relation with other actors as well as the larger structure within which these relations are embedded.

This perspective came by various routes into the social sciences. Urban ecologists in the "Chicago school" led by Park and Burgess (1921) borrowed from the work of biological ecologists to examine "niche space" not only in geographic but in relational terms (McKenzie 1926/1983). Building on gestalt theory from the late 19th century, social psychologist Kurt Lewin (1951: 57) developed his version of field theory in social psychology as a tool to assess an individual's "life space"—encompassing "the person and the psychological environment as it exists for him." Important features of Lewin's approach were his insistence on the mutual interdependence of the many elements and forces surrounding the individual and on the centrality of the individual's perceptive and interpretive processes: life space conceived as a cognitive map of one's social environment (see Mohr, forthcoming).

Another important approach to fields came from sociologically oriented social psychologists in the work of Shibutani (1955), Strauss and colleagues (Strauss 1978; Strauss, Schatzman, Bucher, Erlich, and Sabshin 1964), and Becker (1974; 1982). These symbolic interactionists developed the concept of *social worlds* to refer to groups of actors with "shared commitments to certain activities, sharing resources of many kinds to achieve their goals, and building shared ideologies about how to go about their business" (Clark 1991: 131). These worlds are actor-defined and permit the "identification and analysis of collective activities viewed as meaningful by the actors themselves" (Clark 1991: 135). Studies along these lines in social psychology and Chicago approaches to the sociology of work have developed until recently on a parallel tract to organization fields, but there are increasing signs of convergence (e.g., Clark 1991).

Particularly influential has been the work of sociologist Pierre Bourdieu (1971; 1984), who employed the concept of field to refer "to both the totality of actors and organizations involved in an arena of social or cultural production and the dynamic relationships among them" (DiMaggio, 1979: 1463). Bourdieu insists that "to think in terms of field is to *think relationally*" (Bourdieu and Wacquant, 1992: 96; italics in original), and he employs the analogy of a game, with rules, players, stakes, competition, and contestation, to depict its central features. Fields, for Bourdieu, are not placid and settled social spaces, but arenas of conflict in which all players seek to advance their interests and some are able, for longer or shorter periods, to impose their conception of "the rules of the game" on others. Bourdieu's treatment of field provided the blueprint for DiMaggio and Powell's (1983) founding conception, as well as for the later approach of Fligstein and McAdam (2011; 2012).

Organization Field Conceptions

It was heavy lifting to move organizational scholars to attend to systems above that represented by the individual organizations. After all, it had been difficult enough to convince students of organizations that the organization itself could be studied in ways other than showing it had effects on individual behavior.[1] Very soon after the organization itself had been established as a viable level of analysis, the open systems perspective swept into the arena during the mid-1950s (Scott and Davis 2007: Ch. 4). The environment of an organization took on new importance, and scholars struggled with ways to conceptualize and capture it as a new object of study.

Early investigators (e.g., Dill 1958; Emery and Trist 1965; Lawrence and Lorsch 1967) came to conceive of the environment as a disembodied set of dimensions—such as complexity, stability, munificence—whose states could impact the organization. There was little sense that the organization's environment was *itself organized*. And there was little awareness that organizations operating within the same environment might inhabit quite distinctive locations providing diverse threats and opportunities. Ecologists suggested that community structures could usefully be examined as a network of interorganizational relations (e.g., Galaskiewicz 1979; Warren 1967), but these studies emphasized geographic boundaries. Useful next steps were the identification of the *organization set* (Blau and Scott 1962/2003; Evan 1966)—the organization's primary exchange partners—and the *organization population* (Hannan and Freeman 1977)—a collection of similar organizations that compete for the same resources.

As described in Chapter 4, the concept of *organization field* was crafted by DiMaggio and Powell (1983) to refer to "those organizations that, in the aggregate, constitute a recognized area of institutional life: key suppliers, resource and product consumers, regulatory agencies, and other organizations that produce similar services and products" (p. 148). It thus incorporates both the organization set and organization population frameworks, while adding oversight units. Although based on Bourdieu's work of fields, DiMaggio and Powell gave primary attention to social relational and network components. In their related work, Scott and Meyer (1983) stressed regulative and funding connections, calling attention to the ways in which field complexity affected organizational structure. These frameworks insisted that the fields surrounding organizations were themselves organized in diverse ways that influenced the structure and functioning of organizations embedded within them.

These early formulations, however, overstressed relational systems to the neglect of cultural connections. Building on Bourdieu's work, cultural theorists such as Wuthnow began to remedy this deficiency by pointing to the importance of meaning systems. Rather than pursuing Bourdieu's focus on subjective states, as in his concept of *habitus* (internalized dispositions), Wuthnow (1987) stressed the utility of focusing investigation on objective indicators of culture (e.g., the analysis of texts, discourse, gestures, and cultural products). He noted that approaches may vary from the "structuralist," that examines general patterns in texts that can be seen, recorded and classified; to the "dramaturgic," focusing on rituals, ideologies, and other acts that symbolize and dramatize the nature of social relations; to the "institutional" that calls attention to the roles played by organizations and occupations in producing and disseminating goods and services (e.g., Becker 1982; DiMaggio 1991). Wuthnow (1989) employs the term "discursive field" to characterize the "fundamental categories in which thinking can take place" developed over time by an interacting group of individuals and organizations. As Spillman (1995) argues, "discursive fields mediate between structure and meaningful action."

Or as Snow (2008: 8) points out: "They provide the context within which meaning-making activities, like framing, are embedded." An alternative approach to conceptualizing the symbolic aspects of field structures is, of course, that of *institutional logics,* as discussed in Chapter 4 (see Friedland and Alford 1991; Thornton, Ocasio, and Lounsbury 2012).

Thus, the concept of organization field represents a major step forward in enabling organization scholars to craft a coherent image of the relevant environment for a given organization. By focusing on the examination of specific relational linkages and patterns of activities employing network and other methodologies and by attending to the role of meaning systems as assessed by textual and discourse analysis, the environment can be much more clearly conceptualized and empirically assessed than was previously possible. As Ferguson (1998: 598) indicates, the concept of field allows investigators to "focus on tangible products and identifiable pursuits." Field creation is an admixture of top-down and bottom-up processes. Ferguson also suggests, "a field constructs a social universe in which all participants are at once producers and consumers, caught in a complex web of social, political and cultural relations that they themselves have woven and continue to weave" (p. 598). In a pithy aphorism summarizing their work on a variety of organization fields, Padgett and Powell (2012: 2) conclude: "In the short run, actors create relations; in the long run, relations create actors." I would add: In the short run, actors create and modify meanings; in the long run, meanings create actors, both organizational and individual identities.

While the concept of organization field has proven to be invaluable in helping analysts understand the nature of the environment for a given organization, it is also, as I have noted in previous chapters, in itself a valuable new level of analysis for investigating social systems and processes. Some of the most important organizational scholarship of the past four decades has examined the origin, structuration, and change and/or decline of organization fields. Some of these studies have already been discussed in earlier chapters and additional work is reviewed later in this chapter (see also Fligstein and McAdam 2012; Thornton et al. 2012; Wooten and Hoffman 2008).

As Martin (2011) insists, the existence of a field is a matter to be empirically determined:

> Whether a set of persons [or organizations] or their actions actually forms a field must be an empirical question and cannot be true by definition or methodology. A field theoretic analysis requires

that the positions of persons [or organizations] in a field must be based on their orientations to each other, either directly through their interpersonal relations or in a mediated manner via shared goals. (pp. 269–270)

At the same time, the boundaries of the field are set in part by heuristic processes: allowing investigators to pursue those matters of prime interest to them and/or their subjects.

The concept of organization field celebrates and exploits the insight that "local social orders" constitute the building blocks of contemporary social systems. It urges the benefits of the "meso level of theorizing," which recognizes the centrality of these somewhat circumscribed and specialized realms in the construction and maintenance of social order (Fligstein 2001b: 107). The field concept is productively employed in examining delimited systems ranging from markets to policy domains to the less structured and more contested arenas within which social movements struggle. Thus, as Hoffman (1997) has argued, fields can be created around an issue as well as a set of products or services. The field of environmental protection joins together participants from selected industries, governmental agencies, and environmental activists as, over time, each of these groups attempts to influence and reacts to the control efforts of the others. It is this conception of organization field—as a contested arena within which multiple types of players pursue their interests and defend their turf—that has been adopted and developed by Fligstein and McAdam (2012) as they develop the links between organization studies and social movements (see also Davis, McAdam, Scott, and Zald 2005).

The field concept also fulfills a vital role in connecting organization studies to wider, macro structures—sectoral, societal, and transnational. Organizations are themselves major actors in modern society, but to understand their broader significance, it is necessary to see their role as players in larger networks and systems. As I have argued, most organizations engage with not one, but multiple fields and are subject to multiple institutional logics. Pizarro (2012) suggests that organizations operate within a "sectoral field"—one containing their primary competitors and exchange partners and defined by a shared logic—but also within a "contested field" comprising other types of players in diverse fields motivated by different logics, who attempt to influence the behavior of the focal organization. Organization fields not only reflect many of these conflicts, both in relational patterns and logics, but help to mediate and broker among them as an important component of social change processes. As DiMaggio (1986: 337) asserts, "the organization field has emerged as a critical unit bridging the organizational and the societal levels in the study of social and community change."

❖ KEY COMPONENTS OF ORGANIZATION FIELDS

While it is possible to identify the presence of regulative, normative, and cultural-cognitive elements at work in all organization fields, for empirical purposes it is helpful to focus attention on a number of key components that vary among fields.

Institutional Logics

As discussed in Chapter 4 and elsewhere in this volume, institutional logics call attention to shared conceptual frameworks that provide guidelines for the behavior of field participants (Friedland and Alford 1991; Thornton et al. 2012). They comprise both normative and cultural-cognitive elements. Some of these logics provide the basis for field construction, allowing a "shared understanding of what is going on in the field," while other more limited logics offer different and competing cognitive frames for subsets of participants in varying field locations (Fligstein and McAdam 2012: 10–11). Moreover, as Friedland and Alford (1991) first emphasized, multiple frameworks are available within developed societies, which are differentiated around numerous specialized arenas—political, political, economic, religious, kinship, and so on—and each is governed by a different logic. Organizations, working at a meso level within these arenas, are hence confronted by, and have available to them, multiple often contradictory logics:

> Some of the most important struggles between groups, organizations, and classes are over the appropriate relationships between institutions, and by which institutional logic different activities are to be regulated and to which categories of persons they apply. Is access to housing and health to be regulated by the market or by the state? Are families, churches, or states to control education? Should reproduction be regulated by state, family, or church? (Friedland and Alford 1991: 256)

Thus, institutional logics vary in their content—the nature of beliefs and assumptions—but also in their penetration or "vertical depth" (Krasner, 1988). For example, Fligstein (2001a: 32) distinguishes between "general societal understandings about how to organize firms or markets . . . and specific understandings about how a particular market works." Institutional logics also vary in their breadth or extent of horizontal linkage (Krasner, 1988). One of the most significant predictors of institutional stability and influence is the extent to which it is compatible with or complementary to related institutional arrangements (Hall and Soskice 2001a: 17). Finally, institutional logics within a field vary in terms of their exclusiveness or, conversely, the extent to which they are contested (Scott 1994a: 211).

Another concept that has proven helpful in examining cultural-cognitive systems is that of *cultural frame*. Goffman (1974: 21) first employed the concept to refer to "schemata of interpretation" that enable individuals "to locate, perceive, identify, and label" events occurring to them in ways that establish their meaning. The concept was employed after modification by David Snow and colleagues, who eschewed the noun for the verb, emphasizing *framing processes* in order to better inform social movement theory (Benford and Snow, 2000; Snow, Rochford, Worden, and Benford 1986). As Benford and Snow (2000) note, "This denotes an active, processual phenomenon that implies agency and contention at the level of reality construction. It is active in the sense that something is being done, and processual in the sense of a dynamic, evolving process" (p. 614).

The concept of framing has proved to be useful to social movement theorists who realized that much of the work of activist and reform groups involves a "reframing" of issues and problems in ways that illuminate injustice or identify possible ways forward (McAdam 1996; Zald 1996). In short order, also, the concept was embraced by organizational and institutional scholars.

In their study of the recycling industry, Lounsbury, Ventresca, and Hirsch (2003) describe the contest waged between two competing visions—"field-level frames"—for managing solid waste. Favored during the 1970s was the waste-to-energy (W-T-E) model that involves capturing usable energy from the burning of trash. This approach created opposition among environmental activities who promoted an alternative frame that favored recycling—the collection and breaking down of materials such as paper and glass that can be remanufactured into consumer products. The recycling view remained marginal until it was repackaged from a volunteer model into a for-profit model supported by federal, state, and local legislation to resist the building of incinerators and encourage recycling efforts. Lounsbury and colleagues prefer the concept of framing to that of institutional logic because, for them, the latter is "conceptualized as exogenous to actors," whereas the former emphasizes "the more active struggles over meanings and resources" occurring among actors in the field (p. 72). The researchers tracked changes in discourse reflected in the meetings of the Solid Waste Association of North America and its trade magazine as well as archival sources such as Congressional hearings and to obtain cognitive representation of how key industry issues were thought about and discussed. In addition, multiple interviews were conducted with a variety of field actors. Attention to cultural frames stresses "the interweaving of structures of meaning and resources as well as their wider cultural and political context" (Hoffman and Ventresca 1999).

Frames can unify as well as divide. In closely related work, Beamish and Biggart (2012) employ the term *social heuristic* to refer to an interpretative frame and decision making model that embodies collectively held understandings that provide a socially defensible foundation for actors' decisions. They studied the emergence of a social heuristic within the commercial construction industry that led developers, financiers, construction firms, contractors, and regulators to embrace a "default design" reflecting shared standards and guidelines for developing a commercial building. While this heuristic greatly simplifies decision making and reduces transaction costs among all parties, it framed these buildings as conservative financial investments and inhibited the consideration of innovative practices that could lead to improved energy efficiency, enhanced aesthetics, or improvements in building design.

Another useful concept linking culture and social structure was first introduced into the analysis of social movements by Charles Tilly. Tilly (1978: 143) was among the first to point out that even apparently "disorganized" and disruptive behaviors were likely to take on "well-defined forms already familiar to the participants," including collective actions such as strikes, rallies, and demonstrations. Moreover "given the innumerable ways in which people could, in principle, deploy their resources in pursuit of common ends . . . at any point in time, the *repertoire of collective actions* available to a population is surprisingly limited" (p. 151). If such an observation holds for social movements, which tend to operate under less structured conditions, think how much more applicable it is to the world of everyday organizations operating in settled fields. As Hoffman (1997) observes:

> The institutional environment, in large part, defines the range of the organizational reality. In setting strategy and structure, firms

may choose action from a repertoire of possible options. But the range of that repertoire is bound by the rules, norms, and beliefs of the organizational field. (p. 148)

Clemens (1996; 1997) connects the idea of repertoires of collective action to that of organizational archetype (see Chapter 5 and below). She suggests that any field contains a limited repertoire of organizational forms that themselves contain a limited set of culturally defined tools (Swidler 1986) or repertoires of collective action. Clemens also suggests ways in which social movement organizations participate in inducing institutional change, work I review in a later section.

Concepts such as institutional logics, organizational archetypes, framing processes, and repertoires of collective action help us better understand the ways in which cultural-cognitive models act both to constrain and to empower social action. By providing clear templates for organizing—whether designing structures, strategies, or procedures—institutional forms constrain actors from selecting (or even considering) alternative forms and modes, on the one hand, but, on the other, provide essential support for actors carrying on the selected activities in the guise of comprehensibility, acceptability, and legitimacy.

Actors

A great variety of actors people social landscapes. Although they (we) are biological creatures, they (we) are also social constructions, possessing institutionally defined identities including capacities, rights, and responsibilities. The institutional elements at work are primarily cultural-cognitive, especially in their constitutive capacity, and normative. The types of actors include (1) individuals (e.g., in the health care sector, a specific doctor), (2) associations of individuals (e.g., the American Medical Association), (3) populations of individuals (e.g., patients, physicians, nurses), (4) organizations (e.g., the Stanford University hospital), (5) associations of organizations (e.g., multihospital systems), and (6) populations of organizations (e.g., hospitals or nursing homes; Scott, Ruef, Mendel, and Caronna 2000).

In a typical organization field, one expects to observe a delimited number of models, both for individual actors (roles) and for collective actors (archetypes). As described in Chapter 5, Greenwood and Hinings' (1993) concept of *organization archetype* provides a useful mode of characterizing the ways in which a given interpretive scheme or conceptual model is embodied within organizational structure and its operating systems. Of course, the extent to which organizational activities correspond with the model is always a matter for empirical investigation, but archetypes provide templates around which rules, administrative systems, and accounts of activities can be structured. Following the lead of population ecologists as well as "configurational" arguments (Van de Ven and Drazin, 1985), Greenwood and Hinings (1993: 1058) propose that field-level pressures will encourage organizations to utilize structures and systems that manifest a single underlying interpreting scheme, and that, once adopted, organizations tend to retain the same archetypes.[2]

Attention to the power of organizational archetypes underlines the importance of the constitutive properties of cultural-cognitive elements: their capacity in the guise of typifications, scripts, or conceptions of agency to provide the forms and "categories and understanding that enable us to engage in economic and social action" (Dacin, Ventresca, and Beal 1999: 329; see also DiMaggio 1994: 35). And as emphasized in previous chapters, both individual and collective actors serve as the creator and carrier of institutional elements, including logics as well as ways of thinking and working.

Following Bourdieu (1986), actors control and compete for *capital*, including various forms of economic, social, and cultural resources. What is valued depends on the way in which the field is constructed. Indeed, "a capital does not exist and function except in relation to a field" (Bourdieu and Wacquant 1992: 101). Fligstein and McAdam (2011: 13) emphasize this conception of fields as competitive arenas, insisting that the most important distinction involving actors to be made by field analysts is that between *incumbents*—those actors in control of the most important types of capital—and *challengers*—those actors with relatively little influence but "awaiting new opportunities to challenge the structure and logic of the system." This conception emphasizes the need to take into account the role of peripheral, subjugated actors who may come together in coalitions, as well as less inchoate social movements struggling to mobilize around a collective action project.

Most fields include a limited variety of organizational forms (populations) that constitute the primary modes of producer organizations (e.g., various types of provider organizations in the health care sector, colleges in higher education), along with those different, supporting organizations that supply essential resources, including funding and exercise controls. In addition, it is important not to overlook the critical role played in most fields by a variety of intermediary organizations and occupations, for example, stock analysts in markets or such information brokers as librarians, computer scientists, and rating agencies. For example, Wedlin (2006) examines the surprisingly influential role recently played by media organizations such as the *Financial Times* and *Wall Street Journal* in structuring the international field of management education with their rankings of business schools. These rankings helped to shape the status structure of these programs and to assist in constructing distinctions around which schools shaped their identities, for example, the amount of emphasis placed on academic versus business capital, or the boundary drawn between a European versus an American model (the former more likely to be independent, the latter, inside or tied to a university). Wedlin (2006: 170) argues that "the rankings are not just reflections of the field; they are also part of creating the field and the boundaries of the field . . . [helping to shape] both mental and social structures."

Another example of the importance of intermediaries is provided by research conducted by Jooste and me (Jooste and Scott 2011) in our study of private-public partnerships engaged in infrastructure construction projects. Because such partnerships represent new ways of working for many governmental agencies, they need assistance in creating capacity to negotiate and manage the complex contracts involved. While some of these skills may be available in or added to the public bureaucracy, we observed that in many situations, these skills were lodged in external organizations that emerge to participate in what we term an "enabling field" of project participants. Such organizations include public and nonpublic regulators, transaction advisors, advocacy associations, and local, regional, and multinational development agencies.

> When we talk about the changing "structure" of a field, we refer not only to more regularized patterns of interaction among the main players, but also to growth in the number and importance of organizations whose principal function is to oversee, steer, and mediate the transactions among the primary players. (Jooste and Scott 2011: 389)

Relational Systems

DiMaggio and Powell's (1983) original conception focused much attention on the relational systems linking organizations into larger networks. Similar to DiMaggio and Powell, Meyer and I (Scott and Meyer 1983) stressed relational or structural features at the field (or sector) level, as discussed in Chapter 7. And in a related fashion, in his discussion of business systems, Whitley (1992b) examines the extent of specialization within firms, whether market ties are characterized by arms-length or more relational contracting, and variety of authority and coordination mechanisms at the system level. More so than other organizational scholars at the time, in his examination of corporate systems at the societal level, Fligstein (1991: 314), like Bourdieu, stressed the centrality of power and control processes—"the ability of a given organization or set of organizations to capture or direct the actions of the field." For Fligstein (1990: Ch. 1), the relevant relations for large corporations are (1) those involving other, similar organizations and (2) those with the nation-state, which is in a position to ratify settlements or modify the terms of competition. Other scholars, such as Podolny (1993) and Washington and Zajac (2005), highlight the role of status processes, as more or less prestigious actors work to shape the directions of field development.

An important subset of relational systems are the governance systems that operate at the field level. *Governance systems* are "those arrangements which support the regularized control—whether by regimes created by mutual agreement, by legitimate hierarchical authority or by non-legitimate coercive means—of the actions of one set of actors by another" (Scott et al. 2000: 21). Each organization field is characterized by a somewhat distinctive governance system composed of a combination of public and private actors employing a combination of regulatory and normative controls over activities and actors within the field. Among the common actors exercising these functions are public regulatory bodies, trade associations, unions, professional associations, nongovernmental organizations (NGOs), and judicial systems. For a sampling of empirical studies of field governance systems, see Brunsson and Jacobsson's (2000) examination of standard-setting by professional associations, Campbell and colleagues' study of the governance of economic sectors (Campbell, Hollingsworth, and Lindberg 1991; Campbell and Lindberg 1990; 1991), Djelic and Quack's (2003b) and Djelic and Sahlin-Andersson's (2006) collection of studies of transnational regulatory systems, Holm's (1995) study of Norwegian fishing regimes, and our study of the changing governance systems controlling health care delivery organizations in the United States (Scott et al. 2000).

Organization Field Boundaries

Like all social systems, organization fields are, by nature, open systems. This means that any attempt to determine their boundaries must involve some combination of science and art. As noted, field boundaries must be empirically determined, but because social systems comprise many ingredients, analysts must choose from among a variety of indicators (Scott and Davis 2007: 152–155). These include a focus on actors (e.g., membership boundaries), on activities (e.g., identifying common repertories), on relations (e.g., interaction networks), or on cultural markers (e.g., shared normative frameworks, cultural beliefs, contentious issues). Laumann, Marsden, and Prensky (1983: 21) also identify two approaches to boundary construction: a "realist" approach that adopts the "vantage point of the actors themselves in defining the boundaries" of the system versus a "nominalist" approach in which the investigator "imposes a conceptual framework constructed to serve his own analytic purposes." Moreover, in addition, both spatial and temporal boundaries must be established.

Spatial Boundaries

Actors are located in specific spaces, and for many years space was conceived primarily in geographical dimensions—in terms of propinquity. For many kinds of activities, being physically close, operating in the same locality, remains an important consideration. Indeed, analysts have recently emphasized the continuing importance of co-location for understanding organizational functioning (Marquis, Lounsbury, and Greenwood 2011). Nevertheless, a part of the genius of the field concept is its recognition of the significance of relational and cultural connections, regardless of how distant. For many contemporary organizations, nonlocal ties are more fateful than proximate ones, for example, the relation between local firms and their headquarters office or between companies and state or federal agencies.

The drawing of boundaries is always a somewhat arbitrary process in our highly interconnected social worlds, but the boundaries selected need to serve the analytic focus of the study: What is the primary question being addressed? Sometimes, boundaries are misspecified. McAdam provided an instructive example of this problem when he returned some years later to examine his analysis of the U.S. civil rights movement (McAdam and Scott 2005). He notes that his initial study of the factors leading to the success of this effort focused exclusively on domestic change processes, discounting the importance of the role played by the Cold War (McAdam 1982). Subsequent work by Dudziak (1988), McAdam (1999), and others stressed the role of competition with the Soviet Union in prompting President Truman and other federal officials to embrace civil rights reforms. A full understanding of this movement called for attention to international as well as domestic relations and meanings.

The variety and flexibility of spatial field boundaries can be illustrated with two examples. As noted earlier, Fligstein (1990; 1991) studied changes in the structure of the 100 largest nonfinancial corporations in the United States from the period 1920 to 1980. He began with the more conventional view of a field as demarcated by product or service markets, but during the period of study, organizations began to diversify, entering into multiple markets. Fligstein argues that, over time, the field boundaries of these firms shifted so that the largest corporations increasingly operated in a field comprising other actors like themselves. Fligstein hence constructed his sample of the 100 largest corporations during each decade, even though the composition of this sample changed over time. An important part of his analysis was to ascertain whether the changes observed were due to the changing composition of the top 100 or to the structural adaptations made by the largest corporations. (More details on this study are provided in the next section.)

A second example of setting field boundaries is provided by the research my colleagues and I have conducted on global infrastructure construction projects (Scott, Levitt, and Orr 2011). For some of these studies, we conceptualized three interrelated fields:

1. *the field of global infrastructure players,* comprising a finite collection of multinational corporations that constitute the major players in these projects, a small number of law firms specializing in international construction, a set of key bankers and developers, multilateral agencies such as the World Bank that provide both funding and oversight, and a variety of professional associations and NGOs that help to set standards and safeguard environmental and human rights

2. *the organization field of the host community for a specific project at the time the project commences,* including the specific project company and affiliates; relevant government organizations, possibly at local, regional, and state levels; individuals and organizations residing in the project area; social movement organizations with environmental or human rights concerns; and potential beneficiaries and end-users of the facility being constructed

3. *the new organization field created by the existence and development of the project,* including the project company as it has developed over time, the other types of players included in field 2 as they have changed in response to the developing project, and a set of entirely new players who have arisen in either support of or opposition to the ongoing projects (Scott 2011).

In short, global projects operate at a scale sufficiently large that they always disrupt and may transform the organization fields they enter (see Khagram 2004). It is because such projects are so intrusive and activate new sources of support and resistance that so many of them fail to be successful, in either financial or operational terms. A consideration of the state of a field before and after some event leads naturally to the topic of temporal boundaries.

Temporal Boundaries

Particularly as students of institutional systems have shifted their primary attention from organizational and institutional structures to examine the nature of organizational and institutional change, investigators have been confronted with decisions regarding the appropriate time frame within which to cast their study. Campbell (2004: Ch. 2) provides a helpful discussion of factors affecting this choice, including the differing rhythms exhibited by processes, theoretical orientation, level of analysis, pragmatic methodological considerations (e.g., availability of appropriate data), and attention to critical events affecting the process. I would hazard two generalizations about recent research on organization fields: (1) the most interesting and informative studies of the past several decades of organizations and institutions have been those employing a longitudinal perspective, and (2) too many of these studies suffer from designs whose time periods are too short to enable one to adequately comprehend the processes at work. This failure is especially damaging to scholars interested in assessing the causes and consequences of changes in normative and cultural-cognitive elements. As Roland (2004) reminds us, some institutional elements, such as administrative directives or policy prescriptions (regulative elements), are "fast-moving," while others, such as conventions, routines, habits, and logics (normative and cultural-cognitive elements), are "slow-moving," unfolding over several years or decades, if not centuries.

Paul Pierson (2004: Ch. 3) provides an illuminating discussion of various types of slow-moving causal processes. He begins by differentiating between the time horizons of causes and of outcomes. Some types of causes, such as conditions leading to a revolution, may take place over very long periods; similarly, some types of outcomes, such as state-building, may go on for extended periods. He differentiates between three types of slow-moving causal processes: (1) cumulative causes, involving the long-term build-up of incremental changes; (2) threshold effects—processes that have modest effects until they reach some critical level; and (3) causal chains, in which the particular sequence of development has a strong effect on the outcomes observed. Pierson provides less detail regarding varieties of slow-moving outcomes, but it seems obvious that these are particularly likely to occur in highly institutionalized arenas because of the entrenched nature of many of these arrangements. Work by Greenwood and Hinings (1996) provides some help. They point out that the rate of institutional change is affected by (1) the extent to which a given institutional field is tightly coupled with related fields—the more tightly coupled, the slower the change—and (2) variations in internal organizational dynamics—the more that some subset of actors who have access to power are advantaged by change, the more rapidly changes will occur.

❖ FIELD STRUCTURATION PROCESSES

Multiple Levels

As described in Chapter 4, Giddens (1979; 1984) defines the concept of *structuration* quite broadly to refer to the recursive interdependence or social structures and activities. The verb form is intended to remind us that structures exist only to the extent that actors engage in ongoing activities to produce and reproduce, or change them. In applying the concept to organization fields, DiMaggio and Powell (1983; DiMaggio 1983) employ the term *field structuration* more narrowly to refer to the extent of interaction and the nature of the interorganizational structure that arises at the field level. As noted earlier, the indicators proposed to assess structuration include the extent to which organizations in a field interact and are confronted with larger amount of information to process, the emergence of "interorganizational structures of domination and patterns of coalition," and the development of "mutual awareness among participants in a set of organizations that they are engaged in a common enterprise" (DiMaggio 1983: 148). To these indicators, others can be added, including extent of agreement on the institutional logics guiding activities within the field or on the issues around which participants are engaged, increased isomorphism of structural forms within populations in the field (i.e., organizations embracing a limited repertoire of archetypes and employing a limited range of collective activities), increased structural equivalence of organizational sets within the field, and increased clarity of field boundaries (see Scott 1994a; Scott et al. 2000: Ch. 10).

Earlier I stressed the important locus of the organization field as an intermediate unit between, at micro levels, individual actors and organizations and, at macro levels, systems of societal and trans-societal actors. Figure 8.1 depicts a generalized multilevel model of institutional forms and flows. Trans-societal or societal institutions provide a wider institutional environment within which more specific institutional fields and forms exist and operate, and these, in turn, provide contexts for particular organizations and other types of collective actors, which themselves supply contexts for subgroups and for individual actors. Various top-down processes—constitutive activities, diffusion, translation, socialization, imposition, authorization, inducement, imprinting (see Scott 1987)—allow "higher-level" (more encompassing) structures to shape, both constrain and empower, the structure and actions of "lower-level" actors. But simultaneously, counter-processes are at work by which lower-level actors and structures shape—reproduce and change—the contexts within which they operate. These bottom-up processes include, variously, selective attention, interpretation and sense-making, identity construction, error, invention, conformity and reproduction of patterns, compromise, avoidance, defiance, and manipulation (see Oliver 1991). Research by Schneiberg and Soule (2005) on the changing forms of rate regulation of fire insurance by several U.S. states during the beginning of the 20th century depicts policies resulting from "contested, multilevel" processes as competing regimes developed in different regions of the country. Forces at work in crafting a "middle way," which subsequently became widely adopted, included within-state differences in the power of relevant associations, attention to policies adopted by neighboring states, and decisions at the national level by the U.S. Supreme Court.

Early institutional sociologists emphasized top-down processes, focusing on the ways in which models, menus, and rules constitute and constrain organization-level structures and processes. Institutional economists and rational choice political scientists continue to focus on bottom-up processes as actors pursue their interests by designing institutional frameworks that solve collective action problems or improve the efficiency of economic exchanges. These scholars have now been joined by social movement researchers whose views considerably expand the types of actors, motives, and actions engaged in institutional change. Also, more recent work by a broad range of sociologists and management scholars, described in Chapter 4, has stressed the importance of attending to "institutional work" as actors strive to either reproduce, challenge, or change existing structures. In addition, other scholars emphasize the interweaving of top-down and bottom-up

Figure 8.1   Top-Down and Bottom-Up Process of Institutional Creation
and Diffusion

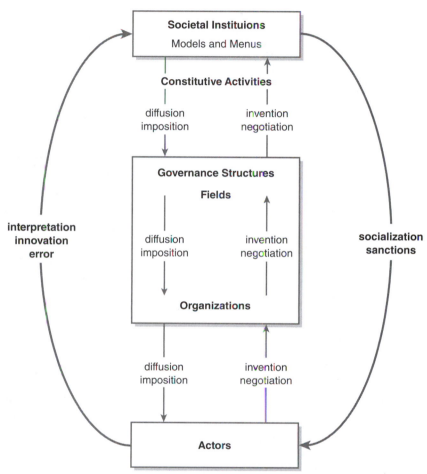

SOURCE: Adapted from Scott 1994c (Figure 3.1, p. 37).

processes as they combine to influence institutional phenomena (Powell
and Colyvas 2008). For example, we previously discussed the studies
by Edelman and associates (Edelman 1992; Edelman et al. 1999) and
Dobbin and associates (Dobbin 2009; Dobbin and Sutton 1998; Dobbin,
Sutton, Meyer, and Scott 1993), who explore how top-down regulative
processes initiated by federal agents trigger collective sense-making
processes among personnel managers, who construct new structures
and procedures that are reviewed and, eventually, authorized by the

federal courts. Regulative (federal laws), normative (professional managerial codes), and cognitive (sense-making) processes are connected in complex and changing mixtures.

In formulating a recursive, iterative model of institutional change, Holm (1995) proposes that it is helpful in examining the processes connecting adjacent levels to distinguish between two nested types of processes: "practical" versus "political" actions. The former are actions taken within a given framework of understandings, norms, and rules, serving to reproduce the institutional structure or, at most, stimulate incremental changes. The latter, political processes are actions whose purpose is to change the rules or frameworks governing actions. For example, explicit rules govern the activities of professional sports teams, but from time to time, team representatives and officials meet to review and make alterations in the rules based on accumulated experiences or specific problems encountered. While in some cases changes in rules are based on collective mobilization and conflict, in many organized systems formal structures are in place to support routine reviews of and revisions in rule systems. The creation of such formalized decision-making and governance systems serves to institutionalize the process of institutional change.

Widening Theoretical Frameworks

In addition to employing more multilevel and recursive models in institutional studies, institutional scholars have begun to widen their theoretical frames, taking advantage of ideas and approaches developed in related areas. I have already discussed, in Chapter 6, the constructive connections being developed between students of the legal environment and institutionalists. Edelman and Suchman (1997) distinguish three dimensions of legal environments relevant to organizational studies. Legal systems offer a "facilitative" environment, supplying tools, procedures and forums that actors can employ to pursue goals, resolve disputes, and control deviant and criminal behavior within and by organizations (see Sitkin and Bies 1994; Vaughn 1999). They provide a "regulatory" environment consisting of a set of "substantive edicts, invoking societal authority over various aspects of organizational life" (Edelman and Suchman 1997: 483; see also Noll 1985). And, most fatefully, they offer a "constitutive" environment that "constructs and empowers various classes of organizational actors and delineates the relationships among them" (Edelman and Suchman 1997: 483; see also Scott 1994c). Edelman and Suchman suggest that we need much more research on the ways in which constitutive legal processes function to construct interorganizational relations (e.g., tort law, bankruptcy law), construct distinctive forms of organization structure (e.g., corporate law), and contribute to an underlying cultural logic of "legal-rationality."

Another rapidly developing intersection, noted earlier, is that between social movement theory and institutional change. For many years, social movement theory has productively borrowed from organizational theory as Mayer Zald, John McCarthy, Charles Tilly, and others showed us how collective movements, if they were to be sustained, required the mobilization of resources and leadership to create social movement *organizations* (Zald and Ash 1966). And as numerous movement organizations pursued similar types of reforms, they identified social movement industries or fields within which such similar organizations competed, cooperated, and learned from each other (McCarthy and Zald 1977). Social movements have become more organized, and as the more nimble and flexible newer forms of organizations become more movement-like, the flow of ideas between the two fields has increased apace as institutional scholars learn from social movement scholars (Davis et al. 2005).

Among their contributions to institutional theory, social movement scholars have called attention to the openings and opportunities provided to suppressed groups and interests by the contradictions or inconsistencies in political institutions or governance structure, the mobilizing processes that give rise to new kinds of organizations, and the reframing processes that involve the creative construction of new meanings and identities enabling new possibilities for collective action (McAdam, McCarthy, and Zald 1996: 2–3; McAdam and Scott 2005: 14–19; Schneiberg and Lounsbury 2008; Snow, Soule, and Kriesi 2004).

All of these ideas are brought to bear by Elisabeth Clemens (1993; 1997) in her analysis of women's political groups at the turn of the 20th century in the United States. Lacking access to normal forms of political action (the right to vote), they "adapted existing nonpolitical models of organization for political purposes" (Clemens 1993: 758). The repertoire of collective action—the "set of organizational models that are culturally or experientially available" for women at this time and place—included unions, clubs, and associations. Employing these conventional models in unconventional ways mobilized around new purposes led to significant institutional change.

At the institutional level, women's groups were central to a broader reworking of the organizational framework of American politics: the decline of competitive political parties and electoral

mass mobilization followed by the emergence of a governing system centered on administration, regulation, lobbying, and legislative politics. (Clemens 1993: 760)

A neglected area of study has been the processes at work in the
transitional period during which successful movement objectives are
"handed off" to legislatures and public agencies for follow-through
and implementation. In our study of advocacy groups for youth development in urban areas, we have observed the ways in which issues and
objectives are reframed and revised as the action moves "from the
streets to the suites" (McLaughlin, Scott, Deschenes, Hopkins, and
Newman 2009).

Institutional theory will benefit greatly by continuing to cultivate
connections with law and society scholars and with social movements theorists, as well as with other rapidly developing research
communities, such as network theorists (Nohria and Eccles 1992;
Smith-Doerr and Powell 2005), students of society and accounting
(Hopwood and Miller 1994), economic sociology (Dobbin 2004;
Smelser and Swedberg 1994; 2005), technical and institutional innovation (Hargrave and Van de Ven 2006; Van de Ven and Garud 1986),
and international and comparative management (Ghoshal and
Westney 1993; Guillén 2001b; Hofstede 1991; House, Hanges, Javidan,
Dorfman, and Gupta 2004; Miller and Lessard 2000; Peng 2003; Scott
et al. 2011). All of these communities can bring theoretical insights
and useful methodologies to our understanding of institutions and
institutional change processes.

Selected Studies of Field Structuration

Evolving Corporate Structures

We can better understand some of the forces and mechanisms at
work in field-level change processes if we approach them as they were
observed in a few studies of particular fields operating in specific times
and places. We begin by revisiting Neil Fligstein's study (1990; 1991) of
changes in the structure of large U.S. corporations during the 20th
century (see Chapter 7). This research is particularly effective in pursuing three aspects of field structuration: the interplay of (1) private
power and public authority, (2) ideas and interests, and (3) field logics
and internal organization processes. We review each.

Recall that Fligstein's study examined a (changing) sample of
the 100 largest nonfinancial corporations during the period 1920 to
1980. These companies became increasingly diversified throughout

this period, but the diversification strategies varied over time, in part due to changing federal antitrust policies.

Whereas Alfred Chandler's (1977) detailed history of changes in corporate structure stresses the role of market forces and managerial strategic decisions, as described in Chapter 5, Fligstein reminds us of the power of the nation-state, not only to ratify institutional settlements enforced by the dominant companies in an industry, but also to establish and change the general rules governing competitive practices and growth strategies for all firms. For Fligstein (2001a) markets are not simply arenas of competition but organization fields whose members, in combination with state agencies, attempt to

> produce a social world stable enough that they can sell [their] goods and services at a price at which their organization will survive. Managing people and uncertain environments to produce stability is a sizable task. . . . The theory of fields implies that the search for stable interactions with competitors, suppliers, and workers is the main cause of social structures in markets. (p. 18)

Fields are vehicles for producing some stability and order for their members.

As for the interplay of ideas and interests, Fligstein (2001a: 15–20), more than most analysts, employs what he terms a "political-cultural" approach melding the role of cultural-cognitive elements or interpretive frameworks with the play of power among actors struggling to achieve a "system of domination" that will serve their interests. Fields are arenas for the interplay of contests between incumbents, who benefit from existing arrangements, and challengers, who seek to change the rules to advance their own interests. Governments, which can be conceived as a "set of fields," interact with markets, another set of fields, imposing rules to help insure stability.

Fligstein asserts that the changing strategies reflect changing institutional logics regarding competitive practices and growth strategies. But what is the process by which field logics result in organizational change? One obvious mechanism is environmental selection: firms not pursuing the favored strategy were more likely to drop out of the sample of largest corporations over time, particularly during the later period (Fligstein 1991: 328). Another mechanism explored by Fligstein is that changes in field logics trigger political processes *within* organizations so that corporations changed the criteria used to select their CEO. Fligstein (1991) categorizes CEOs in terms of their background under the assumption that a manufacturing person will tend to see the organization's problems in production terms, a sales and marketing person will tend to view the nature, size and extent of the market as critical to organizational survival, and a financial person will see the basic profitability of firm activities as crucial. (p. 323)

Empirically, he shows that the hiring of a CEO with a manufacturing background was associated with the subsequent adoption of a "dominant" strategy focusing on a single market; the hiring of a CEO from a sales background was associated with the adoption of a strategy of diversification into related markets; and the hiring of a CEO with a financial background was associated with the adoption of a strategy of diversification into both related and unrelated markets. As we have discussed, Greenwood and Hinings (1996) generalize these arguments by embracing Cyert and March's (1963) conception of organizations as coalitions of participants holding varying interests. Changes in field logics are likely to be viewed as advancing the interests of some types of organizational participants and as undercutting those of others. In this manner they propose to link the "old" institutionalism that focused more on power processes within organizations (think Selznick) with the "new" institutionalism that stresses field-level templates and logics.

Destructuration of a Health Care Field

My colleagues and I (Scott et al. 2000) elected to study health care delivery in the United States because this appeared to represent an instance of a relatively settled and stable institutional arena which, in the past few decades, has become increasingly unstable and conflicted. For our primary empirical data, we focused on changes in health care delivery systems within a limited geographic area—the San Francisco Bay area—but in accounting for these developments we included actors and forces at state and national levels. Data were collected to cover a 50-year period, from 1945 to 1995.

In order to empirically capture changes in the field, we selected three components on which to gather date:

- *changes over time in the types and numbers of social actors—both individual (roles) and collective actors (organizations)*

For example, we measured changes in the number and types (specialties) of physicians, changes in the membership of leading professional associations, and changes in the major organizational forms (archetypes) comprising the delivery systems, including physician groups, hospitals, home health agencies, health maintenance organizations (HMOs), renal dialysis units, and integrated healthcare systems. We also assessed changing relational connections among these various forms, such as clinics and home health agencies contracting with hospitals or hospitals joining integrated healthcare systems (Scott et al. 2000: Ch. 3).

I can think of no better single indicator for assessing change in an organization field than tracking changes in the number and types of organizations that operate within its boundaries. Organization archetypes are critical aspects of the field's "structural vocabulary." During the period of our study, the number and size of medical clinics, home health agencies, HMOs, and specialized treatment units such as dialysis centers expanded greatly, while the overall number and size of hospitals remained relatively stable. Given that the population of the region more than tripled during this time, the lack of expansion in hospitals, the traditional delivery unit, indicates that they were being displaced by other types of organizations. Of equal significance are the new types of organizations that emerged. Newcomers such as home health agencies, staffed largely by nurses who deliver care in patients' homes, and HMOs, which were designed to ensure that physicians are financially at risk for failing to control costs incurred by the care they prescribe, represent radically different approaches to health care delivery. These forms embodied novel organizational archetypes that challenge earlier models.

Of course, it is possible for existing organizations to change their archetype, substituting one template or "interpretive scheme" for another, as Greenwood and Hinings (1993) as well as Fligstein (1990) have demonstrated. However, both of these studies focused attention on a single population of organizations, municipal governments or large corporations. A distinctive advantage of field-level designs is that they widen the lens, allowing researchers to observe the rise of new forms that challenge, and sometime replace, existing forms. And although it appears that we are interested primarily in structural and relational changes—merely counting organizations—we are in fact attending to the constitutive work of changing cultural-cognitive beliefs as reflected in the organization archetypes.

- *changes over time in the institutional logics that guide activities in the field*

Multiple indicators were employed to ascertain changes in logics, including changing patterns in the financing of health care,[3] changes in public policy at the state and federal levels, changes in consumer beliefs regarding health care, and changes in professional discourse as revealed by a textual analysis of articles appearing in physician-oriented and health care administration journals (Scott et al. 2000: Ch. 6). The use of such archival sources to reveal changes over time in the meaning structures employed to interpret and guide actions of field participants provides a promising avenue for assessing the codependence of cultural and structural elements (Ventresca and Mohr 2002).

Composite indicators suggest that three contrasting institutional logics were dominant during different periods. Up to the mid-1960s, the dominant logic was an overriding concern with *quality of care* as defined and assessed by medical providers. In the mid-1960s, this logic was joined with a political logic emphasizing improved *equity of access*—the defining event being the passage of Medicare-Medicaid legislation in 1965. Somewhat later, in the early 1980s, yet another logic was introduced emphasizing the importance of cost containment measures employing both *market and managerial* controls. None of the three logics—each of which was associated with differing types of actors—succeeded in replacing the others. The unresolved contradictions and conflicts among these logics have greatly reduced the coherence and stability of field structure.

- *changes in governance structures that oversee field activities*

As defined earlier in this chapter, governance structures are combinations of public and private, formal and informal systems that exercise control within the field. During the period of our study, dramatic changes were observed in the kinds of actors exercising control and in the mechanisms employed. During the first half of the 20th century, the health care delivery field was firmly under the control of a hegemonic professional group—doctors of medicine. Having warded off a variety of rival claimants for jurisdiction over the field (see Starr 1982), subordinated a variety of ancillary groups (see Freidson 1970), and secured the backing of the several U.S. states exercising their licensure power, the medical establishment ruled by moral authority, exercising normative control, reinforced by state power, over the field.

As already described, by the mid-1960s fragmentation of physician interests and the coming to power of the Democrats resulted in the passage of the Medicare-Medicaid legislation, which overnight made the federal government the largest single purchaser of acute care and hospital services. Paying for a substantial proportion of the bills—which resulted in increasing demands—public authorities became more and more active in regulating health services. The number of health-related regulatory bodies operating at county, state, and national levels governing the Bay Area grew from a handful in 1945 to well over 100 agencies (Scott et al. 2000: 198). The normative power of the medical establishment, while weakened, remained in force but was now joined by public regulative powers.

Beginning in the early 1980s, new approaches to cost containment were introduced based on neoliberal economic assumptions regarding the effectiveness of more businesslike and market-based approaches. For-profit delivery systems were endorsed featuring stronger managerial controls, and incentives were employed to encourage patients to consume fewer services and providers to restrict treatments. New "health plans" emerged to define benefits, collect payments, and enlist panels of eligible providers. Thus, added to the mix of professional and public controls were private market and managerial governance mechanisms (Scott et al. 2000: 217–235).

Some time ago, Meyer and I argued that it is useful to view an organization's legitimacy as varying by the extent of coherence in the cultural environment underlying it—"*the adequacy of an organization as theory.* A completely legitimate organization would be one about which no question may be raised" (Meyer and Scott 1983a: 201; emphasis in original). From this perspective, given the inconsistency of views regarding healthcare expressed by professional, public, and private oversight authorities, the legitimacy of health care systems has markedly declined in this country during the past half-century. This is represented not only in the overelaborated and complex administrative units at the organizational level required to respond to the multiple and conflicting demands, but also in the overgrown jungle of financial and regulatory units and infrastructural apparatus—lawyers, accountants, health economists, actuaries, and insurance brokers—that contribute so much to the costs and confusion marking the current state of this field.

Similar Pressures—Divergent Responses

Nicole Biggart and Mauro Guillén (1999) examined the response of auto industries of four countries—South Korea, Taiwan, Spain, and Argentina—to mounting competitive pressures from the global environment (see also Guillén 2001b). For many decades, manufacturing fields serviced primarily domestic markets and did not have to take into account the productivity or performance of similar fields in other countries. However, in recent decades as a result of numerous political, technological, and economic developments, formerly "local" industries have been compelled to compete for survival with distant producers (Albrow 1997; Berger and Huntington 2002; Ó Riain 2000).

Biggart and Guillén (1999) employ an institutional approach to their study, emphasizing the following:

- the different kinds of actors available in each society (e.g., nature of the state, kinship structures, large firms, small firms, business networks)
- the "pattern of social organization that binds actors to one another" (e.g., the relation of states to industrial firms, of large to small firms, of firms to business networks) (p. 723)
- the organizing logics characteristic of the society: "organizing logics are not merely constraints on the unfolding of otherwise unimpeded social action, but rather are repositories of distinctive capabilities that allow firms and other economic actors to pursue some activities in the global economy more successfully than others" (p. 726)
- the industrial policies pursued by the state; nation-states vary in the development policies they adopt as well as in how actively they intervene in economic matters

Employing a distinction developed by Gereffi (2005), Biggart and Guillén note that societies characterized by more vertical linkages between strong states and firms or between large firms and subordinate units are more likely to excel at "producer-driven" activities linked to the global economy, whereas economies comprising small firms connected by horizontal linkages are more nimble and hence can be more responsive to "buyer-driven" global demands. Thus, for example, South Korea, with its vertically integrated *chaebol* (business units) and strong state has been relatively successful in auto assembly (producer-driven) operations but much less successful in creating a competitive system of components manufacturers. By contrast, Taiwan, with its highly developed small firms economy was unresponsive to state initiatives to promote auto assembly plants and instead has been able to compete globally in its manufacture of (buyer-driven) components. It is also possible for states to bypass their own business community and allow "foreign actors unrestricted access to the country" by encouraging foreign firms to make investments and establish direct ownership ties (Guillén 2001b: 17). This was the policy pursued by Spain. Biggart and Guillén (1999: 743) do not conclude that all strategies pursued are equally successful, but rather that the more successful strategies are those that build on a society's existing institutional logics. Such differences are not obstacles or constraints, but "the very engine of development. . . . Development is about finding a place in the global economy, not about convergence or the suppression of difference."

In short, we have here a situation parallel to that described in Chapter 7, where we considered the reaction of organizations with differing characteristics to similar institutional forces. Like organizations, organization fields are likely to vary substantially in their history, structural features, and capacities so that, when confronted by similar challenges, they are likely to respond not in parallel but divergent ways. This institutionally informed perspective varies considerably from that of a number of global observers, who emphasize the "flattening" of societal differences (Freidman 2005) or the rapid convergence of economic institutions and firm structures (McKenzie and Lee 1991) as the hallmark of globalization. Gray (2005) points out that, in this respect, such neoliberal arguments bear a close relation to earlier Marxist arguments since they assume that "it is technological advances that fuels economic development, and economic forces that shape society. Politics and culture are secondary phenomena." Institutionalists take strong exception to this view.

Identity-Based Fields

Two studies nicely illustrate the ways in which organization fields form around "identity logics." Armstrong (2002) studied the processes leading to the creation of a field of gay/lesbian organizations in San Francisco during the period 1950 to 1994. Early groups attempting to advance gay/lesbian causes, such as the Mattachine Society, borrowed their organizing template from public nonprofit organizations and functioned as conventional interest groups. During the 1970s, organizing models shifted to "identity politics" as groups embraced explicit sexual identity terminology, affirming gay identity often combined with a specific function (e.g., Digital Queers, Gay Democratic Club, Lesbians in Law). "Affirming gay identity and celebrating diversity replaced social transformation as goals, marking the origins of a *gay identity movement*" (Armstrong 2002: 371). The organizing template that was adopted featured developing occasions for identity display and self-expression; modes of organizing favored small, informal, and egalitarian units over more bureaucratic or professionalized forms. One of the more vivid images in the literature on organization fields is Armstrong's description of the colorful spectacle presented by the members of this organization field "on parade" during the gay rights celebration in San Francisco.

Like Armstrong, Rao, Monin, and Durand (2003) creatively combine social movement and institutional theory arguments in a study of "revolutionary" changes occurring in the world of French *haute cuisine*. The study examines the introduction by a rebel breed of chefs of a new culinary rhetoric, replacing classic with nouvelle cuisine. The upstart chefs emerged during the period of general political turmoil associated with student protests against the Vietnam War during 1968, a cause that rapidly became connected to a range of other anti-establishment grievances. I like to think the organizing slogan for this revolution was "Chefs of the world unite. You have nothing to lose but your sauces!"

Rao and colleagues suggest that the two cuisines—classic and nouvelle—represent differing institutional logics (rules of cooking, types of ingredients, bases for naming dishes) as well as contrasting identities for chefs in relation to waiters. Their imaginative method of tracking the progress of the new logic was to examine changes over time in the menus of leading restaurants, coding a random sample of the signature dishes of chefs between the years 1970 and 1997.

Both Armstrong and Rao and colleagues draw on a distinction in social movement theory between "interest group" and "identity politics." Most studies of social movements focus on interest groups pursuing some instrumental goal, for example, increased fairness or equality, whereas identity movements seek opportunities for "authentic" self-expression and opportunities to celebrate and display "who we are." Identity movements seek autonomy, not social justice (Armstrong 2002; Taylor and Whittier 1992). Employing historical materials as well as in-depth interviews, Rao and colleagues examine biographies of selected chefs who personally challenged existing rules—in some cases, rules embraced by their fathers—in order to convert to the new cuisine. However, for such ideas to diffuse into a movement, they needed to be "theorized" (see Chapter 6). This process was greatly facilitated by the media and by the specialized culinary journalists, who developed the "10 commandments"—including "thou shall not overcook," "thou shall use fresh quality products"—guiding the new cuisine and advancing rationales for its adoption. Systematic counts of the number of articles published between 1970 and 1997 extolling nouvelle cuisine in culinary magazines—cultural-cognitive legitimation—were found to correlate with adoption by chefs listed in annual directories of *Guide Michelin.*

Evidence concerning the normative legitimation of the movement came from two sources: the number of highly coveted stars from the *Guide Michelin* received by chefs who added a minimum of one nouvelle cuisine dish as part of his or her signature trio of dishes and the number of nouvelle cuisine activists elected to the executive board of the professional society of French chefs. Both were positively associated with the abandonment of classical for nouvelle cuisine. In short, the new logic was eventually endorsed by the relevant governance systems.

A particularly valuable aspect of this study by Rao and associates is its recognition of the important role played by intermediary actors in field structuration. The contributions of journalists who helped focus and frame and diffuse the new logic as well that of influential arbiters of consumer tastes—the editors of *Guide Michelin*—who gave their all-important stamp of approval to the insurgent band of chefs are systematically incorporated in the design of the study.

The Structuring of Biotech Clusters

Walter Powell and his many collaborators have examined the origins and early structuring processes of biotechnology clusters in the United States during the period 1988 to 2004 (Powell, Koput, and Smith-Doerr 1996; Powell and Owen-Smith 2012; Powell, Packalen, and Whittington 2012; Powell and Sandholtz 2012). Their study design is unusual in that their sample includes 661 biotech firms worldwide and their more than 3,000 partners. They focus on the origins—in their terms, the "emergence"—of successful biotech clusters in the United States, asking why three regional clusters have been so successful compared to firms in other areas. Their approach relies heavily on network approaches due to the fact that networks are an essential ingredient in this arena because all of the relevant capabilities required are rarely found within a single organization or type of organization.

Three clusters—localized organization fields—were most successful in forming during this period: the San Francisco Bay area took the lead in the 1970s and 1980s, the Boston area came later in the 1990s, and the San Diego area developed more slowly and somewhat later. The investigators argue that these more successful clusters emerged because of (1) a rich mixture of diverse organizations, including universities, nonprofit research centers, research hospitals, start-up companies, and venture capitalists; (2) the presence of an "anchor tenant," an organization possessing "the legitimacy to engage with and catalyze others in ways that facilitate the extension of collective resources"; and (3) some form of cross-network mechanism to enable "ideas and models to be transmitted from one domain to another" (Powell, Packalen, and Whittington 2012: 439).

No single model of successful field creation was revealed by the three cases; multiple recipes were employed. Thus, the identity of the anchor tenant varied from case to case: In San Francisco, cluster formation was heavily influenced by the matchmaking efforts of venture capitalists; in Boston, public research organizations, including universities and research institutions, provided significant leadership; and in San Diego, biotech firms, both small start-ups and mature firms, were the most instrumental. In San Diego, a failed acquisition effort between an established firm and a new firm fueled job mobility and information sharing in the area. In all cases, the anchor tenants were able to generate the new types of organizations—hybrid forms—that permitted "boundary crossing": the mixing of institutional logics and practices that allowed the translation of ideas from one realm, basic science, to another, the creation of commercial products. Science and commerce were lashed together in diverse ways as career flows triggered disruption: "Moving energy from one realm into another, or converting reputations and resources in one domain into motivating energy in a new arena, unlocked existing social bonds and expectations, creating space for a new form" (Powell and Sandholtz 2012: 407).

Regional agglomeration occurred in the three successful clusters because of successful collaborations that developed across a diverse array of organization forms. By contrast, in the eight less successful regions examined, single organization forms dominated, resulting in a mixture less capable of spawning successful collaborations among organizations, let alone new organizational forms.

The research by Powell and colleagues differs from previous field studies in part because of the changing nature of organizations and industries. Throughout the 19th and 20th centuries, fields were structured around some focal organizational populations (e.g., healthcare organizations) or an occupation (e.g., gourmet chefs). Students of new industries emerging during the late 20th and early 21st centuries, by contrast, have been compelled to focus on a diverse field of interdependent organizations; no one organization contains the requisite know-how and skills to determine the trajectory of field structure and development. Rather, the focus has been on industrial regions (e.g., Saxenian 1994) and related types of networked systems (Smith-Doerr and Powell 2005). Moreover, in a time of global competition and

rapidly changing demand structures, even more conventional industries, long dominated by Fordist-style, vertically integrated organizations, are being decomposed in favor of a variety of networked forms
and flexible commodity- and value-chain production systems (Gereffi
2005; Harrison 1994).

Thinking Across Fields

A common theme in research on organization fields is the movement of ideas and modes of organizing from one field to another.
Fields are never self-contained; they are always subfields of larger
societal systems and, particularly in contemporary societies, are
obliged to a varying extent to take into account the ideas and actions
taking place in neighboring fields. This is hardly a new idea. As
Marens (2009) emphasizes, some of Karl Marx's foundational ideas
about the engines of change in any political economy deal with the
role played by contradictory logics lodged in institutions (ideologies;
see Chapter 1). Clemens and Cook (1999) invoke Marx to motivate
their argument that many change processes in organization fields
have their origins in "internal contradictions"—instabilities inherent
in coexisting systems of belief and practice. Seo and Creed (2002: 223)
elaborate this argument with a series of hypotheses regarding the
ways in which "institutional arrangements create various inconsistencies and tensions within and between social systems" that transform
actors into change agents.

The Diffusion of Market Logics

While it is not overly apparent in the studies of field structuration
processes just reviewed, many field studies over the past three
decades reveal a common theme. They chronicle the incursion of economic (specifically, market) logics into organization fields previously
organized around other logics. In particular, fields once dominated by
professional (including nonprofit), public (state), or craft logics have
been colonized by neoliberal views emphasizing competition, privati-
zation, cost-benefit analysis, and outcome measures stressing financial
indicators. As a consequence, institutional models for organizing have
been altered: Collegial structures have given way to hierarchical
arrangements, and discretion and power have shifted from professional and craft workers to managers and financial analysts. Such is
the power of ideas!

Originating in Austria, a group of economists surrounding Frederick
Hayek, during the late 1930s became concerned with state expansion,

especially in socialist and fascist regimes, and argued for the value of a more competitive, less regulated economy. These ideas were advanced by Milton Friedman and other economists at the University of Chicago, giving rise of the Chicago school of neoliberalism embraced by many conservative think tanks and politicians (see Harvey 2005; Prasad 2006). They were also fueled by the rapid expansion of global competition among societies, encouraging governments to reduce regulations and taxes on firms and to cut spending on programs these taxes supported, especially welfare spending (Campbell 2004: Ch. 5). Moreover, they became the basis for policy and funding guidelines adopted by a variety of powerful international multilateral financial institutions, such as the World Bank and the International Monetary Fund (IMF), who made the acceptance of these assumptions a criteria for receipt of loans and grants by participating nation-states (Peet 2009).

Among the field studies that I just summarized, the invasion of neoliberal ideas is most apparent in the healthcare study conducted by my colleagues and me, but is also evident in Fligstein's study of the rise of financial criteria to displace manufacturing values in multidivisional corporations and in the study of biotech firms by Powell and colleagues, who describe the rise of commercial logics to supplement and fuse with academic logics. The wider literature provides many additional examples, among them:

- In professional and craft realms, work by Thornton (2004) and Thornton and Ocasio (1999) examines a shift in the higher education publishing industry from an editorial logic to a market logic. These shifts were reflected in a decline in the number of personal imprints (an indicator of editorial control), greater likelihood of becoming a division within a multidivisional firm, and a change in the criteria of executive succession within these firms.

Related work by Greenwood and Suddaby (2006) describes changes in recent decades in corporate accounting firms, as many of them have shifted from operating as single professional organization employing a professional partnership model to multiservice firms structured as a managed professional business form. As a consequence, accountants are subject to more centralized, managerial controls. (For related studies of changes in law, accounting, and healthcare, see Brock, Powell, and Hinings, 1999.)

- Work by a variety of scholars chronicles the incursion of market logics into the public sector. Arguments began in earnest during the

1970s that governments needed to be "run more like a business." Among the reforms introduced are contracting out services or functions to the private sector, the use of "public enterprises" (publically owned organizations that are dependent on nontax revenues), and public-private partnerships (see Brooks, Liebman, and Schelling 1984; Osborne and Gaebler 1992; Smith 1975). Similar attempts to restructure government—to increase accountability, emphasize output controls, employ private sector styles of management, and concentrate power in professional managers rather than civil service officials—have been carried out under the banner of "new public management" in the United Kingdom and its former colonies and in Scandinavia (see Greenwood and Hinings' 1993, study of municipal governments described above; see also Christensen and Laegreid 2001).

Research by Zelner, Henisz, and Holburn (2009) examines the decision by more than 80 countries to privatize electric power utilities involving more than 970 projects during the period 1989 to 2001. The countries experienced strong ideological pressures associated with a growing consensus among economic and political decision makers as well as the lending policies of multilateral agencies such as the World Bank and the IMF to sell off state-owned facilities and encourage private power development. Although large numbers succumbed to these pressures, analysis revealed that during the period of observation, about 20% of the projects involving 37% of the countries experienced retrenchment, restoring the political objectives of the state-centered model without formal repeal of the neoliberal measured adopted. Responding to domestic sociopolitical normative and cognitive forces, a number of states were able to push back on neoliberal "reforms."

- Not only the public sector but the nonprofit and voluntary sector has also been besieged by reformers attempting to restructure them around more "businesslike" models (Powell and Steinberg 2006; Salamon 2002). Hwang and Powell (2009) provide a nuanced study of these rationalization processes occurring in recent decades in a sample of nonprofit organizations in the San Franciscan metropolitan area driven largely by pressures from public agencies and foundations to bring in professional managers. Volunteers have been replaced by paid staff, and managers have introduced systems to improve accountability and "benchmarking" to induce competitive processes and increase efficiency. The discretion once enjoyed by "substantive professionals" (e.g., social workers, mental health personnel) has been curbed in favor of more centralized "strategic" goal setting and managerial controls.

Another example of related processes is provided by the study by Lounsbury and colleagues (2003) described earlier of recycling systems shifting from volunteer to for-profit forms. Also, many studies have been conducted of the conflicts between business and artistic values in cultural industries such as architecture, the performing arts, and film and TV production (e.g., Jones and Thornton 2005; Lampel, Shamsie, and Lant 2006). A different mode of entry by the private sector into fields traditionally associated with nonprofit enterprise is represented by the *social enterprise*—a hybrid form that employs conventional commercial strategies to achieve social ends, such as improving living conditions and protecting the environment (Billis 2010).

- Another field recently impacted by economic logics is that of higher education. There are examples on many fronts, but I focus on three field studies that probe these changes. I already discussed in Chapter 6 Kraatz, Ventresca, and Deng's (2010) study of changes in the organization structure of a number of liberal arts colleges as they introduced "enrollment" management as a way to increase the salience for admissions officers of taking into account a student's ability to pay. But student choices are also reshaping liberal arts programs. Research by Brint and colleagues (Brint 2002; Brint, Proctor, Murphy, and Hanneman 2012) reports that these colleges are increasingly responding to a "market model" in which students are viewed as consumers whose choices should drive the structure of the curriculum. As a consequence, during the period 1980 to 2000, growth in the more institutionalized and "basic" fields of knowledge such as English and mathematics were rapidly outpaced by that in more professionally oriented and "practical" fields of study (e.g., business, engineering, health sciences). These changes were also found to be associated with changes in donor priorities.

The third study marks changes on the research side of universities as technology-transfer offices have grown rapidly to allow universities and their faculties to reap the financial fruits of knowledge creation (Colyvas and Powell 2007). The kinds of activities that once were a cause for expulsion—financially profiting from the knowledge one had created by making it proprietary—were relatively quickly accepted by major universities and led to a redrawing of the boundaries around what kinds of actions and interactions with firms were considered to be legitimate.

Are such changes inevitable? Taking a longer-term historical view, Schneiberg and a variety of collaborators argue they need not be. They point out that in any robust economy, a variety of models for organizing economic activity coexist and compete at any given time. Even during the period of most active industrial development at the turn of the 20th century, which witnessed the dominance of mass production and corporate forms, many associational models, including cooperatives, mutual associations, and municipal utilities, continued to flourish in many sectors of the economy (Berk and Schneiberg 2005; Schneiberg 2007). These alternative organizational templates are available and remain viable in selected contexts. For example, even in the current neoliberal era, a significant number of mutual savings and loan associations well embedded in their communities have successfully resisted conversion to stock company form (Schneiberg, Goldstein, Kraatz, and Moore 2007).

The Diffusion of Religious Logics

Although there have been relatively few studies by institutional scholars dealing with the diffusion of religious logics from their home domain, this clearly represents one of the major arenas of social change in our time. In more traditional societies, we observe that religious beliefs and practices often penetrate and strongly shape others societal sectors, such as politics and education. Thus, in many contemporary Muslim-dominated societies, we observe the playing out of religious doctrines in many non-church contexts. Such trespassing has been largely curtailed in most contemporary secular societies until recent decades.

Much to the surprise of many sociologists who had grown accustomed to the steady march of secularism (e.g., Habermas and colleagues [2010] view with alarm the derailing of the Enlightenment project of modernism), three mainstream religious faiths—Christianity, Islam, and Judaism—have all experienced a major surge of fundamentalism within their ranks. Fundamentalism may be viewed as a religiously based cognitive and affective orientation to the world that entails resistance to change and the ideological orientation of modernization (Antoun 2001; Emerson and Hartman 2006). And, as a consequence, numerous fundamentalist religious leaders and lay believers have become increasingly active in introducing their beliefs into kinship systems, defending traditional gender roles; political contexts, as the basis for supporting particular issues or candidates; and educational systems, as guidelines for revising curricula or selecting teaching personnel.

A useful examination of attempts by religious activists to influence school curricula was conducted by Binder (2002), who studied the efforts of evangelical Christian groups to introduce "creationist" arguments into the science curricula in four public school systems during the period 1981 to 2000. Efforts occurring in three states (Louisiana, California, and Kansas) were chronicled at multiple levels (local, state, national) and across multiple types of actors and forums (activists and school-level professionals, state and federal courts, school boards, and state legislatures). Her research suggests that the efforts of religious groups (challengers) were more successful in cases where the changes advocated were framed not as melding science and religious beliefs but as allowing "all children to feel welcome in publicly paid-for schools and to offer 'balanced' scientific instruction in science classrooms for the good of *science*" (p. 220). Even so, these efforts were observed to be more effective in changing political policies than in changing within-school institutional practice. We need more studies of this important source of institutional change.

❖   A REVISED AGENDA AND FRAMEWORK

Davis and Marquis (2005) have suggested that the time has come to seriously consider whether the organization is the appropriate level of analysis for most of the questions we social scientists want to address and the processes we seek to understand. The view of "an organization" as a relatively independent and self-contained actor engaged in mobilizing resources to accomplish specific goals has always been more applicable to the Anglo-American scene than that of Europe or Asia, where organizations are heavily embedded in state-level or broader collective systems. And even in the United States, as global interdependence increases and new industries emerge, the notion of a stable firm conducting business in regularized ways over time seems less applicable to a wide range of economic activity. As far back as 1937, Coase noted that in a market economy we find "islands of conscious power in this ocean of unconscious cooperation like lumps of butter coagulating in a pail of buttermilk" (p. 388). And the lumps seem to be melting ever more quickly!

In a related vein, a number of social scientists are urging that we turn our attention to the study of processes rather than the study of structure—to *organizing* rather than *organizations* (Scott and Davis 2007: Ch. 14). In preceding chapters, I noted a new emphasis on structuration processes, on institutional "work" rather than institutions, and on social mechanisms. Davis and Marquis (2005) argue that attention to field-level processes may be the salvation of organization studies, suggesting that "an appropriate aspiration for organization theory in the early 21st century is providing a natural history of the changing institutions of contemporary capitalism." While I tend to concur, I would add that others, such as social psychologists, can also usually participate in this project by examining the role of individual actors as they respond to and shape these processes. So, more broadly, this may be an appropriate agenda for all of social science.

A number of these themes are summarized and captured by a discussion of field studies and the natural environment by Hoffman and Ventresca (2002). Their detailed comments will not be reviewed here, but I think it instructive to reproduce their table "expanding" the elements of field-level analysis (see Table 8.1). They celebrate the advantages of adopting this higher, more encompassing level of analysis, emphasize the shift from structure to process, insist on attention to the empowering as well as the constraining effects of institutions, attend to both structural and cultural elements, and recognize a larger role for power processes and strategic action.

Table 8.1   Expanding the Elements of Environmental and Field-Level Analysis

Element	Current View	Expanded View
Level of analsis	Organisation-level activity	Field-level activity
Market activity	Rationally directed	Politically inflected
Fields	Centered on common technology and markets	Centered around issues of debate
	Domains of stability	Domains of contest, conflict, and change
Institutions	Things	Process and Mechanisms
	Constraints	Opportunities *and* Constraints
	Cognitive	Cognitive *and* political
Central organizing concept	Isomorphism	Collective rationalality
Institutions and organizations	Separate levels of analysis	Linked levels of analysis
Field/organization interface	Unidirectional from field to organization	Dual-directional between field and organization

(Continued)

Table 8.1 (Continued)

Element	Current View	Expanded View
	Uniform across organizational contexts	Affected by organizational filtering and enactment processes
Organizational activity	Defined by field-level activity	Negotiated with field-level constituents
	Strategically inert	Strategically active
	Scripted	Entrepreneurial
	Homogeneous	Heterogeneous
Institutional change	Undeveloped	Open to entrepreneurial influence

❖ CONCLUDING COMMENT

The concept of organization field expands the framework of analytic attention to encompass relevant actors, institutional logics, and governance structures that empower and constrain the actions of participants—both individuals and organizations—in a delimited social sphere. It includes within its purview all of these parties that are meaningfully involved in some collective enterprise—whether producing a product or service, carrying out some specific policy, or attempting to resolve a common issue. The concept has not only encouraged attention to a "higher" (more encompassing) level of analysis; it has stimulated interest in organizational processes that take place over longer periods of time. To adequately comprehend the determinants, mechanisms, and effects of significant institutional change—or stability for that matter—demands attention to longer time periods.

Organization fields vary considerably among themselves and over time. The concept of field structuration provides a useful analytic framework, allowing investigators to assess differences among fields and to track changes over time in the extent of the field's cultural coherence and nature of its structural features.

While it would appear that a field-level focus would detract attention from our attempt to understand the behavior of individual organizations and their participants, I believe that this is far from being true.

Just as the attributes and actions of a character in a play are not fully comprehensible apart from knowledge of the wider drama being enacted—including the nature and interest of the other players, their relationships, and the logics that guide their actions—so we can better fathom an individual and organization's behavior by seeing it in the context of the larger action, relational, and meaning system in which it participates.

❖ NOTES

1. For a review of these efforts, see Scott and Davis (2007: 8–10).

2. We consider in a later section processes leading to the replacement of one archetype with another.

3. Financing issues are never just about material resources. In this case, Congress decided that the nation-state, rather than the individual, was responsible for financing medical care for the elderly and the indigent.

9

An Overview, an Observation, a Caution, and a Sermon

> *As a basic orientation toward life, institutional thinking understands itself to be in a position primarily of receiving rather than of inventing or creating. The emphasis is not on thinking up things for yourself, but on thoughtfully taking delivery of and using what has been handed down to you.*
>
> —Hugh Heclo (2008: 98)

I begin this brief coda by commenting on what I see as the distinctive flavor and texture of an institutional approach. Then I attempt to sum up some of the developments during the past half-century that, in my opinion, are signs of progress—indicators of a maturing intellectual field. Third, I note the ways in which institutional theorizing has proceeded in recent decades. Next, I comment on a special type of metaphysical pathos that institutional theory is prone to that we would do well to guard against, and, finally, I conclude with a brief sermon.

❖ DISTINCTIVE FEATURES

Institutional theory differs from alternative approaches to the study of organizations in a number of ways that are important to identify. The following appear to be important:

- Institutionalists eschew a totalistic or monolithic view of organizational and societal structures and processes.

The institutional perspective, more so than others, emphasizes the importance of the social context within which organizations operate. Indeed, the "figure" (organization) is often defocalized to stress the centrality of the "ground" (environment). In many institutional accounts, "the figure is not simply embedded in, but also penetrated and constituted by, the ground" (Scott and Christensen 1995: 310). As suggested in Chapter 8, institutional theorists recognize the value of attending to the larger drama, rather than to the individual player.

In addition, institutionalists are more likely than many other analysts to conditionalize their generalizations. Rather than seeking universal social laws, on the one hand, or reverting to "pure description and story-telling," on the other, they operate at an "intermediary level" that offers "sometimes true theories" of selected social phenomena (Coleman 1964: 516). As Swiss historian and economist Simonde de Sismondi (1837) observed nearly two centuries ago:

> I am convinced that one falls into serious error in wishing always to generalize everything connected with the social sciences. It is on the contrary essential to study human conditions in detail. One must get hold now of a period, now of a country, now of a profession, in order to see clearly what a man is and how institutions act upon him. (p. iv)

This view resonates with our emphasis on the importance of organization fields as a significant unit of study and level of analysis.

- Institutionalists emphasize that even innovative actions make use of preexisting materials and enter into existing contexts which affect them and to which they must adjust

As Tocqueville (1856/1998, 2001) pointed out, the French revolution arose out of central contradictions in *L'Ancien Régime*, and its development was subsequently shaped by this social and political framework (see Chapter 1). A more contemporary example is on offer as the "digital revolution" is beginning to challenge and reshape the contemporary field of higher education (Kamenetz 2010). While new modes of delivering education are being developed and new (primarily for-profit) forms of providers (colleges) have emerged, it is highly likely that, if they are to persist, these new practices and players will be required to accommodate to existing, institutionalized structures and processes (Scott forthcoming). Institutionalists stress the continuing impact of the old on the new, the existing on the becoming.

- Institutionalists insist on the importance of nonlocal, as well as local, forces shaping organizations.

An important addendum to the primacy given to context is the recognition that this concept—particularly in the modern world—can no longer safely be delimited by geographical boundaries. Many, if not the majority of, organizations are affected by and responsive to forces far removed from their local environment. This has long been the case, but is truer in today's world of intensified media and massive migrations (Appadurai 1996). As described in our discussion of institutional carriers in Chapter 4, institutional elements are highly portable and can arrive in the briefcases of consultants or the knapsacks of displaced people, come by the hiring of contract workers, or via the Internet and images of the cinema.

- Institutionalists have rediscovered the important role played by ideas, specifically, and symbolic elements, generally, in the functioning of organizations.

Reigning approaches to organization analysis in our time have for too long privileged the importance of material resources, technological drivers, and exchange/power processes in the shaping of organizations. From contingency theory to resource dependence and population ecology, analysts have examined in detail power and resource constraints to the neglect of cultural forces and cognitive processes. Indeed, throughout much of the 20th century, organizations have been treated as if they were "culture-free" systems driven by instrumental objectives and governed by "natural" economic laws. Political scientists, whose thinking has been dominated by rational models viewing relations between nations or other political actors as reflecting *realpolitik*—self-interested actors driven by material interests—are increasingly attending to the role of ideas in grounding interests (Goldstein and Keohane 1993). Institutional theorists reclaim organizations as creatures of as well as creators of manmade culture.

- Institutionalists accord more attention to types of effects occurring over longer time periods.

Too much of the work in social science concentrates on structures and processes of the here and now. As Pierson (2004) elaborates:

Many important social processes take a long time—sometimes an extremely long time—to unfold. This is a problematic fact for contemporary social science [where] the time horizons of most analysts have become increasingly restricted. Both in what we seek to explain and in our search for explanations, we focus on the immediate—we look for causes and outcomes that are both temporally contiguous and rapidly unfolding. In the process, we miss a lot. There are important things that we do not see at all, and what we do see we often misunderstand. (p. 79)

Pioneering institutional work by Selznick and his students emphasized the value of seeing institutionalization as a process occurring over time (see Clark 1960; 1970; Selznick 1949; Zald and Denton 1963; see also Chapter 2). These quasi-historical studies followed the development of a single organization over a relatively long period of time. Not long after, however, organizational ecologists began to conduct their longitudinal studies of organizational populations, beginning with the birth of the first organization of a given type and following the subsequent development of that population. Such studies emphasized the importance of taking a longer time perspective, ideally capturing the entire history of a given form (Carroll and Hannan 1989). Although this approach recognized the importance of studying organizations through time, these studies collected only minimal data about the organizations being tracked and, as Zucker (1989: 544) emphasized in her critique of this work, ecologists attended to time passing, but not to "historical time," assuming that one year is equivalent to another.

By contrast, during the past two decades, institutionalists have pioneered in the development of what Ventresca and Mohr (2002: 810) label the *new archival tradition*, which "tends to share key sensibilities in the historiographic approach, sharing its concerns for employing the nuanced, meaning-laden, action-oriented foundation of organizational processes." Key features of this work include its reliance on "formal analytic methodologies," "emphasis on the study of relations" rather than attributes, concern with "measuring the shared forms of meaning that underlie social organizational processes," and attention to "the configurational logics" that produce organized activity. The studies by my colleagues and me (Scott et al. 2000) and by Rao, Monin, and Durand (2003), reviewed in Chapter 8, exemplify most of these characteristics.

Still, we have far to go to fully take time seriously. In too many of our change models, time erupts to "punctuate" the equilibrium of our systems, which then return to stability. We need to attend to Streeck's (2010) advice to realize that "time matters," but

> it matters "all the time" and not just once in a while, since institutional change is basically conceived of as an unending process of "learning" about the inevitably imperfect enactment of social rules in interaction with a complex and unpredictable environment. (p. 665)

- Closely related to this concern with time, institutionalists also accord more attention to an examination of social mechanisms.

As described in Chapter 6, interest in mechanisms directs attention away from questions regarding *what* happened to questions of *how* things happen. Attending to processes of various kinds—fueled by environmental, relational, or cognitive mechanisms (McAdam, Tarrow, and Tilly 2001: 25–26)—is also a way of uncovering the sources of agency in institutional change.

- Institutionalists embrace research designs that support attention to examining the interdependence of factors operating at multiple levels to affect the outcomes of interest.

Institutionalists recognize that societies operate within and are affected by transnational processes and structures, organizational fields are affected by societal- as well as organizational-level phenomena, and organizations operate within fields that shape, constrain, and empower them, but are also influenced by the interests and activities of their own participants. In my view, the most interesting institutional studies are those examining the interplay of such top-down and bottom-up processes as they shape our social world.

❖ THE MATURATION OF INSTITUTIONAL THEORY AND RESEARCH[1]

More than 25 years ago, I wrote an article titled "The Adolescence of Institutional Theory" (Scott 1987). In reexamining that article, I think it accurately portrayed, even more than I realized, the undeveloped state of theoretical development of the field at that time, while also recognizing its promise and potential. Taking stock now, I believe it is possible to point to indicators of substantial progress. During the past few decades, we have moved

- from looser to tighter conceptualizations of institutions and their distinctive features

As reviewed in Chapter 1, early formulations about institutions and their effects were literally "all over the map." I believe that by focusing on a few key elements and examining the distinctive mechanisms associated with their operation, we have arrived at a more coherent conception of the phenomena of interest. Institutional forces are recognized to be complex and diverse in their makeup and modes of acting, but identifiable in their manifestation and measurable in their behavior and effects.

- from determinant to interactive arguments

Early formulations saw institutions as being monolithic and uniform in their features and determinant in their consequences. Researchers sought evidence of institutional effects on organizational forms and structures. More recent work recognizes that the institutional environments of many organization fields are fragmented and conflicted; because organizations have varying attributes and occupy different positions within the field, institutional effects are far from uniform. In addition, organizations viewed early as passive victims of institutional pressures are increasingly recognized to exercise varying degrees of agency, responding in diverse ways, ranging from abject conformity to outright defiance. Much attention has shifted from a focus on structure to attention to institutional work.

- from assertions to evidence

Early institutionalists, and I was among them, often simply asserted the existence of institutional effects. Thus, in our early study of U.S. public schools, my colleagues and I (Meyer, Scott, Strang, and Creighton 1988) assembled data over a 40-year period to substantiate increased uniformity of structure. We demonstrated empirically that this evidence of increased structuration was not a consequence of heightened centralization of funding, concluding instead that the changes reflected "the expansion and imposition of standard models" of organizing (p. 166). However, no data were adduced to validate this claim.

Over time, though, as I have tried to demonstrate, institutional researchers have devised imaginative and appropriate ways of testing their arguments. Our study designs and measures are far from perfect, but signs of progress are apparent in contrasting recent with earlier studies.

- from organization-centric to field-level approaches

The earliest organizational studies focused almost exclusive attention on the inner workings of organizations and the behavior of their participants (for a review, see Scott and Davis 2007). When the importance of the environment first became apparent to scholars, during the 1960s, substantial work followed, which adopted an organization-centric perspective—viewing the environment from the vantage point of a single focal organization. The organization's exchanges and strategies became the focus on interest. With the development of organizational ecology and institutional approaches, however, analysis shifted to higher levels, to organizational populations and fields. Attention shifted from the organization *in* an environment to the organization *of* the environment. I tried to describe in Chapter 8, and I elaborate below, why I believe the organization field level to be an especially appropriate venue for the application and testing of institutional arguments.

An interest in more macro approaches has not supplanted, but been supplemented by work at more micro levels. As I have noted, some of the more fruitful designs are those that attend to the interdependence and interaction of actors and forces at multiple levels—individual, organization, population, and field. Studies of top-down structuration processes, together with equal attention to bottom-up processes, have illuminated important facets of organizational life.

- from institutional stability to institutional change

Institutions, by definition, connote stability and change; therefore, it is not surprising that early scholars and researchers focused primarily on settled institutions to observe their effects on organizations. It was not long, however, before organizational researchers began to examine the social processes by which institutional frameworks come into being and by what means the more successful of them became more widely diffused and accepted. Studies attending to construction and convergent change processes were joined, during the 1990s, by new research examining processes of conflict and contention and of divergent change. This latter work was both inspired and infused by parallel studies by social movement scholars; over time, each of these two camps has stimulated and enriched the work of the other.

- from institutions as irrational influences to institutions as frameworks for rational action

A good many early formulations carried the implicit assumption that institutions undercut rational decisions and actions. Terms such as *myth, ceremonial,* and *superficial conformity* all smacked of subterfuge or skullduggery. Many organizational scholars dismissed institutionalists as dealing with superficial aspects of nonserious organizations. Although I believe this was a misreading of some of the early founding texts, it is an interpretation that has been hard to combat and eradicate.

For me, the concept of institution provides a way of examining the complex interdependence of nonrational and rational elements that together comprise any social situation. Values, beliefs, and interests,[2] along with information, habits, and feelings, are critical ingredients of social behavior. Which of us would claim that all our decisions represent "rational" choices? Of course, organizations were thought to be different from ordinary, less disciplined social actors like you and me. As discussed in Chapter 4, the kinds of ideas that gave rise to organizational forms are those that can be formulated as "rule-like principles" that give rise to "means-ends chains"—the basis for rationalized systems. However, as noted, rationalization is a broad tent. These formulations vary enormously in their empirical foundation.

The subtitle of DiMaggio and Powell's (1983) seminal article was "Institutional Isomorphism and Collective Rationality in Organizational Fields." Much attention has been lavished on the first idea, "institutional isomorphism" (see Chapter 7), but far less on the second. Nevertheless, the second idea is the more powerful, and it is the reason that I am so enamored of the possibilities offered by the field level of analysis. As I have tried to argue, it is at the field level where organizations in interaction construct their "collective rationality." It is at this level that one can most readily comprehend the construction of socially constructed frameworks of beliefs, rules, and norms—where we can observe contentious processes involving the participation of various types of actors with varying levels of understanding and influence, and always under the watchful eye and, sometimes, the active intervention of the state. If one looks across the myriad fields that comprise a modern society—banking, manufacturing, mental health, education— one finds multiple worlds of collectively rationalized action, each different from the other. Each defines different interests; each is peopled with actors bearing distinctive identities.

Even within the same field, if one looks across societies, it is to observe the same activities being carried out in diverse, rational ways. This truth is graphically documented in Frank Dobbin's (1994b) comparative study of the building of the railroad industry in the United States, England, and France during the 19th century. Dobbin details the divergent models of organizing, funding, and state involvement that emerged due to what he terms the diverse "political cultures"—I would call them societal and field institutional frameworks—at work in these countries. The institutions in each country constructed an arena of rational action within which individual and collective actors pursued their interests in diverse competitive and cooperative ways as guided by their cognitive frames and cultural assumptions. We observe collective rationality at work.

Progress in a given realm of social inquiry takes many forms, including theoretical elaboration and clarification, broadened scope of application of the ideas, improvement in empirical indications, and strengthened methodological tools. Another type of progress is signified by a growing set of connections intellectually linking the area of study with related fields—in the case of institutional scholarship— with work in organizational ecology, law and society, social movements, technology and society, and cultural sociology. Although there is not cause for complacency, there is much to celebrate in the recent history of our field.

Some observers skeptically wonder whether recent developments in institutional theory may have overly extended the scope of the enterprise (see, e.g., Palmer, Biggart, and Dick 2008). Is there a significant danger that institutional theory will become too broad, too encompassing? Have we staked out too wide a theoretical and empirical domain? Perhaps, but I doubt it. It is true that the range of concepts we employ is large (but the fact is that institutions are complex social systems) and that the levels of analysis to which they are applicable seems boundless. But no one study attempts to comprehend all meanings and levels in a single design. We have devised a rich tool kit of concepts and methods from which scholars may choose as they approach selected problems of interest. Rather than being apprehensive about the direction of our work, I am continually impressed and emboldened by the imagination of my colleagues and the sophistication of their research designs and analytic methods. The fecundity of recent contributions to the field lays to rest any doubts raised in my mind by the skeptics.

However, there is a concern that accompanies one of the major approaches used to construct new theoretical arguments.

❖ FRAGMENTED BY FRACTALS?

Andrew Abbott (2001) has pointed out that all academic disciplines become more complex over time, obviously differentiating among more specialized areas of study (e.g., the sociology of the family, the sociology of religion), but also, less obviously, by creating *fractals*. In this process, distinctions are created by the development of dichotomies (e.g., autonomy vs. control), but then the distinction is reproduced at a lower level, and again at a lower level, in a process of iteration. This process harkens back, as Abbott observed, at least to the work of Kant in the 19th century, but can be observed today in the development of institutional theory (see Figure 9.1).

In the dichotomy, autonomy–control, institutional theory clearly resides on the control side. It emphasizes the sources and uses of stability

Figure 9.1   Theory Development as Fractal Creation

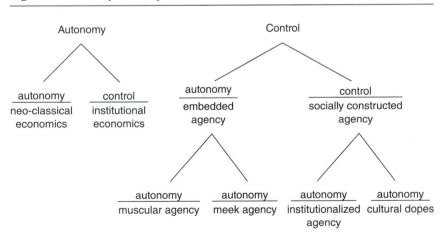

and order. However, as I have documented, as the field developed, we observe the dichotomy repeat itself, as some scholars begin to emphasize the existence and utility of autonomy *within* institutional frameworks (e.g., "embedded agency") (Battilana and D'Aunno 2009) in opposition to those scholars, such as Meyer (2008), who continue to stress the extent to which agency and actors are "socially constructed" by institutional processes. As this dialogue has continued, disputes have begun to break out among those who focus on autonomy within institutions as to how much or how little agency is involved, or, in a parallel fashion among scholars emphasizing control within institutions, how much or how little control is possible (Powell and Colyvas 2008), and so on. The distinctions become ever more fine.

This fractal mode of differentiation has several effects, as Abbott points out. First, scholars pay more attention to others in nearby rather than more distant camps. Thus, over time scholars tend to become more provincial, fine-tuning distinctions to separate themselves from close neighbors and distancing themselves from those working in related but more remote areas. Moreover, arguments between scholars can cause misunderstandings because the distinctions made are relational rather than linear ones.

The use of this approach also creates a now-familiar pattern of (re) discovery when, after burrowing deeper and deeper into territory defined by pursuing an ever-subdividing distinction, we are confronted with important factors we have bracketed out and are compelled to "bring something-or-other back in." And the things brought back in have included both sides of most of the important social scientific dichotomies. Some writers have brought people back in, others behavior. Some have brought social structure back in, others culture. Some have brought ourselves, others the context. Some processes, others structures. Some capitalists, others workers. Some firms, others unions.

A glance at these articles makes one think that sociology and indeed social science more generally consists mainly of rediscovering the wheel. A generation triumphs over its elders, then calmly resurrects their ideas, pretending all the while to advance the cause of knowledge. Revolutionaries defeat reactionaries; each generation plays first the one role, then the other (Abbott 2001: 16–17).

Finally, this pattern produces both change and stability. "Any given group is always splitting up over some fractal distinction. But dominance by one pole of the distinction requires that pole to carry on the analytic work of the other" (Abbott 2001: 21). In short, this pattern of theorizing produces steady work for social scientists, but not necessarily scientific progress.

❖ A CAUTIONARY COMMENT

If one examines the grand march of ideas across the centuries, it is possible to make a case for the regular repetition, and alternating dominance, of either more liberal or more conservative accounts of the human condition. Thus, for example, European intellectual circles during the 18th and 19th centuries experienced the heady period of the Enlightenment, with its celebration of Reason and Nature and Progress as the defining virtues—as espoused by such notables as Voltaire, Hume, Locke, Rousseau, and Mill. This exhilarating and optimistic moment gradually gave way (particularly after the failures of the 1848 revolutions) to a sober consideration of the limits of rational design and the impotence of mere individuals confronted with suprapersonal forces. Scholars such as Burke, Dilthey, Schleiermacher, and, most centrally, Hegel emphasized the overpowering force of History: the constellation of structures and the flow of historical processes as having a life of their own (Berlin 1956; 2006; Collingwood 1948; Dupri 2004; Robinson 1985). Such arguments became incorporated into the work of the early institutionalists—including Marx, Durkheim, Weber, and Schmoller (see Chapter 1)—who stressed the play of larger "historical" forces in the affairs of man.

Fast-forwarding to 20th century organization theory, a period of relatively optimistic work on organization design and strategy by such scholars as Taylor, Galbraith, Lawrence and Lorsch, and Thompson, along with the more strategic, political perspective of resource-dependence theorists, such as Pfeffer and Salancik and Porter, gave way during the late 1970s to much more pessimistic views, crafted by ecologists and institutional theorists, of an organization's ability to control its own destiny. These accounts variously emphasize the importance of imprinting and inertial forces or, alternatively, constitutive and embedding processes that foster increasing returns, commitments, and objectification processes that reinforce current paths of development. These arguments inevitably introduce a sense of constraint and caution to those who would attempt to intervene in or alter trajectories of change.

In short, institutional interpretations seem tailor-made to support conservative forces and voices in the social realm. As Albert Hirschman (1991), the perceptive observer of contemporary economic and political matters, has pointed out in his treatise on *The Rhetoric of Reaction*, conservative critics are poised to employ a "futility thesis" that asserts that any attempt at reform is doomed to failure because of the "intractable" nature of society's social fabric. Let me be clear. This is not a text about social reform. I am not advocating that it is our responsibility to take arms against inequities and injustice in our social structures (although some of us may choose to do so). However, we should see to it that our scholarship does not give aid and comfort to those who would seek to stifle such efforts.

To redress the imbalance, it is important that we recognize and publicize the more complex view of institutions as a double-edged sword. By stressing the role of institutions as curbing and constraining choice and action, we ignore the ways in which institutions also empower actors and enable actions. Those interested in redressing inequalities or pursuing other types of reforms can find inspiration and support from surveying and making judicious use of the variety of schemas, resources, and mechanisms that are to be found in any complex institutional field. Institutional forces can liberate as well as constrain. They can both enable and disarm the efforts of those seeking change. We must call attention to these possibilities in our scholarship.

❖   A BRIEF SERMON

Some of us may prefer to go even further in advancing the cause of institutional analysis. A productive model for doing so has been provided by the lifelong work of Philip Selznick. His work has been discussed in previous chapters, but few organization theorists have followed it beyond its early phases, in particular his study of the Tennessee Valley Authority (Selznick 1949) and his treatise on institutional leadership (Selznick 1957; see Chapter 2). Although as noted, the early thrust of his efforts appeared to focus on the "dark side" of organizations—the forces undermining their original mission—in fact, a close reading of his writings throughout his long career reveals that his work "reflects a peculiar combination of pessimism and optimism, realism and romanticism, resignation and hopefulness" (Kraatz 2009: 66). Krygier (2002; 2012) suggests that Selznick was a "Hobbesian idealist," deeply aware of the pathologies that can plague social organizations and institutions, and yet insisting that our task as analysts and involved participants is to seek and enact measures to strengthen their integrity.

The social sciences are defined by "the values at stake in human experience" (Selznick 1992: xiii). As Weber has long insisted and as I have suggested in the discussion of organization fields and institutional logics, social life is organized into meaningful spheres by the values being upheld and pursued (Friedland 2012). "Each subdiscipline is governed by implicit notions of personal or institutional well-being, which may take the form of economic rationality, administrative rationality, democratic government, cultural integrity, or effective socialization" (Selznick 1992: xiii). Selznick (1980: 215) proposes the development of a "normative theory of social science" that is "not the pursuit of one's 'own thing'"; rather, "it is the study of values in the world and the conditions under which they are fulfilled or frustrated." Employing a medical metaphor, Selznick (1992: 120) insists: "The larger objective of the study of human nature is to discover what personal well-being consists of, what it depends on, and what undermines it." Krygier (2002: 24) adds: "This is so whether one is studying persons, institutions, or groups."

Selznick's work is rooted deeply in American pragmatist philosophy, drawing particularly on the work of John Dewey (Selznick 1992: Ch. 1). In this sense, my sermon suggesting that we take seriously Selznick's approach has secular roots. The message has taken on new salience in a time when worldwide developments dispose us to distrust our institutions (Heclo 2008: Ch. 2; Lipset and Schneider 1987). Evidence of social dysfunction accumulates: the loss of legitimacy and respect for political bodies and public agencies, whether national, state of local; the misdeeds of financial institutions and accounting agencies; corporate corruption; scandals within religious bodies; and the breakdown of family and community structures.

If we examine the bulk of scholarship amassed by institutional theorists over the past half-century, I think it is accurate to say that this work tells us far more about how and why contemporary organizations and institutions fail to work than it does about what might be done to strengthen them.[3] Kraatz (2009) is even more critical, suggesting that the overall effects of the institutional perspective have been to "delegitimate power, to expose hidden forms of domination, and to reveal fragmentation and hypocrisy in the actions of organizations and their elites. It says very little about how to govern, reform, or productively improve any given existing social institution" (pp. 85–86). He suggests that institutional scholars attend more to the institutional work required to design and defend organizational structures, attending carefully to the critical importance of "mundane administrative systems" that preserve "precarious organizational values" (Kraatz, Ventresca, and Deng 2010: 1521). And Heclo (2002: 296) argues that, following Selznick's example, we "ought to think through the problem of maintaining ideals amid grubby organizational realities." Both are, I think, correct that our organizations require thoughtful care and feeding. But if this volume has taught us anything, it is that organizations are subsystems of wider systems. Institutional work is required at not only micro but also macro levels—in subgroups, organizations, organization fields, and societal systems—if values of importance to human life are to be preserved and advanced.

❖ NOTES

1. This section draws from arguments elaborated in Scott (2008a).

2. Hirschman (1996) points out that "interests" are a modern conception, a refined and sanitized version of "passions."

3. I believe this comment applies in particular to sociological work on institutions—my own work and that of my colleagues. Unlike economists, or rational choice political scientists, sociologists have been reluctant to advance suggestions for reform or policy prescriptions based on their analyses.

References

Abbott, Andrew. 1988. *The System of Professions: An Essay on the Division of Expert Labor.* Chicago: University of Chicago Press.

———. 1992. An old institutionalist reads the new institutionalism. *Contemporary Sociology* 21:754–756.

———. 2001. *Chaos of Disciplines.* Chicago: University of Chicago Press.

Abbott, Kenneth W., Robert O. Keohane, Andrew Moravcsik, Anne-Marie Slaughter, and Duncan Snidal 2001. The concept of legalization. In *Legalization and World Politics,* ed. Judith Goldstein, Miles Kahler, Robert O. Keohane, and Anne-Marie Slaugher (pp. 17–35). Cambridge, MA: MIT Press.

Abegglen, James C. 1958. *The Japanese Factory.* Glencoe, IL: Free Press.

Abell, Peter. 1995. The new institutionalism and rational choice theory. In *The Institutional Construction of Organizations: International and Longitudinal Studies,* ed. W. Richard Scott and Søren Christensen (pp. 3–14). London: Sage.

Abernethy, David B. 2000. *The Dynamics of Global Dominance: European Overseas Empires, 1415–1980.* New Haven, CT: Yale University Press.

Abrahamson, Eric. 1991. Managerial fads and fashions: The diffusion and rejection of innovations. *Academy of Management Review* 16:586–612.

Abzug, Rikki, and Stephen J. Mezias. 1993. The fragmented state and due process protections in organizations: The case of comparable worth. *Organization Science* 4:433–453.

Adler, Paul S. 2009. Marx and organization studies today. In *The Oxford Handbook of Sociology and Organization Studies: Classical Foundations,* ed. Paul S. Adler (62–91). Oxford UK: Oxford University Press.

Ahmadjian, Christina L., and Patricia Robinson. 2001. Safety in numbers: Downsizing and the deinstitutionalization of permanent employment in Japan. *Administrative Science Quarterly* 46:622–654.

Ahrne, Göran, and Nils Brunsson. 2008. *Meta-organizations.* Cheltenham, UK: Edward Elgar.

Albert, Stuart, and David A. Whetten. 1985. Organizational identity. In *Research in Organizational Behavior,* vol. 14, ed. L. L. Cummings and Barry M. Staw (pp. 263–295). Greenwich, CT: JAI.

Albrow, Martin. 1997. *The Global Age*. Stanford, CA: Stanford University Press.

Alchian, Armen A. 1950. Uncertainty, evolution and economic theory. *Journal of Political Economy* 58:211–222.

Alchian, Armen A., and Harold Demsetz. 1972. Production, information costs, and economic organization. *American Economic Review* 62:777–795.

Aldrich, Howard E. 2005. Entrepreneurship. In *The Handbook of Economic Sociology*, 2nd ed., ed. Neil J. Smelser and Richard Swedberg (pp. 451–477). Princeton, NJ: Princeton University Press.

Aldrich, Howard E., and Martin Ruef. 2006. *Organizations Evolving*, 2nd ed. Thousand Oaks, CA: Sage.

Alexander, Ernest R. 1995. *How Organizations Act Together: Interorganizational Coordination in Theory and Practice*. Luxembourg: Gordon and Breach.

Alexander, Jeffrey C. 1983. *Theoretical Logic in Sociology*. vols. 1–4. Berkeley: University of California Press.

Alexander, Victoria D. 1996. Pictures at an exhibition: Conflicting pressures in museums and the display of art. *American Journal of Sociology* 101:797–839.

Alford, Robert R., and Roger Friedland. 1985. *Powers of Theory: Capitalism, the State and Democracy*. Cambridge, UK: Cambridge University Press.

Anderson, Benedict. 1983. *Imagined Communities: Reflection on the Origin and Spread of Nationalism*. London: Verso.

Ansell, Christopher. 2005. *Pragmatism and Organization*. Unpublished paper, Department of Political Science, University of California, Berkeley.

———. 2009. Mary Parker Follett and pragmatist organization. In *The Oxford Handbook of Sociology and Organization Studies: Classical Foundations*, ed. Paul S. Adler (pp. 464–485). Oxford, UK: Oxford University Press.

Antoun, Richard T. 2001. *Understanding Fundamentalism: Christian, Islamic, and Jewish Movements*. Walnut Creek, CA: Alta Mira.

Appadurai, Arjun. 1996. *Modernity at Large*. Minneapolis: University of Minnesota Press.

Armour, Henry O., and David Teece. 1978. Organizational structure and economic performance. *Bell Journal of Economics* 9:106–122.

Armstrong, Elizabeth A. 2002. Crisis, collective creativity, and the generation of new organizational forms: The transformation of lesbian/gay organizations in San Francisco. *Social Structure and Organizations Revisited* 19:361–395.

Aronowitz, Stanley. 1992. *The Politics of Identity: Class, Culture and Social Movements*. New York: Routledge.

Arthur, W. Brian. 1994. *Increasing Returns and Path Dependence in the Economy*. Ann Arbor: University of Michigan Press.

Ashforth, Blake E., and Barrie W. Gibbs. 1990. The double-edge of organizational legitimation. *Organization Science* 1:177–194.

Astley, W. Graham. 1985. The two ecologies: Population and community perspectives on organizational evolution. *Administrative Science Quarterly* 30:224–241.

Astley, W. Graham, and Andrew H. Van de Ven. 1983. Central perspectives and debates in organization theory. *Administrative Science Quarterly* 28:245–273.

Axelrod, Robert. 1984. *The Evolution of Cooperation.* New York: Basic Books.

Barley, Stephen R. 1986. Technology as an occasion for structuring: Evidence from observations of CT scanners and the social order of radiology departments. *Administrative Science Quarterly* 31:78–108.

———. 2008. Coalface institutionalism. In *The Sage Handbook of Organizational Institutionalism,* ed. Royston Greenwood, Christine Oliver, Kerstin Sahlin, and Roy Suddaby (pp. 491–518). Thousand Oaks, CA: Sage.

Barley, Stephen R., and Pamela S. Tolbert. 1997. Institutionalization and structuration: Studying the links between action and institution. *Organization Studies* 18:93–117.

Barnard, Chester I. 1938. *The Functions of the Executive.* Cambridge, MA: Harvard University Press.

Barnett, William, and Glenn R. Carroll. 1993. How institutional constraints affected the organization of early U.S. telephony. *Journal of Law, Economics, and Organization* 9:98–126.

Barney, Jay B. 1991. Firm resources and sustained competitive advantage. *Journal of Management* 17:99–120.

Barney, Jay B., Mike Wright, and David J. Ketchen Jr. 2001. The resource-based view of the firm: Ten years after 1991. *Journal of Management* 27:625–641.

Baron, James N., Frank R. Dobbin, and P. Deveraux Jennings. 1986. War and peace: The evolution of modern personnel administration in U.S. industry. *American Journal of Sociology* 92:350–383.

Baron, James N., Michael T. Hannan, and M. Diane Burton. 1999. Building the iron cage: Determinants of managerial intensity in the early years of organizations. *American Sociological Review* 64:527–547.

Baron, James N., P. Deveraux Jennings, and Frank R. Dobbin. 1988. Mission control? The development of personnel systems in U.S. industry. *American Sociological Review* 53:497–514.

Bartley, Tim. 2003. Certifying forests and factories: States, social movements, and the rise of private regulation in the apparel and forest products field. *Politics & Society* 31:433–464.

Battilana, Julie, and Thomas D'Aunno. 2009. Institutional work and the paradox of embedded agency. In *Institutional Work: Actors and Agency in Institutional Studies of Organizations,* ed. Thomas B. Lawrence, Roy Suddaby, and Bernard Leca (pp. 31–58). Cambridge, UK: Cambridge University Press.

Baum, Joel A. C., and Jane E. Dutton. eds. 1996. The embeddedness of strategy. In *Advances in Strategic Management,* vol. 13, ed. Paul Shrivastava, Anne S. Huff, and Jane E. Dutton. Greenwich, CT: JAI Press.

Baum, Joel A. C., and Christine Oliver. 1992. Institutional embeddedness and the dynamics of organizational populations. *American Sociological Review* 57:540–559.

Baum, Joel A. C., and Walter W. Powell. 1995. Cultivating an institutional ecology of organizations: Comment on Hannan, Carroll, Dundon, and Torres. *American Sociological Review* 60:529–538.

Baum, Joel A. C., and Andrew V. Shipilov. 2006. Ecological approaches to orga- nizations. In *The Sage Handbook of Organization Studies,* 2nd ed., ed. Stewart R. Clegg, Cynthia Hardy, Thomas B. Lawrence, and Walter R. Nord (pp. 55–110). London: Sage.

Beamish, Thomas D., and Nicole Woolsey Biggart. 2012. The role of social heuristics in project centered production networks: Insights from the commercial construction industry. *Engineering Project Organization Journal* 2:57–70.

Becker, Howard. 1974. Art as collective action. *American Sociological Review* 39:767–776.

———. 1982. *Art Worlds.* Berkeley: University of California Press.

Becker, Howard S., Blanche Geer, Everett C. Hughes, and Anselm Strauss. 1961. *Boys in White: Student Culture in Medical School.* Chicago: University of Chicago Press.

Becker, Marcus C., and Thorbjørn Knudsen. 2009. Schumpeter and the organi- zation of entrepreneurship. In *Sociology and Organization Studies: Classical Foundations,* ed. Paul S. Adler (pp. 307–326). Oxford, UK: Oxford Univer- sity Press.

Bellah, Robert N., Richard Madsen, William M. Sullivan, Ann Swidler, and Steven M. Tipton. 1985. *Habits of the Heart: Individualism and Commitment in American Life.* Berkeley: University of California Press.

Bendix, Reinhard. 1956/2001. *Work and Authority in Industry: Managerial Ideolo- gies in the Course of Industrialization.* New York: John Wiley. [Reprinted by Transaction, 2001]

———. 1960. *Max Weber: An Intellectual Portrait.* Garden City, NY: Doubleday.

Benford, Robert D., and David A. Snow. 2000. Framing processes and social movements: An overview and assessment. *Annual Review of Sociology* 26:611–639.

Berger, Peter L. 1992. Reflections on the twenty-fifth anniversary of The Social Construction of Reality. Perspectives: The Theory Section Newsletter. *American Sociological Association* 15(2): 1–2, 4.

Berger, Peter L., Brigitte Berger, and Hansfried Kellner. 1973. *The Homeless Mind: Modernization and Consciousness.* New York: Random House.

Berger, Peter L., and Samuel P. Huntington, ed. 2002. *Many Globalizations: Cultural Diversity in the Contemporary World.* Oxford, UK: Oxford Univer- sity Press.

Berger, Peter L., and Hansfried Kellner. 1981. *Sociology Interpreted: An Essay on Method and Vocation.* Garden City, NY: Doubleday Anchor.

Berger, Peter L., and Thomas Luckmann. 1967. *The Social Construction of Reality.* New York: Doubleday Anchor.

Bergesen, Albert J. 2000. A linguistic model of art history. *Poetics* 28:73–90.

———. 2004. Chomsky versus Mead. *Sociological Theory* 22:357–370.

———. 2005. Culture and cognition. In *The Blackwell Companion to the Sociology of Culture,* ed. Mark K. Jacobs and Nancy Weiss Hanrahan (pp. 35–47). Oxford, UK: Blackwell.

Berk, Gerald, and Marc Schneiberg. 2005. Varieties *in* capitalism, varieties of association: Collaborative learning in American industry. *Politics and Society* 13:1–43.

Berkovitz, Nitza. 1999. *From Motherhood to Citizenship.* Baltimore: Johns Hopkins University Press.

Berlin, Isaiah. ed. 1956. *The Age of Enlightenment: The 18th Century Philosophers.* New York: New American Library.

———. 2006. *Political Ideas in the Romantic Age: Their Rise and Influence on Modern Thought.* London: Chatto & Windus.

Berman, Harold J. 1983. *Law and Revolution: The Formation of the Western Legal Tradition.* Cambridge, MA: Harvard University Press.

Biggart, Nicole Woolsey, and Mauro F. Guillén. 1999. Developing difference: Social organization and the rise of the auto industries of South Korea, Taiwan, Spain, and Argentina. *American Sociological Review* 64:722–747.

Biggart, Nicole Woolsey, and Gary G. Hamilton. 1992. On the limits of a firm-based theory to explain business networks: The Western bias of neo-classical economics. In *Networks and Organizations: Structure, Form, and Action,* ed. Nitin Nohria and Robert G. Eccles (pp. 471–490). Boston: Harvard Business School Press.

Bijker, W. E., Thomas Hughes, and Trevor Pinch. eds. 1987. *The Social Construction of Technological Systems: New Directions in the Sociology and History of Technology.* Cambridge, MA: MIT Press.

Bill, James A., and Robert L. Hardgrave Jr. 1981. *Comparative Politics: The Quest for Theory.* Washington, DC: Bell & Howell, University Press of America.

Billis, D. 2010. *Hybrid Organizations in the Third Sector.* Basingstoke, UK: Pelgrave MacMillan.

Binder, Amy J. 2002. *Contentious Curricula: Afrocentrism and Creationism in American Public Schools.* Princeton, NJ: Princeton University Press.

Blake, Judith, and Kingsley Davis. 1964. Norms, values and sanctions. In *Handbook of Modern Sociology,* ed. Robert E. L. Faris (pp. 456–484). Chicago: Rand McNally.

Blau, Peter M. 1955. *The Dynamics of Bureaucracy.* Chicago: University of Chicago Press.

Blau, Peter M., Cecilia McHugh Falbe, William McKinley, and Phelps K. Tracy. 1976. Technology and organization in manufacturing. *Administrative Science Quarterly* 21:20–40.

Blau, Peter M., and W. Richard Scott. 1962/2003. *Formal Organizations: A Comparative Approach.* San Francisco: Chandler. [Reprinted by Stanford University Press, 2003]

Blumer, Herbert. 1969. *Symbolic Interaction: Perspective and Method.* Englewood Cliffs, NJ: Prentice-Hall.

Boas, Franz. 1982. *A Franz Boas Reader: The Shaping of American Anthropology, 1883/1911,* ed. George W. Stocking Jr. Chicago: University of Chicago Press.

Boeker, Warren P. 1989. The development and institutionalization of subunit power in organizations. *Administrative Science Quarterly* 34:388–410.

Boli, John, and George M. Thomas. 1997. World culture in the world polity: A century of international non-governmental organization. *American Sociological Review* 62:171–190.

———. eds. 1999. *Constructing World Culture: International Nongovernmental Organizations Since 1875*. Stanford, CA: Stanford University Press.

Bourdieu, Pierre. 1971. Systems of education and systems of thought. In *Knowledge and Control: New Directions for the Sociology of Education*, ed. M. K. D. Young (pp. 189–207). London: Collier Macmillan.

———. 1973. The three forms of theoretical knowledge. *Social Science Information* 12(1): 53–80.

———. 1977. *Outline of a Theory of Practice*. Cambridge, UK: Cambridge University Press.

———. 1984. *Distinction: A Social Critique of the Judgment of Taste*. Cambridge, UK: Cambridge University Press.

———. 1986. The forms of capital. In *Handbook of Theory and Research for the Sociology of Education*, ed. John G. Richardson (pp. 241–259). New York: Greenwood Press.

———. 1988. *Homo Academicus*. Stanford, CA: Stanford University Press.

Bourdieu, Pierre, and Loïc J. D. Wacquant. 1992. *An Invitation to Reflexive Sociology*. Chicago: University of Chicago Press.

Boxenbaum, Eva, and Stefan Jonsson. 2008. Isomorphism, diffusion, and decoupling. In *The Sage Handbook of Organizational Institutionalism*, ed. Royston Greenwood, Christine Oliver, Kerstin Sahlin, and Roy Suddaby (pp. 78–98). Los Angeles, Sage.

Brint, Stephen. 1994. *In the Age of Experts: The Changing Role of Professionals in Politics and Public Life*. Princeton, NJ: Princeton University Press.

———. 2002. The rise of the "practical arts." In *The Future of the City of Intellect: The Changing American University*, ed. Stephen Brint (pp. 231–259.) Stanford, CA: Stanford University Press.

Brint, Steven, and Jerome Karabel. 1991. Institutional origins and transformations: The case of American community colleges. In *The New Institutionalism in Organizational Analysis*, ed. Walter W. Powell and Paul J. DiMaggio (pp. 337–360). Chicago: University of Chicago Press.

Brint, Stephen, Kristopher Proctor, Scott Patrick Murphy, and Robert A. Hanneman. 2012. The market model and the growth and decline of academic fields in U.S. four-year colleges and universities. *Sociological Forum* 27:275–299.

Brinton, Mary C., and Victor Nee. eds. 1998. *The New Institutionalism in Sociology*. New York: Russell Sage Foundation.

Brock, David, Michael Powell, and C. R. Hinings. eds. 1999. *Restructuring the Professional Organization: Accounting, Health Care and Law*. London: Routledge.

Brogan, Hugh 2006. *Alexis de Tocqueville: A Life*. New Haven, CT: Yale University Press.

Brooks, Harvey, Lance Liebman, and Corinne Schelling. eds. 1984. *Public-Private Partnership: New Opportunities for Meeting Social Needs.* Cambridge, MA: Ballinger.

Brown, John Seely, and Paul Duguid. 1991. Organizational learning and communities-of-practice: Toward a unified view of working, learning, and innovation. *Organization Science* 2:40–57.

———. 2000. *The Social Life of Information.* Boston: Harvard Business School Press.

Brown, Lawrence A. 1981. *Innovation Diffusion: A New Perspective.* London: Methuen.

Brunsson, Nils. 1989. *The Organization of Hypocrisy: Talk, Decisions and Actions in Organizations.* New York: John Wiley & Sons.

Brunsson, Nils, and Bengt Jacobsson. eds. 2000. *A World of Standards.* Oxford, UK: Oxford University Press.

Buchanan, James M., and Gordon Tullock. 1962. *The Calculus of Consent.* Ann Arbor: University of Michigan Press.

Buckley, Walter. 1967. *Sociology and Modern Systems Theory.* Englewood Cliffs, NJ: Prentice Hall.

———. ed. 1968. *Modern Systems Research for the Behavioral Scientist.* Chicago: Aldine.

Burawoy, Michael. 1979. *Manufacturing Consent: Changes in the Labor Process under Monopoly Capitalism.* Chicago: University of Chicago Press.

Burawoy, Michael, and Katherine Verdery. 1999. *Uncertain Transitions: Ethnographies of Change in the Postsocialist World.* Lanham, MD: Rowman & Littlefield.

Burdros, Art. 1997. The new capitalism and organizational rationality: The adoption of downsizing programs, 1979–1994. *Social Forces* 76:229–250.

Burgess, John William. 1902. *Political Science and Comparative Constitutional Law.* Boston: Ginn.

Burke, Peter J., and Donald C. Reitzes. 1981. The link between identity and role performance. *Social Psychology Quarterly* 44:93–92.

Burns, Lawton R., and Douglas R. Wholey. 1993. Adoption and abandonment of matrix management programs: Effects of organizational characteristics and interorganizational networks. *Academy of Management Journal* 36:106–138.

Burrell, Gibson, and Gareth Morgan. 1979. *Sociological Paradigms and Organisational Analysis.* London: Heinemann.

Burt, Ronald S. 1987. Social contagion and innovation: Cohesion versus structural equivalence. *American Journal of Sociology* 92:1287–1335.

———. 1992. *Structural Holes.* Cambridge, MA: Harvard University Press.

Calhoun, Craig. 1991. The problem with identity in collective action. In *Macro-Micro Linkages in Sociology,* ed. Joan Huber (pp. 51–75). Beverly Hills, CA: Sage.

Callon, Michael. ed. 1998. *The Laws of the Markets.* Oxford, UK: Blackwell.

Camic, Charles. 1992. Reputation and predecessor selection: Parsons and the institutionalists. *American Sociological Review* 57:421–445.

Campbell, John L. 2004. *Institutional Change and Globalization.* Princeton, NJ: Princeton University Press.

———. 2005. Where do we stand? Common mechanisms in organizations and social movements research. In *Social Movements and Organization Theory,* ed. Gerald F. Davis, Doug McAdam, W. Richard Scott, and Mayer N. Zald (pp. 41–68). New York: Cambridge University Press.

Campbell, John L., J. Rogers Hollingsworth, and Leon N. Lindberg. eds. 1991. *Governance of the American Economy.* New York: Cambridge University Press.

Campbell, John L., and Leon N. Lindberg. 1990. Property rights and the organization of economic activity by the state. *American Sociological Review* 55:634–647.

———. 1991. The evolution of governance regimes. In *Governance of the American Economy,* ed. John L. Campbell, J. Rogers Hollingsworth, and Leon N. Lindberg (pp. 319–355). New York: Cambridge University Press.

Campbell, John L., and Ove K. Pedersen. eds. 2001. *The Rise of Neoliberalism and Institutional Analysis.* Princeton, NJ: Princeton University Press.

Caronna, Carol. A. 2004. The misalignment of institutional "pillars": Consequences for the U.S. health field. *Journal of Health and Social Behavior* 45:45–58.

Carroll, Glenn R., Jacques Delacroix, and Jerry Goodstein. 1988. The political environments of organizations: An ecological view. In *Research in Organizational Behavior,* vol. 10, ed. Barry M. Staw and L. L. Cummings (pp. 359–392). Greenwich, CT: JAI Press.

Carroll, Glenn R., and Michael T. Hannan. 1989. Density dependence in the evolution of populations of newspaper organizations. *American Sociological Review* 54:524–548.

Casile, Maureen, and Alison Davis-Blake. 2002. When accreditation standards change: Factors affecting differential responsiveness of public and private organizations. *Academy of Management Journal* 45:180–195.

Caves, R. E. 2000. *Creative Industries: Contracts Between Art and Commerce.* Cambridge, MA: Harvard University Press.

Cawson, Alan. ed. 1985. *Organized Interests and the State: Studies in Meso-Corporatism.* Beverly Hills, CA: Sage.

Chandler, Alfred D., Jr. 1962. *Strategy and Structure: Chapters in the History of the American Industrial Enterprise.* Cambridge, MA: MIT Press.

———. 1977. *The Visible Hand: The Managerial Revolution in American Business.* Cambridge, MA: Belknap Press.

———. 1990. *Scale and Scope: The Dynamics of Industrial Capitalism.* Cambridge, MA: Belknap Press.

Child, John. 2000. Theorizing about organization cross-nationally. In *Advances in International Comparative Management,* vol. 13, ed. Joseph C. Cheng and Richard B. Peterson (pp. 27–75). Stamford, CT: JAI Press.

———. 2005. *Organization: Contemporary Principles and Practice.* Malden, MA: Blackwell.

Chomsky, Noam. 1986. *Knowledge of Language*. Westport, CT: Praeger.

Christensen, Søren, Peter Karnøe, Jesper Strandgaard Pedersen, and Frank Dobbin. eds. 1997. Action in institutions. *American Behavioral Scientist* 40:389–538.

Christensen, Tom, and Per Laegreid 2001. *New Public Management: The Transformation of Ideas*. Aldershot, UK: Ashgate.

Cicourel, Aaron V. 1968. *The Social Organization of Juvenile Justice*. New York: Wiley.

Clark, Adele E. 1991. Social worlds/arenas theory as organization theory. In *Social Organization and Social Process: Essays in Honor of Anselm Strauss*, ed. David R. Maines (pp. 119–158). New York: Aldine de Gruyter.

Clark, Burton R. 1960. *The Open Door College*. New York: McGraw-Hill.

———. 1970. *The Distinctive College: Antioch, Reed, and Swarthmore*. Chicago: Aldine.

Clegg, Stewart, and Michael Lounsbury. 2009. Weber: Sintering the iron cage: Translation, domination, and rationality. In *The Oxford Handbook of Sociology and Organization Studies: Classical Foundations*, ed. Paul S. Adler (pp. 118–145). Oxford, UK: Oxford University Press.

Clemens, Elisabeth S. 1993. Organizational repertoires and institutional change: Women's groups and the transformation of U.S. politics, 1890–1920. *American Journal of Sociology* 98:755–798.

———. 1996. Organizational form as frame: Collective identity and political strategy in the American labor movement, 1880–1920. In *Comparative Perspectives on Social Movements: Political Opportunities, Mobilizing Structures, and Cultural Framings*, ed. Doug McAdam, John D. McCarthy, and Mayer N. Zald (pp. 205–226). Cambridge, UK: Cambridge University Press.

———. 1997. *The People's Lobby: Organizational Innovation and the Rise of Interest Group Politics in the United States, 1890–1925*. Chicago: University of Chicago Press.

Clemens, Elisabeth S., and James M. Cook. 1999. Politics and institutionalism: Explaining durability and change. *Annual Review of Sociology* 25:441–466.

Coase, Ronald H. 1937. The nature of the firm. *Economica* 4:385–405.

———. 1972. Industrial organization: A proposal for research. In *Policy Issues and Research Opportunities in Industrial Organization*, ed. Victor R. Fuchs (pp. 59–73). New York: National Bureau of Economic Research.

———. 1983. The new institutional economics. *Journal of Institutional and Theoretical Economics* 140:229–231.

Coburn, Cynthia E. 2004. Beyond decoupling: Rethinking the relationship between the institutional environment and the classroom. *Sociology of Education* 77:211–244.

Cohen, Michael D. 2007. Administrative behavior: Laying the foundation for Cyert and March. *Organization Science* 18:503–506.

———. 2009. Reading Dewey: Some implications for the study of routine. In *The Oxford Handbook of Sociology and Organization Studies: Classical Studies*, ed. Paul S. Adler (pp. 444–463). Oxford, UK: Oxford University Press.

Cohen, Michael D., and Daniel A. Levinthal. 1990. Absorptive capacity: A new perspective on learning and innovation. *Administrative Science Quarterly* 35:128–152.

Cohen, Michael D., James G. March, and Johan P. Olsen. 1972. A garbage can model of organization choice. *Administrative Science Quarterly* 17:1–17.

Cole, Robert E. 1979. *Work, Mobility, and Participation: A Comparative Study of American and Japanese Industry.* Berkeley: University of California Press.

———. 1989. *Strategies for Learning: Small-Group Activities in American, Japanese, and Swedish Industry.* Berkeley: University of California Press.

———. 1999. *Managing Quality Fads: How American Business Learned to Play the Quality Game.* New York: Oxford University Press.

Cole, Robert E., and W. Richard Scott. eds. 2000. *The Quality Movement and Organization Theory.* Thousand Oaks, CA: Sage.

Coleman, James S. 1964. *Introduction to Mathematical Sociology.* New York: Free Press.

———. 1974. *Power and the Structure of Society.* New York: W. W. Norton.

———. 1990. *Foundations of Social Theory.* Cambridge, MA: Belknap Press.

———. 1994. A rational choice perspective on economic sociology. In *The Handbook of Economic Sociology,* ed. Neil J. Smelser and Richard Swedberg (pp. 166–180). Princeton, NJ: Princeton University Press and Russell Sage Foundation.

Collingwood, R. G. 1948. *The Idea of History.* Oxford, UK: Clarendon Press.

Colyvas, Jeannette A., and Stefan Jonsson. 2011. Ubiquity and legitimacy: Disentangling diffusion and institutionalization. *Sociological Theory* 29:27–53.

Colyvas, Jeannette A., and Walter W. Powell. 2007. From vulnerable to venerated: The institutionalization of academic entrepreneurship in the life sciences. In *Research in the Sociology of Organizations* 25:219–259.

Commons, John R. 1924. *The Legal Foundations of Capitalism.* New York: Macmillan.

———. 1950/1970. *The Economics of Collective Action.* Madison: University of Wisconsin Press.

Cooley, Charles Horton. 1902/1956. *Social Organization.* Glencoe, IL: Free Press.

Cooper, David J., Bob Hinings, Royston Greenwood, and John L. Brown. 1996. Sedimentation and transformation in organizational change: The case of Canadian law firms. *Organization Studies* 17:623–647.

Covaleski, Mark A., and Mark W. Dirsmith. 1988. An institutional perspective on the rise, social transformation and fall of a university budget category. *Administrative Science Quarterly* 33:562–587.

Creed, W. E. Douglas, Rich Dejordy, and Jaco Lok. 2010. Being the change: Resolving institutional contradiction through identity work. *Academy of Management Journal* 53:1336–1364.

Cyert, Richard M., and James G. March. 1963. *A Behavioral Theory of the Firm.* Englewood Cliffs, NJ: Prentice Hall.

Czarniawska, Barbara, and Bernward Joerges. 1996. Travels of ideas. In *Translating Organizational Change,* ed. Barbara Czarniawska and Guji Sevón (pp. 13–48). Berlin: Walter de Gruyter.

Dacin, M. Tina. 1997. Isomorphism in context: The power and prescription of institutional norms. *Academy of Management Journal* 40:46–81.

Dacin, M. Tina, and Peter A. Dacin. 2008. Traditions as institutional practice: Implications for deinstitutionalization. In *The Sage Handbook of Organizational Institutionalism*, ed. Royston Greenwood, Christine Oliver, Kerstin Sahlin, and Roy Suddaby (pp. 327–351). Los Angeles: Sage.

Dacin, M. Tina, Jerry Goodstein, and W. Richard Scott. 2002. Institutional theory and institutional change: Introduction to the Special Research Forum. *Academy of Management Journal* 45:43–56.

Dacin, M. Tina, Marc J. Ventresca, and Brent D. Beal. 1999. The embeddedness of organizations: Dialogue and directions. *Journal of Management* 25:317–356.

Daft, Richard, and Karl E. Weick. 1984. Toward a model of organizations as interpretation systems. *Academy of Management Review* 9:284–295.

Dahl, Robert A., and Charles E. Lindblom. 1953. *Politics, Economics, and Welfare.* New York: Harper & Brothers.

D'Andrade, Roy G. 1984. Cultural meaning systems. In *Culture Theory: Essays on Mind, Self, and Emotion*, ed. Richard A. Shweder and Robert A. LeVine (pp. 88–119). Cambridge, UK: Cambridge University Press.

D'Aunno, Thomas, Robert I. Sutton, and Richard H. Price. 1991. Isomorphism and external support in conflicting institutional environments: A study of drug abuse treatment units. *Academy of Management Journal* 14:636–661.

David, Paul A. 1985. Clio and the economics of QWERTY. *American Economic Review* 75:332–337.

———. 1992. *Why are institutions the "carriers of history"? Notes on path-dependence and the evolution of conventions, organizations and institutions.* Paper presented to the Stanford Institute for Theoretical Economics, Stanford University.

———. 2000. Path dependence, its critics, and the quest for "historical economics." In *Evolution and Path Dependence in Economic Ideas: Past and Present*, ed. Pierre Garrouste and Stavros Ionnides. Cheltenham, UK: Edward Elgar.

Davis, Gerald F. 2009. *Managed by the Markets: How Finance Reshaped America.* Oxford, UK: Oxford University Press.

Davis, Gerald F., Kristina A. Diekmann, and Catherine H. Tinsley. 1994. The decline and fall of the conglomerate firm in the 1980s: The deinstitutionalization of an organizational form. *American Sociological Review* 59:547–570.

Davis, Gerald F., and Henrich R. Greve. 1997. Corporate elite networks and governance changes in the 1980s. *American Journal of Sociology* 103:1–37.

Davis, Gerald F., and Christopher Marquis. 2005. Prospects for organization theory in the early 21st century: Institutional fields and mechanisms. *Organization Science* 16:332–343.

Davis, Gerald F., Doug McAdam, W. Richard Scott, and Mayer N. Zald. eds. 2005. *Social Movements and Organization Theory.* Cambridge, UK: Cambridge University Press.

Davis, Kingsley. 1949. *Human Society.* New York: Macmillan.

Deephouse, David L. 1996. Does isomorphism legitimate? *Academy of Management Journal* 39:1024–1039.

Deephouse, David L., and Mark Suchman. 2008. Legitimacy in organizational institutionalism. In *The Sage Handbook of Organizational Institutionalism,* ed. Royston Greenwood, Christine Oliver, Kerstin Sahlin, and Roy Suddaby (pp. 49–77). Los Angeles: Sage.

Dezalay, Yves, and Bryant G. Garth. 1996. *Dealing in Virtue: International Commercial Arbitration and the Construction of a Transnational Legal Order.* Chicago: University of Chicago Press.

Dill, William R. 1958. Environment as an influence on managerial autonomy. *Administrative Science Quarterly* 2:409–443.

DiMaggio, Paul J. 1979. Review essay: On Pierre Bourdieu. *American Journal of Sociology* 84:1460–1474.

———. 1983. State expansion and organizational fields. In *Organizational Theory and Public Policy,* ed. Richard H. Hall and Robert E. Quinn (pp. 147–161). Beverly Hills, CA: Sage.

———. 1986. Structural analysis of organizational fields: A block model approach. In *Research in Organization Behavior*, vol. 8, ed. Barry M. Staw and L. L. Cummings (pp. 335–370). Greenwich, CT: JAI Press.

———. 1988. Interest and agency in institutional theory. In *Institutional Patterns and Organizations: Culture and Environment,* ed. Lynne G. Zucker (pp. 3–21). Cambridge, MA: Ballinger.

———. 1990. Cultural aspects of economic organization and behavior. In *Beyond the Marketplace: Rethinking Economy and Society,* ed. Roger Friedland and A. F. Robertson (pp. 113–136). New York: Aldine de Gruyter.

———. 1991. Constructing an organizational field as a professional project: U.S. art museums, 1920–1940. In *The New Institutionalism in Organizational Analysis,* ed. Walter W. Powell and Paul J. DiMaggio (pp. 267–292). Chicago: University of Chicago Press.

———. 1994. Culture and economy. In *Handbook of Economic Sociology,* ed. Neil J. Smelser and Richard Swedberg (pp. 27–57). Princeton, NJ: Princeton University Press.

———. 1997. Culture and cognition: An interdisciplinary review. *Annual Review of Sociology* 23:263–287.

DiMaggio, Paul J., and Walter W. Powell. 1983. The iron cage revisited: Institutional isomorphism and collective rationality in organizational fields. *American Sociological Review* 48:147–160.

———. 1991. Introduction. In *The New Institutionalism in Organizational Analysis,* ed. Walter W. Powell and Paul J. DiMaggio (pp. 1–38). Chicago: University of Chicago Press.

Djelic, Marie-Laure. 1998. *Exporting the American Model.* Oxford, UK: Oxford University Press.

Djelic, Marie-Laure, and Sigrid Quack. 2003a. Conclusion: Globalization as a double process of institutional change and institution building. In *Globalization and Institutions: Redefining the Rules of the Economic Game*, ed. Marie-Laure Djelic and Sigrid Quack (pp. 302–333). Cheltenham, UK: Edward Elgar.

———. eds. 2003b. *Globalization and Institutions: Redefining the Rules of the Economic Game*. Cheltenham, UK: Edward Elgar.

———. 2003c. Introduction: Governing globalization—bringing institutions back in. In *Globalization and Institutions: Redefining the Rules of the Economic Game*, ed. Marie-Laure Djelic and Sigrid Quack (pp. 1–14). Cheltenham, UK: Edward Elgar.

Djelic, Marie-Laure, and Kerstin Sahlin-Andersson. eds. 2006. *Transnational Governance: Institutional Dynamics of Regulation*. Cambridge, UK: Cambridge University Press.

Dobbin, Frank R. 1994a. Cultural models of organization: The social construction of rational organizing principles. In *The Sociology of Culture: Emerging Theoretical Perspectives*, ed. Diana Crane (pp. 117–141). Oxford, UK: Blackwell.

———. 1994b. *Forging Industrial Policy: The United States, Britain, and France in the Railway Age*. New York: Cambridge University Press.

———. ed. 2004. *The Sociology of the Economy*. New York: Russell Sage Foundation.

———. 2009. *Inventing Equal Opportunity*. Princeton, NJ: Princeton University Press.

Dobbin, Frank R., Lauren B. Edelman, John W. Meyer, W. Richard Scott, and Ann Swidler. 1988. The expansion of due process in organizations. In *Institutional Patterns and Organizations: Culture and Environment*, ed. Lynne G. Zucker (pp. 71–100). Cambridge, MA: Ballinger.

Dobbin, Frank R., and John R. Sutton. 1998. The strength of a weak state: The rights revolution and the rise of human resources management divisions. *American Journal of Sociology* 104:441–476.

Dobbin, Frank R., John R. Sutton, John W. Meyer, and W. Richard Scott. 1993. Equal opportunity law and the construction of internal labor markets. *American Journal of Sociology* 99:396–427.

Dolan, R. J. 2003. Emotion, cognition, and behavior. *Science* 298:1191–1194.

Donald, Merlin. 1991. *Origins of the Modern Mind: Three Stages in the Evolution of Culture and Cognition*. Cambridge, MA: Harvard University Press.

Dore, Ronald. 1973. *British Factory, Japanese Factory: The Origins of National Diversity in Industrial Relations*. Berkeley: University of California Press.

Dornbusch, Sanford M., and W. Richard Scott, with the assistance of Bruce C. Busching and James D. Laing. 1975. *Evaluation and the Exercise of Authority*. San Francisco: Jossey-Bass.

Douglas, Mary. 1982. The effects of modernization on religious change. *Daedalus* (Winter): 1–19.

———. 1986. *How Institutions Think*. Syracuse, NY: Syracuse University Press.

Dowling, John, and Jeffrey Pfeffer. 1975. Organizational legitimacy: Social values and organizational behavior. *Pacific Sociological Review* 18:122–136.

Drori, Gili S., John W. Meyer, and Hokyu Hwang. eds. 2006. *Globalization and Organization: World Society and Organizational Change*. Oxford, UK: Oxford University Press.

Du Gay, Paul 2009. Max Weber and the ethics of office. In *The Oxford Handbook of Sociology and Organization Studies: Classical Foundations*, ed. Paul S. Adler (pp. 146–173). Oxford, UK: Oxford University Press.

Dudziak, Mary L. 1988. Desegregation as a cold war imperative. *Stanford Law Review* 41:61–120.

Dupri, Louis. 2004. *The Enlightenment and the Intellectual Foundations of Modern Culture*. New Haven, CT: Yale University Press.

Durkheim, Émile. 1893/1949. *The Division of Labor in Society*. Glencoe, IL: Free Press.

———. 1901/1950. *The Rules of Sociological Method*. Glencoe, IL: Free Press.

———. 1912/1961. *The Elementary Forms of Religious Life*. New York: Collier Books.

Dutton, Jane E., and Janet M. Dukerich. 1991. Keeping an eye on the mirror: Image and identity in organizational adaptation. *Administrative Science Quarterly* 34:517–554.

Easton, David. 1965. *A Framework for Political Analysis*. Englewood Cliffs, NJ: Prentice Hall.

Eckstein, Harry. 1963. A perspective on comparative politics: Past and present. In *Comparative Politics*, ed. Harry Eckstein and David E. Apter (pp. 3–32). New York: Free Press.

The Economist. 2011, October 29. Review of *Thinking, Fast and Slow*.

Edelman, Lauren B. 1992. Legal ambiguity and symbolic structures: Organizational mediation of civil rights law. *American Journal of Sociology* 97:1531–1576.

Edelman, Lauren B., and Mark C. Suchman. 1997. The legal environment of organizations. *Annual Review of Sociology* 23:479–515.

Edelman, Lauren B., Christopher Uggen, and Howard S. Erlanger. 1999. The endogeneity of legal regulation: Grievance procedures as rational myth. *American Journal of Sociology* 105:406–454.

Eisenstadt, S. N. 1980. Cultural orientations, institutional entrepreneurs, and social change: Comparative analysis of traditional civilizations. *American Journal of Sociology* 85:840–869.

Ellul, Jacques. 1954/1964. *The Technological Society*. New York: Knopf.

Elsbach, Kimberly D. 1994. Managing organizational legitimacy in the California cattle industry: The construction and effectiveness of verbal accounts. *Administrative Science Quarterly* 39:57–88.

———. 2002. Intraorganizational institutions. In *Blackwell Companion to Organizations*, ed. Joel A. C. Baum (pp. 37–57). Oxford, UK: Blackwell.

Elsbach, Kimberly D., and Robert I. Sutton. 1992. Acquiring organizational legitimacy through illegitimate actions: A marriage of institutional and impression management theories. *Academy of Management Journal* 35:699–738.

Elster, Jon. 1983. *Explaining Technical Change: A Case Study in the Philosophy of Science.* Cambridge, UK: Cambridge University Press.

———. 1986. *An Introduction to Karl Marx.* Cambridge, UK: Cambridge University Press.

———. 1989. *Nuts and Bolts for the Social Sciences.* Chicago: University of Chicago Press.

Emerson, Michael O, and David Hartman. 2006. The rise of religious fundamentalism. *Annual Review of Sociology* 32:127–144.

Emery, Fred E., and E. L. Trist. 1965. The causal texture of organizational environments. *Human Relations* 18:21–32.

Emirbayer, Mustafa, and Ann Mische. 1998. What is agency? *American Journal of Sociology* 103:962–1023.

England, Paula, and George Farkas. 1986. *Households, Employment and Gender: A Social, Economic and Demographic View.* Hawthorn, NY: Aldine.

Ertman, Thomas. 1997. *Birth of the Leviathan: Building States and Regimes in Medieval and Early Modern Europe.* Cambridge, UK: Cambridge University Press.

Espeland, Wendy Nelson, and Michael Sauder. 2007. Rankings and reactivity: How public measures recreate social worlds. *American Journal of Sociology* 113:1–40.

Espeland, Wendy Nelson, and Mitchell L. Stevens. 1998. Commensuration as a social process. *Annual Review of Sociology* 24:313–343.

Evan, William M. 1966. The organization set: Toward a theory of interorganizational relations. In *Approaches to Organizational Design,* ed. James D. Thompson (pp. 173–188). Pittsburgh, PA: University of Pittsburgh Press.

Evans, Peter B., Dietrich Rueschemeyer, and Theda Skocpol. eds. 1985. *Bringing the State Back In.* Cambridge, UK: Cambridge University Press.

Fayol, Henri. 1919/1949. *General and Industrial Management.* London: Pittman.

Feldman, Martha S., and Brian T. Pentland. 2003. Reconceptualizing organizational routines as a source of flexibility and change. *Administrative Science Quarterly* 48:94–118.

Ferejohn, John, and Morris Fiorina. 1975. Purposive models of legislative behavior. *American Economic Review, Papers and Proceedings* 65:407–415.

Ferguson, Priscilla Parkhurst. 1998. A cultural field in the making: Gastronomy in 19th century France. *American Journal of Sociology* 104:597–641.

Fine, Gary Alan, and Lori J. Ducharme. 1995. The ethnographic present: Images of institutional control in second-school research. In *A Second Chicago School? The Development of a Postwar American Sociology,* ed. Gary Allan Fine (pp. 108–135). Chicago: University of Chicago Press.

Finnemore, Martha. 1993. International organizations as teachers of norms: The United Nations Educational, Scientific, and Cultural Organization and Science Policy. *International Organizations* 47:567–597.

Fiol, C. Marlene. 2002. Intraorganizational cognition and interpretation. In *The Blackwell Companion to Organizations,* ed. Joel A. C. Baum (pp. 119–137). Oxford, UK: Blackwell.

Fiss, Peer C., and. Edward J. Zajac. 2004. The diffusion of ideas over contested terrain: The (non)adoption of a shareholder value orientation among German firms. *Administrative Science Quarterly* 29:501–534.

———. 2006. The symbolic management of strategic change: Sensegiving via framing and decoupling. *Academy of Management Journal* 49:1173–1193.

Fligstein, Neil. 1985. The spread of the multidivisional form among large firms, 1919–1979. *American Sociological Review* 50:377–391.

———. 1987. The intraorganizational power struggle: The rise of finance presidents in large corporations, 1919–1979. *American Sociological Review* 52:44–58.

———. 1990. *The Transformation of Corporate Control*. Cambridge, MA: Harvard University Press.

———. 1991. The structural transformation of American industry: An institutional account of the causes of diversification in the largest firms, 1919–1979. In *The New Institutionalism in Organizational Analysis*, ed. Walter W. Powell and Paul J. DiMaggio (pp. 311–336). Chicago: University of Chicago Press.

———. 2001a. *The Architecture of Markets: An Economic Sociology of Twenty-First-Century Capitalist Societies*. Princeton, NJ: Princeton University Press.

———. 2001b. Social skill and the theory of fields. *Sociological Theory* 19:105–125.

Fligstein, Neil, and Doug McAdam. 2011. Toward a general theory of strategic action fields. *Sociological Theory* 29:1–26.

———. 2012. *A Theory of Fields*. Oxford, UK: Oxford University Press.

Frank, David John, Ann Hironaka, and Evan Schofer. 2000. The nation-state and the natural environment over the twentieth century. *American Sociological Review* 65:96–110.

Freidson, Eliot. 1970. *Profession of Medicine*. New York: Dodd, Mead.

———. 2001. *Professionalism: The Third Logic*. Chicago: University of Chicago Press.

Friedland, Roger. 2012. Divine institution: Max Weber's value spheres and institutional theory. Unpublished paper, Department of Religious Studies and Sociology, University of California, Santa Barbara.

Friedland, Roger, and Robert R. Alford. 1991. Bringing society back in: Symbols, practices, and institutional contradictions. In *The New Institutionalism in Organizational Analysis*, ed. Walter W. Powell and Paul J. DiMaggio (pp. 232–263). Chicago: University of Chicago Press.

Friedman, Thomas L. 2005. *The World Is Flat: A Brief History of the Twenty-First Century*. New York: Farrar, Straus and Giroux.

Frost, Peter J., Larry F. Moore, Meryl Reis Louis, Craig C. Lundberg, and Joanne Martin. eds. 1985. *Organizational Culture*. Beverly Hills, CA: Sage.

Gagliardi, Pasquale. 1990. Artifacts as pathways and remains of organizational life. In *Symbols and Artifacts: Views of the Corporate Landscape*, ed. Pasquale Gagliardi (pp. 3–38). New York: Walter de Gruyter.

Galaskiewicz, Joseph. 1979. The structure of community organization networks. *Social Forces* 57:1346–1364.

Galaskiewicz, Joseph, and Wolfgang Bielefeld. 1998. *Nonprofit Organizations in an Age of Uncertainty: A Study of Organizational Change.* New York: Aldine De Gruyter.

Galaskiewicz, Joseph, and Ronald S. Burt. 1991. Interorganizational contagion in corporate philanthropy. *Administrative Science Quarterly* 36:88–105.

Garfinkel, Harold. 1967. *Studies in Ethnomethodology.* Englewood Cliffs, NJ: Prentice Hall.

———. 1974. The origins of the term "ethnomethodology." In *Ethnomethodology: Selected Readings,* ed. Roy Turner (pp. 15–18). Harmondworth, UK: Penguin Books.

Geertz, Clifford. 1971. *Islam Observed: Religious Development in Morocco and Indonesia.* Chicago: University of Chicago Press.

———. 1973. *The Interpretation of Cultures.* New York: Basic Books.

Georgopoulos, Basil S. 1972. The hospital as an organization and problem-solving system. In *Organization Research on Health Institutions,* ed. Basil S. Georgopoulos (pp. 9–48). Ann Arbor: Institute for Social Research, University of Michigan.

Gereffi, Gary. 2005. The global economy: Organization, governance and development. In *The Handbook of Economic Sociology,* 2nd ed., ed. Neil J. Smelser and Richard Swedberg (pp. 160–182). Princeton, NJ: Princeton University Press.

Gergen, Kenneth J., and Keith E. Davis. eds. 1985. *The Social Construction of the Person.* New York: Springer-Verlag.

Ghoshal, Sumantra, and D. Eleanor Westney. eds. 1993. *Organization Theory and the Multinational Corporation.* New York: St. Martin's Press.

Gibbons, Robert 1992. *Game Theory for Applied Economists.* Princeton, NJ: Princeton University Press.

Giddens, Anthony. 1979. *Central Problems in Social Theory: Action, Structure and Contradiction in Social Analysis.* Berkeley: University of California.

———. 1984. *The Constitution of Society.* Berkeley: University of California Press.

Gioia, Dennis A., and Kumar Chittipeddi. 1991. Sensemaking and sensegiving in strategic change initiation. *Strategic Management Journal* 12:433–448.

Glassman, Robert. 1973. Persistence and loose coupling in living systems. *Behavioral Science* 18:83–98.

Glynn, Mary Ann. 2000. When cymbals becomes symbols: Conflict over organizational identity within a symphony orchestra. *Organization Science* 11:285–298.

———. 2008. Beyond constraint: How institutions enable identities. In *The Sage Handbook of Organizational Institutionalism,* ed. Royston Greenwood, Christine Oliver, Kerstin Sahlin, and Roy Suddaby (pp. 413–430). Los Angeles: Sage.

Goffman, Erving. 1961. *Asylums.* Garden City, NY: Doubleday, Anchor Books.

———. 1974. *Frame Analysis.* Cambridge, MA: Harvard University Press.

———. 1983. The interaction order. *American Sociological Review* 48:1–17.

Goldstein, Judith, and Robert O. Keohane. eds. 1993. *Ideas and Foreign Policy: Beliefs, Institutions and Political Change.* Ithaca, NY: Cornell University Press.

Goodrick, Elizabeth, and Gerald R. Salancik. 1996. Organizational discretion in responding to institutional practices: Hospitals and Cesarean births. *Administrative Science Quarterly* 41:1–28.

Gopnik, Alison, Andrew N. Melzoff, and Patricia K. Kuhl. 1999. *The Scientist in the Crib: What Early Learning Tells Us About the Mind.* New York: Morrow.

Gouldner, Alvin W. 1954. *Patterns of Industrial Bureaucracy.* Glencoe, IL: Free Press.

Granovetter, Mark. 1973. The strength of weak ties. *American Journal of Sociology* 78:1360–1380.

———. 1985. Economic action and social structure: The problem of embeddedness. *American Journal of Sociology* 91:481–510.

Gray, John. 2005, August 11. The world is round: Review of "The World Is Flat: A Brief History of the Twenty-First Century" by Thomas L. Friedman. *The New York Review of Books* 52, no. 13.

Greening, Daniel W., and Barbara Gray. 1994. Testing a model of organizational response to social and political issues. *Academy of Management Journal* 37:467–498.

Greenwood, Royston, and C. R. Hinings. 1993. Understanding strategic change: The contribution of archetypes. *Academy of Management Journal* 36:1052–1081.

———. 1996. Understanding radical organizational change: Bringing together the old and the new institutionalism. *Academy of Management Review* 21:1022–1054.

Greenwood, Royston, Mia Raynard, Farah Kodeih, Evelyn R. Micelotta, and Michael Lounsbury 2011. Institutional complexity and organizational responses. *Academy of Management Annals* 5: 317-71.

Greenwood, Royston, and Roy Suddaby. eds. 2006. *Professional Service Firms Research in the Sociology of Organizations,* vol. 24. Amsterdam: Elsevier.

Greenwood, Royston, Roy Suddaby, and C. R. Hinings. 2002. Theorizing change: The role of professional association in the transformation of institutional fields. *Academy of Management Journal* 45:58–80.

Greif, Avner. 2003. Review essay of *The Architecture of Markets: An Economic Sociology of Twenty-First-Century Capitalist Societies* by Neil Fligstein. *Contemporary Sociology* 32:148–152.

———. 2006. *Institutions and the Path to the Modern Economy: Lessons From Medieval Trade.* Cambridge, UK: Cambridge University Press.

Greve, Henrich R. 1995. Jumping ship: The diffusion of strategy abandonment. *Administrative Science Quarterly* 40:444–473.

———. 1998. Managerial cognition and the mimetic adoption of market positions: What you see is what you do. *Strategic Management Journal* 19:967–988.

Griswold, Wendy. 1992. Recent developments in the sociology of culture: Four good arguments (and one bad one). *Acta Sociologica* 35:323–328.

Gronow, Antti. 2008. Not by rules of choice alone: A pragmatist critique of institutional theories in economics and sociology. *Journal of Institutional Economics* 4:351–373.

Guillén, Mauro F. 1994. *Models of Management: Work, Authority, and Organization in a Comparative Perspective.* Chicago: University of Chicago Press.

———. 2001a. Introduction to the transaction edition. In *Reinhold Bendix, Work and Authority in Industry* (pp. xvii–lxv). New Brunswick, NJ: Transaction.

———. 2001b. *The Limits of Convergence: Globalization and Organizational Change in Argentina, South Korea, and Spain.* Princeton, NJ: Princeton University Press.

Gusfield, Joseph R. 1955. Social structure and moral reform: A study of the Women's Christian Temperance Union. *American Journal of Sociology* 61:221–232.

Guthrie, Doug, and Louise Marie Roth. 1999. The state, courts, and maternity policies in U.S. organizations: Specifying institutional mechanisms, *American Sociological Review* 64:41–63.

Habermas, Jürgen, et al. 2010. *An Awareness of What Is Missing: Faith and Reason in a Post-Secular Age.* Oxford, UK: Oxford University Press.

Hall, Peter A. 1986. *Governing the Economy: The Politics of State Intervention in Britain and France.* New York: Oxford University Press.

Hall, Peter A., and David Soskice. 2001a. An introduction to varieties of capitalism. In *Varieties of Capitalism: The Institutional Foundation of Comparative Advantage,* ed. Peter A. Hall and David Soskice (pp. 1–68). Oxford, UK: Oxford University Press.

———. eds. 2001b. *Varieties of Capitalism: The Institutional Foundations of Comparative Advantage.* New York: Oxford University Press.

Hall, Peter A., and Rosemary C. R. Taylor. 1996. Political science and the three new institutionalisms. *Political Studies* 44:936–957.

Hall, Richard H. 1992. Taking things a bit too far: Some problems with emergent institutional theory. In *Issues, Theory and Research in Industrial Organizational Psychology,* ed. Kathryn Kelley (pp. 71–87). Amsterdam: Elsevier.

Hallett, Tim, and Marc J. Ventresca. 2006. Inhabited institutions: Social interactions and organizational forms in Gouldner's *Patterns of Industrial Bureaucracy. Theory and Society* 35:213–236.

Halliday, Terence C., Michael J. Powell, and Mark W. Granfors. 1993. After minimalism: Transformation of state bar associations from market dependence to state reliance, 1918 to 1950. *American Sociological Review* 58:515–535.

Hamilton, Gary G., and Misha Petrovic 2009. Thorstein Veblen and the organization of the capitalist economy. In *The Oxford Handbook of Sociology and Organization Studies: Classical Foundations,* ed. Paul S. Adler (pp. 351–374). Oxford, UK: Oxford University Press.

Hanks, William F. 1991. Foreword. In *Situated Learning: Legitimate Peripheral Participation,* Jean Lave and Etienne Wenger (pp. 13–26). Cambridge, UK: Cambridge University Press.

Hannan, Michael T., and Glenn R. Carroll. 1987. The ecology of organizational founding: American labor unions, 1836–1985. *American Journal of Sociology* 92:910–943.

Hannan, Michael T., Glenn R. Carroll, Elizabeth A. Dundon, and John Charles Torres. 1995a. Organizational evolution in a multinational context: Entries of automobile manufacturers in Belgium, Britain, France, Germany, and Italy. *American Sociological Review* 60:509–528.

———. 1995b. Response to Baum and Powell. *American Sociological Review* 57:539–540.

Hannan, Michael T., and John Freeman. 1977. The population ecology of organizations. *American Journal of Sociology* 82:929–964.

———. 1984. Structural inertia and organizational change. *American Sociological Review* 49:149–164.

———. 1989. *Organizational Ecology.* Cambridge, MA: Harvard University Press.

Hannan, Michael T., Laszlo Pólos, and Glenn R. Carroll. 2007. *The Logics of Organizational Theory: Social Codes and Ecologies.* Princeton, NJ: Princeton University Press.

Hargrave, Timothy J., and Andrew H. Van de Ven. 2006. A collective action model of institutional innovation. *Academy of Management Review* 31:864–888.

Harrison, Bennett. 1994. *Lean and Mean: The Changing Landscape of Corporate Power in the Age of Flexibility.* New York: Basic Books.

Harvey, Bruce. 2005. *A Brief History of Neoliberalism.* Oxford, UK: Oxford University Press.

Hasenclever, Andreas, Peter Mayer, and Volker Rittberger. 1997. *Theories of International Regimes.* Cambridge: Cambridge University Press.

Haunschild, Pamela R. 1993. Interorganizational imitation: The impact of interlocks on corporate acquisition activity. *Administrative Science Quarterly* 38:564–592.

Haunschild, Pamela R., and Christine M. Beckman. 1998. When do interlocks matter? Alternative sources of information and interlock influence. *Administrative Science Quarterly* 43:815–844.

Haunschild, Pamela, and David Chandler. 2008. Institution-level learning: Learning as a source of institutional change. In *The Sage Handbook of Organizational Institutionalism,* ed. Royston Greenwood, Christine Oliver, Kerstin Sahlin, and Roy Suddaby (pp. 624–649). Los Angeles: Sage.

Haunschild, Pamela R., and Anne S. Miner. 1997. Modes of interorganizational imitation: The effects of outcome salience and uncertainty. *Administrative Science Quarterly* 42:472–500.

Haveman, Heather A. 1993. Follow the leader: Mimetic isomorphism and entry into new markets. *Administrative Science Quarterly* 38:593–627.

Haveman, Heather A., and Hayagreeva Rao. 1997. Structuring a theory of moral sentiments: Institutional and organizational coevolution in the early thrift industry. *American Journal of Sociology* 102:1606–1651.

Hawley, Amos. 1950. *Human Ecology.* New York: Ronald Press.

———. 1968. Human ecology. *International Encyclopedia of the Social Sciences,* vol. 4, ed. David L. Sills (pp. 328–337). New York, NY: Macmillan.

Hay, Peter. 1993. Royal treatment. *Performing Arts* (March): 70.

Hayek, Friedrich A. 1948. *Individualism and Economic Order.* Chicago: University of Chicago Press.

Hechter, Michael. 1987. *Principles of Group Solidarity.* Berkeley: University of California Press.

Hechter, Michael, Karl-Dieter Opp, and Reinhard Wippler. eds. 1990. *Social Institutions: Their Emergence, Maintenance and Effects.* New York: Aldine de Gruyter.

Heclo, Hugh. 2002. The statesman: Revisiting *Leadership in Administration.* In *Legality and Community: On the Intellectual Legacy of Philip Selznick,* ed. Robert A. Kagan, Martin Krygier, and Kenneth Winston (pp. 295–310). Lanham, MA: Rowman & Littlefield.

———. 2008. *On Thinking Institutionally.* Boulder, CO: Paradigm.

Hegel, Georg W. F. 1807/1967. *The Phenomenology of Mind.* New York: Harper & Row.

Heilbroner, Robert L. 1985. *The Nature and Logic of Capitalism.* New York: W. W. Norton.

Heimer, Carol A. 1999. Competing institutions: Law, medicine, and family in neonatal intensive care. *Law and Society Review* 33:17–66.

Heimer, Carol A., and Lisa R. Staffen. 1998. *For the Sake of the Children: The Social Organization of Responsibility in the Hospital and Home.* Chicago: University of Chicago Press.

Heise, David R. 1979. *Understanding Events: Affect and the Construction of Social Action.* Cambridge, UK: Cambridge University Press.

Helper, Susan, John Paul MacDuffie, and Charles Sabel. 2000. Pragmatic collaborations: Advancing knowledge while controlling opportunism. Unpublished paper, Wharton School, University of Pennsylvania.

Hemenway, David. 1975. *Industrywide Voluntary Product Standards.* Cambridge, MA: Ballinger.

Hernes, Gudmund. 1998. Real virtuality. In *Social Mechanisms: An Analytical Approach to Social Theory,* ed. Peter Hedström and Richard Swedberg (pp. 74–101). New York: Cambridge University Press.

Hirsch, Paul M. 1972. Processing fads and fashions: An organization-set analysis of cultural industry systems. *American Sociological Review* 77:639–659.

———. 1985. The study of industries. In *Research in the Sociology of Organizations,* vol. 4, ed. Sam B. Bacharach and S. M. Mitchell (pp. 271–309). Greenwich, CT: JAI Press.

———. 1997. Review essay: Sociology without social structure: Neoinstitutional theory meets brave new world. *American Journal of Sociology* 102:1702–1723.

Hirsch, Paul M., and Michael D. Lounsbury. 1996. Rediscovering volition: The institutional economics of Douglass C. North. *Academy of Management Review* 21:872–884.

———. 1997. Ending the family quarrel: Toward a reconciliation of "old" and "new" institutionalism. *American Behavioral Scientist* 40:406–418.

Hirschman, Albert O. 1991. *The Rhetoric of Reaction.* Cambridge, MA: Belknap Press.

———. 1996. *The Passions and the Interests: Political Arguments for Capitalism Before its Triumph.* Princeton, NJ: Princeton University Press.

Hodgson, Geoffrey M. 1991. Institutional economic theory: The old versus the new. In *After Marx and Sraffa: Essays in Political Economy*, ed. Geoffrey M. Hodgson (pp. 194–213). New York: St. Martin's Press.

———. ed. 1993. *The Economics of Institutions.* Aldershot, UK: Edward Elgar.

———. 1994. The return of institutional economics. In *The Handbook of Economic Sociology*, ed. Neil J. Smelser and Richard Swedberg (pp. 58–76). Princeton, NJ: Princeton University Press.

Hoffman, Andrew J. 1997. *From Heresy to Dogma: An Institutional History of Corporate Environmentalism.* San Francisco: New Lexington Press.

———. 1999. Institutional evolution and change: Environmentalism and the U.S. chemical industry. *Academy of Management Journal* 42:351–71.

———. 2001. Linking organizational and field level analysis. *Organization & Environment* 14:133–156.

Hoffman, Andrew J., and Marc J. Ventresca. 1999. The institutional framing of policy debates: Economics versus the environment. *American Behavioral Scientist* 42:1368–1392.

———. eds. 2002. *Organizations, Policy, and the Natural Environment: Institutional and Strategic Perspectives.* Stanford, CA: Stanford University Press.

Hofstede, Geert. 1984. *Culture's Consequences: International Differences in Work-Related Values.* Beverly Hills, CA: Sage.

———. 1991. *Culture and Organizations: Software of the Mind.* New York: McGraw-Hill.

Hollingsworth, J. Rogers, and Robert Boyer. eds. 1997. *Contemporary Capitalism: The Embeddedness of Institutions.* Cambridge, UK: Cambridge University Press.

Holm, Petter. 1995. The dynamics of institutionalization: Transformation processes in Norwegian fisheries. *Administrative Science Quarterly* 40:398–422.

Hopwood, Anthony, and Peter Miller. 1994. *Accounting as a Social and Institutional Practice.* Cambridge: Cambridge University Press.

House, Robert J., Paul J. Hanges, Mansour Javidan, Peter W. Dorfman, and Vipin Gupta. 2004. *Culture, Leadership, and Organization: The GLOBE Study of 62 Societies.* Thousand Oaks, CA: Sage.

Hughes, Everett C. 1936. The ecological aspect of institutions. *American Sociological Review* 1:180–189.

———. 1939. Institutions. In *An Outline of the Principles of Sociology*, ed. Robert E. Park (pp. 218–330). New York: Barnes & Noble.

———. 1958. *Men and Their Work.* Glencoe, IL: Free Press.

———. 1962/1971. "Going concerns": The study of American institutions. In *The Sociological Eye: Selected Papers*, ed. Everett C. Hughes (pp. 52–64). Chicago: Aldine.

———. 1984. *The Sociological Eye: Selected Papers*. New Brunswick, NJ: Transaction Books.

Hwang, Hokyu, and Walter W. Powell. 2009. The rationalization of charity: The influences of professionalism in the nonprofit sector. *Administrative Science Quarterly* 54:268–298.

Hybels, Ralph C., and Alan R. Ryan. 1996. The legitimation of commercial biotechnology through the business press, 1974–1989. Presented at the annual meetings of the Academy of Management, Cincinnati, Ohio.

Ingram, Paul. 2002. Interorganizational learning. In *The Blackwell Companion to Organizations*, ed. Joel A. C. Baum (pp. 642–663). Oxford, UK: Blackwell.

Innis, Harold A. 1972. *Empire and Communications*. Toronto: University of Toronto Press.

———. 1995. *Staples, Markets, and Cultural Change: Selected Essays*, ed. Daniel Drache. Montreal: McGill-Queen University Press.

Jacobsson, Bengt, and Kerstin Sahlin-Andersson. 2006. Dynamics of soft regulations. In *Transnational Governance: Institutional Dynamics of Regulation*, ed. Marie-Laure Djelic and Kerstin Sahlin-Andersson (pp. 247–265). Cambridge, UK: Cambridge University Press.

Jacoby, Sanford M. 1990. The new institutionalism: What can it learn from the old? *Industrial Relations* 29:316–359.

Janowitz, Morris. ed. 1966. *W. I. Thomas on Social Organization and Social Psychology*. Chicago: University of Chicago Press.

Jensen, Michael C., and William H. Meckling. 1976. Theory of the firm: Managerial behavior, agency costs, and ownership structure. *Journal of Financial Economics* 3:305–360.

Jepperson, Ronald L. 1991. Institutions, institutional effects, and institutionalization. In *The New Institutionalism in Organizational Analysis*, ed. Walter W. Powell and Paul J. DiMaggio (pp. 143–163). Chicago: University of Chicago Press.

Jepperson, Ronald L., and John W. Meyer. 1991. The public order and the construction of formal organizations. In *The New Institutionalism in Organizational Analysis*, ed. Walter W. Powell and Paul J. DiMaggio (pp. 204–231). Chicago: University of Chicago Press.

Jepperson, Ronald L., and Ann Swidler. 1994. What properties of culture should we measure? *Poetics* 22:359–371.

Johnson, Carthryn, Timothy J. Dowd, and Cecilia L. Ridgeway. 2006. Legitimacy as a social process. *Annual Review of Sociology* 32:53–78.

Johnson, Victoria 2007. What is organizational imprinting? Cultural entrepreneurship in the founding of the Paris opera. *American Journal of Sociology* 113:97–127.

Jones, Candace, and Patricia H. Thornton. eds. 2005. *Transformation in Cultural Industries* in *Research in the Sociology of Organizations*, vol. 23. Amsterdam: Elsevier.

Jooste, Stephan F., and W. Richard Scott 2011. Organizations enabling public-private partnerships: An organization field approach. In *Global Projects:*

Institutional and Political Challenges, ed. W. Richard Scott, Raymond E. Levitt, and Ryan J. Orr (pp. 377–402). Cambridge, UK: Cambridge University Press.

Kahneman, Daniel 2011. *Thinking, Fast and Slow.* New York: Farrar, Straus & Gireaux.

Kalberg, Stephen. 1980. Max Weber's types of rationality: Cornerstones for the analysis of rationalization processes in history. *American Journal of Sociology* 85:1145–1179.

Kalleberg, Arne L., David Knoke, Peter V. Marsden, and Joe L. Spaeth. 1996. *Organizations in America: Analyzing Their Structures and Human Resource Practices.* Thousand Oaks, CA: Sage.

Kamenetz, Anya. 2010. *DIY U: Edupunks, Edupreneurs, and the Coming Transformation of Higher Education.* White River Junction, VT: Chelsea Green.

Kaplan, Marilyn R., and J. Richard Harrison. 1993. Defusing the director liability crisis: The strategic management of legal threats. *Organization Science* 4:412–432.

Karl, Terry Lynn. 1997. *The Paradox of Plenty: Oil Booms and Petro-States.* Berkeley: University of California Press.

Katz, Daniel, and Robert L. Kahn. (1966). *The Social Psychology of Organizations.* New York: Wiley.

Katz, Michael L., and Carl Shapiro. 1985. Network externalities, competition, and compatibility. *American Economic Review* 75:424–440.

Katzenstein, Peter J., Robert O. Keohane, and Stephen D. Krasner. 1998. International organization and the study of world politics. *International Organization* 52:645–686.

Kellogg, Katherine C. 2011. *Challenging Operations: Medical Reform and Resistance in Surgery.* Chicago: University of Chicago Press.

Keohane, Robert O. ed. 1989. *International Institutions and State Power: Essays in International Relations Theory.* Boulder, CO: Westview Press.

Keohane, Robert, and Joseph S. Nye. 1977. *Power and Interdependence: World Politics in Transition.* Boston: Little, Brown.

Kerr, Clark, John T. Dunlop, Frederick Harbison, and Charles A. Myers. 1964. *Industrialism and Industrial Man,* 2nd ed. New York: Oxford University Press.

Khagram, Sanjeev 2004. *Dams and Development: Transnational Struggles for Water and Power.* Ithaca, NY: Cornell University Press.

Kilduff, Martin. 1993. The reproduction of inertia in multinational corporations. In *Organization Theory and the Multinational Corporation*, ed. Sumantra Ghoshal and D. Eleanor Westney (pp. 259–274). New York: St. Martin's Press.

King, Brayden G., Elizabeth S. Clemens, and Melissa Fry. 2011. Identity, realization and organizational forms: Differentiation and consolidation of identities among Arizona's charter schools. *Organization Science* 22:554–572.

Kiser, Larry L., and Elinor Ostrom 1982. The three worlds of action: A metatheoretical synthesis of institutional approaches. In *Strategies of Political Inquiry*, ed. Elinor Ostrom (pp. 179–222). Beverly Hills, CA: Sage.

Knorr-Certina, Karin. 1999. *Epistemic Cultures: How the Sciences Make Knowledge.* Cambridge, MA: Harvard University Press.

Knudsen, Christian. 1993. Modelling rationality: Institutions and processes in economic theory. In *Rationality, Institutions and Economic Methodology,* ed. Uskali Mäki, Bo Gustafsson, and Christian Knudsen (pp. 265–299). London: Routledge.

———. 1995a. The competence view of the firm: What can modern economists learn from Philip Selznick's sociological theory of leadership? In *The Institutional Construction of Organizations: International and Longitudinal Studies,* ed. W. Richard Scott and Søren Christensen (pp. 135–163). Thousand Oaks, CA: Sage.

———. 1995b. Theories of the firm, strategic management, and leadership. In *Resource-Based and Evolutionary Theories of the Firm: Toward a Synthesis,* ed. Cynthia A. Montgomery (pp. 179–217). Boston: Kluwer.

Kostova, Tatiana, and Srilata Zaheer. 1999. Organizational legitimacy under conditions of complexity: The case of the multinational enterprise. *Academy of Management Review* 24:64–81.

Kraatz, Matthew S. 1998. Learning by association? Interorganizational networks and adaptation to environmental change. *Academy of Management Journal* 41:621–643.

———. 2009. Leadership as institutional work: A bridge to the other side. In *Institutional Work: Actors and Agency in Institutional Studies of Organizations,* ed. Thomas B. Lawrence, Roy Suddaby, and Bernard Leca (pp. 59–91). Cambridge, UK: Cambridge University Press.

Kraatz, Matthew S., and Emily S. Block 2008. Organizational implications of institutional pluralism. In *The Sage Handbook of Organizational Institutionalism,* ed. Royston Greenwood, Christine Oliver, Kerstin Sahlin, and Roy Suddaby (pp. 243–275). Los Angeles: Sage.

Kraatz, Matthew S., Marc J. Ventresca, and Lina Deng. 2010. Precarious values and mundane innovations: Enrollment management in American liberal arts colleges. *Academy of Management Journal* 53:1521–1545.

Kraatz, Matthew S., and Edward J. Zajac. 1996. Exploring the limits of the new institutionalism: The causes and consequences of illegitimate organizational change. *American Sociological Review* 61:812–836.

Krasner, Stephen D. ed. 1983. *International Regimes.* Ithaca, NY: Cornell University Press.

———. 1988. Sovereignty: An institutional perspective. *Comparative Political Studies* 21:66–94.

———. 1993. Westphalia and all that. In *Ideas and Foreign Policy,* ed. Judith Goldstein and Robert Keohane (pp. 235–264). Ithaca, NY: Cornell University Press.

Kroeber, Alfred L., and Clyde Kluckhohn. 1952. Culture: A critical review of concepts and definitions. *Peabody Museum Papers* 47. Cambridge, MA: Harvard University Press.

Kroeber, Alfred L., and Talcott Parsons. 1958. The concepts of culture and of social systems. *American Sociological Review* 23:582–583.

Krygier, Martin. 2002. Philip Selznick, normative theory and the rule of law. In *Legality and Community: On the Intellectual Legacy of Philip Selznick*, ed. Robert A. Kagan, Martin Krygier, and Kenneth Winston (pp. 19-48). Lanham, MD: Rowman & Littlefield.

———. 2012. *Philip Selznick: Ideals in the World.* Stanford, CA: Stanford Law Books, Stanford University Press.

Kuhn, Thomas. 1970. *The Structure of Scientific Revolutions.* 2nd ed. Chicago: University of Chicago Press.

Kunda, Gideon. 1992. *Engineering Culture: Control and Commitment in a High-Tech Corporation.* Philadelphia: Temple University Press.

Lampel, Joseph, Jamal Shamsie, and Theresa K. Lant. eds. 2006. *The Business of Culture: Strategic Perspectives on Entertainment and Media.* Mahwah, NJ: Lawrence Erlbaum.

Landy, Marc K., Marc J. Roberts, and Stephen R. Thomas. 1990. *The Environmental Protection Agency: Asking the Wrong Questions.* New York: Oxford University Press.

Langlois, Richard N. 1986a. The new institutional economics: An introductory essay. In *Economics as a Process: Essays in the New Institutional Economics,* ed. Richard N. Langlois (pp. 1–25). New York: Cambridge University Press.

———. 1986b. Rationality, institutions and explanations. In *Economics as a Process: Essays in the New Institutional Economics,* ed. Richard N. Langlois (pp. 225–255). New York: Cambridge University Press.

Lasswell, Harold. 1936. *Politics: Who Gets What, When, and How?* New York: Whittlesey House.

Latour, Bruno. 1986. The powers of association. In *Power, Action, and Belief,* ed. John Law (pp. 164–180). London: Routledge and Kegan Paul.

———. 1987. *Science in Action.* Cambridge, MA: Harvard University Press.

Laumann, Edward O., Joseph Galaskiewicz, and Peter V. Marsden. 1978. Community structure as interorganizational linkage. *Annual Review of Sociology* 4:455–484.

Laumann, Edward O., and David Knoke. 1987. *The Organizational State: Social Choice in National Policy Domains.* Madison: University of Wisconsin Press.

Laumann, Edward O., Peter V. Marsden, and David Prensky. 1983. The boundary specification problem in network analysis. In *Applied Network Analysis,* ed. Ronald S. Burt and Michael J. Minor (pp. 18–34). Beverly Hills, CA: Sage.

Lave, Jean, and Etienne Wenger. 1991. *Situated Learning: Legitimate Peripheral Participation.* Cambridge, UK: Cambridge University Press.

Lawrence, Paul R., and Jay W. Lorsch. 1967. *Organization and Environment: Managing Differentiation and Integration.* Boston: Graduate School of Business Administration, Harvard University.

Lawrence, Thomas B. 2008. Power, institutions and organizations. In *The Sage Handbook of Organizational Institutionalism,* ed. Royston Greenwood, Christine Oliver, Kerstin Sahlin, and Roy Suddaby (pp. 170–197). Los Angeles: Sage

Lawrence, Thomas B., and Roy Suddaby. 2006. Institutions and institutional work. In *The Sage Handbook of Organization Studies*, 2nd ed., ed. Stewart R. Clegg, Cynthia Hardy, Thomas B. Lawrence, and Walter R. Nord (pp. 215–254). London: Sage.

Lawrence, Thomas B., Roy Suddaby, and Bernard Leca. eds. 2009. *Institutional Work: Actors and Agency in Institutional Studies of Organizations*. Cambridge, UK: Cambridge University Press.

Leblebici, Husayin, Gerald R. Salancik, Anne Copay, and Tom King. 1991. Institutional change and the transformation of interorganizational fields: An organizational history of the U.S. radio broadcasting industry. *Administrative Science Quarterly* 36:333–363.

Lecours, André. 2005. New institutionalism: Issues and questions. In *New Institutionalism Theory and Analysis*, ed. André Lecours. Toronto: University of Toronto Press.

LeDoux, J. E. 1996. *The Emotional Brain*. New York: Simon and Schuster.

Levi-Strauss, Claude. 1966. *The Savage Mind*. Chicago: University of Chicago Press.

Levitt, Barbara, and James G. March. 1988. Organization learning. *Annual Review of Sociology* 14:319–340.

Lewin, Kurt. 1951. *Field Theory in Social Psychology*. New York: Harper.

Lindblom, Charles E. 1977. *Politics and Markets: The World's Political-Economic Systems*. New York: Basic Books.

Lipset, Seymour Martin, and William Schneider. 1987. *The Confidence Gap: Business, Labor, and Government in the Public Mind*. rev. ed. Baltimore: John Hopkins University Press.

Lipset, Seymour Martin, Martin A. Trow, and James S. Coleman. 1956. *Union Democracy*. Glencoe, IL: Free Press.

Lipsky, Martin. 1980. *Street-Level Bureaucracy*. New York: Russell Sage Foundation.

Lounsbury, Michael, Marc J. Ventresca, and Paul M. Hirsch. 2003. Social movements, field frames, and industry emergence: A cultural-political perspective on recycling. *Socio-Economic Review* 1:70–104.

Loya, Thomas A., and John Boli. 1999. Standardization in the world polity: Technical rationality over power. In *Constructing World Culture: International Nongovernmental Organizations Since 1875*, ed. John Boli and George M. Thomas (pp. 169–197). Stanford, CA: Stanford University Press.

Macaulay, Stewart. 1963. Non-contractual relations in business. *American Sociological Review*, 28:55–70.

Macneil, I. 1985. Relational contract: What we do and do not know. *Wisconsin Law Review* 3:483–526.

Maguire, Steve, Cynthia Hardy, and Thomas B. Lawrence. 2004. Institutional entrepreneurship in emerging fields: HIV/AIDS treatment advocacy in Canada. *Academy of Management Journal* 47:657–669.

Maines, David R. 1977. Social organization and social structure in symbolic interactionist thought. *Annual Review of Sociology* 3:235–259.

Mäki, Uskali, Bo Gustafsson, and Christian Knudsen. eds. 1993. *Rationality, Institutions and Economic Methodology*. London: Routledge.

March, James G. ed. 1965. *Handbook of Organizations*. Chicago: Rand McNally.

———. 1981. Decisions in organizations and theories of choice. In *Perspectives on Organization Design and Behavior*, ed. Andrew H. Van de Ven and William F. Joyce (pp. 205–244). New York: John Wiley & Sons.

———. 1994. *A Primer on Decision Making: How Decisions Happen*. New York: Free Press.

March, James G., and Johan P. Olsen. 1984. The new institutionalism: Organizational factors in political life. *American Political Science Review* 78:734–749.

———. 1989. *Rediscovering Institutions: The Organizational Basis of Politics*. New York: Free Press.

March, James G., and Herbert A. Simon. 1958. *Organizations*. New York: Wiley.

Marens, Richard. 2009. It's not just for communists anymore: Marxian political economy and organization theory. In *The Oxford Handbook of Sociology and Organization Studies: Classical Foundations*, ed. Paul S. Adler (pp. 92–117). Oxford, UK: Oxford University Press.

Markus, Hazel, and R. B. Zajonc. 1985. The cognitive perspective in social psychology. In *The Handbook of Social Psychology*, vol. 1, 3rd ed., ed. Gardner Lindzey and Elliot Aronson (pp. 137–230). New York: Random House.

Marquis, Christopher, Michael Lounsbury, and Royston Greenwood. eds. 2011. *Communities and Organizations*. Bingley, UK: Emerald Group.

Martin, Joanne. 1992. *Cultures in Organizations: Three Perspectives*. New York: Oxford University Press.

———. 1994. The organization of exclusion: The institutionalization of sex inequality, gendered faculty jobs, and gendered knowledge in organizational theory and research. *Organizations* 1:401–431.

———. 2002. *Organizational Culture: Mapping the Terrain*. Thousand Oaks, CA: Sage.

Martin, John Levi. 2011. *The Explanation of Social Action*. Oxford, UK: Oxford University Press.

Marx, Karl. 1844/1972. Economic and philosophic manuscripts of 1944: Selections. In *The Marx-Engels Reader*, ed. Robert C. Tucker (pp. 52–106). New York: W. W. Norton.

———. 1845–1846/1972. The German ideology: Part I. In *The Marx-Engels Reader*, ed. Robert C. Tucker (pp. 110–164). New York: W. W. Norton.

———. 1852/1963. *The Eighteenth Brumaire of Louis Bonaparte*. New York: International.

Masten, Scott E. 1986. The economic institutions of capitalism: A review article. *Journal of Institutional and Theoretical Economics* 142:445–451.

———. 1994. Culture and social movements. In *New Social Movements*, ed. Enrique Laraña, Hank Johnson, and Joseph R. Gusfield (pp. 36–57). Philadelphia, PA: Temple University Press.

Mayo, Elton 1945. *The Social Problems of an Industrial Civilization*. Boston: Graduate School of Business Administration, Harvard University.

McAdam, Doug 1982. *Political Process and the Development of Black Insurgency 1930–1970*. Chicago: University of Chicago Press.

———. 1996. The framing function of movement tactics: Strategic dramaturgy in the American civil rights movement. In *Comparative Perspectives on Social Movements*, ed. Doug McAdam, John D. McCarthy, and Mayer N. Zald (pp. 338–355). Cambridge, UK: Cambridge University Press.

———. 1999. Introduction. In *Political Process and the Development of Black Insurgency 1930–1970* (2nd ed., pp. vii–xlii). Chicago: University of Chicago Press.

McAdam, Doug, John D. McCarthy, and Mayer N. Zald. 1996. Introduction: Opportunities, mobilizing structures, and framing processes—Toward a synthetic, comparative perspective on social movements. In *Comparative Perspectives on Social Movements: Political Opportunities, Mobilizing Structures, and Cultural Framings*, ed. Doug McAdam, John D. McCarthy, and Mayer N. Zald (pp. 1–22). Cambridge, UK: Cambridge University Press.

McAdam, Doug, and W. Richard Scott. 2005. Organizations and movements. In *Social Movements and Organization Theory*, ed. Gerald F. Davis, Doug McAdam, W. Richard Scott, and Mayer N. Zald (pp. 4–40). Cambridge, UK: Cambridge University Press.

McAdam, Doug, Sidney Tarrow, and Charles Tilly. 2001. *Dynamics of Contention*. Cambridge, UK: Cambridge University Press.

McCarthy, John D., and Mayer N. Zald. 1977. Resource mobilization and social movements: A partial theory. *American Journal of Sociology* 82:1212–1241.

McDonough, Patricia M., Marc J. Ventresca, and Charles Outcalt. 2000. Field of dreams: Organization field approaches to understanding the transformation of college access, 1965–1995. In *Higher Education: Handbook of Theory and Research*, vol. 15, ed. John C. Smart (pp. 371–405). New York: Agathon Press.

McKelvey, Bill. 1982. *Organizational Systematics*. Berkeley: University of California Press.

McKenzie, Richard B., and Dwight R. Lee. 1991. *Quicksilver Capital*. New York: Free Press.

McKenzie, Roderick D. 1926/1983. The scope of human ecology. In *Origins of Human Ecology*, ed. Gerald L. Young (pp. 35–48). Stroudsburg, PA: Hutchinson Ross.

McLaughlin, Milbrey W. 1975. *Evaluation and Reform: The Elementary and Secondary Education Act of 1965*. Cambridge, MA: Ballinger.

McLaughlin, Milbrey, W. Richard Scott, Sarah Deschenes, Kathryn Hopkins, and Anne Newman. 2009. *Between Movement and Establishment: Organizations Advocating for Youth*. Stanford, CA: Stanford University Press.

Mead, George Herbert. 1934. *Mind, Self and Society*. Chicago: University of Chicago Press.

Mehler, Jacques, and Emmanuel Dupoux. 1994. *What Infants Know: The New Cognitive Science of Early Development*. Oxford, UK: Blackwell.

Melnick, R. Shep. 1983. *Regulation and the Courts: The Case of the Clean Air Act*. Washington, DC: Brookings Institution.

Menand, Louis. ed. 1997. *Pragmatism: A Reader*. New York: Vintage Books.

———. 2001. *The Metaphysical Club: A Story of Ideas in America*. New York: Farrar, Straus and Giroux.

Menger, Carl. 1883/1963. *Problems of Economics and Sociology*, ed. Louis Schneider. Urbana: University of Illinois Press.

Merton, Robert K. 1936. The unanticipated consequences of purposive social action. *American Sociological Review* 1:894–904.

———. 1940/1957. Bureaucratic structure and personality. In *Social Theory and Social Structure*, 2nd ed., ed. Robert K. Merton (pp. 195–206). Glencoe, IL: Free Press.

Merton, Robert K., Ailsa P. Gray, Barbara Hockey, and Hanan C. Selvin. eds. 1952. *Reader in Bureaucracy*. Glencoe, IL: Free Press.

Meyer, Heinz-Dieter 2003. Tocqueville's cultural institutionalism. *Journal of Classical Sociology* 3:197–220.

Meyer, John W. 1983. Conclusion: Institutionalization and the rationality of formal organizational structure. In *Organizational Environments: Ritual and Rationality*, ed. John W. Meyer and W. Richard Scott (pp. 261–282). Beverly Hills, CA: Sage.

———. 1994. Rationalized environments. In *Institutional Environments and Organizations: Structural Complexity and Individualism*, ed. W. Richard Scott and John W. Meyer (pp. 28–54). Thousand Oaks, CA: Sage.

Meyer, John W. 1996. "Otherhood": The transmission of ideas in the modern organizational environment. In *Translating Organizational Change*, ed., Barbara Czarniawsky and Guji Sevon (pp. 241–252). Berlin: Walter de Gruyter.

———. 2008. Reflections on institutional theories of organizations. In *The Sage Handbook of Organizational Institutionalism*, ed. Royston Greenwood, Christine Oliver, Kerstin Sahlin, and Roy Suddaby (pp. 790–811). Los Angeles: Sage.

Meyer, John W., John Boli, and George M. Thomas. 1987. Ontology and rationalization in the Western cultural account. In *Institutional Structure: Constituting State, Society, and the Individual*, ed. George M. Thomas, John W. Meyer, Francisco O. Ramirez, and John Boli (pp. 12–37). Newbury Park, CA: Sage.

Meyer, John W., John Boli, George M. Thomas, and Francisco O. Ramirez. 1997. World society and the nation state. *American Journal of Sociology* 103:144–181.

Meyer, John W., Gili S. Drori, and Hokyu Hwang. 2006. World society and the proliferation of formal organization. In *Globalization and Organization: World Society and Organizational Change*, ed. Gili S. Drori, John W. Meyer, and Hokyu Hwang (pp. 25–49). Oxford, UK: Oxford University Press.

Meyer, John W., and Brian Rowan. 1977. Institutionalized organizations: Formal structure as myth and ceremony. *American Journal of Sociology* 83:340–363.

Meyer, John W., and W. Richard Scott. 1983a. Centralization and the legitimacy problems of local government. In *Organizational Environments: Ritual and Rationality*, ed. John W. Meyer and W. Richard Scott (pp. 199–215). Beverly Hills, CA: Sage.

Meyer, John W., and W. Richard Scott, with the assistance of Brian Rowan and Terrence E. Deal. 1983b. *Organizational Environments: Ritual and Rationality.* Beverly Hills, CA: Sage. (Updated in 1992)

Meyer, John W., W. Richard Scott, and David Strang. 1987. Centralization, fragmentation, and school district complexity. *Administrative Science Quarterly* 32:186–201.

Meyer, John W., W. Richard Scott, David Strang, and Andrew L. Creighton. 1988. Bureaucratization without centralization: Changes in the organizational system of U.S. public education, 1940–80. In *Institutional Patterns and Organizations: Culture and Environment,* ed. Lynne G. Zucker (pp. 139–168). Cambridge, MA: Ballinger.

Meyer, Renate E., Kerstin Sahlin, Marc Ventresca, and Peter Walgenbach. 2009a. Ideology and institutions: Introduction. In *Institutions and Ideology: Research in the Sociology of Organizations,* vol. 27, ed. Renate E. Meyer, Kerstin Sahlin, Marc Ventresca, and Peter Walgenbach (pp. 1–15). Bingley, UK: Emerald.

———. ed. 2009b. *Institutions and Ideology: Research in the Sociology of Organizations,* vol. 27. Bingley, UK: Emerald.

Mezias, Stephen J. 1990. An institutional model of organizational practice: Financial reporting at the Fortune 200. *Administrative Science Quarterly* 35:431–457.

———. 1995. Using institutional theory to understand for-profit sectors: The case of financial reporting standards. In *The Institutional Construction of Organizations: International and Longitudinal Studies,* ed. W. Richard Scott and Soren Christensen (pp. 164–196). London: Sage.

Michels, Robert. 1915/1949. *Political Parties.* Tr. Eden and Cedar Paul. Glencoe, IL: Free Press.

Micklethwait, John, and Adrian Wooldridge. 2003. *The Company: A Short History of a Revolutionary Idea.* New York: Modern Library, Random House.

Miles, Robert H. 1982. *Coffin Nails and Corporate Strategy.* Englewood Cliffs, NJ: Prentice Hall.

Milgrom, Paul, and John Roberts. 1992. *Economics, Organization and Management.* Englewood Cliffs, NJ: Prentice Hall.

Miller, Jon. 1994. *The Social Control of Religious Zeal: A Study of Organizational Contradictions.* New Brunswick, NJ: Rutgers University Press.

Miller, Roger, and Donald Lessard. 2000. *The Strategic Management of Large Engineering Projects: Shaping Institutions, Risks, and Governance.* Cambridge, MA: MIT Press.

Mindl, James R., Charles Stubbart, and Joseph F. Porac. 1996. *Cognition Within and Between Organizations.* London: Sage.

Miner, Anne S. 1991. The social ecology of jobs. *American Sociological Review* 56:772–785.

Moe, Terry M. 1984. The new economics of organization. *American Journal of Political Science* 28:739–777.

———. 1989. The politics of bureaucratic structure. In *Can the Government Govern?* ed. John Chubb and Paul Peterson (pp. 267–329). Washington, DC: Brookings Institution.

———. 1990a. Political institutions: The neglected side of the story. *Journal of Law, Economics and Organizations* 6:213–253.

———. 1990b. The politics of structural choice: Toward a theory of public bureaucracy. In *Organization Theory: From Chester Barnard to the Present and Beyond*, ed. Oliver E. Williamson (pp. 116–153). New York: Oxford University Press.

Mohr, John W. 1994. Soldiers, mothers, tramps and others: Discourse roles in the 1907 New York City Charity Directory. *Poetics* 22:327–357.

———. Forthcoming. Implicit terrains: Meaning, measurement, and spatial metaphors in organization theory. In *Constructing Industries and Markets*, ed. Joseph Porac and Marc Ventresca. Amsterdam: Elsevier.

Mohr, John W., and Vincent Duquenne. 1997. The duality of culture and practice: Poverty relief in New York City, 1888–1917. *Theory and Society* 26:305–356.

Mohr, Lawrence B. 1982. *Explaining Organizational Behavior*. San Francisco: Jossey-Bass.

Morgenthau, Henry J. 1948. *Politics Among Nations: The Struggle for Power and Peace*. New York: Knopf.

Morrill, Calvin. Forthcoming. Institutional change through interstitial emergence: The growth of alternative dispute resolution in American law, 1965–1995. In *How Institutions Change*, ed. Walter W. Powell and Daniel L. Jones. Chicago: University of Chicago Press.

Mörth, U. ed. 2004. *Soft Law in Governance and Regulation*. Cheltenham, UK: Edward Elgar.

National Commission on Excellence in Education. 1983. *A Nation at Risk: The Imperative for Educational Reform*. Washington, DC: Government Printing Office.

Nee, Victor. 1998. Sources of the new institutionalism. In *The New Institutionalism in Sociology*, ed. Mary C. Brinton and Victor Nee (pp. 1–16). New York: Russell Sage Foundation.

Nee, Victor, and Peng Lian. 1994. Sleeping with the enemy: A dynamic model of declining political commitment to state socialism. *Theory and Society* 23:253–296.

Nelson, Richard R., and Sidney G. Winter. 1982. *An Evolutionary Theory of Economic Change*. Cambridge, MA: Belknap Press.

Nisbett, Richard, and Lee Ross. 1980. *Human Inference: Strategies and Shortcomings of Social Judgment*. Englewood Cliffs, NJ: Prentice Hall.

Nohria, Nitin, and Robert G. Eccles. eds. 1992. *Networks and Organizations: Structure, Form, and Action*. Boston: Harvard Business School Press.

Noll, Roger T. ed. 1985. *Regulatory Policy and the Social Sciences*. Berkeley: University of California Press.

North, Douglass C. 1989. Institutional change and economic history. *Journal of Institutional and Theoretical Economics* 145:238–245.

———. 1990. *Institutions, Institutional Change and Economic Performance*. Cambridge, UK: Cambridge University Press.

———. 2005. *Understanding the Process of Economic Change*. Princeton, NJ: Princeton University Press.

North, Douglass C., and Robert Paul Thomas. 1973. *The Rise of the Western World: A New Economic History*. Cambridge: Cambridge University Press.

Ó Riain, Seán. 2000. States and markets in an era of globalization. *Annual Review of Sociology* 26:187–213.

Oliver, Christine. 1991. Strategic responses to institutional processes. *Academy of Management Review* 16:145–179.

———. 1992. The antecedents of deinstitutionalization. *Organization Studies* 13:563–588.

Orlikowski, Wanda J. 1992. The duality of technology: Rethinking the concept of technology in organizations. *Organization Science* 3:398–427.

Orr, Ryan J., and W. Richard Scott 2008. Institutional exceptions on global projects: A process model. *Journal of International Business Studies* 38:562–588.

Orren, Karen, and Stephen Skowronek. 1994. Beyond the iconography of order: Notes for "new" institutionalism. In *The Dynamics of American Politics*, ed. Lawrence C. Dodd and Calvin Jillson (pp. 311–332). Boulder, CO: Westview.

Orton, J. Douglas, and Karl E. Weick. 1990. Loosely coupled systems: A reconceptualization. *Academy of Management Review* 15:203–223.

Osborne, David, and Ted Gaebler. 1992. *Reinventing Government: How the Entrepreneurial Spirit Is Transforming the Public Sector From Schoolhouse to Statehouse, City Hall to the Pentagon*. Reading, MA: Addison-Wesley.

Ostrom, Elinor 2005. *Understanding Institutional Diversity*. Princeton, NJ: Princeton University Press.

Ouchi, William G. 1981. *Theory Z: How American Business Can Meet the Japanese Challenge*. New York: Addison-Wesley.

Owen-Smith, Jason. Forthcoming. *Structural components of institutional change: Science and commerce in academe*. Unpublished paper, University of Michigan.

Owen-Smith, Jason, and Walter W. Powell. 2008. Networks and institutions. In *The Sage Handbook of Organizational Institutionalism*, ed. Royston Greenwood, Christine Oliver, Kerstin Sahlin, and Roy Suddaby (pp. 596–623). Los Angeles: Sage.

Oxley, Joanne E. 1999. Institutional environment and the mechanisms of governance: The impact of intellectual property protection on the structure of inter-firm alliances. *Journal of Economic Behavior & Organization* 38:283–309.

Pache, A., and Filipe Santos. 2010. When worlds collide: The internal dynamics of organizational responses to conflicting institutional demands. *Academy of Management Review* 35:455–476.

Padgett, John F., and Christopher K. Ansell. 1993. Robust action and the rise of the Medici, 1400–1434. *American Journal of Sociology* 98:1259–1318.

Padgett, John F., and Walter W. Powell. 2012. The problem of emergence. In *The Emergence of Organizations and Markets*, ed. John F. Padgett and Walter W. Powell (pp. 1–29). Princeton, NJ: Princeton University Press.

Palmer, Donald, Nicole Biggart, and Brian Dick. 2008. Is the new institutionalism a theory? In *The Sage Handbook of Organizational Institutionalism*, ed. Royston Greenwood, Christine Oliver, Kerstin Sahlin, and Roy Suddaby (pp. 739–768). Los Angeles: Sage.

Palmer, Donald A., P. Devereaux Jennings, and Xueguang Zhou. 1993. Late adoption of the multidivisional form by large U.S. corporations: Institutional, political, and economic accounts. *Administrative Science Quarterly* 38:100–131.

Park, Robert E., and Ernest Burgess. 1921. *Introduction to the Science of Sociology.* Chicago: University of Chicago Press.

Parsons, Talcott. 1934/1990. Prolegomena to a theory of social institutions. *American Sociological Review* 55:319–339.

———. 1937. *The Structure of Social Action.* New York: McGraw-Hill.

———. 1951. *The Social System.* New York: Free Press.

———. 1953. A revised analytical approach to the theory of social stratification. In *Class, Status and Power: A Reader in Social Stratification*, ed. Reinhard Bendix and Seymour Martin Lipset (pp. 92–129). Glencoe, IL: Free Press.

———. 1956/1960a. A sociological approach to the theory of organizations. In *Structure and Process in Modern Societies* (pp. 16–58). Glencoe, IL: Free Press.

———. 1956/1960b. Some ingredients of a general theory of formal organization. In *Structure and Process in Modern Societies* (pp. 59–96). Glencoe, IL: Free Press.

Parsons, Talcott, Robert F. Bales, and Edward A. Shils. 1953. *Working Papers in the Theory of Action.* Glencoe, IL: Free Press.

Pedersen, Jesper Strandgaard, and Frank Dobbin. 1997. The social invention of collective actors: On the rise of the organization. *American Behavioral Scientist* 40:431–443.

Peet, Richard. 2009. *Unholy Trinity: The IMF, World Bank and WTO.* 2nd ed. London: Zed Books,

Peng, Mike. 2003. Institutional transitions and strategic choices. *Academy of Management Review* 28:275–296.

Penrose, Edith. 1959/1995. *The Theory of the Growth of the Firm.* Oxford, UK: Oxford University Press.

Perrow, Charles. 1961. The analysis of goals in complex organizations. *American Sociological Review* 26:854–866.

———. 1985. Review essay: Overboard with myth and symbols. *American Journal of Sociology* 91:151–155.

———. 1986. *Complex Organizations: A Critical Essay*, 3rd ed. New York: Random House.

Peters, B. Guy. 1999. *Institutional Theory in Political Science: The "New Institutionalism."* London: Pinter.

Peterson, Paul E., Barry G. Rabe, and Kenneth K. Wong. 1986. *When Federalism Works.* Washington, DC: Brookings Institution.

Pfeffer, Jeffrey. 1981. Management as symbolic action: The creation and maintenance of organizational paradigms. In *Research in Organizational Behavior*, vol. 13, ed. Barry M. Staw and L. L. Cummings (pp. 1–52). Greenwich, CT: JAI Press.

———. 1992. *Managing With Power: Politics and Influence in Organizations.* Boston: Harvard Business School Press.

Pfeffer, Jeffrey, and Yinon Cohen. 1984. Determinants of internal labor markets in organizations. *Administrative Science Quarterly* 29:550–572.

Pfeffer, Jeffrey, and Gerald Salancik. 1978. *The External Control of Organizations.* New York: Harper & Row.

Phillips, Nelson, and Namrata Malhotra. 2008. Taking social construction seriously: Extending the discursive approach in institutional theory. In *The Sage Handbook of Organizational Institutionalism,* ed. Royston Greenwood, Christine Oliver, Kerstin Sahlin, and Roy Suddaby (pp. 702–720). Los Angeles: Sage.

Pierson, Paul. 2004. *Politics in Time: History, Institutions, and Social Analysis.* Princeton, NJ: Princeton University Press.

Pizarro, Rodrigo Gariazzo. 2012. The global diffusion of conservation policy: An institutional analysis. Unpublished doctoral dissertation, Interdisciplinary Program in Environment and Resources, Stanford University.

Podolny, Joel M. 1993. A status-based model of market competition. *American Journal of Sociology* 98:829–872.

Porac, Joseph F., James B. Wade, and Timothy G. Pollock. 1999. Industry categories and the politics of the comparable firm in CEO compensation. *Administrative Science Quarterly* 44:112–144.

Powell, Walter W. 1988. Institutional effects on organizational structure and performance. In *Institutional Patterns and Organizations: Culture and Environment,* ed. Lynne G. Zucker (pp. 115–136). Cambridge, MA: Ballinger.

———. 1990. Neither market nor hierarchy: Network forms of organization. In *Research in Organizational Behavior,* vol. 12, ed. Barry M. Staw and L. L. Cummings (pp. 295–336). Greenwich, CT: JAI Press.

———. 1991. Expanding the scope of institutional analysis. In *The New Institutionalism in Organizational Analysis,* ed. Walter W. Powell and Paul J. DiMaggio (pp. 183–203). Chicago: University of Chicago Press.

———. 1999. The social construction of an organizational field: The case of biotechnology. *International Journal of Biotechnology* 1:42–66.

Powell, Walter W., and Jeannette A. Colyvas. 2008. Microfoundations of institutional theory. In *The Sage Handbook of Organizational Institutionalism,* ed. Royston Greenwood, Christine Oliver, Kerstin Sahlin, and Roy Suddaby (pp. 276–298). Thousand Oaks, CA: Sage

Powell, Walter W., and Paul J. DiMaggio. eds. 1991. *The New Institutionalism in Organizational Analysis.* Chicago: University of Chicago Press.

Powell, Walter W., Kenneth W. Koput, and Laurel Smith-Doerr. 1996. Interorganizational collaboration and the locus of innovation: Networks of learning in biotechnology. *Administrative Science Quarterly* 41:116–145.

Powell, Walter W., and Jason Owen-Smith. 2012. An open elite: Arbiters, catalysts, or gatekeepers in the dynamics of industry evolution? In *The Emergence of Organizations and Markets,* ed. John F. Padgett and Walter W. Powell (pp. 466–495). Princeton, NJ: Princeton University Press,

Powell, Walter W., Kelley Packalen, and Kjersten Whittington. 2012. Organizational and institutional genesis: The emergence of high-tech clusters in the life sciences. In *The Emergence of Organizations and Markets,* ed. John F. Padgett and Walter W. Powell (pp. 434–465). Princeton, NJ: Princeton University Press.

Powell, Walter W., and Kurt Sandholtz. 2012. Chance, nécessité, et naïveté. In *The Emergence of Organizations and Markets,* ed. John F. Padgett and Walter W. Powell (pp. 379–433). Princeton, NJ: Princeton University Press.

Powell, Walter W., and R. Steinberg. eds. 2006. *The Nonprofit Sector.* 2nd ed. New Haven, CT: Yale University Press.

Powell, Walter W., Doug White, Kenneth Koput, and Jason Owen-Smith. 2005. Network dynamics and field evolution: The growth of interorganizational collaboration in the life sciences. *American Journal of Sociology* 110:1132–1205.

Prasad, Monica. 2006. *The Politics of Free Markets: The Rise of Neoliberal Economic Policies in Britain, France, Germany and the United States.* Chicago: University of Chicago Press.

Pratt, John W., and Richard J. Zeckhauser. eds. 1985. *Principals and Agents: The Structure of Business.* Boston: Harvard Business School Press.

President's Research Committee on Social Trends. 1934. *Recent Social Trends in the United States.* New York: McGraw-Hill.

Rao, Hayagreeva. 1998. Caveat emptor: The construction of nonprofit consumer watchdog organizations. *American Journal of Sociology* 103:912–961.

Rao, Hayagreeva, and Martin Kenney. 2008. New forms as settlements. In *The Sage Handbook of Organizational Institutionalism,* ed. Royston Greenwood, Christine Oliver, Kerstin Sahlin, and Roy Suddaby (pp. 352–370). Los Angeles: Sage.

Rao, Hayagreeva, Philippe Monin, and Rodolphe Durand. 2003. Institutional change in Toque Ville: Nouvelle cuisine as an identity movement in French gastronomy. *American Journal of Sociology* 108:795–843.

Rao, Havagreeva, and Kumar Sivakumar. 1999. Institutional sources of boundary-spanning structures: The establishment of investor relations departments in the Fortune 500 industrials. *Organization Science* 10:27–42.

Reddy, Michael. 1979. The conduit metaphor. In *Metaphor and Thought,* ed. Andrew Ortney (pp. 284–324). New York: Cambridge University Press.

Reed, Michael. 1985. *Redirections in Organizational Analysis.* London: Tavistock.

Richardson, Richard, Jr., and Mario Martinez. 2009. *Policy and Performance in American Higher Education: An Examination of Cases across State Systems.* Baltimore, MD: Johns Hopkins University Press.

Ridley, Matt. 2003. *Nature via Nurture: Genes, Experience and What Makes Us Human.* New York: HarperCollins.

Riker, William. 1980. Implications from the disequilibrium of majority rules for the study of institutions. *American Political Science Review* 74:432–447.

Rittberger, V. 1993. *Regime Theory and International Relations.* Oxford, UK: Clarendon Press.

Rivers, W. H. R. 1914. *The History of Melanesian Society.* Cambridge, UK: Cambridge University Press.

Robinson, Paul. 1985. *Opera and Ideas: From Mozart to Strauss.* Ithaca, NY: Cornell University Press.

Roethlisberger, Fritz J., and William J. Dickson. 1939. *Management and the Worker.* Cambridge, MA: Harvard University Press.

Rogers, Everett. 1995. *Diffusion of Innovation.* 4th ed. New York: Free Press.

Roland, Gérard. 2004. Understanding institutional change: Fast-moving and slow-moving institutions. *Studies in Comparative International Development* 4:109–131.

Rorty, Richard. 1989. *Contingency, Irony and Solidarity.* New York: Cambridge University Press.

Rosenberg, Morris. 1979. *Conceiving the Self.* New York: Basic Books.

Rosenberg, Nathan, and L. E. Birdzell Jr. 1986. *How the West Grew Rich: The Economic Transformation of the Industrial World.* New York: Basic Books.

Rowan, Brian. 1982. Organizational structure and the institutional environment: The case of public schools. *Administrative Science Quarterly* 27:259–279.

Roy, Donald. 1952. Quota restriction and goldbricking in a machine shop. *American Journal of Sociology* 57:427–442.

Roy, William G. 1997. *Socializing Capital: The Rise of the Large Industrial Corporation in America.* Princeton, NJ: Princeton University Press.

Ruef, Martin, and Michael Lounsbury. 2007a. Introduction: The sociology of entrepreneurship. In *The Sociology of Entrepreneurship, Research in the Sociology of Organizations,* vol. 25, ed. Martin Ruef and Michael Lounsbury (pp. 1–29). Amsterdam: Elsevier.

———. eds. 2007b. *The Sociology of Entrepreneurship, Research in the Sociology of Organizations,* vol. 25. Amsterdam: Elsevier.

Ruef, Martin, and W. Richard Scott. 1998. A multidimensional model of organizational legitimacy: Hospital survival in changing institutional environments. *Administrative Science Quarterly* 43:877–904.

Sahlin, Kerstin, and Linda Wedlin. 2008. Circulating ideas: Imitation, translation and editing. In *The Sage Handbook of Organizational Institutionalism,* ed. Royston Greenwood, Christine Oliver, Kerstin Sahlin, and Roy Suddaby (pp. 218–242). London: Sage.

Sahlin-Andersson, Kerstin. 1996. Imitating by editing success: The construction of organization fields. In *Translating Organizational Change,* ed. Barbara Czarniawska and Bernward Joerges (pp. 69–92). New York: Walter de Gruyter.

Sahlin-Andersson, Kerstin, and Lars Engwall. eds. 2002. *The Expansion of Management Knowledge: Carriers, Flows and Sources.* Stanford, CA: Stanford University Press.

Salaman, Graeme. 1978. Toward a sociology of organisational structure. *The Sociological Review* 26:519–554.

Salamon, Lester. ed. 2002. *The State of Nonprofit America.* Washington, DC: Bookings Institution.

Saxenian, Annalee. 1994. *Regional Advantage: Culture and Competition in Silicon Valley and Route 128.* Cambridge, MA: Harvard University Press.

Scharpf, Fritz W. 1997. *Games Real Actors Play: Actor-Centered Institutionalism in Policy Research.* Boulder, CO: Westview Press.

Schein, Edgar H. 1985. *Organization Culture and Leadership.* San Francisco: Jossey-Bass.

Schmitter, Philippe. 1990. Sectors in modern capitalism: Models of governance and variations in performance. In *Labour Relations and Economic Performance,* ed. Renato Brunetta and Carlo Dell'Aringa (pp. 3–39). Houndmills, UK: Macmillan.

Schmitter, Philippe C., and Gerhard Lehmbruch. eds. 1979. *Trends Toward Corporatist Intermediation.* Beverly Hills, CA: Sage.

Schmoller, Gustav von. 1900–1904. *Grundriss der Allgemeinen Volkswirtschaftslehre.* Leipzig: Duncker & Humbolt.

Schneiberg, Marc. 2002. Organizational heterogeneity and the production of new forms: Politics, social movements and mutual companies in American fire insurance, 1900–1930. In *Social Structure and Organizations Revisited: Research in the Sociology of Organizations,* vol. 19 (pp. 39–89). Amsterdam: Elsevier.

———. 2007. What's on the path? Path dependence, organizational diversity and the problem of institutional change in the U.S. economy, 1900–1950. *Socio-Economic Review* 5:47–80.

Schneiberg, Marc, and Elisabeth S. Clemens. 2006. The typical tools for the job: Research strategies in institutional analysis. *Sociological Theory* 24:195–227.

Schneiberg, Marc, Adam Goldstein, Matt Kraatz, and James Moore. 2007. Embracing market liberalism? Community embeddedness and mutual savings and loan conversions to stock company form. Unpublished paper.

Schneiberg, Marc, and Michael Lounsbury. 2008. Social movements and institutional analysis. In *The Sage Handbook of Organizational Institutionalism,* ed. Royston Greenwood, Christine Oliver, Kerstin Sahlin, and Roy Suddaby (pp. 650–672). Los Angeles: Sage.

Schneiberg, Marc, and Sarah Soule. 2005. Institutionalization as a contested multilevel process. In *Social Movements and Organization Theory,* ed. Gerald F. Davis, Doug McAdam, W. Richard Scott, and Mayer N. Zald (pp. 122–160). Cambridge, UK: Cambridge University Press.

Schneider, David. 1976. Notes toward a theory of culture. In *Meaning in anthropology,* ed. Keith M. Basso and Henry L. Silby (pp. 197–220). Albuquerque: University of New Mexico Press.

Schoonhoven, Claudia Bird, and Frank Dobbin, ed. 2010. *Stanford's Organization Theory Renaissance, 1970–2000, Research in the Sociology of Organizations,* vol. 28. Bingley, UK: Emerald.

Schotter, Andrew 1986. The evolution of rules. In *Economics as a Process: Essays in the New Institutional Economics,* ed. Richard N. Langlois (pp. 117–134). New York: Cambridge University Press.

Schrödinger, Erwin. 1945. *What Is Life?* New York: Cambridge University Press.

Schumpeter, Joseph A. 1926/1961. *The Theory of Economic Development.* New York: Oxford University Press.

———. 1942/1975. *Capitalism, Socialism and Democracy.* 2nd ed. New York: Harper and Row.

Schutz, Alfred. 1932/1967. *The Phenomenology of the Social World,* tr. George Walsh and Frederick Lehnert. Evanston, IL: Northwestern University Press.

Scott, W. Richard. 1987. The adolescence of institutional theory. *Administrative Science Quarterly* 32:493–511.

———. 1992. *Organizations: Rational, Natural, and Open Systems.* 3rd ed. Englewood Cliffs, NJ: Prentice Hall.

———. 1994a. Conceptualizing organizational fields: Linking organizations and societal systems. In *Systemrationalität und Partialinteresse* [Systems Rationality and Partial Interests], ed. Hans-Ulrich Derlien, Uta Gerhardt, and Fritz W. Scharpf (pp. 203–221). Baden-Baden, Germany: Nomos Verlagsgesellschaft.

———. 1994b. Institutions and organizations: Toward a theoretical synthesis. In *Institutional Environments and Organizations: Structural Complexity and Individualism,* ed. W. Richard Scott and John W. Meyer (pp. 55–80). Thousand Oaks, CA: Sage.

———. 1994c. Law and organizations. In *The Legalistic Organization,* ed. Sim B. Sitkin and Robert J. Bies (pp. 3–18). Thousand Oaks, CA: Sage.

———. 2003a. Institutional carriers: Reviewing modes of transporting ideas over time and space and considering their consequences. *Industrial and Corporate Change* 12:879–894.

———. 2003b. *Organizations: Rational, Natural and Open Systems,* 5th ed. Upper Saddle River, NJ: Prentice Hall.

———. 2005. Institutional theory: Contributing to a theoretical research program. In *Great Minds in Management: The Process of Theory Development,* ed. Ken G. Smith and Michael A. Hitt (pp. 460–484). Oxford, UK: Oxford University Press.

———. 2008a. Approaching adulthood: The maturing of institutional theory. *Theory and Society* 37:427–442.

———. 2008b. Lords of the dance: Professionals as institutional agents. *Organization Studies* 29:219–238.

———. 2010. Entrepreneurs and professionals: The mediating role of institutions. In *Institutions and Entrepreneurship, Research in the Sociology of Work,* vol. 21, ed. Westley D. Sine and Robert J. David (pp. 27–49). Bingley, UK: Emerald.

———. 2011. The institutional environment of global projects. In *Global Projects: Institutional and Political Challenges,* ed. W. Richard Scott, Raymond E. Levitt, and Ryan J. Orr (pp. 52–85). Cambridge, UK: Cambridge University Press.

———. Forthcoming. Higher education in America: Multiple field perspectives. In *Remaking College: Broad-Access Higher Education for a New Era,* ed. Mitchell L. Stevens and Michael W. Kirst. Stanford, CA: Stanford University Press.

Scott, W. Richard, and Elaine V. Backman. 1990. Institutional theory and the medical care sector. In *Innovations in Health Care Delivery: Insights for Organization Theory,* ed. Stephen S. Mick (pp. 20–52). San Francisco: Jossey-Bass.

Scott, W. Richard, and Søren Christensen. eds. 1995. *The Institutional Construction of Organizations: International and Longitudinal Studies.* Thousand Oaks, CA: Sage.

Scott, W. Richard, and Gerald F. Davis. 2007. *Organizations and Organizing: Rational, Natural, and Open System Perspectives.* Upper Saddle River, NJ: Pearson Prentice Hall.

Scott, W. Richard, Sarah Deschenes, Kathryn Hopkins, Anne Newman, and Milbrey McLaughlin. 2006. Advocacy organizations and the field of youth development: Dynamics of early stages of field structuration. *Nonprofit and Voluntary Sector Quarterly* 35:691–714.

Scott, W. Richard, Raymond E. Levitt, and Ryan J. Orr. eds. 2011. *Global Projects: Institutional and Political Challenges.* Cambridge, UK: Cambridge University Press.

Scott, W. Richard, and John W. Meyer. 1983. The organization of societal sectors. In *Organizational Environments: Ritual and Rationality,* ed. John W. Meyer and W. Richard Scott (pp. 129–153). [Revised version in *The New Institutionalism in Organizational Analysis,* ed. Walter W. Powell and Paul J. DiMaggio (pp. 108–140). Chicago: University of Chicago Press, 1991.]

———. 1987. Environmental linkages and organizational complexity: Public and private schools. In *Comparing Public and Private Schools,* vol 1, ed. Thomas James and Henry M. Levin (pp. 128–160). New York: Falmer Press.

———. eds. 1994. *Institutional Environments and Organizations: Structural Complexity and Individualism.* Thousand Oaks, CA: Sage.

Scott, W. Richard, Martin Ruef, Peter J. Mendel, and Carol A. Caronna. 2000. *Institutional Change and Healthcare Organizations: From Professional Dominance to Managed Care.* Chicago: University of Chicago Press.

Scully, Maureen A., and W. E. Douglas Creed. 2005. Subverting our stories of subversion. In *Social Movements and Organization Theory,* ed. Gerald F. Davis, Doug McAdam, W. Richard Scott, and Mayer N. Zald (pp. 310–332). Cambridge, UK: Cambridge University Press.

Searle, John R. 1995. *The Construction of Social Reality.* New York: Free Press.

Seashore, Stanley E. 1954. *Group Cohesiveness in the Industrial Work Group.* Ann Arbor: Institute for Social Research, University of Michigan.

Seavoy, Ronald E. 1982. *The Origins of the American Business Corporation, 1784–1855: Broadening the Concept of Public Service during Industrialization.* Westport, CT: Greenwood Press.

Selznick, Philip. 1948. Foundations of the theory of organization. *American Sociological Review* 13:25–35.

———. 1949. *TVA and the Grass Roots.* Berkeley: University of California Press.

———. 1957. *Leadership in Administration.* New York: Harper & Row.

———. 1969. *Law, Society, and Industrial Justice.* New York: Russell Sage Foundation.

———. 1980. Jurisprudence and social policy: Aspirations and perspectives. *California Law Review* 68:206–220.

———. 1992. *The Moral Commonwealth: Social Theory and the Promise of Community.* Berkeley: University of California Press.

———. 1996. Institutionalism "old" and "new." *Administrative Science Quarterly* 41:270–277.

Seo, Myeong-Gu, and W. E. Douglas Creed. 2002. Institutional contradictions, praxis, and institutional change: A dialectical perspective. *Academy of Management Review* 27:222–247.

Sewell, William H., Jr. 1992. A theory of structure: Duality, agency, and transformation. *American Journal of Sociology* 98:1–29.

Shank, Roger C., and Robert P. Abelson. 1977. *Scripts, Plans, Goals, and Understanding: An Inquiry into Human Knowledge Structures.* Hillsdale, NJ: Lawrence Erlbaum.

Shenhav, Yehouda. 1995. From chaos to systems: The engineering foundations of organizational theory, 1879–1932. *Administrative Science Quarterly* 40:557–586.

———. 1999. *Manufacturing Rationality: The Engineering Foundations of the Managerial Revolution.* Oxford, UK: Oxford University Press.

Shepsle, Kenneth A. 1989. Studying institutions: Lessons from the rational choice approach. *Journal of Theoretical Politics* 1:131–147.

Shepsle, Kenneth A., and Barry Weingast. 1987. The institutional foundations of committee power. *American Political Science Review* 81:85–104.

Sherif, Muzafer. 1935. A study of some social factors in perception. *Archives of Psychology,* 187:1–60.

Shibutani, Tomatsu. 1955. Reference groups as perspectives. *American Journal of Sociology* 60:562–569.

Shonfield, Alfred. 1965. *Modern Capitalism.* London: Oxford University Press.

Silverman, Brian S. 2002. Organizational economics. In *The Blackwell Companion to Organizations,* ed. Joel A. C. Baum (pp. 477–493). Oxford, UK: Blackwell.

Silverman, David. 1971. *The Theory of Organisations: A Sociological Framework.* New York: Basic Books.

———. 1972. Some neglected questions about social reality. In *New Directions in Sociological Theory,* ed. Paul Filmer, Michael Phillipson, David Silverman, and David Walsh (pp. 165–182). Cambridge, MA: MIT Press.

Silverman, David, and Jill Jones. 1976. *Organizational Work: The Language of Grading and the Grading of Language.* London: Macmillan.

Simon, Herbert A. 1945/1997. *Administrative Behavior: A Study of Decision-Making Processes in Administrative Organization.* New York: Macmillan. [Reprinted by Free Press, 1997]

———. 1991. *Models of My Life.* New York: Basic Books.

Simonde de Sismondi, J. C. L. 1837. *Études sur L'économie Politique,* vol. 1. Paris: Treuttel et Würtz.

Simons, Tal, and Paul Ingram. 1997. Organization and ideology: Kibbutzim and hired labor, 1951–1965. *Administrative Science Quarterly* 42:784–813.

Sine, Wesley D., and Robert J. David. eds. 2010. *Institutions and Entrepreneurship, Research in the Sociology of Work,* vol. 21. Bingley, UK: Emerald.

Sine, Wesley D., and Pamela S. Tolbert. 2006. *Institutions in Action: Tenure Systems and Faculty Employment in Colleges and Universities.* Unpublished paper, Cornell University, Ithaca, NY.

Singh, Jitendra V., David J. Tucker, and Robert J. House. 1986. Organizational legitimacy and the liability of newness. *Administrative Science Quarterly* 31:171–193.

Sitkin, Sim B., and Robert J. Bies. eds. 1994. *The Legalistic Organization.* Thousand Oaks, CA: Sage.

Sjöstrand, Sven-Erik. 1995. Toward a theory of institutional change. In *On Economic Institutions: Theory and Applications*, ed. John Groenewegen, Christos Pitelis, and Sven-Erik Sjöstrand (pp. 19–44). Aldershot, UK: Edward Elgar.

Skocpol, Theda. 1979. *States and Social Revolutions.* Cambridge, UK: Cambridge University Press.

———. 1985. Bringing the state back in: Strategies of analysis in current research. In *Bringing the State Back In*, ed. Peter B. Evans, Dietrich Rueschemeyer, and Theda Skocpol (pp. 3–37). Cambridge, UK: Cambridge University Press.

Skowronek, Stephen. 1982. *Building a New American State: The Expansion of National Administrative Capacities, 1877–1920.* Cambridge, UK: Cambridge University Press.

Smelser, Neil J., and Richard Swedberg. eds. 1994. *The Handbook of Economic Sociology.* Princeton, NJ: Princeton University Press.

———. eds. 2005. *The Handbook of Economic Sociology.* 2nd ed. Princeton, NJ: Princeton University Press.

Smith, Bruce L. ed. 1975. *The New Political Economy.* New York: John Wiley.

Smith, Jackie. 2005. Globalization and transnational social movement organizations. In *Social Movements and Organization Theory*, ed. Gerald F. Davis, Doug McAdam, W. Richard Scott, and Mayer N. Zald (pp. 226–248). Cambridge, UK: Cambridge University Press.

Smith-Doerr, Laurel, and Walter W. Powell. 2005. Networks and economic life. In *The Handbook of Economic Sociology*, ed. Neil J. Smelser and Richard Swedberg (pp. 379–402). Princeton, NJ: Princeton University Press.

Snow, David A. 2008. Elaborating the discursive contexts of framing: Discursive fields and spaces. In *Symbolic Interaction: A Research Annual*, vol. 30, ed. Norman K. Denzin (pp. 3–28). Bingley, UK: Emerald.

Snow, David A., and Robert D. Benford. 1992. Master frames and cycles of protest. In *Frontiers in Social Movement Theory*, ed. Aldon Morris and Carol McClurg Mueller (pp. 133–155). New Haven, CT: Yale University Press.

Snow, David A., E. Burke Rochford Jr., Steven K. Worden, and Robert D. Benford. 1986. Frame alignment processes, micromobilization, and movement participation. *American Sociological Review* 51:464–481.

Snow, David A., Sarah A. Soule, and Hanspeter Kriesi. eds. 2004. *The Blackwell Companion to Social Movements.* Oxford, UK: Blackwell.

Somers, Ann R. 1969. *Hospital Regulation: The Dilemma of Public Policy.* Princeton, NJ: Industrial Relations Section.

Somers, Margaret R., and Gloria Gibson. 1994. Reclaiming the epistemological "other": Narrative and the social constitution of identity. In *Social Theory and the Politics of Identity*, ed. Craig Calhoun (pp. 37–99). Oxford, UK: Basil Blackwell.

Sorokin, Peterim A. 1937–1941. *Social and Cultural Dynamics.* New York: American Book.

Spencer, Herbert. 1876, 1896, 1910. *The Principles of Sociology,* vols 1–3. London: Appleton-Century-Crofts.

Spillman, Lyn. 1995. Culture, social structure and discursive fields. In *Current Perspectives in Social Theory,* vol. 15, ed. Ben Agger (pp. 129–154). Greenwich, CT: JAI.

Stark, David. 1996. Recombinant property in East European capitalism. *American Journal of Sociology* 101:993–1027.

Starr, Paul. 1982. *The Social Transformation of American Medicine.* New York: Basic Books.

Steinmo, Sven, Kathleen Thelen, and F. Longstreth. 1992. *Structuring Politics: Historical Institutionalism in Comparative Analysis.* Cambridge, UK: Cambridge University Press.

Stern, Robert N. 1979. The development of an interorganizational control network: The case of intercollegiate athletics. *Administrative Science Quarterly* 24:242–266.

Stigler, George J. 1968. *The Organization of Industry.* Homewood, IL: Richard D. Irwin.

Stinchcombe, Arthur L. 1965. Social structure and organizations. In *Handbook of Organizations,* ed. James G. March (pp. 142–193). Chicago: Rand McNally.

———. 1968. *Constructing Social Theories.* Chicago: University of Chicago Press.

———. 1997. On the virtues of the old institutionalism. *Annual Review of Sociology* 23:1–18.

Strang, David. 2010. *Learning by Example: Imitation and Innovation at a Global Bank.* Princeton, NJ: Princeton University Press.

Strang, David, and John W. Meyer. 1993. Institutional conditions for diffusion. *Theory and Society* 22:487–511.

Strang, David, and Wesley D. Sine. 2002. Interorganizational institutions. In *The Blackwell Companion to Organizations,* ed. Joel A. C. Baum (pp. 497–519). Oxford, UK: Blackwell.

Strang, David, and Sarah A. Soule. 1998. Diffusion in organizations and social movements: From hybrid corn to poison pills. *Annual Review of Sociology* 24:265–290.

Strauss, Anselm L. 1978. A social worlds perspective. In *Studies in Symbolic Interaction,* vol. 1, ed. Norman Denzin (pp. 119–128). Greenwich, CT: JAI Press.

———. 1993. *Continual Permutations of Action.* New York: Aldine de Gruyter.

Strauss, Anselm L., Leonard Schatzman, Rue Bucher, Danuta Erlich, and Melvin Sabshin. 1964. *Psychiatric Ideologies and Institutions.* Glencoe, IL: Free Press.

Streeck, Wolfgang. 2010. Institutions in history: Bringing capitalism backing in. In *The Oxford Handbook of Comparative Institutional Analysis,* ed. Glenn Morgan, John L. Campbell, Colin Crouch, Ove Kaj Pedersen, and Richard Whitley (pp. 659–686). Oxford, UK: Oxford University Press.

Streeck, Wolfgang, and Philippe C. Schmitter. 1985. Community, market, state—and associations? The prospective contribution of interest governance to social order. In *Private Interest Government: Beyond Market and State*, ed. Wolfgang Streeck and Philippe C. Schmitter (pp. 1–29). Beverly Hills, CA: Sage.

Stryker, Robin. 1994. Rules, resources and legitimacy processes: Some implications for social conflict, order, and change. *American Journal of Sociology* 99:847–910.

———. 2000. Legitimacy processes as institutional politics: Implications for theory and research in the sociology of organizations. In *Research in the Sociology of Organizations*, vol. 17, ed. Samuel B. Bacharach (pp. 179–223). Greenwich, CT: JAI Press.

Stryker, Sheldon. 1980. *Symbolic Interactionism: A Social Structural Version*. Menlo Park, CA: Cummings.

Suchman, Mark C. 1995a. Localism and globalism in institutional analysis: The emergence of contractual norms in venture finance. In *The Institutional Construction of Organizations: International and Longitudinal Studies*, ed. W. Richard Scott and Søren Christensen (pp. 39–63). Thousand Oaks, CA: Sage.

———. 1995b. Managing legitimacy: Strategic and institutional approaches. *Academy of Management Review* 20:571–610.

———. 2003. The contract as social artifact. *Law & Society Review* 37:91–142.

Suchman, Mark C., and Mia L. Cahill. 1996. The hired-gun as facilitator: The case of lawyers in Silicon Valley. *Law and Social Inquiry* 21:837–874.

Suchman, Mark C., and Lauren B. Edelman. 1997. Legal rational myths: The new institutionalism and the law and society tradition. *Law and Social Inquiry* 21:903–941.

Suchman, Mark C., Daniel J. Steward, and Clifford A. Westfall. 2001. The legal environment of entrepreneurship: Observations on the legitimation of venture finance in Silicon Valley. In *The Entrepreneurship Dynamic: Origins of Entrepreneurship and the Evolution of Industries*, ed. Claudia Bird Schoonhoven and Elaine Romanelli (pp. 349–382). Stanford, CA: Stanford University Press.

Sumner, William Graham. 1906. *Folkways*. Boston: Ginn.

Sutton, John R., Frank R. Dobbin, John W. Meyer, and W. Richard Scott. 1994. The legalization of the workplace. *American Journal of Sociology* 99:944–971.

Swedberg, Richard. 1991. Major traditions of economic sociology. *Annual Review of Sociology* 17:251–276.

———. 1998. *Max Weber and the Idea of Economic Sociology*. Princeton, NJ: Princeton University Press.

———. 2009. Tocqueville as a pioneer in organization theory. In *Oxford Handbook of Sociology and Organizations: Classical Foundations*, ed. Paul S. Adler (pp. 39–61). Oxford, UK: Oxford University Press.

Swidler, Ann. 1986. Culture in action: Symbols and strategies. *American Sociological Review* 51:273–286.

Tate, Jay. 2001. National varieties of standardization. In *Varieties of Capitalism*, ed. Peter A. Hall and David Soskice (pp. 442–473). Oxford, UK: Oxford University Press.

Taylor, Frederick Winslow. 1911. *The Principles of Scientific Management*. New York: Harper.

Taylor, Serge. 1984. *Making Bureaucracies Think: The Environment Impact Statement Strategy of Administrative Reform*. Stanford, CA: Stanford University Press.

Taylor, Verta, and Nancy Whittier. 1992. Collective identity in social movement communities: Lesbian feminist mobilization. In *Frontiers in Social Movement Theory*, ed. Aldon D. Morris and Carol McClurg Mueller (pp. 104–130). New Haven, CT: Yale University Press.

Teece, David J. 1981. Internal organization and economic performance: An empirical study of the profitability of principal firms. *Journal of Industrial Economics* 30:173–200.

———. 1982. Toward an economic theory of the multiproduct firm. *Journal of Economic Behavior and Organization* 3:39–63.

———. 2009. *Dynamic Capabilities and Strategic Management: Organizing for Innovation and Growth*. Oxford, UK: Oxford University Press.

Thelen, Kathleen. 1999. Historical institutionalism in comparative politics. *Annual Review of Political Science* 2:369–404.

Thelen, Kathleen, and Sven Steinmo. 1992. Historical institutionalism in comparative politics. In *Structuring Politics: Historical Institutionalism in Comparative Analysis*, ed. Sven Steinmo, Kathleen Thelen, and Frank Longstreth (pp. 1–32). Cambridge: Cambridge University Press.

Thoits, Peggy A. 1989. The sociology of emotions. *Annual Review of Sociology* 15:317–342.

Thomas, George M., John W. Meyer, Francisco O. Ramirez, and John Boli. eds. 1987. *Institutional Structure: Constituting State, Society, and the Individual*. Newbury Park, CA: Sage.

Thomas, William I., and Dorothy Swaine Thomas. 1928. *The Child in America*. New York: Knopf.

Thompson, James D. 1967/2003. *Organizations in Action*. New York: McGraw-Hill. [Reprinted by Transaction Publishers, 2003]

Thompson, John B. 1996. *Ideology and Modern Culture*. Cambridge, MA: Polity Press.

Thornton, Patricia H. 2002. The rise of the corporation in a craft industry: Conflict and conformity in institutional logics. *Academy of Management Journal* 45:81–101.

———. 2004. *Markets From Culture: Institutional Logics and Organizational Decisions in Higher Education Publishing*. Stanford, CA: Stanford University Press.

Thornton, Patricia H., Candace Jones, and Kenneth Kury. 2005. Institutional logics and institutional change: Transformation in accounting, architecture, and publishing. In *Research in the Sociology of Organizations*, ed. Candace Jones and Patricia Thornton (*Transformation in Cultural Industries*, vol. 23: 125–170). Greenwich, CT: JAI Press.

Thornton, Patricia H., and William Ocasio. 1999. Institutional logics and the historical contingency of power in organizations: Executive succession in the higher education publishing industry, 1958–1990. *American Journal of Sociology* 105:801–843.

———. 2008. Institutional logics. In *The Sage Handbook of Organizational Institutionalism,"* ed. Royston Greenwood, Christine Oliver, Kerstin Sahlin, and Roy Suddaby (pp. 99–129). Los Angeles: Sage.

Thornton, Patricia H., William Ocasio, and Michael Lounsbury. 2012. *The Institutional Logics Perspective: A New Approach to Culture, Structure, and Process.* Oxford, UK: Oxford University Press.

Tilly, Charles. 1978. *From Mobilization to Revolution.* Reading, MA: Addison-Wesley.

———. 1984. *Big Structures, Large Processes, Huge Comparisons.* New York: Russell Sage Foundation.

Tocqueville, Alexis de. 1835–1840/1969. *Democracy in America,* trans. George Lawrence, ed. J. P. Mayer. New York: Doubleday, Anchor Books.

———. 1835/2004. *Democracy in America,* tr. Arthus Goldhammer. New York: Library of America.

———. 1856/1998, 2001. *The Old Regime and the Revolution,* vols. 1–2, tr. A. S. Kahan. Chicago: University of Chicago Press.

Tolbert, Pamela S. 1988. Institutional sources of organizational culture in major law firms. In *Institutional Patterns and Organizations: Culture and Environment,* ed. Lynne G. Zucker (pp. 101–113). Cambridge, MA: Ballinger.

Tolbert, Pamela S., and Lynne G. Zucker. 1983. Institutional sources of change in the formal structure of organizations: The diffusion of civil service reform, 1880–1935. *Administrative Science Quarterly* 28:22–39.

———. 1996. The institutionalization of institutional theory. In *Handbook of Organization Studies,* ed. Stewart R. Clegg, Cynthia Hardy, and Walter R. Nord (pp. 175–190). London: Sage.

Trank, Christine Quinn, and Marvin Washington. 2009. Maintaining an institution in a contested organizational field: The work of the AACSB and its constituents. In *Institutional Work: Actors and Agency in Institutional Studies of Organizations,* ed. Thomas B. Lawrence, Roy Suddaby, and Bernard Leca (pp. 236–261). Cambridge, UK: Cambridge University Press.

Trice, Harrison M., and Janice M. Beyer. 1993. *The Cultures of Work Organizations.* Englewood Cliffs, NJ: Prentice Hall.

Tucker, Robert C. 1972. Introduction: The writings of Marx and Engels. In *The Marx-Engels Reader,* ed. Robert C. Tucker (pp. xv–xxiv). New York: Norton.

Tullock, Gordon. 1976. *The Vote Motive.* London: Institute for Economic Affairs.

Turner, Roy. ed. 1974. *Ethnomethodology: Selected Readings.* Harmondsworth, UK: Penguin.

Tushman, Michael L., and Philip Anderson. 1986. Technological discontinuities and organizational environments. *Administrative Science Quarterly* 31:439–465.

Tversky, Amos, and Daniel Kahneman. 1974. Judgment under uncertainty. *Science* 185:1124–1131.

Uzzi, Brian D. 1996. The sources and consequences of embeddedness for the economic performance of organizations: The network effect. *American Sociological Review* 61:674–698.

Van de Ven, Andrew H. 1993. The institutional theory of John R. Commons: A review and commentary. *Academy of Management Review* 18:129–152.

Van de Ven, Andrew H., and Robert Drazin. 1985. The concept of fit in contingency theory. In *Research in Organizational Behavior*, vol. 7, ed. L. L. Cummings and Barry M. Staw (pp. 171–222). Greenwich, CT: JAI Press.

Van de Ven, Andrew, and Raghu Garud. 1986. A framework for understanding the emergence of new industries. *Research on Technological Innovation Management and Policy* 4:195–225.

———. 1994. The coevolution of technical and institutional events in the development of an innovation. In *Evolutionary Dynamics of Organizations*, ed. Joel A. C. Baum and Jitendra Singh (pp. 425–443). New York: Oxford University Press.

Van de Ven, Andrew H., and George P. Huber. 1990. Longitudinal field research methods for studying processes of organizational change. *Organization Science* 1:213–219.

Van Dijk, T. A. 2001. Discourse, ideology and context. *Folio Linguistica* 25:11–40.

Vanberg, Viktor. 1989. Carl Menger's evolutionary and John R. Commons' collective action approach to institutions: A comparison. *Review of Political Economy* 1:334–360.

Vaughn, Diane. 1996. *The Challenger Launch Decision: Risky Technology, Culture, and Deviance at NASA*. Chicago: University of Chicago Press.

———. 1999. The dark side of organizations: Mistakes, misconduct, and disaster. *Annual Review of Sociology* 25:271–305.

Veblen, Thorstein B. 1898. Why is economics not an evolutionary science? *Quarterly Journal of Economics* 12:373–397.

———. 1909. The limitations of marginal utility. *Journal of Political Economy* 17:235–245.

———. 1919. *The Place of Science in Modern Civilization and Other Essays*. New York: B. W. Huebsch.

Ventresca, Marc J., and Willam N. Kaghan 2008. Routines, "going concerns" and innovation: Towards an evolutionary economic sociology. In *Handbook of Organizational Routines*, ed. M. Becker (pp. 52–86). Cheltenham, UK: Edward Elgar.

Ventresca, Marc J., and John W. Mohr. 2002. Archival research methods. In *The Blackwell Companion to Organizations*, ed. Joel A. C. Baum (pp. 805–828). Oxford, UK: Blackwell.

Ventresca, Marc J., Dara Szliowicz, and M. Tina Dacin. 2003. Innovations in governance: Global structuring and the field of public exchange-traded markets. In *Globalization and Institutions: Redefining the Rules of the Economic Game*, ed. Marie-Laure Djelic and Sigrid Quack (pp. 243–277). Cheltenham, UK: Edward Elgar.

Vogus, Timothy J., and Gerald F. Davis. 2005. Elite mobilization for antitakeover legislation, 1982–1990. In *Social Movements and Organization Theory*, ed. Gerald F. Davis, Doug McAdam, W. Richard Scott, and Mayer N. Zald (pp. 96–121). New York: Cambridge University Press.

Voronov, Maxim, and Russ Vince. 2012. Integrating emotions into the analysis of institutional work. *Academy of Management Review* 37:58–81.

Walker, Gordon, and David Weber. 1984. A transaction cost approach to make-or-buy decisions. *Administrative Science Quarterly* 29:373–391.

Wallerstein, Immanuel. 1974. *The Modern World System*, vol. 1. New York: Academic Press.

———. 1979. From feudalism to capitalism: Transition or transitions. In *The Capitalist World-Economy: Essays by Immanuel Wallerstein* (pp. 138–151). Cambridge: Cambridge University Press.

Warren, Roland L. 1967. The interorganizational field as a focus for investigation. *Administrative Science Quarterly* 12:396–419.

———. 1972. *The Community in America*. Chicago: Rand McNally.

Warren, Roland L., Stephen M. Rose, and Ann F. Bergunder. 1974. *The Structure of Urban Reform: Community Decision Organizations in Stability and Change*. Lexington, MA: Lexington Books.

Washington, Marvin, and Ed J. Zajac. 2005. Status evolution and competition: Theory and evidence. *Academy of Management Journal* 48:282–296.

Weber, Max. 1904–1918/1949. *The Methodology of the Social Sciences*, tr. and ed. Edward A. Shils and Henry A. Finch. Glencoe, IL: Free Press.

———. 1906–1924/1946. *Max Weber: Essays in Sociology*, tr. and ed. Hans H. Gerth and C. Wright Mills. New York: Oxford University Press.

———. 1924/1947. *The Theory of Social and Economic Organization*, tr. and ed. A. M. Henderson and Talcott Parsons. New York: Oxford University Press.

———. 1924/1968. *Economy and Society: An Interpretive Sociology*, vols. 1–3, ed. Guenther Roth and Claus Wittich. New York: Bedminister Press.

Wedlin, Linda. 2006. *Ranking Business Schools: Forming Fields, Identities and Boundaries in International Management Education*. Cheltenham, UK: Edward Elgar.

Weick, Karl E. 1969/1979. *The Social Psychology of Organizing*. 2nd ed. Reading, MA: Addison-Wesley.

———. 1976. Educational organizations as loosely coupled systems. *Administrative Science Quarterly* 21:1–19.

———. 1995. *Sensemaking in Organizations*. Thousand Oaks, CA: Sage.

———. 2000. Quality improvement: A sensemaking perspective. In *The Quality Movement and Organization Theory*, ed. Robert E. Cole and W. Richard Scott (pp. 155–172). Thousand Oaks, CA: Sage.

Weingast, Barry R. 1989. The political institutions of representative government. *Working Papers in Political Science P-89–14*. Stanford, CA: Hoover Institution, Stanford University.

———. 2002. Rational choice institutionalism. In *The State of the Discipline*, ed. Ira Katznelson and Helen Milner (pp. 660–692). New York: W. W. Norton.

Westney, D. Eleanor. 1987. *Imitation and Innovation: The Transfer of Western Organizational Patterns to Meiji Japan*. Cambridge, MA: Harvard University Press.

Westphal, James D., Ranjay Gulati, and Stephen M. Shortell. 1997. Customization or conformity? An institutional and network perspective on the content and consequences of TQM adoption. *Administrative Science Quarterly* 42:366–394.

Westphal, James D., and Edward J. Zajac. 1994. Substance and symbolism in CEOs' long-term incentives plans. *Administrative Science Quarterly* 39:367–390.

———. 1998. The symbolic management of stockholders: Corporate governance reforms and shareholder reactions. *Administrative Science Quarterly* 43:127–153.

Whetten, David A., and Paul C. Godfrey. eds. 1999. *Identity in Organizations: Building Theory Through Conversations.* Thousand Oaks, CA: Sage.

White, William D. 1982. The American hospital industry since 1900: A short history. In *Advances in Health Economics and Health Services Research*, vol. 3, ed. Richard M. Scheffler (pp. 143–170). Greenwich, CT: JAI Press.

Whitley, Richard D. 1987. Taking firms seriously as economic actors: Toward a sociology of firm behaviour. *Organisation Studies* 8:125–147.

———. 1992a. *Business Systems in East Asia: Firms, Markets, and Societies.* London: Sage.

———. 1992b. The social construction of organizations and markets: The comparative analysis of business recipes. In *Rethinking Organizations: New Directions in Organization Theory and Analysis*, ed. Michael Reed and Michael Hughes (pp. 120–143). Newbury Park, CA: Sage.

———. 1992c. Societies, firms, and markets: The social structuring of business systems. In *European Business Systems: Firms and Markets in Their National Contexts*, ed. Richard Whitley (pp. 5–44). London: Sage.

———.1999. *Divergent Capitalisms: The Social Structuring and Change of Business Systems.* Oxford, UK: Oxford University Press.

Widmaier, Wesley, Mark Blyth, and Leonard Seabrooke. 2007. Exogenous shocks or endogenous constructions? The meaning of wars and crises. *International Studies Quarterly* 51:747–759.

Wiley, Mary Glenn, and Mayer N. Zald. 1968. The growth and transformation of educational accrediting agencies: An exploratory study in social control of institutions. *Sociology of Education* 41:36–56.

Williamson, Oliver E. 1975. *Markets and Hierarchies: Analysis and Antitrust Implications.* New York: Free Press.

———. 1981. The economics of organization: The transaction cost approach. *American Journal of Sociology* 87:548–577.

———. 1985. *The Economic Institutions of Capitalism.* New York: Free Press.

———. 1991. Comparative economic organization: The analysis of discrete structural alternatives. *Administrative Science Quarterly* 36:269–296.

———. 1994. Transaction cost economics and organization theory. In *The Handbook of Economic Sociology*, ed. Neil J. Smelser and Richard Swedberg (pp. 77–107). Princeton, NJ: Princeton University Press and Russell Sage Foundation.

———. 2005. Transaction cost economics: The process of theory development. In *Great Minds in Management: The Process of Theory Development*, ed. Ken G. Smith and Michael A. Hitt (pp. 485–508). Oxford, UK: Oxford University Press.

Willoughby, Westel Woodbury. 1896. *An Examination of the Nature of the State.* New York: Macmillan.

———. 1904. *The American Constitutional System.* New York: Century.

Wilson, James Q. ed. 1980. *The Politics of Regulation.* New York: Basic Books.

Wilson, Woodrow. 1889. *The State and Federal Governments of the United States.* Boston: D. C. Heath.

Winter, Sidney F. 1964. Economic "natural selection" and the theory of the firm. *Yale Economic Essays* 4:225–272.

———. 1990. Survival, selection, and inheritance in evolutionary theories of organization. In *Organizational Evolution: New Directions*, ed. Jitndra V. Singh (pp. 269–297). Newbury Park, CA: Sage.

———. 2005. Developing evolutionary theory for economics and management. In *Great Minds in Management: The Process of Theory Development*, ed. Ken G. Smith and Michael A. Hitt (pp. 509–546). Oxford, UK: Oxford University Press.

Womack, James P., Daniel T. Jones, and Daniel Roos. 1991. *The Machine That Changed the World: The Story of Lean Production.* New York: HarperCollins.

Woodward, Joan. 1958. *Management and Technology.* London: H.M.S.O.

Wooten, Melissa, and Andrew J. Hoffman. 2008. Organizational fields: Past, present, and future. In *The Sage Handbook of Organizational Institutionalism*, ed. Royston Greenwood, Christine Oliver, Kerstin Sahlin, and Roy Suddaby (pp. 130–147). Los Angeles: Sage.

Wuthnow, Robert. 1987. *Meaning and Moral Order: Explorations in Cultural Analysis.* Berkeley: University of California Press.

———. 1989. *Communities of Discourse: Ideology and Social Structure in the Reformation, the Enlightenment and European Socialism.* Cambridge, MA: Harvard University Press.

———. 2005. *America and the Challenge of Religious Diversity.* Princeton, NJ: Princeton University Press.

Wuthnow, Robert, James Dividson Hunter, Albert J. Bergesen, and Edith Kurzwell. 1984. *Cultural Analysis: The Work of Peter L. Berger, Mary Douglas, Michel Foucault, and Jurgen Habermas.* Boston: Routledge & Kegan Paul.

Zajac, Edward J., and James D. Westphal. 2002. Intraorganizational economics. In *The Blackwell Companion to Organizations*, ed. Joel A. C. Baum (pp. 233–255). Oxford, UK: Blackwell.

Zald, Mayer N. 1996. Culture, ideology and strategic framing. In *Comparative Perspectives on Social Movements*, ed. Doug McAdam, John D. McCarthy, and Mayer N. Zald (pp. 261–274). Cambridge, UK: Cambridge University Press.

Zald, Mayer N., and Roberta Ash. 1966. Social movement organizations: Growth, decay, and change. *Social Forces* 44:327–340.

Zald, Mayer N., and Patricia Denton. 1963. From evangelism to general service: The transformation of the YMCA. *Administrative Science Quarterly* 8:214–234.

Zelditch, Morris, Jr., and Henry A. Walker. 1984. Legitimacy and the stability of authority. In *Advances in Group Processes* vol. 1, ed. Edward J. Lawler (pp. 1–25). Greenwich, CT: JAI Press.

Zelner, Bennet A., Witold J. Henisz, and Guy L. F. Holburn. 2009. Contentious implementation and retrenchment in neoliberal policy reform: The global electric power industry, 1989–2001. *Administrative Science Quarterly* 54:379–412.

Zilber, Tammar B. 2002. Institutionalization as an interplay between actions, meanings, and actors: The case of a rape crisis center in Israel. *Academy of Management Journal* 45:234–254.

Zimmerman, Donald H. 1969. Record-keeping and the intake process in a public welfare agency. In *On Record: Files and Dossiers in American Life*, ed. Stanton Wheeler (pp. 319–354). New York: Russell Sage Foundation.

Znaniecki, Florian. 1945. Social organization and institutions. In *Twentieth Century Society*, ed. Gerges Gurvitch and Wilbert E. Moore (pp. 172–217). New York: Philosophical Library.

Zuboff, Shoshana. 1985. Technologies that informate: Implications for human resource management in the computerized industrial workplace. In *Human Resources, Management Trends and Challenges*, ed. Richard E. Walton and Raul R. Lawrence (pp. 103–139). Boston: Harvard Business School Press.

———. 1988. *In the Age of the Smart Machine*. New York: Basic Books.

Zucker, Lynne G. 1977. The role of institutionalization in cultural persistence. *American Sociological Review* 42:726–743.

———. 1983. Organizations as institutions. In *Research in the Sociology of Organizations*, vol. 2, ed. Samuel B. Bacharach (pp. 1–47). Greenwich, CT: JAI Press.

———. ed. 1988a. *Institutional Patterns and Organizations: Culture and Environment*. Cambridge, MA: Ballinger.

———. 1988b. Where do institutional patterns come from? Organizations as actors in social systems. In *Institutional Patterns and Organizations: Culture and Environment*, ed. Lynne G. Zucker (pp. 23–49). Cambridge, MA: Ballinger.

———. 1989. Combining institutional theory and population ecology: No legitimacy, no history (Comment on Carroll and Hannan, 1989). *American Sociological Review* 54:542–545.

———. 1991. Postscript: Microfoundations of institutional thought. In *The New Institutionalism in Organizational Analysis*, ed. Walter W. Powell and Paul J. DiMaggio (pp. 103–106). Chicago: University of Chicago Press.

Zuckerman, Ezra W. 1999. The categorical imperative: Securities analysts and the illegitimacy discount. *American Journal of Sociology* 104:1398–1438.

Zysman, John. 1983. *Governments, Markets and Growth: Finance and the Politics of Industrial Change*. Ithaca, NY: Cornell University.

Index

Abbott, Andrew, 270, 271
Abernethy, David B., 96
Accreditation:
    institutional pressures and, 202
    legitimacy and, 73, 191, 192–193
    as a normative process, 162–163
Action, voluntaristic theory of, 16
Activities, as carriers of institutional
    elements, 96 (table), 100–102,
    176–177
Actors and action:
    action theory of organization, 49
    actors and organization fields,
        228–230, 232, 237 (figure)
    collective, 79–80, 81, 88–89, 91, 146
    collective, repertoire of, 227–228
    institutionalized system of
        action, 16
    social construction of, 39, 77–78, 91,
        238, 271
    social structure and, 11–12, 57
    types of actors, 228
    See also Agency and agents;
        Institutional work
Administrative behavior, theory of, 29
Administrative systems, typology of, 14
Adoptive behavior:
    early versus late adopters, 188, 202,
        203–204
    organizational factors and, 204–207
Affect. See Emotion
Agency and agents:
    agency defined, 94
    agency in the analytic framework,
        92–95
    institutional change and, 114–126
    institutional construction and,
        114–126
    social construction of agency, 271
    types of agents, 119–126

Agency theory, 61, 63
Agent-based versus naturalistic
        accounts of construction, 114–118
Ahmadjian, Christina L., 170–171
Aldrich, Howard E., 117
Alexander, Jeffrey C., 2, 16, 75
Alexander, Victoria D., 211–212
Alford, Robert R., 90, 197, 225
Analysis levels. See Levels of analysis
Anderson, Benedict, 98
Ansell, Christopher, 83
Anthropology, cultural, 45–47, 48
Appadurai, Arjun, 98
Archetypes, organization, 89, 133,
        228–229, 235, 243
Arena, organization. See Field,
        organization
Armour, Henry O., 136
Armstrong, Elizabeth A., 247–248
Arthur, W. Brian, 144, 145
Artifacts, as carriers of institutional
        elements, 96 (table), 102–104,
        177–178
Art museums, 132, 162, 197, 211
Associations, as institutional agents,
        123–124
Austrian School, 2, 18, 19n1
Authority:
    legitimacy and, 14, 71, 72–73, 74
    moral, 14, 16, 244
    regulative elements and, 60, 61
Authority systems, types of, 14
Autonomy-control dichotomy,
        270–271, 270 (figure)
Axelrod, Robert, 139–140

Barley, Stephen R., 103, 177
Barnard, Chester I., 24–25, 32, 185
Barney, Jay B., 37, 100
Baron, James N., 120–121, 195

329

About the Author

W. Richard (Dick) Scott received his PhD from the University of Chicago and is currently Professor Emeritus in the Department of Sociology with courtesy appointments in the Graduate School of Business, Graduate School of Education, and School of Medicine at Stanford University. He has spent his entire professional career at Stanford, serving as chair of the Sociology Department (1972–1975), as director of the Training Program on Organizations and Mental Health (1972–1989), and as director of the Stanford Center for Organizations Research (1988–1996).

Scott is an organizational sociologist who has concentrated his work on the study of professional organizations, including educational, engineering, medical, research, social welfare, and nonprofit advocacy organizations. During the past three decades, he has concentrated his writing and research on the relation between organizations and their institutional environments. He is the author or editor of about a dozen books and more than 200 articles and book chapters.

He was elected to membership in the Institute of Medicine (1975), served as editor of the *Annual Review of Sociology* (1987–1991), and as president of the Sociological Research Association (2006–2007). Scott was the recipient of the Distinguished Scholar Award from the Management and Organization Theory Division of the Academy of Management in 1988, the Distinguished Educator Award from the same Division in 2013, and of the Richard D. Irwin Award for Distinguished Scholarly Contributions to Management from the Academy of Management in 1996. In 2000, the Section on Organization, Occupations and Work of the American Sociological Association created the W. Richard Scott Award to annually recognize an outstanding article-length contribution to the field. He has received honorary doctorates from the Copenhagen School of Business (2000), the Helsinki School of Economics and Business (2001), and Aarhus University in Denmark (2010).

⑤SAGE research**methods**

The essential online tool for researchers from the world's leading methods publisher

Find exactly what you are looking for, from basic explanations to advanced discussion

More content and new features added this year!

"I have never really seen anything like this product before, and I think it is really valuable."

John Creswell, University of Nebraska–Lincoln

Discover **Methods Lists**— methods readings suggested by other users

Watch video interviews with leading methodologists

Explore the **Methods Map** to discover links between methods

Search a custom-designed taxonomy with more than 1,400 qualitative, quantitative, and mixed methods terms

Uncover more than 120,000 pages of book, journal, and reference content to support your learning

Find out more at
www.sageresearchmethods.com